THE
50 GREATEST PLAYERS
IN
PHILADELPHIA PHILLIES
HISTORY

ROBERT W. COHEN

LYONS
PRESS

GUILFORD, CONNECTICUT

An imprint of Globe Pequot, the trade division of
The Rowman & Littlefield Publishing Group, Inc.
4501 Forbes Blvd., Ste. 200
Lanham, MD 20706
www.rowman.com

Distributed by NATIONAL BOOK NETWORK

British Library Cataloguing in Publication Information available

Library of Congress Cataloging-in-Publication Data

Names: Cohen, Robert W, author.
Title: The 50 greatest players in Philadelphia Phillies history / Robert W.
  Cohen.
Other titles: Fifty greatest players in Philadelphia Phillies history
Description: Guilford, Connecticut : Lyons Press, 2022. | Includes
  bibliographical references.
Identifiers: LCCN 2021038089 (print) | LCCN 2021038090 (ebook) | ISBN
  9781493062782 (cloth) | ISBN 9781493066964 (epub)
Subjects: LCSH: Philadelphia Phillies (Baseball team)—History. | Baseball
  players—Pennsylvania—Philadelphia—Biography.
Classification: LCC GV875.P45 C65 2022 (print) | LCC GV875.P45 (ebook) |
  DDC 796.357/640974811—dc23
LC record available at https://lccn.loc.gov/2021038089
LC ebook record available at https://lccn.loc.gov/2021038090

♾️™ The paper used in this publication meets the minimum requirements of American
National Standard for Information Sciences—Permanence of Paper for Printed Library
Materials, ANSI/NISO Z39.48-1992.

CONTENTS

ACKNOWLEDGMENTS

I would like to express my gratitude to the grandchildren of Leslie Jones, who, through the Trustees of the Boston Public Library, Print Department, supplied some of the photos included in this book.

I also wish to thank Troy R. Kinunen of MEARSonlineauctions.com, Kate of RMYauctions.com, Keith Allison, Matthew Straubmuller, Bryan Green, Scott Ableman, Dirk Hansen, and Richard Albersheim, each of whom generously contributed to the photographic content of this work.

INTRODUCTION

THE PHILLIES LEGACY

Originally founded by sporting goods manufacturer Al Reach and attorney John Rogers, the Philadelphia Quakers came into being in 1883, when they replaced the Worcester (Massachusetts) Ruby Legs in the eight-team National League after the Ruby Legs disbanded following the conclusion of the previous campaign. Performing dreadfully in their inaugural season, the Quakers posted a record of just 17-81, prompting owners Reach and Rogers to recruit Harry Wright, the former manager of baseball's first openly professional team, the Cincinnati Red Stockings, to pilot their squad. Gradually improving the fortunes of the ballclub over the course of the next few seasons, Wright led the Quakers to a winning record four times from 1884 to 1889, with their mark of 75-48 in 1887 placing them second in the NL standings. During that same period, the Quakers became better known as the "Phillies," although their original moniker continued to be used interchangeably with that sobriquet until 1890, when they adopted "Phillies" as their official nickname. Meanwhile, after spending the first four years of their existence playing their home games at Recreation Park, the Phillies moved into the newly constructed Philadelphia Base Ball Grounds in 1887.

Later renamed the Baker Bowl, the Phillies' new ballpark, located in North Philadelphia, on Broad Street, between West Huntingdon Street and West Lehigh Avenue, ended up serving as home to them for the next 52 years. Built to fit inside a city block, the 18,000-seat stadium, as originally configured, featured extremely unusual dimensions, with the 20-foot-high right field wall standing just 310 feet from home plate and the wall in left standing nearly 500 feet away.

Harry Wright continued to manage the Phillies until three consecutive fourth-place finishes prompted ownership to replace him at the helm with

1

former big-league shortstop and Boston Reds manager Arthur Irwin at the end of the 1893 season. Faring no better the next five years under managers Irwin, Billy Nash, George Stallings, and Bill Shettsline, the Phillies finished as high as third just once, although they featured some truly exceptional players, including Hall of Famers "Sliding" Billy Hamilton, "Big Ed" Delahanty, and Sam Thompson, who comprised the only all-.400-hitting outfield in baseball history in 1894. In fact, the right-handed-swinging Delahanty batted over .400 three times, hit four homers in one game in 1896, won a batting title, and led the league in several other offensive categories on multiple occasions. Meanwhile the left-handed-hitting Thompson topped the circuit in homers and RBIs twice each, once driving in 165 runs, while fellow lefty Hamilton not only won two batting titles and four stolen base crowns but set a major-league record that still stands by scoring 198 runs in 1894.

After Reach sold his interest in the team to Rogers prior to the start of the 1899 campaign, the Phillies emerged as one of the NL's strongest clubs over the course of the next three seasons, earning one second-place finish and ranking third in the league the other two years under Shettsline. But following the formation of the American League in 1901, the Phillies' three best players—Delahanty, Nap Lajoie, and Elmer Flick—all defected to the junior circuit, resulting in a lengthy period of mediocrity that lasted 13 seasons. Although the Phillies posted a winning record six times between 1902 and 1914, they finished higher than fourth in the NL just twice, as Shettsline (1902), Charles Zimmer (1903), Hall of Fame outfielder Hugh Duffy (1904–1906), Bill Murray (1907–1909), and longtime Phillies catcher Red Dooin (1910–1914) all took turns managing the team. The Phillies also experienced a considerable amount of instability in the front office during that time, as ownership of the club passed from Rogers to James Potter (1903–1904), to Charles P. Taft (1905–1913), and, finally, to former New York City police commissioner William Baker, who retained controlling interest of the team from 1913 to 1930. Yet, even in mediocrity, the Phillies presented to the opposition one of the league's more formidable lineups that included slugging first baseman Fred Luderus and star outfielders Sherry Magee and Gavvy Cravath, who won six home run titles during his time in Philadelphia.

Following the hiring of former player-coach Pat Moran as manager prior to the start of the 1915 campaign, the Phillies enjoyed a brief three-year run as one of the NL's elite teams, winning their first pennant in 1915, before finishing second in the league in each of the next two seasons. Although the powerful bat of Cravath contributed greatly to the success the

Phillies experienced during that time, Hall of Fame hurler Grover Cleveland Alexander proved to be the team's most dominant performer, posting more than 30 victories three straight times, and giving the Phillies their only win over the Boston Red Sox in the 1915 World Series.

Unfortunately, concerns over Alexander's future availability following the nation's entrance into World War I and William Baker's unwillingness to increase his salary caused the Phillies owner to trade his star pitcher to the Chicago Cubs prior to the start of the 1918 campaign, ushering in a dark period in franchise history during which the Phillies consistently placed at, or near, the bottom of the NL standings. Finishing last in the senior circuit seven times from 1918 to 1928 while being managed by Pat Moran (1918), Jack Coombs (1919), Gavvy Cravath (1919–1920), Bill Donovan (1921), Kaiser Wilhelm (1921–1922), Art Fletcher (1923–1926), Stuffy McInnis (1927), and Burt Shotton (1928), the Phillies developed into the laughingstock of the NL, despite the efforts of outfielder Cy Williams, who led the league in home runs on three separate occasions. And even though outstanding players such as Chuck Klein, Lefty O'Doul, Dolph Camilli, and Pinky Whitney graced the Phillies' roster in subsequent seasons, the team continued to struggle on the field, finishing no higher than fourth from 1929 to 1948, as Burt Shotton (1929–1933), Jimmie Wilson (1934–1938), Doc Prothro (1939–1941), Hans Lobert (1942), Bucky Harris (1943), Freddie Fitzsimmons (1943–1945), Ben Chapman (1945–1948), and Eddie Sawyer (1948) entered the Phillies' managerial carousel. When all was said and done, the Phillies had finished last 16 times and next-to-last 8 times from 1918 to 1948, posting just one winning record over the course of those 31 seasons.

Certainly, the penurious ways of William Baker contributed significantly to the lack of success the Phillies experienced during the 1920s. But the team fared no better after Baker died in 1930 and left half his estate to his wife and the other half to longtime team secretary Mae Mallen, whose husband, Gerald Nugent, assumed full control of the ballclub after Baker's widow passed away in 1932. While Nugent yearned to build a winning program, he lacked the financial means to do so, forcing him to trade away what little talent the team had to make ends meet. Furthermore, with the aging Baker Bowl in poor condition by 1938, the Phillies moved five blocks west into Shibe Park as tenants of the Athletics, who also played in Philadelphia at the time. Although Shibe Park (later renamed Connie Mack Stadium), which first opened in 1909, seated 33,000 patrons, the Phillies had a difficult time drawing more than 3,000 fans to their new home, thereby adding to their financial woes.

No longer able to field a representative team by 1943, Nugent sold the Phillies to a group of investors headed by lumber baron William D. Cox, who soon found himself being banned from baseball by Commissioner Kenesaw Mountain Landis for betting on the sport. Cox subsequently sold the Phillies to DuPont heir Robert R. M. Carpenter, who turned over control of the team to his son, Bob Jr.

With the Carpenters in charge, the Phillies began signing talented young players, enabling them to develop one of the better farm systems in all of baseball before long. Finally emerging from the depths of the NL in 1949, the Phillies finished third in the league with a record of 81-73 under second-year manager Eddie Sawyer, posting in the process their first winning mark in 17 seasons. Led by veteran reliever Jim Konstanty, who captured NL MVP honors, and a core of youngsters that included shortstop Granny Hamner, third baseman Willie Jones, pitcher Curt Simmons, slugging outfielder Del Ennis, and future Hall of Famers Richie Ashburn and Robin Roberts, the Philadelphia "Whiz Kids" subsequently stunned everyone by winning the pennant in 1950, doing so in dramatic fashion, with Dick Sisler's three-run homer in the bottom of the 10th inning giving them a 4–1 victory over Brooklyn on the final day of the regular season that eliminated the Dodgers from contention. However, the "Whiz Kids" came up short against the Yankees in the World Series, losing to their AL counterparts in four games.

Although the Phillies remained competitive the next seven years under managers Sawyer (1951–1952), Steve O'Neill (1952–1954), Terry Moore (1954), and Mayo Smith (1955–1957), finishing .500 or better four times, they failed to regain the magic that carried them to the 1950 pennant, eventually reverting to form by finishing last in the NL four straight times from 1958 to 1961, with their 23 consecutive losses in the last of those campaigns representing the longest such streak in the majors since 1900. But, after performing horribly under rookie manager Gene Mauch in 1961, the Phillies began to turn things around the next two seasons, posting a winning mark each year, before nearly capturing the NL pennant in 1964, when a late-season collapse deprived them of their third league championship. Holding a 6 1/2-game lead in the pennant race with just 12 games remaining, the Phillies lost 10 straight contests, relegating them to a close second-place finish behind the St. Louis Cardinals.

It took another 12 years for the Phillies to mount a serious challenge for a postseason berth, as managers Mauch (1965–1968), Bob Skinner (1968–1969), George Myatt (1969), Frank Lucchesi (1970–1972), Paul Owens (1972), and Danny Ozark (1973–1975) all failed in their attempts to return the team to prominence. Yet even though the Phillies struggled as a team for much of the period, especially after the major leagues instituted divisional play in 1969, several players distinguished themselves while donning the team's colors, with sluggers Dick Allen and Johnny Callison, and pitchers Jim Bunning, Chris Short, and Steve Carlton all earning All-Star honors on multiple occasions. Meanwhile, after spending the previous 33 years playing their home games at Connie Mack Stadium, the Phillies moved into newly constructed Veterans Stadium in 1971. Located at 3501 South Broad Street in South Philadelphia, Veterans Stadium, which featured an artificial playing surface and a seating capacity of 62,623, remained home to the Phillies for the next 33 years. The Phillies also experienced a change in ownership during that time, with Ruly Carpenter assuming control of the team after his father, Bob Carpenter Jr., retired in 1972.

Emerging as a contender again under Danny Ozark in 1976, the Phillies began an outstanding eight-year run during which they advanced to the playoffs six times, won five division titles and two pennants, and captured their first world championship. Surpassing 100 victories for the first time in franchise history in 1976, the Phillies concluded the regular season with a record of 101-61, before being swept by the eventual World Series champion Cincinnati Reds in three straight games in the NLCS. The Phillies captured the division title in each of the next two seasons as well, only to lose to the Los Angeles Dodgers in four games in the NLCS both times. After the Phillies finished a disappointing fourth in the NL East in 1979, ownership replaced Ozark at the helm with Dallas Green, who led the team to its fourth division title, a hard-fought five-game victory over the Houston Astros in the NLCS, and a six-game win over the Kansas City Royals in the World Series his first year in charge. Although the Phillies advanced to the playoffs once again in 1981, the Montreal Expos defeated them in five games when the two teams met in the NLDS to determine the division champion after a players' strike split the season into two halves. Ownership subsequently replaced Green with Pat Corrales, who led the Phillies to a close second-place finish in 1982, before surrendering his duties to GM Paul Owens midway through the 1983 campaign. After adding the title of field manager to his job description, Owens guided the Phillies to the division title and a four-game victory over the Dodgers in the 1983 NLCS. However, the Baltimore Orioles handled the Phillies rather easily in the World Series, defeating them in five games.

The Phillies teams of the mid- to late 70s and early 80s featured many outstanding players, with Larry Bowa starring at shortstop, Bob Boone excelling behind home plate, Garry Maddox performing brilliantly in center field, Greg Luzinski establishing himself as one of the foremost sluggers in the game, and free agent acquisition Pete Rose providing a solid bat and some much-needed leadership. But third baseman Mike Schmidt and pitcher Steve Carlton stood out above all others. Arguably the league's finest all-around player throughout the period, Schmidt excelled both at the bat and in the field, winning eight home run crowns, six Silver Sluggers, 10 Gold Gloves, and three NL MVP Awards. Meanwhile, Carlton rivaled Tom Seaver as the finest pitcher of the era, winning the Cy Young Award on four separate occasions.

Although the Phillies advanced to the playoffs in both 1981 and 1983, the subsequent departures of Carlton, Rose, Luzinski, Maddox, Bowa, and Boone led to another period of mediocrity that coincided with the reign of longtime Phillies executive Bill Giles, who purchased the team from Ruly Carpenter for $32.5 million early in 1981. Hampered by a lack of talent, the Phillies compiled just one winning record from 1984 to 1992, a period during which six different men managed the team. But, after finishing last in the NL East the previous year, a Phillies squad piloted by Jim Fregosi and dubbed "Macho Row" for its shaggy, unkempt, and gruff appearance surprised everyone by capturing the division title in 1993. Led by catcher Darren Daulton, center fielder Lenny Dykstra, first baseman John Kruk, and pitcher Curt Schilling, the Phillies compiled a regular-season record of 97-65 that earned them a berth in the NLCS, where they defeated the Atlanta Braves in six games. However, they subsequently suffered a six-game defeat at the hands of the Toronto Blue Jays in the World Series, with Joe Carter's three-run walkoff homer off Mitch Williams in Game 6 sealing their fate.

Proving to be just a one-year wonder, the Phillies finished well below .500 in each of the next seven seasons, forcing Fregosi to surrender his managerial duties to Terry Francona in 1997, the same year that minority owner David P. Montgomery replaced Bill Giles as team president and principal owner. Seeking to restore the Phillies to prominence, Montgomery spent the next several years replenishing the organization's farm system with talented players such as Bobby Abreu, Jimmy Rollins, Pat Burrell, Chase Utley, Ryan Howard, and Cole Hamels, most of whom played huge roles in the team's return to glory. Montgomery also replaced Francona at the helm with Larry Bowa in 2001, before turning to Charlie Manuel in 2005 after Bowa failed to deliver a division title in his four years in charge. Meanwhile, the Phillies moved across the street from Veterans Stadium into Citizens Bank Park, which officially opened on April 3, 2004. Boasting a seating capacity of close to 43,000, Citizens Bank Park lies on the northeast corner of the South Philadelphia Sports Complex, which also includes Lincoln Financial Field, the Wells Fargo Center, and Xfinity Live!

After guiding the Phillies to a pair of second-place finishes his first two years in charge, Manuel led them to five consecutive division titles, two pennants, and one world championship, with the maturation of Ryan Howard, Chase Utley, Jimmy Rollins, Pat Burrell, and Cole Hamels into top performers and the additions by new general manager Pat Gillick of outfielder Shane Victorino and pitchers Jamie Moyer, Cliff Lee, and Roy Halladay contributing greatly to the success the team experienced during that time. Beginning their exceptional run in 2007, the Phillies captured the NL East title by winning 13 of their final 17 contests, overcoming in the process a seven-game deficit to the New York Mets, who went just 4-11 down the stretch. However, the Phillies subsequently exited the postseason tournament quickly, losing to the Colorado Rockies in the NLDS in three straight games. After finishing first in the division once again in 2008, the Phillies redeemed themselves for their poor showing in the playoffs the previous year by defeating Milwaukee three games to one in the NLDS and Los Angeles four games to one in the NLCS, before laying claim to their second world championship by disposing of the Tampa Bay Rays in five games in the World Series. Remaining the class of the NL East following the retirement of Pat Gillick and the subsequent promotion to GM of Rubén Amaro Jr., the Phillies captured their third straight division title in 2009, finishing six games ahead of the second place Florida Marlins with a record of 93-69, before earning their second consecutive trip to the World Series by eliminating Colorado and Los Angeles in the playoffs. However, they faltered against the Yankees in the Fall Classic, losing to their AL counterparts in six games. Despite posting the NL's best record in each of the next two seasons, the Phillies failed to make it back to the World Series, losing to the San Francisco Giants in six games in the 2010 NLCS, before suffering a five-game defeat at the hands of the St. Louis Cardinals in the 2011 NLDS.

Manuel continued to manage the Phillies for most of the next two seasons, before being replaced by third base coach Ryne Sandberg during the latter stages of the 2013 campaign after the team failed to live up to expectations. Having led the Phillies to an overall record of 780-636 in his eight-plus years as skipper, Manuel left Philadelphia with more wins than any other manager in franchise history.

Sandberg's tenure as Phillies manager lasted until the midway point of the 2015 campaign, when he handed in his resignation after guiding the club to an overall mark of just 119-159 over parts of the previous three seasons. Unfortunately, the Phillies fared no better under his replacement, bench coach Pete Mackanin, posting a composite record of 174-238 over the course of the next two-and-a-half years, as ownership of the team passed from David Montgomery to John S. Middleton, who replaced Amaro Jr. as GM with Matt Klentak and named Andy MacPhail president of baseball operations. MacPhail remained in that position until 2020, when Middleton hired Dave Dombrowski to assume the same role.

Meanwhile, following the firing of Mackanin, former Dodgers director of player development Gabe Kapler spent two seasons managing the Phillies to a pair of mediocre finishes, before Middleton replaced him with former New York Yankees manager Joe Girardi following the conclusion of the 2019 campaign. The Phillies have continued to play uninspired baseball under Girardi the past two seasons, compiling a record of 28-32 during the pandemic-shortened 2020 campaign, before posting a mark of 82–80in 2021. But, with a talented roster that includes star outfielder Bryce Harper, slugging first baseman Rhys Hoskins, standout catcher J. T. Realmuto, and a solid starting rotation anchored by Aaron Nola and Zack Wheeler, the Phillies figure to be strong contenders in the NL East for years to come. Their next division title will be their 12th. The Phillies have also won seven pennants and two World Series.

Despite their storied past, the Phillies have proven to be one of the National League's less successful franchises through the years, compiling a winning record just 55 times in their 139-year history, losing more games than any other American professional sports team, and failing to win a world championship in the first 97 years of their existence. Still, a significant number of men have attained notable individual honors while wearing a Phillies uniform, with eight players having won the MVP award during their time in the City of Brotherly Love. The franchise also boasts seven Cy Young Award winners, 29 home-run champions, and eight batting champions. Six players have had their number retired by the team. Meanwhile, 27 members of the Baseball Hall of Fame spent at least one full season playing for the Phillies, 14 of whom had several of their finest seasons as a member of the team.

FACTORS USED TO DETERMINE RANKINGS

It should come as no surprise that selecting the 50 greatest players ever to perform for a team with the rich history of the Phillies presented a difficult and daunting task. Even after I narrowed the field down to a mere 50 men, I found myself faced with the challenge of ranking the elite players that remained. Certainly, the names of Mike Schmidt, Steve Carlton, Grover Cleveland Alexander, Richie Ashburn, Robin Roberts, and Chase Utley would appear at, or near, the top of virtually everyone's list, although the order might vary somewhat from one person to the next. Several other outstanding performers have gained general recognition through the years as being among the greatest players ever to wear a Phillies uniform, with Chuck Klein, Dick Allen, Ryan Howard, and Jimmy Rollins heading the list of other Phillies icons. But how does one differentiate between the all-around brilliance of Mike Schmidt and the offensive dominance of Chuck Klein, or the pitching greatness of Robin Roberts and the exceptional slugging ability of Ryan Howard? After initially deciding whom to include on my list, I then needed to determine what criteria to use when formulating my final rankings.

The first thing I decided to examine was the level of dominance a player attained during his time in Philadelphia. How often did he lead the National League in some major offensive or pitching statistical category? How did he fare in the annual MVP and/or Cy Young voting? How many times did he make the All-Star team?

I also needed to weigh the level of statistical compilation a player achieved while wearing a Phillies uniform. Where does a batter rank in team annals in the major offensive categories? How high on the all-time list of Phillies hurlers does a pitcher rank in wins, ERA, complete games, innings pitched, shutouts, and saves? Of course, I also needed to consider the era in which the player performed when evaluating his overall numbers. For example, modern-day starting pitchers such as Cole Hamels and Cliff Lee are not likely to throw nearly as many complete games or shutouts as either Grover Cleveland Alexander or Robin Roberts, who anchored the Phillies starting rotation during the 1910s and 1950s, respectively. Meanwhile, Chuck Klein had a distinct advantage over Dick Allen in that he competed during an era that was far more conducive to posting huge offensive numbers. Klein had the additional benefit of playing his home games at the Baker Bowl, a veritable paradise for left-handed hitters. And Dead Ball Era stars such as Sherry Magee and Gavvy Cravath were not likely to hit nearly as many home runs as the players who performed for the team after the major leagues began using a livelier ball.

Other important factors I needed to consider were the overall contributions a player made to the success of the team, the degree to which he improved the fortunes of the ballclub during his time in Philadelphia, and the manner with which he impacted the team, both on and off the field. While the number of pennants or division titles the Phillies won during a particular player's years with the club certainly entered into the equation, I chose not to deny a top performer his rightful place on the list if his years in the City of Brotherly Love happened to coincide with a lack of overall success by the team. As a result, the names of players such as Tony Taylor and Johnny Callison will appear in these rankings.

There are two other things I wish to mention. Firstly, I only considered a player's performance while playing for the Phillies when formulating my rankings. That being the case, the names of exceptional players such as Pete Rose and Jim Thome, both of whom had many of their best years for other teams, may appear lower on this list than one might expect. In addition, since several of the rules that governed 19th-century baseball (including permitting batters to dictate the location of pitches until 1887, situating the pitcher's mound only 50 feet from home plate until 1893, and crediting a stolen base to a runner any time he advanced from first to third base on a hit) differed dramatically from those to which we have become accustomed, I elected to include only those players who competed after 1900, which is generally considered to be the beginning of baseball's "modern era." Doing so eliminated from consideration 19th-century standouts such as Sam Thompson, "Sliding" Billy Hamilton, and Ed Delahanty.

Having established the guidelines to be used throughout this book, we are ready to begin our review of the 50 greatest players in Phillies history, starting with number one and working our way down to number 50.

MIKE SCHMIDT

Mike Schmidt received stiff competition from Steve Carlton and Grover Cleveland Alexander for the number 1 position in these rankings, with both Hall of Fame hurlers performing magnificently during their time in Philadelphia. En route to earning seven All-Star nominations, four Cy Young awards, and five top-10 finishes in the NL MVP voting, Carlton won more games and recorded more strikeouts than any other pitcher in team annals. Meanwhile, Alexander surpassed 30 victories three times, set several single-season franchise records that still stand, and won the pitcher's version of the Triple Crown three straight times, with his brilliant mound work prompting the *Sporting News* to place him at number 12 on its 1999 list of Baseball's 100 Greatest Players. However, Schmidt also boasts an extremely impressive list of credentials that includes 13 seasons with more than 30 home runs, nine years with more than 100 RBIs, eight home run championships, three NL MVP awards, one World Series MVP trophy, six Silver Sluggers, 10 Gold Gloves, and franchise records in eight different offensive categories. Equally significant, though, is the fact that, while both Carlton and Alexander spent several seasons pitching for other teams, Schmidt spent his entire 18-year big-league career in Philadelphia, making him the only possible choice for the top spot here.

Widely considered the greatest all-around third baseman in baseball history, Mike Schmidt excelled in every aspect of the game. A tremendous offensive player who possessed extraordinary physical strength and good running speed, Schmidt, in addition to his previously mentioned achievements, batted over .300 once, stole more than 20 bases twice, scored more than 100 runs seven times, and posted an OPS over .900 on 12 separate occasions. A superb fielder as well, Schmidt led all NL third basemen in assists seven times, double plays turned six times, and fielding percentage once, with his outstanding all-around play earning him 12 All-Star selections, *Sporting News* NL Player of the Year honors twice, and recognition from that same publication as Player of the Decade for the 1980s.

And following the conclusion of his playing career, Schmidt received the additional distinctions of being named to Major League Baseball's All-Century Team, having his #20 retired by the Phillies, and gaining induction into the Baseball Hall of Fame in his first year of eligibility.

Born in Dayton, Ohio, on September 27, 1949, Michael Jack Schmidt grew up a huge fan of Frank Robinson and the Cincinnati Reds. That Schmidt lived long enough to see Robinson play is something of a miracle. Spending most of his youth in a sleepy, tree-lined, middle-class neighborhood in

Mike Schmidt hit more homers, drove in more runs, and scored more times than anyone else in team annals.
Courtesy of MearsonlineAuctions.com

Dayton, Schmidt almost lost his life at the age of five when he foolishly climbed a tree in his backyard and grabbed on to a 4,000-volt power line. Knocked unconscious by the shock, young Michael fell limp to the ground, before the impact of the fall fortunately restarted his heart. Reflecting back on his brush with death years later, Schmidt said, "I've never thought that I was given a second chance because I was supposed to do something great in my life. But I've looked back and wondered why that stupid little kid didn't die. Maybe that's the reason I've always worked so hard—because I don't want to think that I wasted that chance."

Eventually emerging as a standout athlete at local Fairview High School, Schmidt starred in baseball and basketball, proving to be equally proficient in both sports. Continuing to compete in multiple sports at Ohio University, which he entered in the hope of becoming an architect, Schmidt won a starting job as a guard on the school's freshman basketball team, before knee problems forced him to focus exclusively on baseball. Recalling the events that transpired at the time, Schmidt said, "All I cared about was basketball at that point in time. I got called into the varsity coach's office one day and he said, 'Mike, your knees just aren't going to make it.' I was playing with a brace on each knee, and it just wasn't pretty. Even though I could compete, there was no way, over the long haul, I was going to be able to make it in basketball. So, I just kind of fell back on baseball."

After spending his early days at Ohio switch-hitting, Schmidt chose to concentrate solely on developing his skills as a right-handed batter, remembering, "I was not a prospect as a switch-hitter. My power was righthanded, basically raw power, everything to the pull side."

After leading Ohio to the College World Series in 1970, Schmidt hit 10 home runs and batted .331 in 37 games in 1971, prompting the Phillies to select him in the second round of that year's Amateur Draft, with the 30th overall pick. In discussing the impression that Schmidt made on him during his time at Ohio, Phillies scout Tony Lucadello said, "Sometimes he would do things that would amaze me. Other times, he would make errors or just look terrible up at the plate. This gave me an edge right away, see, because other scouts, they'd see him, and they'd pick at all those flaws. But I sensed Mike Schmidt would be a late bloomer."

Ultimately signing with the Phillies for $32,500, plus $2,500 for each minor-league level he passed, Schmidt also received an invitation to formalize the deal at Veterans Stadium, recalling, "That was more important than the money. Veterans Stadium was new; it was the talk of baseball. The red shoes and the pinstriped uniforms and the artificial turf, going into the major league locker room and putting the uniform on—if that wasn't enough to entice you to sign a major league contract, nothing would."

After playing mostly shortstop in college, Schmidt moved to third base while advancing through the Phillies' farm system. Promoted to the parent club after less than two full seasons in the minors, Schmidt arrived in Philadelphia for the first time during the latter stages of the 1972 campaign. Appearing in 13 games in September, Schmidt batted just .206 but hit the first home run of his big-league career. Continuing to struggle at the plate the following year after laying claim to the Phillies' starting third base job, Schmidt batted just .196, knocked in only 52 runs, and struck out 136 times, although he finished third on the team with 18 homers.

Improving his offensive production dramatically in 1974 after learning to hit the slider while playing winter ball in Caguas, Puerto Rico, Schmidt earned his first All-Star selection and a sixth-place finish in the NL MVP voting by leading the league with 36 home runs and a .546 slugging percentage; ranking among the leaders with 116 RBIs, 108 runs scored, 310 total bases, 106 walks, an on-base percentage of .395, and an OPS of .941; batting .282; stealing 23 bases; and leading all players at his position with a career-high 404 assists. However, Schmidt also struck out a league-leading 138 times, frequently incurring the wrath of the hometown fans with his propensity for whiffing in crucial situations.

Schmidt subsequently topped the senior circuit in homers in each of the next two seasons as well, reaching the seats 38 times in both 1975 and

1976, with his 107 RBIs, 112 runs scored, .900 OPS, and league-leading 306 total bases in the second of those campaigns earning him his second All-Star nomination and a third-place finish in the NL MVP balloting. Meanwhile, Schmidt's excellent defensive work at third in 1976 earned him Gold Glove honors for the first of nine straight times. Nevertheless, Schmidt continued to draw the ire of the Philly Faithful by leading the league in strikeouts both years, with totals of 180 and 149, respectively, while posting batting averages of just .249 and .262.

Schmidt gained All-Star recognition once again in 1977 by driving in 101 runs; batting .274; placing near the top of the league rankings with 38 homers, 114 runs scored, and an OPS of .967; and leading all NL third basemen in assists. But, when Schmidt slumped somewhat at the plate the following year, hitting just 21 homers, knocking in only 78 runs, and batting just .251 during the regular season, before posting a batting average of .200 and collecting just one RBI during the Phillies' four-game loss to the Dodgers in the NLCS, Phillies fans grew increasingly hostile toward him, prompting the beleaguered third baseman to state on one occasion, "You're trying your damndest, you strike out and they boo you. I act like it doesn't bother me, like I don't hear anything the fans say, but the truth is, I hear every word of it, and it kills me."

Yet, for the most part, Schmidt took his lack of popularity in stride, rarely displaying any emotion on the field and demonstrating no ill will toward the fans at Veterans Stadium, to whom he once paid tribute by saying, "They read their sports pages, know their statistics and either root like hell or boo their butts off. I love it. Give me vocal fans, pro or con, over the tourist types who show up in Houston or Montreal and just sit there."

And, after calling Veterans Stadium a "mob scene" on another occasion, Schmidt ingratiated himself to Phillies fans the next time he took the field at his home ballpark by emerging from the dugout wearing a wig and sunglasses, as if trying to hide from the "boo-birds." In response, the Philly fanatics erupted in laughter and gave Schmidt a standing ovation.

Schmidt's acceptance of his plight enabled him to focus solely on his on-field performance, thereby allowing him to further develop his all-around game. In addition to his prodigious power at the plate, the right-handed-hitting Schmidt, who stood 6'2" and weighed 205 pounds, possessed a keen batting eye, drawing more than 100 bases on balls in a season seven times. Also blessed with good speed on the basepaths and outstanding range and a powerful throwing arm in the field, Schmidt proved to be particularly adept at barehanding slowly hit grounders and firing laser beams across the diamond to nip opposing batters at first base.

Following his poor showing in 1978, Schmidt earned All-Star honors for the fourth time in the ensuing campaign by placing near the top of the NL rankings with 45 homers, 114 RBIs, 109 runs scored, a slugging percentage of .564, and an OPS of .950, while also leading the league with 120 walks. Yet, despite his outstanding offensive production, Schmidt's tremendous determination and will to succeed did not permit him to rest on his laurels. And Pete Rose, whom the Phillies signed as a free agent during the subsequent offseason, provided further motivation to his new teammate when he stated, "Mike Schmidt is the best player in the National League today. There's no question about that. He honestly doesn't realize how much ability he has. All he has to do is get the most out of those abilities on a daily basis because, believe me, he can play. He can do it all, and he's just starting to want to, more and more."

Having already established himself as the National League's top slugger, Schmidt developed into an even better hitter after tinkering with his batting style prior to the start of the 1980 campaign. Schmidt, a dead pull hitter the first half of his career, studied the hitting style of the late Roberto Clemente, who tended to lean in toward the pitcher's delivery and drive the ball with power to all fields. Standing deep in the batter's box and turning his back slightly toward the opposing pitcher while wiggling his posterior ever so slightly, Schmidt adopted a similar batting style to that of Clemente, enabling him to hit for a higher batting average, increase his on-base percentage, and reduce his strikeout total. He posted the following numbers over the course of the next eight seasons:

YEAR	HR	RBI	RUNS	AVG	OBP	SLG	OPS
1980	**48**	**121**	104	.286	.380	**.624**	**1.004**
1981	**31**	**91**	**78**	.316	**.435**	**.644**	**1.080**
1982	35	87	108	.280	**.403**	**.547**	**.949**
1983	**40**	109	104	.255	**.399**	.524	.923
1984	**36**	**106**	93	.277	.383	.536	**.919**
1985	33	93	89	.277	.375	.532	.907
1986	**37**	**119**	97	.290	.390	**.547**	**.937**
1987	35	113	88	.293	.388	.548	.936

* Please note that any numbers printed in bold throughout this book indicate that the player led the league in that statistical category that year.

In addition to leading the NL in home runs and OPS five times, RBIs and slugging percentage four times, on-base percentage three times, and runs scored once, Schmidt topped the senior circuit in total bases twice and walks three times, earning in the process six Silver Sluggers, seven All-Star selections, and three league MVP trophies. Continuing to perform exceptionally well in the field as well, Schmidt also won another six Gold Gloves. Particularly outstanding in 1980 and 1981, Schmidt earned NL MVP honors in the first of those campaigns by leading the Phillies to the pennant, before homering twice, driving in seven runs, and batting .381 during their six-game win over the Kansas City Royals in the World Series. Although a players' strike in 1981 prevented Schmidt from surpassing the totals he posted the previous season, he performed brilliantly once again, earning MVP honors for the second straight time by leading the league in nine different offensive categories. Schmidt won his third MVP award in 1986, when, in addition to his outstanding offensive production, he led all NL third basemen with a .980 fielding percentage, committing just eight errors in the field all year.

Unfortunately, the 1987 campaign proved to be Schmidt's last as a truly dominant player. Limited to just 108 games by an injured rotator cuff in 1988, the 38-year-old third baseman hit just 12 homers, knocked in only 62 runs, and batted just .249. After Schmidt began the following season in similar fashion, homering just six times, driving in only 28 runs, and batting just .203 in his first 42 games, his great pride forced him to suddenly announce his retirement at a hastily called news conference held at San Diego's Jack Murphy Stadium on May 30. Making his decision known to the public during an emotional speech punctuated by frequent pauses, a tearful Schmidt stated, "Over the years, I've set high standards for myself as a player. I've always said that, when I don't feel I can perform up to those standards, it would be time for me to retire. My skills to do the things on the field, to make the adjustments needed to hit, to make the routine plays on defense, and to run the bases aggressively have deteriorated."

Schmidt continued, "This is something I have been mulling over for about a week. It's been a week, maybe a little bit longer that I felt a deterioration of my skills. I prayed about it, thought about it, talked to my family and my advisers about it. I gave it a period of time to turn around. On the field, I looked for signs. Every night, I looked for reasons to continue as an active player, and they weren't there."

Schmidt then added, "I feel like I could easily ask the Phillies to make me a part-time player, to hang around for a couple of years to add to my statistical totals. However, my respect for the game, my teammates, and the fans won't allow me to do that. For that reason, I have decided to retire as an active player."

Retiring with career totals of 548 home runs, 1,595 RBIs, 1,506 runs scored, 2,234 hits, 408 doubles, 59 triples, and 174 stolen bases, a lifetime batting average of .267, an on-base percentage of .380, and a slugging percentage of .527, Schmidt continues to hold the major-league record for most homers by a third baseman.

In assessing the career of his longtime teammate, Steve Carlton said, "Schmitty provided what the relief pitchers need most, home runs and great defense. He's the best third baseman that I ever played with, and maybe of all-time. Obvious Hall of Famer, even then. He retired while on top of his game. I thought for sure he was going to hit 600 home runs."

Shortly after he retired as an active player, Schmidt spent one year serving as a member of the Phillies broadcast team on the now-defunct PRISM network. More than a decade later, the Phillies hired him to work for several weeks each spring training as a hitting coach. Schmidt also spent one season managing in the Phillies' farm system, before handing in his resignation.

Schmidt has remained in the public spotlight in subsequent years, occasionally expressing his thoughts on various baseball controversies. In addition to supporting the reinstatement of Pete Rose to baseball, Schmidt addressed the subject of steroids during a July 2005 appearance on Bob Costas's HBO show, *Costas Now*, raising a few eyebrows when he stated, "Let me go out on a limb and say that if I had played during that era, I would have taken steroids. . . . We all have these things we deal with in life, and I'm surely not going to sit here and say to you guys, 'I wouldn't have done that.'" Later, though, Schmidt recanted that statement somewhat, saying in his 2006 book, *Clearing the Bases: Juiced Players, Shrinking Ballparks, Sham Records, and a Hall of Famer's Search for the Soul of Baseball*, that he understood the desire to get a competitive advantage even though he could not condone breaking the rules to do so.

Mike Schmidt, who overcame a bout with stage-3 melanoma in 2013, did not need a competitive edge over his opponents during his playing days, as noted sportswriter Dave Anderson suggested when he wrote in the *New York Times* shortly after Schmidt announced his retirement from the game: "No other third baseman ever did what he [Schmidt] did with both his bat and his glove. Not Brooks Robinson, not Eddie Mathews, not Pie Traynor."

CAREER HIGHLIGHTS

Best Season

Schmidt likely would have compiled the best numbers of his career in 1981 had the season not been abbreviated by a players' strike. Appearing in 102 of the Phillies' 107 games, Schmidt batted a career-high .316 and led the NL with 31 homers, 91 RBIs, 78 runs scored, 73 walks, 228 total bases, a .435 on-base percentage, a .644 slugging percentage, and an OPS of 1.080, with each of the last three figures also representing career-high marks. But, with the season being halted for nearly two months, Schmidt posted his most impressive stat-line the previous year, earning NL MVP honors for the first of three times in 1980 by batting .286, scoring 104 runs, and leading the league with 48 homers, 121 RBIs, 342 total bases, a slugging percentage of .624, and an OPS of 1.004.

Memorable Moments/Greatest Performances

Schmidt helped the Phillies complete a doubleheader sweep of the St. Louis Cardinals on April 22, 1973, by hitting a two-out, game-winning solo home run off Bob Gibson in the bottom of the ninth inning of the nightcap.

Schmidt led the Phillies to a 5–3 win over the Dodgers on August 10, 1973, by driving in four runs with a pair of home runs, delivering the game's big blow in the top of the seventh inning when he homered off Tommy John with two men on base.

Schmidt, who hit several tape-measure home runs, delivered probably the longest blast of his career during a 12–0 pasting of the Astros in Houston on June 10, 1974, when he hit a pitch into a public address speaker suspended 117 feet above and 329 feet away from home plate. The ball then fell to the field, where, by the Astrodome's ground rules, it remained in play. Although Schmidt only reached first base, experts subsequently estimated that the ball likely would have traveled more than 500 feet had its progress not been impeded.

Schmidt entered the record books on April 17, 1976, when he became just the 10th player in major-league history to hit four home runs in one game, going 5-for-6, with eight RBIs and 17 total bases during a 10-inning, 18–16 win over the Chicago Cubs.

Schmidt helped lead the Phillies to a 7–5 win over the Atlanta Braves on June 10, 1977, by homering twice and knocking in five runs, with his three-run blast off Dave Campbell in the top of the seventh inning providing the margin of victory.

Schmidt contributed to a 10–2 win over the Cubs on August 14, 1977, by going 4-for-5, with two homers, six RBIs, and four runs scored.

Schmidt had another big game against the Cubs on May 17, 1979, hitting a pair of homers, knocking in four runs, and scoring three times during a 23–22, 10-inning Phillies win, with his solo shot off Bruce Sutter in the top of the 10th providing the margin of victory.

Although the Phillies lost to the Giants 8–6 on July 7, 1979, Schmidt hit three home runs and knocked in five runs, homering twice off John Montefusco and once off Pedro Borbon.

Schmidt led the Phillies to a 14–8 win over the Mets on April 22, 1980, by homering twice and driving in six runs, securing the victory with a grand slam homer in the bottom of the eighth inning.

Schmidt clinched the NL East title for the Phillies on the next-to-last day of the 1980 regular season when he homered off Stan Bahnsen with one man aboard in the top of the 11th inning, giving them a 6–4 victory over the Montreal Expos.

Schmidt contributed to an 11–7 win over the San Diego Padres on May 8, 1981, by going 4-for-5, with two homers, five RBIs, and three runs scored.

Schmidt gave the Phillies a 2–1 win over the Houston Astros on September 3, 1982, by hitting a solo homer off Joe Niekro with two men out in the bottom of the ninth inning.

Schmidt delivered another walkoff win on May 28, 1983, giving the Phillies a 5–3 victory over the Expos by hitting a two-out, two-run homer in the bottom of the ninth inning after striking out in his four previous plate appearances.

Schmidt provided further heroics on July 11, 1983, when, after reaching the seats with no one on base earlier in the contest, he gave the Phillies an 11–7 victory over the Reds by homering with the bases loaded with two men out in the top of the 11th inning.

Schmidt became the 14th member of the 500 Home Run Club on April 18, 1987, when his two-out, three-run homer off Don Robinson in the top of the ninth inning gave the Phillies an 8–6 win over the Pittsburgh Pirates.

Schmidt led the Phillies to an 11–6 win over the Montreal Expos on June 14, 1987, by hitting three home runs and knocking in six runs, with his homers coming off three different pitchers.

Notable Achievements

- Hit more than 30 home runs 13 times, surpassing 40 homers on three occasions.
- Knocked in more than 100 runs nine times.
- Scored more than 100 runs seven times.
- Batted over .300 once.
- Finished in double digits in triples once.
- Surpassed 30 doubles three times.
- Stole more than 20 bases twice.
- Drew at least 100 bases on balls seven times.
- Compiled on-base percentage over .400 twice.
- Posted slugging percentage over .500 13 times, finishing with mark above .600 twice.
- Compiled OPS over .900 12 times, finishing with mark above 1.000 twice.
- Hit four home runs in one game vs. Chicago Cubs on April 17, 1976.
- Hit three home runs in one game twice (vs. San Francisco Giants on July 7, 1979, and vs. Montreal Expos on June 14, 1987).
- Led NL in home runs eight times, RBIs four times, runs scored once, extra-base hits five times, total bases three times, walks four times, on-base percentage three times, slugging percentage five times, OPS five times, and sacrifice flies twice.
- Finished second in NL in home runs once, RBIs once, runs scored twice, triples once, extra-base hits twice, total bases twice, walks twice, slugging percentage twice, and OPS twice.
- Finished third in NL in home runs twice, RBIs four times, runs scored six times, extra-base hits three times, walks three times, slugging percentage twice, and OPS twice.
- Led NL third basemen in assists seven times, double plays turned six times, and fielding percentage once.
- Ranks among MLB all-time leaders in assists (4th) and double plays (5th) by a third baseman.
- Holds Phillies career records for most home runs (548), RBIs (1,595), runs scored (1,506), extra-base hits (1,015), total bases (4,404), bases on balls (1,507), intentional bases on balls (201), sacrifice flies (108), games played (2,404), and plate appearances (10,062).
- Ranks among Phillies career leaders in hits (2nd), doubles (3rd), slugging percentage (5th), OPS (7th), and at-bats (2nd).
- Five-time division champion (1976, 1977, 1978, 1980, and 1983).

- Two-time NL champion (1980 and 1983).
- 1980 world champion.
- Six-time NL Player of the Week.
- Five-time NL Player of the Month.
- Two-time *Sporting News* NL Player of the Year (1980 and 1986).
- Three-time NL MVP (1980, 1981, and 1986).
- Finished in top 10 in NL MVP voting six other times, placing third twice.
- 1980 World Series MVP.
- Six-time Silver Slugger Award winner (1980, 1981, 1982, 1983, 1984, and 1986).
- 10-time Gold Glove Award winner (1976, 1977, 1978, 1979, 1980, 1981, 1982, 1983, 1984, and 1986).
- 1983 Lou Gehrig Memorial Award winner.
- 10-time *Sporting News* NL All-Star selection (1974, 1976, 1977, 1979, 1980, 1981, 1982, 1983, 1984, and 1986).
- 12-time NL All-Star (1974, 1976, 1977, 1979, 1980, 1981, 1982, 1983, 1984, 1986, 1987, and 1989).
- *Sporting News* 1980s Player of the Decade.
- Member of Major League Baseball's All-Century Team.
- Number 28 on the *Sporting News'* 1999 list of Baseball's 100 Greatest Players.
- Member of Philadelphia Baseball Wall of Fame.
- Member of Philadelphia Sports Hall of Fame.
- Named to Phillies Centennial Team in 1983.
- #20 retired by Phillies.
- Elected to Baseball Hall of Fame by members of the Baseball Writers' Association of America (BBWAA) in 1995.

2

STEVE CARLTON

aving fallen just short of earning the top spot on our list, Steve Carlton lays claim to the number 2 position, barely edging out Grover Cleveland Alexander for that distinction. One of the greatest left-handed pitchers in baseball history, Carlton won a total of 329 games over the course of his 24-year major-league career that he spent primarily with the Phillies and Cardinals. Having most of his finest seasons for the Phillies, Carlton won at least 20 games five times and struck out more than 200 batters on seven separate occasions, en route to setting franchise records for most wins and strikeouts. Also ranking extremely high in team annals in several other categories, "Lefty," as he came to be known, compiled an ERA under 3.00 five times, completed 30 of his starts once, and threw more than 250 innings 10 times, with his brilliant mound work helping the Phillies capture five division titles, two pennants, and one world championship. A four-time NL Cy Young Award winner, Carlton also earned five top-10 finishes in the league MVP voting and seven All-Star nominations during his time in Philadelphia, before being further honored following the conclusion of his playing career by having his #32 retired by the Phillies and being elected to the Baseball Hall of Fame.

Born in Miami, Florida, on December 22, 1944, Steven Norman Carlton developed his pitching skills while playing Little League and American Legion baseball in his home state, before emerging as a multisport star at North Miami High School, where he excelled in both baseball and basketball. After quitting the basketball team his senior year to focus exclusively on baseball, Carlton performed so well on the mound that he began to draw the attention of pro scouts, who followed him to Miami-Dade Community College the following year. Offered a $5,000 signing bonus by the St. Louis Cardinals while still just a freshman at Miami-Dade, Carlton decided to turn pro at the tender age of 18, after which he began his career with Rock Hill of the Class A Western Carolinas League in 1964.

Although Carlton initially found his velocity being questioned by some scouts, he advanced rapidly through the St. Louis farm system after instituting a rigorous workout regimen that enabled him to add some much-needed bulk onto his lean 6'4" frame, leaving him at close to 210 pounds. Having developed a decent curveball and a well-above-average fastball, Carlton spent part of the 1965 campaign in St. Louis, appearing in a total of 15 games, but failing to record a decision. Receiving a more extensive look from the Cardinals the following year,

Steve Carlton won more games and recorded more strikeouts than anyone else in franchise history.

Carlton started nine contests and compiled a record of 3-3.

Arriving in the big leagues to stay in 1967, Carlton became a regular member of the Cardinals' starting rotation, helping them win the NL pennant for the first of two straight times by going 14-9 with a 2.98 ERA and 168 strikeouts. After earning his first All-Star selection the following year by going 13-11 with a 2.99 ERA, Carlton emerged as one of the senior circuit's top pitchers in 1969, when he finished 17-11 with 210 strikeouts and an ERA of 2.17 that placed him second in the league rankings. Ironically, Carlton turned in arguably his most dominant performance of the year during a 4–3 loss to the eventual world champion New York Mets on September 15, when, despite surrendering a pair of two-run homers to Ron Swoboda, he recorded a then-record 19 strikeouts.

After engaging in a lengthy contract dispute with the Cardinals during the subsequent offseason, Carlton suffered through a dismal 1970 campaign during which he compiled a record of just 10-19 and an ERA of 3.73. But he rebounded the following year, earning his third All-Star nomination by posting 20 victories for the first time in his career.

Coming off his big year, Carlton asked the Cardinals for a $10,000 raise, prompting St. Louis general manager Bing Devine to trade him to the Phillies for right-hander Rick Wise, in what turned out to be one of the worst trades the Redbirds ever made. In attempting to explain his thinking at the time, Devine, who made the deal at the behest of Cardinals owner

Auggie Busch, later said, "We hadn't been able to sign Carlton. There was no free agency, so he didn't have the freedom to say, 'Sign me or else.' He was being very difficult to sign for the ridiculous amount of $10,000 between what he wanted and what we'd give him. Many times, Mr. Busch gave me a little leeway in the budget, but, in the case of Carlton, Mr. Busch developed the feeling that Carlton was a 'smart-aleck young guy,' and I'm not used to having smart-alecks tell me what to do."

Initially incensed over being dealt to the Phillies, Carlton later shared his recollections of the trade that sent him to Philadelphia, saying, "Auggie Busch traded me to the last-place Phillies over a salary dispute. I was mentally committed to winning 25 games with the Cardinals and now I had to re-think my goals. I decided to stay with the 25-win goal and won 27 of the Phillies' 59 victories. I consider that season my finest individual achievement."

Carlton's 1972 campaign must be considered one of the finest ever turned in by any pitcher. By compiling a record of 27-10 for the last-place Phillies, Carlton established a major-league record by posting 46 percent of his team's victories. In addition to leading all NL hurlers in wins, he finished first in ERA (1.97), strikeouts (310), complete games (30), and innings pitched (346), winning in the process the pitcher's version of the Triple Crown, his first Cy Young Award, and the Hickok Belt as the top professional athlete of the year. Carlton also finished fifth in the league MVP voting despite the Phillies' poor showing as a team.

In discussing some of the qualities that enabled Carlton to perform so magnificently, former Phillies teammate Larry Bowa stated, "He had a way of elevating everyone's game. . . . He was never indecisive on the mound. Before the game, he'd go over the hitters and say, 'This is how I'm going to pitch, and this is where I want you to play him.' He had a game plan of how to pitch to each hitter and he stuck to it. And he wanted you in a certain spot, and if they didn't hit it there, it was his responsibility. That's how he wanted it."

Meanwhile, Carlton later attributed the tremendous success he experienced in 1972 to his grueling training regimen, which included Eastern martial arts techniques, the most famous of which involved twisting his fist to the bottom of a five-gallon bucket of rice. Carlton also credited the further development of his three primary pitches—a rising fastball, a long looping curveball, and a legendary slider that he relied on more heavily than ever before. Typically breaking down-and-in to right-handed batters,

Carlton's slider proved to be virtually impossible for them to hit since it looked like a fastball until the last split-second, resulting in countless check-swings and swings-and-misses, with Carlton stating, "I threw all my pitches over the top, which was important for me because my slider was hard to tell from my fastball at release."

Describing what it was like trying to hit Carlton's slider, former Houston Astros third baseman Doug Rader said, "I had three choices when he threw it. Hit it off my ankle, miss it, or hit it foul."

Former Giants catcher Bob Brenly claimed, "It was like he had remote control on that pitch. He could put it wherever he wanted it. If you took it, it would stay in the strike zone. And if you swung, it would break down by your ankles or in the dirt."

And Tim McCarver, who made a career out of catching Carlton, first with the Cardinals and, later, as a member of the Phillies, noted, "When I played for other teams against Steve, I could hear the righthanded hitters saying, 'He may have gotten me out, but at least he didn't throw me the slider.'"

Although Carlton proved to be a workhorse once again in 1973, leading all NL hurlers with 40 starts, 293 1/3 innings pitched, and 18 complete games, he didn't pitch nearly as well, finishing the season with a record of 13-20 and an ERA of 3.90. While at least part of Carlton's relative ineffectiveness could be attributed to occasional soreness in his left elbow, articles began appearing in the local newspapers questioning his somewhat unusual training techniques and fondness for fine wine. Growing increasingly indignant over his treatment by the members of the press corps, Carlton severed all ties with the media at the conclusion of the 1973 campaign, vowing to never again answer their questions. Looking back at his acrimonious relationship with the media, Carlton suggested, "It [not talking to the media from 1974 through the end of his career] was perfect for me at the time. It took me two years to make up my mind. I was tired of getting slammed. To me, it was a slap in the face. But it [his silence] made me concentrate better."

Still bothered by occasional pain in his pitching elbow, Carlton posted a combined record of 31-27 from 1974 to 1975, earning All-Star honors in the first of those campaigns by going 16-13, with a 3.22 ERA and a league-leading 240 strikeouts. Fully healthy by the start of the 1976 season, Carlton began an exceptional seven-year run during which he posted the following numbers:

YEAR	W-L	ERA	SO	SHO	CG	IP	WHIP
1976	20-7	3.13	195	2	13	252.2	1.172
1977	**23**-10	2.64	198	2	17	283	1.124
1978	16-13	2.84	161	3	12	247.1	1.177
1979	18-11	3.62	213	4	13	251	1.159
1980	**24**-9	2.34	**286**	3	13	**304**	1.095
1981	13-4	2.42	179	1	10	190	1.126
1982	**23**-11	3.10	**286**	**6**	**19**	**295.2**	1.147

Consistently ranking among the NL leaders in wins, strikeouts, complete games, and innings pitched, Carlton topped the senior circuit in each of those categories at least once, while also leading the league in shutouts once and finishing second in ERA in 1980, when he came within 14 percentage points of winning the pitcher's version of the Triple Crown for the second time. Performing especially well in 1977, 1980, and 1982, Carlton earned NL Cy Young honors and a top-10 finish in the league MVP voting all three years, placing fifth in the balloting in both 1977 and 1980. Meanwhile, the Phillies won four division titles, one pennant, and the 1980 World Series, with Carlton posting a perfect 3-0 record during that year's postseason.

Revealing the tremendous amount of confidence that Carlton inspired in his teammates every time he took the mound, Jim Kaat said, "There was no better feeling than thinking about how important the game was going to be tomorrow and knowing, 'Lefty's pitching.' When you knew that, you knew, 'The bullpen's going to get a night off.' And you knew, 'We've got a win in the bag.' When this team played behind Lefty, everybody thought, 'We're gonna win,' every night. And that epitomizes what a No. 1, Hall of Fame pitcher is all about."

Admired by his teammates for more than just his pitching skills, Carlton also drew praise for the extraordinary focus he exhibited on the mound, with former Phillies third baseman and coach John Vukovich saying, "When I think of Lefty, the first thing I think of is his presence on the mound and the way he carried himself. Lefty never had excuses. He would get a questionable call from the umpire and his reaction was no different than if it was a called strike. He just got the ball back and was ready to throw again."

Vukovich continued, "I hear that word focus now, and I laugh. Lefty didn't just focus. He was in a zone all his own. . . . He had that mystique about him, even among us. On days he pitched, about the only conversation you'd ever have with him was, 'Hi, Lefty.' We left him alone."

Meanwhile, Larry Bowa related the following story: "I saw Billy Williams hit a line drive at Wrigley Field that hit him right in the neck. And this was not a broken-bat job. This was a line drive. Most guys would have crumbled. I mean, you could see the laces from the ball on his neck. But Lefty just picked the ball up, threw it to first and got the out. Then everybody started running out, and he just waved his glove, like, 'Get out of here.'"

Carlton pitched well for the Phillies for two more years, going 15-16, with a 3.11 ERA and a league-leading 275 strikeouts and 283 2/3 innings pitched in 1983, before compiling a record of 13-7 and an ERA of 3.58 the following season. But, after getting off to a 1-8 start in 1985, Carlton spent most of the season's second half on the disabled list with a strained rotator cuff. Beginning the ensuing campaign in similar fashion, Carlton won just 4 of his first 12 decisions and compiled an ERA of 6.18 in his 16 starts, prompting the Phillies to ask him to retire. Carlton, though, refused to do so, forcing the team to finally release him on June 24. Carlton then broke more than a decade of silence in the media to voice his reasons for not speaking and thank the Philadelphia fans for their support. In his 15 years with the Phillies, Carlton compiled an overall record of 241-161, an ERA of 3.09, and a WHIP of 1.211, struck out 3,031 batters, and threw 3,697 1/3 innings, 185 complete games, and 39 shutouts.

After leaving Philadelphia, Carlton split the remainder of the 1986 campaign between the San Francisco Giants and the Chicago White Sox, before pitching for the Cleveland Indians and the Minnesota Twins the following year, experiencing very little success with all four teams. Released by the Twins early in 1988, Carlton announced his retirement, ending his career with a record of 329-244, an ERA of 3.22, a WHIP of 1.247, 4,136 strikeouts, 5,217 2/3 innings pitched, 254 complete games, and 55 shutouts. At the time of his retirement, Carlton ranked second all-time only to Nolan Ryan in strikeouts (he has since slipped to fourth). More than 30 years later, Carlton remains the last NL pitcher to win as many as 25 games in a season and the last pitcher in either league to throw more than 300 innings in a season.

Expressing his admiration for Carlton, former Phillies outfielder and longtime broadcaster Richie Ashburn said, "Lefty was a craftsman, an artist. He was a perfectionist. He painted a ballgame. Stroke, stroke, stroke, and when he got through [pitching a game] it was a masterpiece."

Author Peter Golenbock wrote in *The Spirit of St. Louis*: "Carlton was not your normal guy. Communicating with him was not always easy. On the mound, he would tune out all distractions. Off the mound, he did the same. If he considered you the distraction, he'd direct at you an icy stare. Teammates considered him to be a recluse. He hated to sign autographs. He refused to talk to reporters for long stretches at a time. He was devoted to the martial arts. He studied Far East religions. He was a wine connoisseur. He pissed people off with his stand-offishness and arrogance. Carlton was also the finest lefthanded pitcher of his generation. . . . Unfortunately, most of his career was not spent in St. Louis but rather in Philadelphia."

Following his playing days, Carlton retreated to Durango, Colorado, where he spent much of his time riding motorcycles and dirt bikes, skiing, and making public appearances at charity golf outings. Carlton, who gained induction into the Baseball Hall of Fame the very first time his name appeared on the ballot in 1994, later received the additional honor of being ranked number 30 by the *Sporting News* on its 1999 list of Baseball's 100 Greatest Players.

Waxing philosophical about his playing career many years later, Carlton stated, "Everything I was, physically and mentally, that's what I put on that field. . . . So, what I did on the field was the essence of what I am. Remember me like that."

Meanwhile, when asked during an interview with Roy Firestone why he believes he was put on this earth, Carlton responded, "To teach the world how to throw a slider."

PHILLIES CAREER HIGHLIGHTS

Best Season

As well as Carlton pitched throughout most of his 15-year tenure in Philadelphia, his performance in 1972 stands out above all others. Establishing career-best marks in every major pitching category, Carlton earned Cy Young honors for the first of four times by going 27-10, with eight shutouts, a WHIP of 0.993, and a league-leading 1.97 ERA, 310 strikeouts, 30 complete games, 346 1/3 innings pitched, and strikeouts-to-walks ratio of 3.56. Particularly effective from mid-July to mid-August, Carlton threw 31 consecutive scoreless innings from July 19 to August 1. Then, after surrendering a run in the fourth inning of a 4–1 win over the Mets on August 1, he began another string of 27 consecutive scoreless innings that lasted until August 13.

Memorable Moments/Greatest Performances

Carlton excelled in his first start as a member of the Phillies, allowing just two runs on four hits in eight innings of work during a 4–2 win over the Chicago Cubs in the opening game of the 1972 regular season.

Carlton followed that up by winning a 1–0 pitchers' duel with former Cardinals teammate Bob Gibson on April 19, 1972, yielding just three hits to his old team.

Carlton proved to be even more dominant in his next start, recording 14 strikeouts, walking one batter, and allowing just a first-inning leadoff single to Chris Speier during a 3–0, one-hit shutout of the Giants on April 25, 1972.

In addition to recording 12 strikeouts and surrendering just three hits during a 2–0 win over the Pirates on August 9, 1972, Carlton hit a solo homer off Steve Blass in the top of the third inning.

Carlton tossed another three-hit shutout on July 14, 1973, helping his own cause by hitting a two-run homer off Jerry Reuss during a 7–0 win over the Houston Astros.

Carlton allowed just a fourth-inning single to Jim Wynn and a pinch-hit single in the top of the eighth inning to Manny Mota during a 4–0, two-hit shutout of the Dodgers on June 7, 1975.

Carlton struck out nine batters, issued five walks, and surrendered just one hit during an 8–1 victory over the Mets on September 27, 1975, yielding just a sixth-inning RBI double by Félix Millán.

Carlton experienced one of his greatest thrills when he homered off Don Sutton with two men on base in the top of the second inning of a 9–4 win over the Dodgers in Game 3 of the 1978 NLCS.

Carlton threw a one-hit shutout against the Houston Astros on June 5, 1979, allowing just four walks and a seventh-inning single by Jeffrey Leonard during an 8–0 Phillies win.

Carlton tossed another one-hit shutout one month later, recording nine strikeouts, issuing no walks, and yielding just a seventh-inning double to Elliott Maddox during a 1–0 victory over the Mets on July 4, 1979, also scoring the game's only run in the bottom of the third inning, when, after doubling to right field, he came home on an RBI double by Bake McBride.

Carlton again surrendered just one hit during a 7–0 shutout of the Cardinals on April 26, 1980, allowing just a second-inning single to Ted Simmons.

Carlton turned in another dominant performance on October 1, 1980, recording 10 strikeouts, issuing two walks, and yielding just two hits during a 5–0 win over the Cubs, who failed to get their first hit until the top of the eighth inning, when Mike Vail delivered a leadoff single to center field.

Carlton shut out the Giants on just two hits on May 14, 1982, allowing only back-to-back singles to Bob Brenly and Johnnie LeMaster with two men out in the top of the eighth inning during a 2–0 win.

Although Carlton surrendered 10 hits and issued two walks during a complete-game 4–2 victory over the Cubs on June 9, 1982, he recorded 16 strikeouts, which represented his highest single-game total as a member of the Phillies.

Carlton punctuated a 2–0 shutout of the Cardinals on September 13, 1982, during which he allowed just three hits and recorded 12 strikeouts, by hitting a solo homer off Bob Forsch in the bottom of the fifth inning.

Carlton tossed a two-hit shutout against the Montreal Expos on September 29, 1982, yielding just a fifth-inning single by Joel Youngblood and a ninth-inning leadoff single by Tim Raines during a 4–0 Phillies win.

Carlton recorded the 300th victory of his career on September 23, 1983, striking out 12 batters in eight innings of work during a 6–2 win over the Cardinals.

Carlton delivered the key blow of a 7–2 victory over the Dodgers on May 16, 1984, when he homered off Fernando Valenzuela with the bases loaded in the top of the fourth inning.

Notable Achievements

- Won at least 20 games five times, surpassing 25 victories once.
- Posted winning percentage over .600 eight times, topping the .700-mark on four occasions.
- Compiled ERA under 3.00 five times, finishing with mark under 2.00 once.
- Posted WHIP under 1.000 once.
- Struck out more than 200 batters seven times, recording more than 300 strikeouts once.
- Threw more than 250 innings 10 times, tossing more than 300 frames twice.

- Threw at least 17 complete games five times, completing 30 of his starts once.
- Tossed eight shutouts in 1972.
- Led NL pitchers in wins four times, winning percentage once, ERA once, strikeouts five times, complete games three times, innings pitched five times, shutouts once, strikeouts-to-walks ratio twice, and starts four times.
- Finished second among NL pitchers in wins once, winning percentage twice, ERA once, strikeouts three times, complete games three times, innings pitched once, shutouts once, WHIP once, and starts twice.
- Finished third among NL pitchers in wins once, winning percentage once, complete games twice, innings pitched twice, WHIP once, strikeouts-to-walks ratio once, and assists once.
- Ranks among MLB all-time leaders in wins (11th), strikeouts (4th), innings pitched (9th), and games started (6th).
- Holds Phillies career records for most wins (241), strikeouts (3,031), and starts (499).
- Ranks among Phillies career leaders in winning percentage (tied for 10th), complete games (3rd), innings pitched (2nd), shutouts (2nd), and pitching appearances (2nd).
- Five-time division champion (1976, 1977, 1978, 1980, and 1983).
- Two-time NL champion (1980 and 1983).
- 1980 world champion.
- Three-time NL Player of the Week.
- May 1980 NL Pitcher of the Month.
- Won pitcher's version of Triple Crown in 1972.
- 1981 Gold Glove Award winner.
- Finished in top 10 in NL MVP voting five times, placing fifth on three occasions.
- Four-time NL Cy Young Award winner (1972, 1977, 1980, and 1982).
- Four-time *Sporting News* NL Pitcher of the Year (1972, 1977, 1980, and 1982).
- Five-time *Sporting News* NL All-Star selection (1972, 1977, 1979, 1980, and 1982).
- Seven-time NL All-Star (1972, 1974, 1977, 1979, 1980, 1981, and 1982).
- Number 30 on the *Sporting News'* 1999 list of Baseball's 100 Greatest Players.
- Member of Philadelphia Baseball Wall of Fame.

- Member of Philadelphia Sports Hall of Fame.
- Named to Phillies Centennial Team in 1983.
- #32 retired by Phillies.
- Elected to Baseball Hall of Fame by members of BBWAA in 1994.

3

GROVER
CLEVELAND ALEXANDER

Had Grover Cleveland Alexander spent more time in Philadelphia, he likely would have laid claim to the top spot in these rankings. One of the greatest pitchers in baseball history, Alexander posted 373 victories over the course of his 20-year major-league career, tying him with Christy Mathewson for the third most wins in MLB history. Amassing 190 of those victories for the Phillies from 1911 to 1917, the man affectionately known to his teammates as "Old Pete" won more than 20 games six times as a member of the team, surpassing 30 victories on three separate occasions. Alexander also compiled an ERA under 2.00 three times, threw more than 30 complete games five times, tossed more than 10 shutouts twice, and recorded more than 200 strikeouts four times, en route to winning the pitcher's version of the Triple Crown on three separate occasions and leading the Phillies to their first pennant. The franchise's all-time leader in shutouts (61) and winning percentage (.676), Alexander continues to rank extremely high in team annals in virtually every major statistical category for pitchers more than a century after he won his last game in a Phillies uniform.

Born in the farming community of Elba, Nebraska, on February 26, 1887, Grover Cleveland Alexander owed his name to US president Grover Cleveland, who was in his first term of office at the time. Growing up on a farm with his 12 siblings, Alexander later described his youth as "more or less a matter of long days of work and short nights of sleep." Yet, the many chores that Alexander performed during his formative years contributed greatly to the success he eventually experienced on the pitcher's mound, with his father later crediting the exceptional movement on his curveball to the powerful right wrist he developed while shucking corn. Meanwhile, young Grover developed the pinpoint control that later became his trademark by throwing stones at clothespins and chickens.

After graduating from nearby St. Paul High School, Alexander chose to discontinue his education to become a telephone lineman so that he

Grover Cleveland Alexander's 16 shutouts in 1916 represent the highest single-season total in MLB history.

could play baseball on weekends. Alexander subsequently spent the next few years playing for several semipro teams, before signing his first professional contract with Galesburg of the Illinois-Missouri League in 1909. Performing extremely well in his first year of pro ball, Alexander compiled a record of 15-8, before a throw made by the opposing shortstop while attempting to complete a double play struck him in the head, knocking him unconscious for two days. Awakening with double vision, Alexander found himself unable to pitch until the following year, by which time his contract had been sold to the Syracuse Chiefs of the New York State League. Although Alexander's condition improved sufficiently to allow him to win 29 games for the Chiefs in 1910, it is believed that the long-term effects of the incident may well have caused the epilepsy that haunted him for the rest of his life.

Impressed with Alexander's exceptional pitching at the minor-league level, the Phillies purchased his contract for $750 prior to the start of the 1911 campaign. Proving to be a huge bargain, Alexander earned a third-place finish in the NL MVP voting in his very first season by compiling an ERA of 2.57, finishing second in the league with 227 strikeouts, and topping the circuit with 28 victories (against 13 losses), 31 complete games, 367 innings pitched, and seven shutouts, with his 28 wins setting a 20th-century record for rookies that stood the test of time.

Alexander followed up his extraordinary first-year performance with three more outstanding seasons, compiling an overall record of 68-40 from 1912 to 1914. Performing especially well in 1914, Alexander posted an ERA of 2.38, threw six shutouts, and led the NL with 27 wins, 214 strikeouts, 32 complete games, and 355 innings pitched. Having established himself as one of the finest pitchers in all of baseball, Alexander subsequently began an incredible three-year run during which he posted the following numbers:

YEAR	W-L	ERA	SO	SHO	CG	IP	WHIP
1915	31-10	1.22	241	12	36	376.1	0.842
1916	33-12	1.55	167	16	38	389	0.959
1917	30-13	1.83	200	8	34	388	1.010

Leading all NL hurlers in wins, ERA, and strikeouts all three years, Alexander captured the pitcher's version of the Triple Crown each season, doing so even though he pitched half his games at the hitter-friendly Baker Bowl. Alexander's fabulous performance in 1915 led the Phillies to their first pennant, after which he gave them their only win of the World Series, which resulted in a five-game loss to the Boston Red Sox. Holding Boston's lineup in check in each of his two starts, Alexander finished the Series with a record of 1-1 and an ERA of 1.53.

Alexander then led the Phillies to a second-place finish in each of the next two seasons, with his 16 shutouts in 1916 setting a single-season major-league record that still stands. Neither the AL nor the NL presented a Most Valuable Player award in any of those seasons. But, had they done so, Alexander would have been a serious contender for NL honors each year.

Although the 6'1", 185-pound Alexander had outstanding movement on his pitches, which included a live fastball that moved in on right-handed batters and a sharp-breaking curveball, the secret of his success lay primarily with his exceptional control. Employing a seemingly effortless pitching motion, a minimal windup, a short stride, and a three-quarters overhand delivery to home plate, Alexander appeared to be able to spot the ball to any place he so desired, with legendary sportswriter Grantland Rice once commenting, "He could pitch into a tin can. His control was always remarkable—the finest I have ever seen."

Meanwhile, in describing Alexander's smooth delivery to the plate, one teammate said, "He looked like he was hardly working at all, like he was throwing batting practice."

Johnny Evers, who spent several seasons hitting against Alexander before briefly managing him in Chicago following the conclusion of his playing career, expressed the sense of helplessness he felt every time he faced "Old Pete," revealing, "He made me want to throw my bat away when I went to the plate. He fed me pitches I couldn't hit. If I let them go, they were strikes. He made you hit bad balls. He could throw into a tin can all day long."

The picture of grace and efficiency on the mound, Alexander often completed games in 90 minutes or less, once telling a reporter who asked him why he worked so quickly, "What, and give him [the batter] a chance to think on my time?"

And, as to why he typically completed his starts having thrown so few pitches, Alexander responded, "What's the use of doing in three pitches what you can do in one?"

Yet, despite the brilliance Alexander displayed on the mound during his time in Philadelphia, Phillies owner William Baker elected to trade him to the Chicago Cubs for two nondescript players and $55,000 prior to the start of the 1918 campaign. Although Baker claimed at the time that he made the move because he needed the money, he later revealed that he parted ways with his team's best player because he feared that the nation's involvement in World War I would inevitably result in Alexander joining the military.

Proving Baker to be prophetic, Alexander enlisted in the US Army early in 1918, after which he spent the remainder of the year serving as an artillery officer in France. Under constant bombardment during the seven weeks that he spent at the front, Alexander experienced a series of events that traumatized him for the rest of his life. Suffering from shell shock, deafness in his left ear, muscle damage to his pitching arm, and increasingly worse seizures, Alexander also returned from the war with shrapnel in his right ear, which may have led to his bout with cancer years later. Always a heavy drinker, Alexander turned to the bottle even more, often as a means of concealing his epilepsy from others.

Somehow managing to pull himself together after he returned to the Cubs on May 11, 1919, Alexander went on to win 16 games and lead the league with nine shutouts and an ERA of 1.72. He followed that up by winning his fourth Triple Crown in 1920, concluding the campaign with a league-leading 27 wins, 173 strikeouts, and 1.91 ERA, while also topping the circuit with 33 complete games and 363 1/3 innings pitched.

Although Alexander remained an effective pitcher for several more years, surpassing 20 victories two more times and winning at least 15 games on four other occasions, his inability to throw the ball with the same velocity he once had turned him into more of a finesse pitcher who relied primarily on guile, changing speeds, pitch location, and his extraordinary control. Further hampered by an ever-increasing dependency on alcohol,

Alexander, it was said, "drank to relive the past, forget the present, and forestall the future." Ungainly even as a youth, with a uniform that never seemed to fit properly and a cap that always looked a size too small, Alexander appeared even more out of place on a baseball diamond during the latter stages of his career.

Nevertheless, Alexander won a total of 80 games for mediocre Cubs teams from 1921 to 1925, performing especially well in 1923, when, at the age of 36, he finished 22-12, with a 3.19 ERA, 26 complete games, 305 innings pitched, and a league-leading 1.108 WHIP. But, after Alexander grew increasingly insubordinate under new Chicago manager Joe McCarthy in 1926, the Cubs sold him to the St. Louis Cardinals for the waiver price at midseason. Thriving in his new surroundings, Alexander helped the Cardinals capture the NL pennant by winning nine games over the season's final three months. He then performed brilliantly in the World Series, leading St. Louis to a seven-game upset victory over the Yankees by earning complete-game wins in Games 2 and 6, before making an unexpected appearance in the decisive seventh contest.

With the Cardinals ahead 3–2, the bases loaded, two men out in the bottom of the seventh inning, and Yankees slugger Tony Lazzeri due to hit, Alexander entered the game (according to legend) with a huge hangover he acquired the previous evening after pitching his team to victory. Alexander struck out Lazzeri and then threw two more hitless innings to wrap up the world championship for his team, with the 39-year-old right-hander's performance remaining one of the most memorable in the history of the Fall Classic. Asked years later why he chose to bring Alexander into the game under such extenuating circumstances, Cardinals player-manager Rogers Hornsby said, "I'd rather him pitch a crucial game for me drunk than anyone I've ever known sober. He was that good."

Alexander had two more good years for the Cardinals, winning 21 games in 1927 and another 16 the following year, before his skills finally left him. After posting only nine victories in 1929, Alexander found himself headed back to Philadelphia when St. Louis traded him to the Phillies at season's end. The 42-year-old hurler subsequently ended his major-league career in the same place it began, making his final mound appearance on May 28, 1930, before being released by the Phillies a few days later after getting off to a 0-3 start. Over the course of 20 big-league seasons, Alexander compiled a record of 373-208, an ERA of 2.56, and a WHIP of 1.121. He also recorded 2,198 strikeouts, threw 5,190 innings and 436 complete games, and tossed 90 shutouts—a figure that places him second all-time only to Washington Senators great Walter Johnson. In addition to tossing 61 shutouts and posting an overall record of 190-91 as a member of the Phillies, Alexander compiled an ERA of 2.18 and a WHIP of 1.075, registered 1,409 strikeouts, and threw 2,513 2/3 innings and 219 complete games during his time in Philadelphia.

Although Alexander experienced one more moment of glory when he gained induction into the Baseball Hall of Fame in 1938, his remaining days proved to be extremely unhappy ones. After leaving the majors, Alexander pitched in demeaning circumstances with touring teams for another 10 years. Unable to cure his drinking problem even though he visited numerous sanitariums in an effort to do so, Alexander roamed the country, staying in cheap hotels and falling in and out of poverty, while taking on several odd jobs. After suffering a heart attack in 1946, Alexander injured himself while falling down a flight of stairs during an epileptic seizure the following year. Doctors discovered cancer on his right ear, which subsequently had to be removed. Three years later, Alexander attended Game 3 of the 1950 World Series at Yankee Stadium, where he saw the Phillies lose to the Yankees. He died less than a month later, on November 4, 1950, in St. Paul, Nebraska, at the age of 63.

Following Alexander's passing, Grantland Rice called him the "most cunning, the smartest, and the best control pitcher that baseball had ever seen," adding, "Above everything else, Alex had one terrific feature to his pitching—he knew just what the batter didn't want—and he put it there to the half-inch."

PHILLIES CAREER HIGHLIGHTS

Best Season

Alexander established himself as baseball's preeminent pitcher from 1915 to 1917, leading all NL hurlers in wins, ERA, strikeouts, shutouts, complete games, and innings pitched three straight times. Certainly, a strong case could be made for identifying any of those seasons as the finest of Alexander's career, with his major-league record 16 shutouts in 1916 making that year a particularly plausible selection. Nevertheless, I opted to go with 1915 instead, since, in addition to winning 31 games, completing 36 of his starts, tossing 12 shutouts, and throwing 376 1/3 innings, Alexander established career-best marks in ERA (1.22), strikeouts (241), and WHIP (0.842), with his fabulous performance leading the Phillies to the NL pennant.

Memorable Moments/Greatest Performances

Alexander put together a pair of impressive scoreless-innings streaks in 1911, throwing 27 consecutive scoreless frames from June 21 to June 30, before tossing another 41 straight scoreless innings from September 7 to September 24.

Alexander turned in the first truly dominant performance of his career on May 8, 1911, allowing just three hits and recording nine strikeouts during a 5–0 shutout of the Brooklyn Superbas.

Alexander earned a 2–1, 15-inning complete-game victory over the Superbas on June 21, 1911, yielding nine hits and three walks along the way.

Alexander won a 1–0 pitchers' duel with Cy Young of the Boston Rustlers on September 7, 1911, issuing no walks and allowing just a single by outfielder Dock Miller in the process.

An extremely capable hitter who posted a lifetime batting average of .209, hit 11 home runs, and knocked in a total of 163 runs, Alexander homered for the first time in his career during a 10–2 win over the Cincinnati Reds on August 10, 1912.

Alexander surrendered just two hits, issued no walks, and recorded 11 strikeouts during a 7–0 victory over the St. Louis Cardinals on September 19, 1912, allowing only a single by center fielder Walton Cruise and a double by right fielder Chief Wilson.

Alexander punctuated a 7–0, two-hit shutout of the Superbas on September 26, 1912, by driving in a pair of runs with a double.

Alexander yielded just two hits and struck out nine batters during a 3–0 win over the Cubs on May 25, 1915.

Alexander amazingly threw four one-hitters in 1915, allowing just a two-out single in the bottom of the ninth inning by shortstop Art Butler during a 3–0 win over the Cardinals on June 5, a single by Hall of Fame outfielder Zack Wheat during a 4–0 victory over the Brooklyn Robins on June 26, a double by first baseman Fred Merkle during a 2–0 shutout of the Giants on July 5, and a single by former Phillies teammate Sherry Magee during a 5–0 win over the Braves on September 29.

Alexander fashioned another lengthy pair of scoreless-innings streaks in 1916, keeping the opposition off the scoreboard for 30 consecutive frames from May 8 to May 22, before throwing another 30 2/3 straight scoreless innings from August 5 to August 21.

Alexander shut out the Reds, 6–0, on two hits on July 20, 1916, yielding just a pair of harmless singles to third baseman Heinie Groh and pinch-hitter Clarence Mitchell.

Alexander started and won both ends of a doubleheader against the Reds on September 23, 1916, allowing two earned runs and 13 hits during a complete-game 7–3 victory in Game 1, before tossing a 4–0, eight-hit shutout in the nightcap.

Alexander turned in an outstanding all-around effort on May 23, 1917, recording eight strikeouts and surrendering just two hits during a 5–1 win over the Reds, while also going 3-for-3 at the plate, with a homer and two runs scored.

Notable Achievements

- Won more than 20 games six times, surpassing 30 victories on three occasions.
- Posted winning percentage over .600 six times, finishing with mark above .700 three times.
- Compiled ERA under 2.50 four times, finishing with mark below 2.00 on three occasions.
- Struck out at least 200 batters four times.
- Finished in double digits in shutouts twice.
- Threw more than 300 innings seven times, tossing more than 350 frames five times.
- Threw more than 20 complete games seven times, completing more than 30 of his starts on five occasions.
- Posted WHIP under 1.000 twice.
- Led NL pitchers in wins five times, winning percentage once, ERA three times, strikeouts five times, shutouts five times, innings pitched six times, complete games five times, WHIP twice, strikeouts-to-walks ratio twice, games started twice, putouts four times, and assists twice.
- Finished second among NL pitchers in ERA once, winning percentage once, strikeouts once, strikeouts-to-walks ratio twice, and starts twice.
- Finished third among NL pitchers in winning percentage once, strike-outs once, shutouts once, innings pitched once, complete games once, WHIP once, and starts twice.
- Holds MLB single-season record for most shutouts (16 in 1916).
- Ranks among MLB all-time leaders in wins (tied for 3rd), shutouts (2nd), innings pitched (10th), and assists by a pitcher (3rd).
- Holds Phillies single-season records for lowest ERA (1.22 in 1915), most shutouts (16 in 1916), lowest WHIP (0.842 in 1915), and fewest hits allowed per nine innings pitched (6.050 in 1915).

- Holds Phillies career records for most shutouts (61) and highest winning percentage (.676).
- Ranks among Phillies career leaders in wins (3rd), ERA (3rd), strikeouts (6th), complete games (2nd), innings pitched (3rd), WHIP (2nd), pitching appearances (9th), and starts (5th).
- 1915 NL champion.
- Won pitcher's version of Triple Crown three straight times (1915, 1916, and 1917).
- Finished in top 10 in NL MVP voting twice, placing as high as third in 1911.
- Number 12 on the *Sporting News'* 1999 list of Baseball's 100 Greatest Players.
- Member of Philadelphia Baseball Wall of Fame.
- Member of Philadelphia Sports Hall of Fame.
- Elected to Baseball Hall of Fame by members of BBWAA in 1938.

4

CHUCK KLEIN

Nicknamed the "Hoosier Hammer" for his Indiana roots and tremendous power at the plate, Chuck Klein proved to be the National League's preeminent slugger from 1929 to 1933, topping the senior circuit in virtually every major offensive category at least once. A four-time home-run champion, Klein also led the league in total bases four times, runs scored and slugging percentage three times, RBIs, hits, doubles, and OPS twice, and batting average, stolen bases, and on-base percentage once each, earning in the process one NL MVP award, two runner-up finishes in the balloting, and one All-Star selection. Spending parts of 15 seasons with the Phillies in three tours of duty with the club, Klein continues to rank among the franchise's career leaders in most offensive categories nearly 80 years after he played his last game in Philadelphia. A solid defender as well, Klein led all NL outfielders in assists three times and double plays once, with his excellent all-around play eventually earning him a bust in Cooperstown and a number 92 ranking on the *Sporting News*' 1999 list of Baseball's 100 Greatest Players.

Born to German-immigrant parents in Indianapolis, Indiana, on October 7, 1904, Charles Herbert Klein grew up on a farm, where he discovered at an early age that he preferred playing baseball to attending class, recalling years later, "I worked on a farm. Played ball and loafed along the fishing and swimming holes of the White River, and my boyhood was not a lot different from that of other youngsters. I avoided as much work as possible in the classroom but did all the work possible on the ball field."

Emerging as a star athlete at Southport High School, Klein established himself as the school's best baseball player before long, excelling on the mound, in the outfield, and at the plate. Nevertheless, due to poor grades and a lack of money, Klein never seriously considered going to college, instead taking a job on a construction road gang, before going to work at a nearby steel mill, where he spent three long years heaving 200-pound white-hot ingots into a blast furnace six days a week. Later crediting his unusual physical strength to his work at the mill, Klein stated, "There is one thing I can say about working in a steel mill. If it does not kill you, it will make a man out of you."

Playing baseball after his shift and on weekends, Klein starred in the outfield for a local semipro team, performing so well that in 1927 he left the mill and signed a minor-league contract with Evansville of the Three-I League. Continuing to excel in the minors, Klein moved on to the Central League, where he compiled a batting average of .331 for Fort Wayne in 1928, prompting the Phillies to purchase his contract at midseason. Arriving in Philadelphia at the end of July, Klein started

Chuck Klein earned NL MVP honors in 1932.
Courtesy of RMYAuctions.com

64 games for the Phillies in right field over the season's final three months, batting .360, hitting 11 homers, driving in 34 runs, and scoring 41 times, before beginning an extraordinary five-year run during which he posted the following numbers:

YEAR	HR	RBI	RUNS	HITS	AVG	OBP	SLG	OPS
1929	**43**	145	126	219	.356	.407	.657	1.065
1930	40	170	**158**	250	.386	.436	.687	1.123
1931	**31**	**121**	**121**	200	.337	.398	**.584**	.982
1932	38	137	**152**	**226**	.348	.404	**.646**	**1.050**
1933	28	**120**	101	**223**	.368	.422	.602	1.025

In addition to placing at, or near, the top of the NL rankings in each of those categories all five years, Klein led the league in stolen bases once, doubles twice, and total bases and extra-base hits four times each, with his 170 RBIs, 59 doubles, 445 total bases, and 107 extra-base hits in 1930 all setting single-season franchise records that still stand. Klein, who accomplished the rare feat of amassing more than 400 total bases in a season on three separate occasions, also consistently ranked among the league leaders in outfield assists, with his 44 assists in 1930 remaining a modern major-league record. Even though the Phillies finished fourth in the NL in 1932, 12 games out of first, Klein earned league MVP honors with his outstanding performance. He also finished second in the voting in both 1931 and 1933, winning the Triple Crown in the second of those campaigns, while also earning the distinction of being named to the National League's inaugural All-Star team.

Quite surprised by the tremendous amount of success he experienced so early in his career, Klein told reporters at the end of 1929, "I find it very difficult to realize that I, Chuck Klein, the chap who was working in a steel mill three years ago, am the same fellow who led the National League in home runs this season. Isn't that a laugh?"

Yet, the powerfully built Klein, who stood 6 foot and weighed 190 pounds, remained extremely confident in his own abilities, telling a reporter from the *Philadelphia Evening Bulletin* when he arrived at spring training the following year, "I think I can hit 50 home runs this year. Last year, I didn't really try for homers until I realized I had a chance for the [NL] record. I'm going to try this year right from the start, and I'm sure I can beat my own record."

Certainly, the National League's experimentation with the use of a livelier ball in 1929 and 1930 contributed greatly to the exceptional numbers that Klein posted in his first two full seasons. The left-handed-hitting Klein also had the good fortune of playing his home games at the Baker Bowl, whose right field wall stood only 280 feet from home plate down the line and just 300 feet to the power alley in right-center. In fact, even though the fence in right stood 60 feet high, Klein's home and away splits from 1928 to 1933 serve as a clear indication of just how much he benefited from playing half his games at the Baker Bowl. While Klein batted .420, hit 131 homers, and knocked in 469 runs at home, he batted just .296, hit only 60 homers, and drove in just 259 runs in virtually the same number of games on the road. Nevertheless, Klein posted a composite batting average of .359 and averaged 36 home runs, 139 RBIs, 132 runs scored, 224 hits, 46 doubles, and 396 total bases over the course of his first five full seasons—impressive figures in any ballpark.

Klein also gradually developed into an above-average defensive outfielder with the help of Phillies manager Burt Shotton, who suggested that he employ a quicker release when attempting to throw out runners on the basepaths. Recalling the lessons that he learned from Shotton, Klein said, "Shotton told me: 'From the outfield, you never throw a man out by more than a step. If you take a step before you throw, that's the step which allows the runner to tie you. You probably lose him. If you take two steps, you're sure to lose him.'" Meanwhile, Klein became extremely adept at playing the tricky caroms off the high right field wall at the Baker Bowl.

Unfortunately, Klein played for losing teams in Philadelphia, and, with attendance dwindling following the onset of the Great Depression, Phillies owner Gerald Nugent found it necessary to trade away his team's best player to help meet the club's debts. Completing a deal with the Cubs on November 21, 1933, Nugent sent Klein to Chicago for shortstop Mark Koenig, outfielder Harvey Hendrick, pitcher Ted Kleinhans, and $65,000 in cash.

Klein subsequently got off to a fast start following his arrival in Chicago in 1934, hitting 14 homers, driving in 40 runs, scoring 38 times, and batting .333 in his first 41 games with the Cubs. But, after injuring his leg on May 30, Klein failed to maintain that same torrid pace, telling a reporter years later, "When I joined the Cubs, I started out doing good work. I thought I was set for one of my best years, but on the 30th of May, while I was running the bases, I tore a muscle loose in the back of one of my legs. It bothered me, but I stayed on my feet for some time until I discovered that I was making a bad matter worse. Without any hesitation, I'll say that my disappointing work in 1934 was mainly due to my leg. It hurt me in 1935 too."

Finally forced to surrender his spot in the starting lineup after continuing to play on his injured leg for nearly two months, Klein slumped badly the rest of the year, finishing the season with just 20 home runs, 80 RBIs, 78 runs scored, and a batting average of .301. Still hampered by the injury in 1935, Klein appeared in only 119 games, hitting 21 homers, driving in 73 runs, scoring 71 times, and batting .293.

Yet, even in his somewhat diminished state, Klein made an extremely favorable impression on Cubs teammate Billy Herman, who later said, "Klein was strong—very, very strong. And a hell of a competitor." Herman then added, "No player would have played with the injured leg that Chuck had with the Cubs."

While Klein's ailing leg contributed greatly to the subpar numbers he compiled during his time in Chicago, he later admitted that the intense pressure he felt to produce as the Cubs' "next great slugger" after leaving the friendly confines of Philadelphia adversely affected his performance as well. Klein also found his play being compromised somewhat by a growing dependency on alcohol that continued to plague him for the remainder of his career.

When Klein got off to another slow start in 1936, the Cubs included him in a four-player trade they completed with the Phillies on May 21 that netted them outfielder Ethan Allen and pitcher Curt Davis. Experiencing something of a rebirth upon his return to Philadelphia, Klein ended up finishing the season with 25 home runs, 104 RBIs, 102 runs scored, and a batting average of .306. He followed that up by hitting 15 homers, driving in 57 runs, scoring 74 times, and batting .325 in 1937, despite missing more than a month of the season due to injury.

With the Phillies moving from the Baker Bowl into more spacious Shibe Park in 1938, and with age, injuries, and a growing drinking problem continuing to take their toll on Klein, the 33-year-old outfielder experienced his worst season to date, finishing the year with just eight home runs, 61 RBIs, 53 runs scored, and a .247 batting average. Klein subsequently spent the first two months of the ensuing campaign serving the Phillies primarily as a backup, before being released by the team on June 6.

Recalling his feelings upon learning that he had been cut loose, Klein later told sportswriter Jack Singer, "I didn't sleep that night. I was out of a job and didn't know what the future held in store for me. I got up early the next day and bought the papers. 'Klein Released by Phillies' mocked the headlines. I crumpled them up savagely and threw them into the waste basket."

Still only 34 years old, Klein refused to believe that he had nothing left, telling Singer, "'I can't be through as a major league player,' I said to myself again and again. 'All I need is a chance to play regularly.'"

Feeling the same way, the Pittsburgh Pirates signed Klein just one day later and inserted him into their everyday lineup, giving him the chance that he craved. Making the most of his opportunity, Klein performed well the rest of the year, hitting 11 homers, driving in 47 runs, and batting .300 in 85 games, only to be released again prior to the start of the 1940 season.

Ironically, Klein subsequently re-signed with the Phillies, with whom he spent the next five seasons assuming the role of a player-coach, serving them primarily during games as a pinch-hitter, although he occasionally played the outfield as well. Relinquishing his coaching duties at the end of 1945 after making his last appearance as a player midway through the 1944 campaign, Klein ended his major-league career with 300 home runs, 1,201 RBIs, 1,168 runs scored, 2,076 hits, 398 doubles, 74 triples, 79 stolen bases, a .320 batting average, a .379 on-base percentage, and a .543 slugging percentage. In his three tours of duty with the Phillies, Klein hit 243 homers, knocked in 983 runs, scored 963 times, stole 71 bases, batted .326, compiled an on-base percentage of .382, posted a slugging percentage of .553, and amassed 1,705 hits, 336 doubles, and 64 triples.

After leaving the game, Klein briefly operated a neighborhood tavern at the corner of Coral and York Streets in the Kensington section of

Philadelphia before his health began to deteriorate. Though still a relatively young man, Klein suffered a stroke in 1947 that left him, according to his brother, "in a semi-coma." Almost unable to walk, barely able to speak, and experiencing lapses in memory, Klein was diagnosed with a disease of the central nervous system that had been aggravated by alcohol and a poor diet. Subsequently cared for by his mother and brother, Klein gave up drinking and made a partial recovery, although he never returned to full health. Unable to work his final years, Klein divorced his wife in 1956. Two years later, on March 28, 1958, he died of a cerebral hemorrhage at age 53.

Kept out of the Baseball Hall of Fame for years by those who questioned the legitimacy of the numbers he compiled while playing in the Baker Bowl, Klein never came close to gaining induction into Cooperstown until his followers embarked on a campaign to get him elected. Finally admitted by the Veterans Committee in 1980, Klein later received the following words of praise from author Michael Francis Mann in his book *Baseball's Rare Triple Crown*: "It was unfortunate that it took the Hall of Fame until 1980, well after his death on March 28, 1958, to recognize his greatness. But no longer does he go unnoticed for his greatness, and the plaque in Cooperstown is testament to that. And in Philadelphia, he will always be remembered as the superstar who had five of the greatest seasons ever produced in baseball history, and as the favorite Phillie of 1933."

PHILLIES CAREER HIGHLIGHTS

Best Season

Klein compiled an incredibly impressive stat-line in 1930, when he posted career-high marks in nine different offensive categories. But, at least to some degree, those numbers could be attributed to the senior circuit's use of a livelier ball, which caused an offensive explosion throughout the league. As a result, Klein finished first in the NL in just three offensive categories. On the other hand, Klein led the league in seven different categories when he earned NL MVP honors two years later, topping the circuit with 38 homers, 152 runs scored, 226 hits, 420 total bases, 20 stolen bases, a slugging percentage of .646, and an OPS of 1.050, while also ranking among the leaders with 137 RBIs, 15 triples, 50 doubles, and a batting average of .348. By leading the NL in both home runs and stolen bases, Klein became the only post-1920 player to finish first in his league in both categories in the same season. Factoring everything into the equation, the 1932 campaign would have to be considered the finest of Klein's career.

Memorable Moments/Greatest Performances

Klein led the Phillies to an 11–6 win over the Pirates on May 11, 1929, by going 4-for-4, with two homers, five RBIs, and three runs scored.

Klein contributed to a 13–4 victory over the Boston Braves on May 22, 1929, by going 5-for-6, with four RBIs and three runs scored.

Klein again hit safely five times during a 14–12 win over the Brooklyn Robins on July 4, 1929, this time going a perfect 5-for-5, with two RBIs and one run scored.

Klein followed that up by giving the Phillies a 10–9 victory over the Cardinals on July 5, 1929, by leading off the bottom of the ninth inning with a home run off Hall of Fame right-hander Jesse Haines.

Klein fashioned two 26-game hitting streaks in 1930, hitting safely in every game from May 18 to June 17, and again from July 12 to August 3. Particularly impressive during the first of those streaks, Klein batted .486 (53-for-109), with 11 homers, two triples, nine doubles, 43 RBIs, and 29 runs scored.

Klein hit for the cycle for the first of two times on July 1, 1931, going 4-for-5, with five RBIs and three runs scored during an 11–6 win over the Cubs.

Klein accomplished the feat again on May 26, 1933, going 4-for-6, with two RBIs and two runs scored during a 5–4, 14-inning loss to the Cardinals.

Klein led the Phillies to a 6–4 win over the Pirates on June 29, 1933, by going 4-for-4, with two homers and six RBIs.

Klein had another huge day against the Pirates on July 10, 1936, hitting four homers and knocking in six runs during a 9–6 Phillies win, going deep for the fourth and final time during Philadelphia's game-winning, three-run rally in the top of the 10th inning.

Klein defeated the Reds almost single-handedly on June 20, 1940, driving in every run the Phillies scored during a 4–3 victory with a homer and two singles, with his RBI single in the bottom of the 12th inning plating the game's winning run.

Notable Achievements

- Surpassed 20 home runs six times, topping 30 homers four times and 40 homers twice.
- Knocked in more than 120 runs five times.

- Scored more than 100 runs five times, topping 120 runs scored on four occasions.
- Batted over .300 eight times, surpassing the .330-mark on six occasions.
- Topped 200 hits five times.
- Finished in double digits in triples twice.
- Surpassed 30 doubles six times, topping 40 two-baggers four times and 50 two-baggers twice.
- Surpassed 400 total bases three times.
- Stole 20 bases once.
- Compiled on-base percentage over .400 four times.
- Posted slugging percentage over .500 seven times, finishing with mark above .600 four times.
- Compiled OPS over .900 six times, finishing with mark above 1.000 on four occasions.
- Amassed more than 20 outfield assists three times, topping 40 assists once.
- Hit for the cycle twice (vs. Chicago on July 1, 1931, and vs. St. Louis on May 26, 1933).
- Hit four home runs in one game vs. Pittsburgh on July 10, 1936.
- Led NL in home runs four times, RBIs twice, runs scored three times, batting average once, doubles twice, hits twice, extra-base hits four times, total bases four times, stolen bases once, on-base percentage once, slugging percentage three times, OPS twice, and games played twice.
- Finished second in NL in home runs once, RBIs twice, runs scored once, doubles once, hits once, extra-base hits once, total bases once, slugging percentage twice, and OPS once.
- Finished third in NL in home runs once, batting average twice, triples once, total bases once, and OPS once.
- Led NL outfielders in assists three times and double plays once.
- Led NL right fielders in putouts once, assists three times, and double plays twice.
- Led NL left fielders in assists once.
- Holds Phillies single-season records for most RBIs (170 in 1930), doubles (59 in 1930), total bases (445 in 1930), and extra-base hits (107 in 1930).
- Ranks among Phillies career leaders in home runs (5th), RBIs (5th), runs scored (5th), batting average (7th), slugging percentage (2nd),

OPS (2nd), triples (tied-11th), doubles (7th), hits (7th), extra-base hits (5th), total bases (6th), and on-base percentage (tied-13th).

- Won NL Triple Crown in 1933.
- 1932 NL MVP.
- Finished second in NL MVP voting twice (1931 and 1933).
- Two-time *Sporting News* MLB All-Star selection (1932 and 1933).
- 1933 NL All-Star.
- Number 92 on the *Sporting News*' 1999 list of Baseball's 100 Greatest Players.
- Member of Philadelphia Baseball Wall of Fame.
- Member of Philadelphia Sports Hall of Fame.
- Elected to Baseball Hall of Fame by members of Veterans Committee in 1980.

5

ROBIN ROBERTS

A true workhorse who led all NL hurlers in wins four times and innings pitched and complete games five times each, Robin Roberts spent 14 of his 19 big-league seasons in Philadelphia, throwing more innings and tossing more complete games during that time than any other pitcher in franchise history. Also ranking extremely high in team annals in wins, strikeouts, and shutouts, Roberts helped bring a level of respectability to the Phillies for much of the 1950s by posting at least 20 victories six straight times. Relying on just two pitches and his tremendous control to navigate his way through opposing lineups, Roberts compiled an ERA under 3.00 three times, threw more than 300 innings six times, and completed more than 20 of his starts on eight separate occasions, earning in the process five top-10 finishes in the NL MVP voting, seven All-Star nominations, and four *Sporting News* MLB All-Star selections. And, following the conclusion of his playing career, Roberts received the additional honors of having his #36 retired by the Phillies, being ranked number 74 by the *Sporting News* on its 1999 list of Baseball's 100 Greatest Players, and gaining induction into the Baseball Hall of Fame.

Born in Springfield, Illinois, on September 30, 1926, Robin Evan Roberts grew up with his five siblings in a small farmhouse, where he spent much of his free time playing catch with his brothers. A huge fan of the Chicago Cubs in his youth, Roberts displayed his competitive nature and passion for sports at an early age, with his older brother, John, recalling, "When he was a kid, he played all the sports. If you played against him, you better play your hardest because he played his hardest. He wanted to win."

After getting his start in organized sports at nearby East Pleasant Hill School, Roberts began to make a name for himself while attending Springfield High School, starring in baseball, basketball, and football for two years, before being relocated to Lanphier High School when the boundaries changed. With the nation engaged in World War II by the time Roberts graduated from Lanphier in 1944, he enrolled in the Reserve Air

Corps program, hoping to become a fighter pilot. Sent to Michigan State University, where he attended regular college classes and received his initial military training, Roberts spent two years playing baseball and basketball for the Spartans, before re-enrolling at MSU when the war ended. While completing his education, Roberts also spent his summers playing semipro baseball for the Twin Cities Trojans, whose manager, Ray Fisher, taught him how to throw a serviceable curveball and tutored him on the art of changing speeds.

Having compiled an overall record of 29-11 in his two years with the Trojans, Roberts received a contract offer from the Phillies,

Robin Roberts holds franchise records for most innings pitched and complete games thrown.
Courtesy of MearsonlineAuctions.com

who signed him for $25,000 in 1948. Subsequently sent to Wilmington of the Class B Eastern League, Roberts won 9 of 10 decisions, earning him a promotion to the parent club in mid-June. Performing well the rest of the year for a Phillies club that finished the season 22 games under .500, Roberts went 7-9, with a 3.19 ERA, nine complete games, and 84 strikeouts in 146 2/3 innings of work. Roberts followed that up by winning 15 of his 30 decisions and compiling an ERA of 3.69 in 1949, before beginning an exceptional six-year run during which he posted the following numbers:

YEAR	W-L	ERA	SO	SHO	CG	IP	WHIP
1950	20-11	3.02	146	5	21	304.1	1.180
1951	21-15	3.03	127	6	22	315	1.105
1952	28-7	2.59	148	3	30	330	1.021
1953	23-16	2.75	198	5	33	346.2	1.111
1954	23-15	2.97	185	4	29	336.2	1.025
1955	23-14	3.28	160	1	26	305	1.131

Consistently ranking among the league leaders in every major pitching category, the right-handed-throwing Roberts led all NL hurlers in innings pitched in each of the final five seasons and topped the senior circuit in wins and complete games in each of the final four years, amazingly completing 28 games in a row from July 1952 to June 1953. Roberts also finished either first or second in the league in WHIP and started more games than any other NL pitcher all six years, with his fabulous work earning him six consecutive All-Star selections and *Sporting News* NL Pitcher of the Year honors in both 1952 and 1955. Especially dominant in 1952, Roberts also earned a runner-up finish in the NL MVP voting by winning 10 more games than any other pitcher in the league and surrendering only 45 walks in 330 innings of work. More importantly, Roberts helped the Phillies post a winning record in three of those six seasons, contributing significantly to the team's unexpected run to the NL pennant in 1950.

A two-pitch pitcher who threw a fastball that consistently registered in the mid-to-high 90s and a curveball with a nice, sharp break, the 6-foot, 190-pound Roberts drew praise for his ability to throw his high, hard one past opposing batters, with Hall of Fame slugger Ralph Kiner saying, "Probably the best fastball I ever saw was Robin Roberts'. His ball would rise around six or eight inches, and with plenty on it."

Meanwhile, Red Schoendienst once remarked that Roberts's fastball "seemed to skid across the strike zone as though it were on a sheet of ice."

Yet, despite his outstanding velocity, Roberts preferred to pitch to contact, with his relatively high strikeout totals resulting from his ability to work so many innings. In discussing his approach to pitching, Roberts told *Time* magazine in 1956, "You don't have to make a big study of batters beforehand. When I have good stuff, I throw four fastballs out of five pitches. When you take up a hitter in a clubhouse meeting, no matter what his weakness is, it's going to end up low and away or high and tight, and the curveball must be thrown below the belt. That's the whole story of pitching. Keep your life and your pitching real simple and you'll get along."

Working quickly and employing a drop-and-drive pitching motion later adopted by fellow Hall of Fame hurler Tom Seaver, Roberts used his strong legs to push off when he delivered the ball to home plate, virtually dragging his right knee on the ground. Although Roberts typically gave up a lot of home runs, most of them came with no one on base since he rarely walked anyone.

In discussing Roberts, Stan Musial stated that "there was no pretense, no trickery. He was going to come after you with that fastball of his that rose, hopped, or slid. I never saw another fastball pitcher with such good control."

Musial also marveled at the competitiveness that Roberts displayed on the mound, suggesting, "He enjoyed those tight spots and had a unique ability to find something extra with the game on the line."

Jackie Robinson expressed similar sentiments when he said, "You can't hit him when it counts. There isn't a tougher competitor in the business."

Meanwhile, Curt Simmons addressed his former teammate's tremendous stamina and durability when he commented, "He was like a diesel engine. The more you used him, the better he ran. I don't think you could wear him out. The end of the 1950 season, I was in the Army and I think Bob Miller had a bad back. I know Robin had to throw almost every day."

Frequently criticized for not pitching inside and knocking hitters down, Roberts became known to some as "the pitcher who was too polite." Yet, even though Dizzy Dean, who served as a broadcaster on television's *Game of the Week* during the 1950s, and Phillies pitching coach Whitlow Wyatt both urged him to brush back hitters, Roberts did not have it in him to do so, preferring instead to rely on his outstanding velocity, unique ability to block out any outside distractions, and exceptional control to retire opposing batters.

Although Roberts earned his seventh consecutive All-Star nomination in 1956 by leading the league with 22 complete games and finishing second in the circuit with 297 1/3 innings pitched, his overall performance began to decline as the tremendous workload he assumed the previous six seasons began to take its toll on his pitching arm. Losing some of the pop on his fastball, Roberts finished just 19-18 with a 4.45 ERA, before suffering through a horrendous 1957 campaign during which he went 10-22 with an ERA of 4.07.

No longer able to rely on the velocity, movement, and control of his fastball, Roberts changed his pitching style in 1958 and evolved into more of a finesse pitcher. Rebounding in a big way for a Phillies team that finished last in the NL standings, the 31-year-old Roberts compiled a record of 17-14 and ranked among the league leaders with a 3.24 ERA, 21 complete games, and 269 2/3 innings pitched. Unfortunately, Roberts's renaissance lasted just that one season, and, after going a combined 27-33 with an ERA over 4.00 the next two years, he tried to pitch through the pain of a sore knee in 1961, resulting in an embarrassing 1-10 performance during which he compiled an ERA of 5.85. Feeling that Roberts had very little left, the Phillies sold him to the Yankees during the subsequent offseason, ending his 14-year association with the ballclub. Roberts left Philadelphia with a record of 234-199, an ERA of 3.46, a WHIP of 1.171, 35 shutouts,

272 complete games, 24 saves, and 1,871 strikeouts in 3,739 1/3 innings pitched.

Unable to earn a roster spot in New York, Roberts turned down an offer to play for the Tokyo Giants in Japan, before signing with the Baltimore Orioles in May 1962. Performing well for the Orioles over the course of the next three seasons, Roberts posted an overall record of 37-29 from 1962 to 1964, twice compiling an ERA under 3.00 and throwing more than 200 innings, before being released midway through the 1965 campaign after getting off to a slow start. Roberts then split the next year-and-a-half between the Houston Astros and Chicago Cubs, going a combined 10-10 during that time, before announcing his retirement in the spring of 1967. Over parts of 19 major-league seasons, Roberts compiled a record of 286-245, an ERA of 3.41, and a WHIP of 1.170; threw 305 complete games and 45 shutouts; recorded 25 saves; and struck out 2,357 batters in 4,688 2/3 innings of work.

Looking back on Roberts's career some years later, noted author James A. Michener wrote in the *New York Times*: "When he won, he was gracious. When he lost, so often in extra innings with his teammates giving him no runs, he did not pout. Day after day he went out there and threw that high, hard one down the middle, a marvelously coordinated man doing his job. If he had pitched for the Yankees, he might have won 350 games."

Following his playing days, Roberts, who spent six years serving as the NL representative in the Players Association during the 1950s, worked in the investment field until 1977, when he became the head baseball coach at the University of South Florida in Tampa. Roberts remained at USF until 1986, when he retired to private life. Roberts subsequently spent his remaining years in Temple Terrace, Florida, where he died of natural causes at the age of 83 on May 6, 2010. To honor Roberts, the Phillies wore a commemorative #36 patch on their uniforms the rest of the season and hung a jersey bearing his name in their dugout during home and away games.

Upon learning of Roberts's passing, Phillies pitcher Brad Lidge spoke of the personal relationship he developed with the Hall of Fame hurler during his time in Philadelphia, saying, "Every time he came around the clubhouse, he would start talking about pitching. He talked with me about my slider, and anything he had to say, I was all ears. Another thing about Robbie was that he never talked about the way things were when he played the game. He realized that the game changed with time. I was really fortunate to be able to talk with a living legend about pitching."

Then–Phillies owner Bill Giles also spoke fondly of Roberts when he stated, "When I think of Robin, there is definitely one word that comes quickly to mind—class. He was a class act both on and off the field. He was definitely one of the most consistent quality pitchers of all time, and the way he lived his life was exemplary. Every young baseball player should model their life after Robin."

PHILLIES CAREER HIGHLIGHTS

Best Season

Roberts pitched his best ball for the Phillies from 1950 to 1955, with the 1952 campaign standing out as the finest of his career. In addition to ranking among the NL leaders with a winning percentage of .800, an ERA of 2.59, a WHIP of 1.021, and 148 strikeouts, Roberts led the league with 28 wins, 330 innings pitched, and 30 complete games, with his fabulous performance earning him a runner-up finish in the NL MVP voting and recognition from the *Sporting News* as the Major League Player of the Year.

Memorable Moments/Greatest Performances

In addition to allowing just five hits during a 6–2 complete-game victory over the Cardinals on August 7, 1948, Roberts hit the first of his five career home runs.

Roberts yielded just two hits and three walks during a 1–0 shutout of the Reds on May 16, 1950, with only outfielder Ron Northey reaching him for a second-inning double and fourth-inning single.

Roberts threw 33 2/3 consecutive scoreless innings from July 18, 1950, to August 4, 1950, tossing three straight shutouts during that time.

Making his third start in five days, Roberts came up big for the Phillies in the final game of the 1950 regular season, allowing just one run on five hits during a 4–1, 10-inning victory over the Brooklyn Dodgers that clinched the pennant for the "Whiz Kids."

Roberts tossed another two-hit shutout on May 6, 1952, surrendering just a second-inning infield single to second baseman Jack Merson and an eighth-inning single to right field by outfielder Bobby Del Greco during a 6–0 win over the Pirates.

Roberts again allowed just two hits during a 6–0 shutout of the Cubs on June 24, 1952, yielding only singles to outfielder Gene Hermanski and catcher Toby Atwell in the top of the fourth inning.

Although Roberts surrendered five earned runs, 18 hits, and three walks during a 7–6 win over the Boston Braves on September 6, 1952, he performed heroically, working all 17 innings of a game the Phillies won on a walkoff homer by Del Ennis.

Roberts allowed just one hit and three walks during a 4–0 shutout of the Braves on April 29, 1954, yielding only a third-inning double to Del Crandall.

Roberts hurled a gem on May 13, 1954, allowing just one hit during an 8–1 victory over the Reds that saw him retire 27 consecutive batters after yielding a leadoff home run to Cincinnati third baseman Bobby Adams in the top of the first inning.

Roberts displayed his strength and stamina by working all 15 innings of a 3–2 win over the Cardinals on June 17, 1954, allowing 10 hits, issuing no walks, recording seven strikeouts, and scoring the game-winning run himself on a single to center field by Del Ennis in the bottom of the 15th.

Roberts threw 8 1/3 innings of no-hit ball during a 4–2 win over the Giants in the 1955 regular-season opener, before finally yielding three hits and two unearned runs in the top of the ninth.

Roberts tossed a three-hit shutout against the Cardinals on June 9, 1955, issuing no walks and recording nine strikeouts during a 2–0 Phillies win.

In addition to yielding just three hits during a 7–1 win over the Pirates on July 9, 1955, Roberts went 2-for-3 at the plate, with a solo home run.

Roberts again surrendered just three hits during a 4–2 victory over the Cubs on May 2, 1957, registering a career-high 13 strikeouts in the process.

Roberts turned in one of his finest performances on July 21, 1960, recording eight strikeouts and yielding just one hit and one walk during a 3–0 win over the Giants, whose only hit came on a fifth-inning single by Felipe Alou.

Notable Achievements

- Won at least 20 games six times, topping 25 victories once.
- Posted winning percentage of better than .600 four times.
- Compiled ERA under 3.00 three times.
- Threw more than 300 innings six times, tossing more than 250 frames another three times.

- Threw more than 20 complete games eight times, completing more than 30 of his starts twice.
- Led NL pitchers in wins four times, strikeouts twice, innings pitched five times, complete games five times, shutouts once, WHIP once, strikeouts-to-walks ratio five times, and starts six times.
- Finished second among NL pitchers in wins once, ERA once, winning percentage once, strikeouts once, innings pitched twice, complete games twice, shutouts three times, strikeouts-to-walks ratio four times, WHIP six times, and putouts twice.
- Finished third among NL pitchers in ERA once, winning percentage once, strikeouts once, strikeouts-to-walks ratio twice, WHIP once, putouts three times, assists once, and starts once.
- Holds Phillies career records for most innings pitched (3,739 1/3), complete games (272), and pitching appearances (529).
- Ranks among Phillies career leaders in wins (2nd), strikeouts (2nd), shutouts (3rd), strikeouts-to-walks ratio (12th), and starts (2nd).
- 1950 NL champion.
- Finished in top 10 in NL MVP voting five times, placing as high as second in 1952.
- 1952 *Sporting News* Major League Player of the Year.
- Two-time *Sporting News* NL Pitcher of the Year (1952 and 1955).
- Four-time *Sporting News* MLB All-Star selection (1952, 1953, 1954, and 1955).
- Seven-time NL All-Star (1950, 1951, 1952, 1953, 1954, 1955, and 1956).
- Number 74 on the *Sporting News'* 1999 list of Baseball's 100 Greatest Players.
- Member of Philadelphia Baseball Wall of Fame.
- Member of Philadelphia Sports Hall of Fame.
- Named to Phillies Centennial Team in 1983.
- #36 retired by Phillies.
- Elected to Baseball Hall of Fame by members of BBWAA in 1976.

6

RICHIE ASHBURN

One of the most beloved figures in Philadelphia sports history, Richie Ashburn spent more than four decades serving the Phillies in one capacity or another, starring for them in center field for 12 seasons, before spending more than 30 years providing color commentary on their television and radio broadcasts. Known for his speed, defensive prowess, tremendous bat control, and superior knowledge of the strike zone, Ashburn earned four All-Star nominations and two top-10 finishes in the NL MVP voting by collecting more than 200 hits three times, batting over .300 eight times, and compiling an on-base percentage over .400 on four separate occasions, before splitting his final three seasons between the Chicago Cubs and New York Mets. A two-time NL batting champion who accumulated more hits (1,875) than any other player during the 1950s, Ashburn proved to be even more outstanding in the field, leading all NL outfielders in putouts a record nine times, en route to amassing the sixth-most putouts of any outfielder in major-league history. Adding to his legacy with his excellent work in the broadcast booth, Ashburn eventually gained induction into the Baseball Hall of Fame and earned the additional honor of having his uniform #1 retired by the Phillies.

Born in Tilden, Nebraska, on March 19, 1927, Donald Richard Ashburn grew up on a farm about 150 miles northwest of Omaha, where he acquired a love of baseball from his father, Neil, who made his living working as a blacksmith. Nicknamed "Whitey" for his light blonde hair, Ashburn excelled in sports from an early age, starring as a catcher in the midget leagues, before eventually joining an American Legion team in neighboring Neligh. While competing in Neligh, Ashburn also played baseball and basketball for Tilden High School, with one of his basketball teammates, Jim Kelly, recalling years later that the undersized Ashburn had the ability to dribble down the court faster than the other players could run end-to-end without the ball.

After wowing scouts in attendance at the American Legion East-West All-Star Game played at New York's Polo Grounds during his final year at Neligh, Ashburn enrolled at Norfolk Junior College. However, he ended up signing with the Phillies after just one semester, with team scout, Ed Krajinick, reportedly saying at the time, "Something tells me this is about the most important deal I ever made."

Beginning his professional career with the Class A Utica Blue Sox in 1945, Ashburn helped lead the Sox to the Eastern League pennant by batting .312, while also exhibiting so much quickness behind the plate and speed on the basepaths that his manager, future Phillies skipper Eddie Saw-

Richie Ashburn amassed more hits during the 1950s than any other player in the game.
Courtesy of Boston Public Library, Leslie Jones Collection

yer, decided to convert him into a center fielder. However, before Ashburn had an opportunity to fully grasp the intricacies of his new position, he entered the military after being drafted by the US Army. Ashburn subsequently missed the entire 1946 campaign while serving in Alaska, later commenting, "Sending a ballplayer to Alaska was like sending a dog sledder to the Sahara Desert."

Returning to Utica following his discharge in 1947, Ashburn batted .362, scored 107 runs, and stole 27 bases, before completing a second semester at Norfolk Junior College at season's end. Promoted to the big leagues the following year, the 21-year-old Ashburn spent most of the season batting leadoff and playing center field for the Phillies, before missing the final 37 games with a broken thumb. Nevertheless, Ashburn led the league with 32 stolen bases, ranked among the leaders with a .333 batting average and a .410 on-base percentage, and scored 78 runs, earning in the process his first All-Star selection, an 11th-place finish in the NL MVP voting, and a third-place finish in the official Rookie of the Year balloting. Meanwhile, the *Sporting News* named Ashburn its Rookie of the Year. Ashburn followed that up by batting .284, scoring 84 runs, and placing near the top of the league rankings with 188 hits and 11 triples in 1949, while also leading all NL outfielders in putouts for the first of six straight times, with his 514 putouts setting a new major-league record that he broke just two years later.

Continuing his excellent play in 1950, Ashburn helped the Phillies capture the NL pennant by batting .303, scoring 84 runs, and leading the league with 14 triples, before beginning an outstanding eight-year run during which he posted the following numbers:

YEAR	RUNS	HITS	AVG	OBP	SLG	OPS
1951	92	**221**	.344	.393	.426	.819
1952	93	173	.282	.362	.357	.720
1953	110	**205**	.330	.394	.408	.802
1954	111	175	.313	**.441**	.376	.817
1955	91	180	**.338**	**.449**	.448	.897
1956	94	190	.303	.384	.384	.768
1957	93	186	.297	.390	.364	.754
1958	98	**215**	**.350**	**.440**	.441	.881

Establishing himself as the National League's premier leadoff hitter, Ashburn consistently ranked among the league leaders in batting average, on-base percentage, hits, and runs scored, topping the senior circuit in each of the first three categories on multiple occasions. The left-handed-hitting Ashburn also typically placed near the top of the league rankings in bases on balls, triples, and stolen bases, leading the league in walks three times and three-baggers once, with his excellent hitting, keen batting eye, exceptional baserunning, and superb defense earning him three All-Star nominations and a pair of seventh-place finishes in the NL MVP voting. Furthermore, Ashburn proved to be extremely durable, missing a total of just 17 games over the course of those eight seasons, at one point appearing in 731 consecutive contests.

Possessing very little power at the plate, the 5'10", 170-pound Ashburn hit just 29 home runs over the course of his career. Nevertheless, he became an elite table-setter by using his great speed, bunting ability, and knowledge of the strike zone to reach base in any number of ways, prompting one sportswriter to remark during his rookie campaign of 1948, "He's no .300 hitter—he hits .100 and runs .200." However, Brooklyn Dodgers Hall of

Fame manager Leo Durocher expressed a greater appreciation for Ashburn's speed on the basepaths when he said that same season, "Ashburn is the fastest man I've ever seen getting down to first base. He's even faster than Pete Reiser in his prime. Anybody who's faster than Ashburn isn't running. He's flying."

Also making excellent use of his tremendous quickness in the outfield, Ashburn later drew praise for his ability to gather in virtually everything hit to center field from longtime teammate Robin Roberts, who stated, "The only complaint I have about him is he wasn't tall enough to catch the balls that went into the seats. He caught everything else."

And even though the hustling Ashburn lacked a strong throwing arm, he did an outstanding job of charging balls hit to him and throwing on the run, enabling him to lead all NL center fielders in assists on four separate occasions, with his 23 outfield assists in 1952 representing the highest single-season total of his career.

After leading the league in five different offensive categories in 1958, Ashburn experienced a precipitous decline in production the following year, finishing the season with just 20 RBIs, 86 runs scored, 150 hits, and a batting average of .266. Convinced that the 32-year-old outfielder had already seen his best days, the Phillies traded him to the Chicago Cubs during the subsequent offseason for a package of three players that included veteran shortstop Alvin Dark, right-handed starting pitcher John Buzhardt, and infield prospect Jim Woods. In addition to hitting 22 homers, driving in 499 runs, scoring 1,114 times, collecting 2,217 hits, 287 doubles, and 97 triples, stealing 199 bases, batting .311, compiling an on-base percentage of .394, and posting a slugging percentage of .388 during his time in Philadelphia, Ashburn established MLB records for most times leading his league in outfield chances (9), most years with 500 or more putouts (4), and most seasons with 400 or more putouts (9).

After leaving Philadelphia, Ashburn performed well his first year in Chicago, batting .291, scoring 99 runs, and leading the league with 116 walks and a .415 on-base percentage. However, after Ashburn batted just .257 and scored only 49 runs in 1961, the Cubs left him unprotected in the expansion draft, allowing the New York Mets to claim him. Ashburn then spent one season in New York, batting .306, compiling an on-base percentage of .424, scoring 60 runs, and hitting a career-high seven homers for a team that finished in last place with a record of 40-120, before announcing his retirement at the end of the year. In explaining Ashburn's decision, noted journalist Jimmy Breslin claimed that the prospect of eventually assuming a backup role in New York convinced him to hang up his cleats, stating, "He sat on the bench for a while with another team once and it bothered him badly. And he said that if he ever had to be a benchwarmer for the New York Mets he'd commit suicide."

Retiring with career totals of 29 home runs, 586 RBIs, 1,322 runs scored, 2,574 hits, 317 doubles, 109 triples, 234 stolen bases, 1,198 walks, and only 571 strikeouts, a batting average of .308, an on-base percentage of .396, and a slugging percentage of .382, Ashburn transitioned seamlessly into a career in broadcasting, returning to Philadelphia, where he spent the next nine seasons working with play-by-play man Bill Campbell, before teaming up with Harry Kalas for the next 26 years. Developing tremendous chemistry with Kalas, who became one of his closest friends, Ashburn provided expert analysis, while also entertaining Phillies fans with his keen wit and dry sense of humor. In fact, Ashburn, whose hustle and competitive nature made him a favorite of the Philly Faithful during his playing days, became even more popular with the hometown fans after he retired, with Tim McCarver stating, "He has such a powerful connection with the city of Philadelphia because he not only played there but broadcast there for so long. But I think the reason for the warmth fans felt for him was that everyone had a chance to experience his wonderful sense of humor."

Ashburn, whom the members of the Veterans Committee elected to the Hall of Fame in 1995, continued to serve as an announcer for the Phillies until September 9, 1997, when he died of a heart attack at the age of 70, just hours after broadcasting a Phillies-Mets game in New York. The Phillies later honored his memory by erecting a statue of him at Citizens Bank Park and naming a long, concession-filled broad walk behind center field "Ashburn Alley."

PHILLIES CAREER HIGHLIGHTS

Best Season

Ashburn had most of his finest seasons for the Phillies from 1951 to 1955, batting well over .300 four times during that five-year stretch, while also compiling an OPS in excess of .400, scoring more than 100 runs, collecting more than 200 hits, and drawing more than 100 bases on balls twice each. Nevertheless, I chose to identify the 1958 campaign as the finest of Ashburn's career since, in addition to ranking among the NL leaders with 98 runs scored and 30 stolen bases, he topped the senior circuit with 215 hits,

13 triples, 97 walks, a batting average of .350, and an on-base percentage of .440.

Memorable Moments/Greatest Performances

Ashburn hit safely in 23 consecutive games from May 9 to June 5, 1948, going 43-for-98 (.439), with a homer, five doubles, 11 stolen bases, and 23 runs scored during that time.

Ashburn made one of the most significant defensive plays in franchise history in the final game of the 1950 regular season, when, with no outs in the bottom of the ninth inning, the score tied at 1–1, and the Phillies needing a victory over the Dodgers to prevent a best two-out-of-three play-off between the two teams for the NL pennant, he threw out Cal Abrams at home plate when the latter attempted to score from second base on a single to center field by Duke Snider. Ashburn's fielding gem ultimately forced the game to go into extra innings, where the Phillies won the pennant on a three-run homer by Dick Sisler in the top of the 10th.

Ashburn led the Phillies to a doubleheader sweep of the Pirates on May 20, 1951, during which they posted wins of 17–10 and 12–4, by going 8-for-11, with four RBIs and four runs scored.

In addition to singling and scoring the game's only run, Ashburn helped preserve a 1–0 victory over the Pirates on June 20, 1951, by making a sensational catch in center field. In attendance at Forbes Field that day was Hall of Famer George Sisler, who commented afterward, "I've been around major-league baseball for 35 years. I've seen every great center fielder since [Tris] Speaker. I thought I had seen every sort of impossible catch. But that's the greatest piece of center fielding I ever saw anywhere by any fielder. I still don't believe it."

Ashburn had a hand in both runs the Phillies scored during a 2–0 win over the Pirates on July 14, 1951, going 4-for-4, with an RBI and a run scored.

In addition to stealing three bases during a 1–0 victory over the Cubs on July 28, 1951, Ashburn drove home the game's only run with an opposite field single in the top of the fifth inning.

Ashburn helped lead the Phillies to a 12–7 win over the Pirates on August 5, 1951, by going 4-for-5, with a triple, double, stolen base, three RBIs, and two runs scored.

Ashburn delivered the big blow in a 4–0 victory over the Pirates on June 29, 1954, when he broke a scoreless tie in the top of the eighth inning with a three-run homer.

Ashburn homered twice, knocked in four runs, and scored three times during a 10–8 win over the Cardinals on June 21, 1955, with his two-run homer in the top of the ninth inning providing the margin of victory.

Taking full advantage of the Polo Grounds' short right field porch, Ashburn hit two homers and drove in four runs during a 6–2 victory over the Giants on April 28, 1956.

Ashburn collected five hits in one game for the only time in his career during a 9–3 win over the Cardinals on June 3, 1956, finishing the game 5-for-5, with two doubles, one RBI, and three runs scored.

Ashburn had another big day against the Cardinals on July 10, 1958, going 4-for-5, with a double, stolen base, three RBIs, and three runs scored during a 13–3 Phillies win.

Ashburn laid claim to the 1958 NL batting title by going 3-for-4, with a walk and two runs scored, during a 6–4 victory over the Pittsburgh Pirates on the final day of the regular season, finishing three points ahead of runner-up Willie Mays with an average of .350.

Notable Achievements

- Batted over .300 eight times, topping the .330 mark on five occasions.
- Scored more than 100 runs twice.
- Surpassed 200 hits three times.
- Finished in double digits in triples three times.
- Surpassed 30 doubles three times.
- Stole more than 20 bases three times, topping 30 thefts twice.
- Drew more than 100 bases on balls twice.
- Compiled on-base percentage over .400 four times.
- Led NL in batting average twice, hits three times, triples twice, stolen bases once, bases on balls three times, on-base percentage three times, games played twice, plate appearances four times, and at-bats once.
- Finished second in NL in batting average twice, hits once, stolen bases twice, bases on balls once, sacrifice hits twice, plate appearances three times, and at-bats twice.
- Finished third in NL in on-base percentage once, sacrifice hits once, games played once, and at-bats four times.
- Led NL outfielders in putouts nine times, assists three times, and double plays three times.
- Led NL center fielders in putouts nine times, assists four times, fielding percentage twice, and double plays three times.

- Ranks sixth all-time among major-league outfielders with 6,089 putouts.
- Ranks among Phillies career leaders in batting average (11th), runs scored (4th), hits (3rd), triples (5th), doubles (9th), total bases (8th), bases on balls (tied-3rd), stolen bases (11th), sacrifice hits (12th), on-base percentage (9th), games played (3rd), plate appearances (3rd), and at-bats (3rd).
- 1950 NL champion.
- 1948 *Sporting News* Major League Rookie of the Year.
- Finished seventh in NL MVP voting twice (1951 and 1958).
- Four-time NL All-Star (1948, 1951, 1953, and 1958).
- Member of Philadelphia Baseball Wall of Fame.
- Member of Philadelphia Sports Hall of Fame.
- Named to Phillies Centennial Team in 1983.
- #1 retired by Phillies.
- Elected to Baseball Hall of Fame by members of Veterans Committee in 1995.

7

CHASE UTLEY

A throwback of sorts who played the game with an old-school mentality, Chase Utley teamed up with Jimmy Rollins for more than a decade to give the Phillies the National League's top double-play combination. Starting alongside Rollins at second base for 10 seasons, Utley led all players at his position in putouts four times and assists twice, while also establishing himself as the finest hitting second sacker in the senior circuit. Surpassing 20 homers five times, knocking in more than 100 runs four times, batting over .300 twice, and posting a slugging percentage in excess of .500 on five separate occasions, Utley won four Silver Sluggers, in helping to lead the Phillies to five division titles, two pennants, and one world championship. A six-time NL All-Star, Utley also earned three top-10 finishes in the league MVP voting, with his outstanding on-field performance and aggressive style of play making him one of the most beloved and well-respected players in franchise history.

Born in Pasadena, California, on December 17, 1978, Chase Cameron Utley first developed his love for baseball when he picked up a Wiffle ball shortly after he celebrated his fourth birthday. Although not particularly big or fast as a child, Chase displayed amazing instincts and a tremendous feel for the sport at an early age, while also exhibiting a never-ending desire to improve himself in every aspect of the game.

Already pondering a career in the major leagues by the time he entered Long Beach Polytechnic High School in the fall of 1993, Utley spent four seasons starring for the Jackrabbits at shortstop, performing especially well his senior year, when, after growing a few inches and adding some much-needed bulk onto his lean frame, he gained consensus All-America recognition by hitting 12 homers, driving in 48 runs, and batting .525. Subsequently selected by the Los Angeles Dodgers in the second round of the June 1997 MLB Draft, Utley faced a difficult decision when he also received several offers to play baseball in college. Ultimately deciding that he needed a few more years of seasoning, Utley turned down $850,000 from the Dodgers and accepted an athletic scholarship from the University of California, Los Angeles.

Continuing to excel at UCLA, Utley hit 15 homers while playing shortstop for the Bruins as a freshman, before earning First-Team All-America honors his junior year by batting .382, hitting 22 homers, and driving in 69 runs in 64 games after moving to second base the previous season. Impressed with Utley's exceptional play, the Phillies selected him with the 15th overall pick of the 2000 MLB Draft, after which they inked him to a $1.78 million signing bonus.

Chase Utley helped lead the Phillies to five NL East titles, two pennants, and one world championship.
Courtesy of Matthew Straubmuller

Utley subsequently spent the next three years playing exclusively in the minor leagues, performing especially well at Triple-A Scranton in 2002, when he hit 17 homers and set a team record by amassing 39 doubles. But even though Utley appeared ready to compete at the major-league level, the presence of standout second baseman Plácido Polanco in Philadelphia forced him to shuttle back-and-forth between Scranton and Philly the next two seasons. Appearing in a total of 137 games with the Phillies during that time, Utley hit 15 homers, knocked in 78 runs, and posted a composite batting average of .257, while committing a total of seven errors in the field, with his solid play at second prompting then–Phillies manager Larry Bowa to say, "He's still got some work to do defensively, but he's going to be a good second baseman."

Finally displacing Polanco as the team's starting second baseman in 2005, Utley emerged as arguably the league's best player at his position, hitting 28 homers, driving in 105 runs, scoring 93 times, stealing 16 bases, batting .291, and compiling an OPS of .915, before posting the following numbers over the course of the next four seasons:

YEAR	HR	RBI	RUNS	2B	AVG	OBP	SLG	OPS
2006	32	102	**131**	40	.309	.379	.527	.906
2007	22	103	104	48	.332	.410	.566	.976
2008	33	104	113	41	.292	.380	.535	.915
2009	31	93	112	28	.282	.397	.508	.905

Establishing himself as one of the most productive offensive players in the senior circuit, Utley consistently ranked among the league leaders in runs scored, finished second in hits once (203 in 2006), and placed third in batting average and doubles once each. Reaching the seats 32 times in 2006, Utley combined with Jimmy Rollins to become the first pair of middle infielders in NL history to each hit at least 25 home runs in the same season. Utley posted similarly impressive overall numbers the following year, even though he ended up missing a month of action after having the fourth metacarpal bone in his right hand broken by a pitch thrown by Washington Nationals southpaw John Lannan. In addition to gaining All-Star recognition and winning the Silver Slugger Award in each of those four seasons, Utley earned three top-10 finishes in the NL MVP voting. Meanwhile, the Phillies won three NL East titles, two pennants, and one world championship.

Employing a slightly open batting stance, the left-handed-hitting Utley, who stood 6'1" and weighed 195 pounds, derived much of his power from his tremendous bat speed, which made a strong impression on former Phillies second baseman Mickey Morandini, who said, "He generates that bat speed by having a great work ethic, strong forearms and hands, and the ability to keep his bottom half calm while hitting."

Possessing a short, compact swing that enabled him to drive the ball to all fields, Utley displayed good knowledge of the strike zone, rarely chasing balls in the dirt or above his shoulders. In describing his approach at the plate, Utley said, "The majority of the time with two strikes, I'll choke up on the bat a little to try to stay as short as possible. It doesn't always work out like that, but that's the goal."

Particularly tough with men on base, Utley drew praise from Phillies batting coach Milt Thompson for his ability to hit in the clutch, with Thompson stating, "He's an RBI guy like Ryne Sandberg or Jeff Kent. That's what makes Chase so special. That, and those quick hands."

In discussing his teammate, Jim Thome said, "He's a gamer. And I think the bigger the situation, he thrives on it. And you can't teach that. Either you have it or you don't."

Phillies manager Charlie Manuel also spoke of Utley's ability to perform well under pressure when he said, "He loves to hit, and he wants to be up there. He wants to be up there when the game is on the line, and when there's a time to knock people in. Once you know him, you realize that. He's exactly what you look for in a player. He's definitely my kind of player."

Although not a Gold Glove–caliber second baseman, Utley also acquitted himself extremely well in the field, displaying decent range and soft hands that enabled him to consistently rank among the top players at his position in both putouts and assists. A solid baserunner as well, Utley set a major-league record in 2009 by stealing 23 bases without being caught.

As much as anything, though, Utley became known for his strong work ethic, ability to lead by example, and fierce competitive spirit, with former Phillies teammate Aaron Rowand stating, "He's not a pretty-boy style flashy player, he's old school. He just goes out and plays hard and continues to get better. It's nice to have guys like that on your team."

Utley also received high praise from two of his managers for his aggressive style of play, with Larry Bowa saying, "He plays every game like it's the seventh game of the World Series."

Meanwhile, Charlie Manuel suggested, "I think his hustle, determination, and Pete Rose style make people look to him as a leader, and as a vocal leader. His opinion counts. He's learning to voice it."

Phillies clubhouse attendant Phil Sheridan added, "Even if this guy doesn't get a hit, he still gets his uniform dirty. I mean, it's filthy."

Sportswriter Michael Farber expressed his admiration for the manner with which Utley played the game in a piece entitled "Grime Pays" that appeared in the August 14, 2006, edition of *Sports Illustrated*, when he wrote, "If some Phillies do lack big league industriousness . . . Utley is beyond reproach, conspicuous in his effort. The 27-year-old second baseman dives for all grounders in his zip code. He grinds out at bats and bursts out of the box as if someone had fired a starter's pistol, even when he's not trying to extend a hitting streak."

In discussing the attitude that he brought with him to the playing field, Utley said, "I'm definitely not the most graceful person out there. I've always been taught to play the game hard. I don't know how not to play hard. But for some guys it just looks easier. For me, it's not that natural. . . . I never want to look in the mirror and say, 'What if? What if I had run harder? What if I had dived for that groundball?'"

Despite missing a significant amount of playing time in 2010 with a sprained thumb, Utley earned his fifth consecutive All-Star selection by hitting 16 homers, driving in 65 runs, scoring 75 others, and batting .275.

Plagued by chronic knee problems in each of the next two seasons, Utley appeared in a total of only 186 games, limiting him to just 22 homers, 89 RBIs, and batting averages of .259 and .256. Although still slowed somewhat by injuries in 2013, Utley managed to hit 18 homers, knock in 69 runs, and bat .284, before earning All-Star honors for the final time the following year by hitting 11 homers, driving in 78 runs, and batting .270. But after Utley got off to a slow start in 2015, the Phillies traded him to the Dodgers on August 19 for Darnell Sweeney and John Richy, ending his lengthy stint in Philadelphia.

Following the trade, Utley told reporters, "Three weeks ago or so, I had a conversation with Ruben [Phillies GM Rubén Amaro Jr.]. We put our heads together and decided it might be best for us to part ways. I gave them a list of a handful of teams that I would consider playing for, and then it was Ruben's job to find the best deal he could for the organization. And ultimately it came down to the Dodgers, a team I grew up watching."

Meanwhile, Amaro expressed his appreciation for everything Utley had contributed to the success of the Phillies during his time in the City of Brotherly Love when he said, "Chase is an iconic, generational player here in Philadelphia, and arguably one of the most popular and most successful players we've ever had in our organization. To have to take him away from our organization and put him in another one is not what I'd consider to be particularly gratifying. But I can say that I believe this is the best thing for all parties at this stage of the Phillies' development and this stage of Chase's career."

Utley, who left Philadelphia with career totals of 233 home runs, 916 RBIs, 949 runs scored, 1,623 hits, 346 doubles, 49 triples, and 142 stolen bases, a .282 batting average, a .366 on-base percentage, and a .481 slugging percentage, ended up spending the next three-plus years in Los Angeles, contributing to Dodger teams that won four division titles and two pennants, before announcing his retirement following the conclusion of the 2018 campaign. Over the course of 16 big-league seasons, Utley hit 259 homers, knocked in 1,025 runs, scored 1,103 times, stole 154 bases, batted .275, compiled an on-base percentage of .358, posted a slugging percentage of .465, and collected 1,885 hits, 411 doubles, and 58 triples.

Upon learning of Utley's decision to retire, Phillies principal owner John Middleton said, "Fans sense that his commitment to the team, to the thing that's bigger than he is, was absolutely 100 percent, and people respected that and loved him for it, and still do. I don't know how much longer I'm going to live and how many more baseball players I'm going to see, but he's one of my absolute favorite people I've ever met in my life, and certainly one of my favorite baseball players."

When asked how he would like to be remembered by the fans, Utley, who currently serves as a TV baseball analyst at SportsNet LA, said, "Playing the game the right way. That's all that really matters to me, that every single day I played the game the right way—to win."

PHILLIES CAREER HIGHLIGHTS

Best Season

Had Utley not missed a month of the 2007 campaign with a broken hand, he likely would have had his finest statistical season, since, as it is, he hit 22 homers, knocked in 103 runs, scored 104 times, and established career-high marks in doubles (48), batting average (.332), on-base percentage (.410), and slugging percentage (.566). But, with Utley missing only two contests the previous year, he posted the best overall numbers of his career, hitting 32 homers, driving in 102 runs, batting .309, compiling an OPS of .906, ranking among the league leaders with 203 hits and 347 total bases, and topping the circuit with 131 runs scored.

Memorable Moments/Greatest Performances

Utley made his first big-league hit a memorable one, homering off Aaron Cook with the bases loaded in the bottom of the third inning of a 9–1 win over the Colorado Rockies on April 24, 2003.

Utley delivered the big blow in a 10–6 win over the Giants on June 1, 2005, hitting a pinch-hit grand slam homer in the bottom of the eighth inning.

After hitting a solo homer during the earlier stages of an 11–10 win over the Reds on September 23, 2005, Utley sparked a five-run ninth-inning rally that enabled the Phillies to overcome a four-run deficit by homering with two men on, finishing the game with three hits, five RBIs, and three runs scored.

Utley led the Phillies to an 8–6 win over the Dodgers on June 2, 2006, by going 4-for-4, with a homer and three runs scored.

Utley fashioned the second-longest hitting streak in franchise history from June 23 to August 3, 2006, hitting safely in 35 consecutive games during that time. Compiling a .405 batting average over the course of those 35 contests, Utley went 62-for-153, with nine homers, two triples, 14 doubles, 30 RBIs, and 35 runs scored.

Utley contributed to a 9–3 victory over the Washington Nationals on April 25, 2007, by going 5-for-5, with two doubles and three RBIs.

Utley provided most of the offensive firepower when the Phillies defeated the Mets, 5–4, on April 20, 2008, knocking in four runs with a pair of homers.

Utley helped lead the Phillies to a 20–5 pasting of the Colorado Rockies on May 26, 2008, by going 3-for-6, with a homer, six RBIs, and two runs scored.

Utley homered twice during a 5–4 win over the Mets on June 10, 2009, with his two-run blast off Bobby Parnell in the top of the 11th inning providing the margin of victory.

Although the Phillies lost the 2009 World Series to the Yankees in six games, Utley performed exceptionally well, going 6-for-21 (.286), with five home runs, eight RBIs, seven runs scored, a .400 on-base percentage, and a 1.048 slugging percentage. The driving force behind both Phillies wins, Utley homered twice off C. C. Sabathia during a 6–1 victory in Game 1, before reaching the seats twice, driving in four runs, and scoring three times during an 8–6 win in Game 5.

Notable Achievements

- Hit more than 20 home runs five times, topping 30 homers on three occasions.
- Knocked in more than 100 runs four times.
- Scored more than 100 runs four times.
- Batted over .300 twice, topping the .330 mark once.
- Topped 200 hits once.
- Surpassed 30 doubles five times, amassing more than 40 two-baggers on three occasions.
- Stole more than 20 bases once.
- Compiled on-base percentage over .400 once.
- Posted slugging percentage over .500 five times.
- Compiled OPS over .900 five times.
- Led NL in runs scored once, hit-by-pitch three times, and assists once.
- Finished second in NL in hits once and intentional bases on balls once.
- Finished third in NL in batting average once, runs scored once, doubles once, sacrifice flies once, and hit-by-pitch twice.
- Led NL second basemen in putouts four times and assists twice.
- Ranks among Phillies career leaders in home runs (6th), RBIs (7th), runs scored (6th), doubles (5th), hits (9th), extra-base hits (7th), total

bases (7th), bases on balls (10th), intentional bases on balls (11th), sacrifice flies (2nd), games played (9th), plate appearances (7th), and at-bats (9th).

- Five-time division champion (2007, 2008, 2009, 2010, and 2011).
- Two-time NL champion (2008 and 2009).
- 2008 world champion.
- Five-time NL Player of the Week.
- Two-time NL Player of the Month.
- Finished in top 10 in NL MVP voting three times.
- Four-time Silver Slugger Award winner (2006, 2007, 2008, and 2009).
- Four-time *Sporting News* NL All-Star selection (2006, 2007, 2008, and 2009).
- Six-time NL All-Star (2006, 2007, 2008, 2009, 2010, and 2014).

8

DEL ENNIS

One of the top sluggers and run producers of his era, Del Ennis spent 11 years in Philadelphia, hitting the third-most home runs and driving in the fourth-most runs of any player in franchise history while splitting his time between left field and right. Surpassing 20 homers eight times and 100 RBIs on six separate occasions, Ennis ranked second only to the incomparable Stan Musial among major-league players in runs batted in from 1948 to 1956, knocking in a total of 970 runs over the course of those nine seasons. More than just a slugger, Ennis also batted over .300 three times and led all players at his position in putouts five times, assists four times, and fielding percentage twice, with his excellent all-around play earning him three All-Star selections and two top-10 finishes in the NL MVP voting. Yet, despite his many contributions to the Phillies, Ennis often found himself being booed by the hometown fans, who tended to blame him for the failures of the team.

Born in the Crescentville section of Philadelphia, Pennsylvania, on June 8, 1925, Delmer Ennis starred in multiple sports at Olney High School, earning All-State honors as a fullback in football, while also excelling as an outfielder, first baseman, and catcher on the school's baseball team. Coerced into signing with the Phillies at only 17 years of age after scout Jocko Collins attended a game in which he hit three home runs and delivered a bases loaded double, Ennis prepared to join the team's Canadian American League affiliate, when the league ceased operations due to World War II. Signed by Collins again when play resumed in 1943, Ennis spent the year with the Trenton Packers of the B-Level Interstate League, for whom he batted .346, hit 18 home runs, and collected 197 hits, 37 doubles, and 16 triples, earning him a late-season callup to the parent club. However, Ennis instead chose to enlist in the US Navy, where he spent the next two years serving as a petty officer third class, seeing action in the Pacific, while also honing his baseball skills alongside major leaguers Billy Herman, Johnny Vander Meer, and Schoolboy Rowe in the Honolulu League.

Discharged from the military on April 5, 1946, Ennis re-signed with the Phillies after turning down a much larger offer from the Yankees and reported directly to his hometown team. Recalling the earliest days of his big-league career, Ennis said, "I really didn't expect to stay with the Phillies, but they had to give me a 30-day trial because I was on the National Defense List. I never had spring training, and I pinch hit in Pittsburgh in my first game, then I got into the starting lineup. In my second game in left field, I hit a bases loaded double to beat the Pirates. A few days later in Chicago against the Cubs, I hit two homers in one game."

Ennis ended up starting 138 games in left field for the Phillies in

Del Ennis proved to be one of the top sluggers and run producers of his time.
Courtesy of Boston Public Library, Leslie Jones Collection

1946, earning a spot on the NL All-Star team, an eighth-place finish in the league MVP voting, and *Sporting News* Major League Rookie of the Year honors by driving in 73 runs, scoring 70 times, placing near the top of the league rankings with 17 homers, 30 doubles, a .313 batting average, a .485 slugging percentage, and an OPS of .849, while also leading all players at his position in putouts, assists, double plays, and fielding percentage.

Impressed with Ennis's hitting style and strong performance his first year in the league, St. Louis Cardinals manager Gabby Street said, "He's got the best-looking wrist action of any player I ever saw."

Ennis followed up his outstanding rookie campaign by hitting 12 homers, driving in 81 runs, and batting .275 in 1947, before establishing himself as one of the league's most feared hitters by posting the following numbers the next three seasons:

YEAR	HR	RBI	RUNS	2B	AVG	OBP	SLG	OPS
1948	30	95	86	40	.290	.345	.525	.869
1949	25	110	92	39	.302	.367	.525	.892
1950	31	**126**	92	34	.311	.372	.551	.923

In addition to placing near the top of the league rankings in home runs, RBIs, doubles, slugging percentage, and OPS all three years, Ennis ranked among the leaders in batting average twice and total bases each season, with his outstanding performance for the Phillies' 1950 pennant-winning team earning him a fourth-place finish in the NL MVP voting. Ennis also did a solid job wherever the Phillies put him in the outfield, leading all NL right fielders in putouts in both 1948 and 1950, while amassing more putouts and assists than any other left fielder in the league in 1949.

The right-handed-hitting Ennis, who stood 6 foot and weighed 195 pounds, possessed strong shoulders, arms, and wrists that enabled him to drive the ball with power to all parts of the ballpark. Standing square in the batter's box, Ennis held the bat still and stepped toward the pitcher as he delivered the ball to home plate. Particularly tough with men on base, Ennis said, "I was a better hitter with men on base. I studied the pitchers, and I always knew I would get the pitcher's best pitch when he was in a jam."

An outstanding two-strike hitter, Ennis also excelled when down in the count, with former Phillies GM Herb Pennock once suggesting, "He's just as dangerous then as when he stepped to the plate. And he hits to all fields. They can't throw up a special defense against him."

Although Ennis proved to be somewhat erratic in the field, leading all players at his position in errors on seven separate occasions, he possessed above-average speed and a strong throwing arm that often enabled him to overcome his mistakes. In fact, Ennis played the outfield with a certain flair, with Robin Roberts recalling one particularly spectacular catch he made during a game against the Dodgers in 1950, when, after overrunning a drive hit to right field by Jackie Robinson, he reached out and caught the ball barehanded. Upset over losing a sure extra-base hit, Robinson ran into right field, yelling at Ennis all the way, "How did you catch that ball?" Commenting on his teammate's remarkable grab, Richie Ashburn observed, "Ennis reached up and caught the ball barehanded on the dead run, like picking an apple off a tree. He never cracked a smile, just like it was a routine play."

Even though Ennis hit just 15 homers, knocked in only 73 runs, and batted just .267 in 1951, he gained All-Star recognition for the second time, before beginning an outstanding four-year run during which he averaged 26 home runs and 118 RBIs. Performing especially well in 1953 and 1955, Ennis hit 29 homers, drove in 125 runs, and batted .285 in the first of those campaigns, before earning his final All-Star selection two years later by reaching the seats 29 times, knocking in 120 runs, and batting .296.

Yet, despite his outstanding offensive production, Ennis became a whipping boy for Phillies fans, who never forgave him for his poor showing against the Yankees in the 1950 World Series (2-for-14, with one double and one run scored) and struggles at the plate the following year. Ridiculed for every mistake he made, Ennis often incurred the wrath of the Philly Faithful, with pitcher Steve Ridzik recalling how the crowd reacted after his teammate dropped a flyball in the third inning of a 1954 contest:

We had a packed house, and the fans started to boo him unmercifully. It was terrible. The next inning when he went out to left field they booed and booed and booed. They booed him when he ran off the field at the end of the inning. Unmerciful. I looked over at him sitting in the dugout, and he's got his hands clenched and he's just white. He's just livid. Here he is a hometown guy and everything. . . . He came to bat in the last of the eighth inning with the score still tied and two outs. The fans just booed and booed, and all our guys on the bench are just hotter than a pistol. We were ready to fight the 30-some thousand. He didn't deserve that. So, Del hits one on top of the roof, and, as he's rounding the bases, the crowd goes crazy. They cheered and cheered and cheered. They were standing and wouldn't sit down. They wanted him to come out of the dugout. But he wouldn't move. He just sat there as white as a ghost, mad as hell. When he went out in the ninth inning, the fans stood up and applauded again. I had to step back off the rubber a couple of times because they wouldn't sit down. That was one of the greatest thrills of my career, watching something like that happen to somebody else. It was beautiful.

Choosing to take the high road when discussing the shabby treatment that he received from Phillies fans, Ennis stated, "They've stung me a few times with personal insults, but I never really let them bother me. I figured they're paying their way into the park and have the right to boo."

On another occasion, Ennis told *Sport* magazine, "Sometimes they threw food. If I spotted a good orange, I would pick it up, peel it, and eat it. One night a paper bag landed at my feet. I looked inside and found a peanut butter and jelly sandwich all wrapped up in wax paper. I unwrapped it and then started to eat it. You should have heard them howl."

Still unable to fully understand some 50 years later why the fans of Philadelphia derived so much pleasure out of jeering her husband, Ennis's widow, Liz Ennis, told the *Philadelphia Inquirer* in 2003: "The booing, that's the age-old question. I still get asked it all the time. His children get asked. His grandchildren get asked. . . . When there was a lot written about Mike Schmidt being booed, Del couldn't believe it. He'd say, 'They think that's booing? That's nothing.' He didn't think that was anything compared to what he got every game, every at-bat, every move he made. Del was just lucky that he was a strong person. A lot of people couldn't have survived in this town with the abuse he took. . . . He was the hometown boy. You'd have thought he'd have been worshipped."

After Ennis hit 26 homers, knocked in 95 runs, scored 80 times, and batted .260 in 1956, his years of abuse finally ended when the Phillies traded him to the St. Louis Cardinals for infielder Bobby Morgan and out-fielder Rip Repulski during the following offseason. Leaving Philadelphia with career totals of 259 home runs, 1,124 RBIs, 891 runs scored, 1,812 hits, 310 doubles, and 65 triples, a batting average of .286, an on-base percentage of .344, and a slugging percentage of .479, Ennis continues to rank extremely high in team annals in each of the first six categories more than 60 years after he donned a Phillies uniform for the last time.

Ennis ended up spending two seasons in St. Louis, hitting 24 homers, driving in 105 runs, and batting .286 for the Cardinals in 1957, before appearing in a total of just 31 games with the Cincinnati Reds and Chicago White Sox through the first three months of the 1959 campaign. Released by the White Sox on June 20 of that year, Ennis announced his retirement, ending his career with 288 home runs, 1,284 RBIs, 985 runs scored, 2,063 hits, 358 doubles, 69 triples, a .284 batting average, a .340 on-base percentage, and a .472 slugging percentage.

Following his retirement, Ennis returned to Philadelphia and the bowling-alley business he started with former Phillies traveling secretary John Wise during his playing days. He also bred greyhound race dogs and spent a year coaching baseball at Penn State University. Ennis lived until February 8, 1996, when he died of complications from diabetes at the age of 70.

PHILLIES CAREER HIGHLIGHTS

Best Season

Although Ennis also posted outstanding numbers in each of the previous two seasons, concluding the 1948 campaign with 30 homers, 95 RBIs, and a .290 batting average, before hitting 25 homers, driving in 110 runs, and batting .302 in 1949, he had the finest all-around season of his career in 1950, earning a fourth-place finish in the NL MVP voting by ranking among the league leaders in 10 different offensive categories, including home runs (31), RBIs (126), batting average (.311), hits (185), total bases (328), and OPS (.923). Particularly outstanding during the month of July, Ennis knocked in 38 runs in 35 games.

Memorable Moments/Greatest Performances

Ennis led the Phillies to a 7–1 win in the second game of a doubleheader split with the Chicago Cubs on May 5, 1946, by driving in four runs with the first two homers of his career.

Although the Phillies suffered a 7–0 defeat at the hands of the Cardinals on June 8, 1946, Ennis prevented them from being no-hit by St. Louis starter Red Barrett by singling to left field with one man out in the top of the eighth inning.

Ennis gave the Phillies a 12–11 win over the Giants on April 26, 1949, by homering with one man aboard with two men out in the bottom of the 11th inning.

Ennis led the Phillies to a lopsided 13–3 victory over the Cubs on July 27, 1950, by collecting a career-high seven RBIs, four of which came on an eighth-inning grand slam off Johnny Vander Meer.

Ennis gave the Phillies an 8–7 win over the Reds on September 15, 1950, by singling with the bases loaded in the bottom of the 19th inning, finishing the game with five hits in 10 at-bats.

Ennis helped lead the Phillies to an 8–7 win over the Boston Braves on September 26, 1950, by going 4-for-5, with a homer and four RBIs.

Ennis gave the Phillies a 7–6 win over the Braves on September 6, 1952, when he led off the bottom of the 17th inning with a home run.

Ennis contributed to a 17–8 victory over the Reds on July 30, 1953, by going 4-for-6, with two homers, six RBIs, and four runs scored.

Ennis's RBI single to center field in the bottom of the 10th inning gave the Phillies an 8–7 win over the Cubs on May 11, 1954.

Ennis provided further heroics when he gave the Phillies a 3–2 win over the Cardinals on June 17, 1954, by delivering a walkoff single to center field with two men out in the bottom of the 15th inning.

Ennis proved to be a one-man wrecking crew on June 23, 1955, hitting three home runs and knocking in all seven runs during a 7–2 victory over the Cardinals.

Ennis gave the Phillies an 8–5 win over the Milwaukee Braves on July 21, 1956, by homering with two men aboard in the top of the 15th inning.

Notable Achievements

- Surpassed 20 home runs eight times, topping 30 homers twice.
- Knocked in more than 100 runs six times, topping 120 RBIs on three occasions.
- Batted over .300 three times.
- Finished in double digits in triples twice.
- Surpassed 30 doubles five times, amassing 40 two-baggers once.
- Posted slugging percentage over .500 four times.
- Compiled OPS over .900 once.
- Hit three home runs in one game vs. St. Louis Cardinals on July 23, 1955.
- Led NL with 126 RBIs in 1950.
- Finished second in NL in doubles twice, extra-base hits once, slugging percentage once, intentional bases on balls twice, sacrifice flies twice, and at-bats once.
- Finished third in NL in RBIs twice, extra-base hits three times, total bases three times, OPS once, and at-bats once.
- Led NL outfielders in assists once.
- Led NL left fielders in putouts three times, assists four times, fielding percentage twice, and double plays four times.
- Led NL right fielders in putouts twice and double plays once.
- Ranks among Phillies career leaders in home runs (3rd), RBIs (4th), runs scored (tied-10th), triples (10th), doubles (8th), hits (5th), extra-base hits (6th), total bases (4th), intentional bases on balls (4th), games played (6th), plate appearances (6th), and at-bats (6th).
- 1950 NL champion.
- 1946 *Sporting News* Major League Rookie of the Year.
- Finished in top 10 in NL MVP voting twice, placing as high as fourth in 1950.
- Three-time NL All-Star (1946, 1951, and 1955).
- Member of Philadelphia Baseball Wall of Fame.
- Member of Philadelphia Sports Hall of Fame.
- Named to Phillies Centennial Team in 1983.

9
RYAN HOWARD

A tremendous force in the middle of the Phillies lineup for much of his 13-year major-league career, which he spent entirely in Philadelphia, Ryan Howard established himself as one of the most prolific sluggers in the game, surpassing 30 homers and 100 RBIs six straight times, while also compiling a slugging percentage over .500 on seven separate occasions. Possessing extraordinary power to all fields, the left-handed-hitting Howard hit at least 45 homers in four consecutive seasons, with his 58 round-trippers in 2006 setting a single-season franchise record. A three-time NL All-Star and one-time league MVP, Howard topped the senior circuit in home runs twice and RBIs three times, with his outstanding run production helping to lead the Phillies to five division titles, two pennants, and one world championship.

Born in St. Louis, Missouri, on November 19, 1979, Ryan James Howard grew up in the northern suburb of Florissant, where he spent much of his youth playing baseball, football, basketball, and soccer. Despite his athletic pursuits, though, Howard remained dedicated to excelling in the classroom at the urging of his parents, who stressed to him and his three siblings the importance of going to college and earning a degree.

Sharing a love of baseball with his father, Ron, who had grown up amid poverty and racism in the segregated South, young Ryan excelled in his favorite sport during his formative years, before further developing his skills at Lafayette High School in Wildwood, Missouri. Nevertheless, Howard garnered little interest from pro scouts and major college programs, forcing him to ultimately enroll at nearby Southwest Missouri State University in Springfield. After initially making the Bears' roster as a walk-on, Howard eventually earned a scholarship with his outstanding play that won him 1999 Missouri Valley Conference Freshman of the Year honors. Continuing to perform extremely well over the course of the next two seasons, Howard ended his college career with a .335 batting average, 50 home runs, and 183 RBIs in 172 games played. Particularly outstanding his junior year, Howard hit a school-record 19 home runs, prompting the Phillies to select him in the fifth round of the 2001 MLB Amateur Draft.

Looking back on his time at SMSU years later, Howard said, "I got to Missouri State and, with coach (Brent) Thomas and coach (Paul) Evans, everything was great. That's where I learned to hit to the opposite field. . . . They helped me a lot, and I tried to rise to the occasion."

After signing with the Phillies, Howard spent most of the next four seasons advancing through their farm system, making stops at low Class A Batavia, Class A Lake-wood, Class A-Advanced Clear-

Ryan Howard ranks second only to Mike Schmidt in franchise history with 382 career home runs.
Courtesy of Matthew Straubmuller

water, Double-A Reading, and Triple-A Scranton. Yet, despite earning two All-Star selections and one league MVP trophy, Howard found his path to the big leagues being blocked by All-Star first baseman Jim Thome, who joined the Phillies as a free agent prior to the start of the 2003 campaign.

After Howard made a brief appearance with the Phillies during the final month of the 2004 season, his situation changed dramatically the following year when Thome developed a sore right elbow that forced him onto the disabled list in early May. Subsequently called up from the minors, Howard failed to make much of an impression during his second tour of duty with the club, prompting the Phillies to option him back to Scranton when Thome returned to action three weeks later. However, after Howard launched a 24-game hitting streak at Scranton and Thome continued to experience health problems, the Phillies recalled the 25-year-old first sacker from the minors in early July. Performing magnificently the rest of the year, Howard earned NL Rookie of the Year honors by hitting 22 homers, driving in 63 runs, scoring 52 times, batting .288, and posting a slugging percentage of .567, although he also struck out 100 times in only 348 plate appearances.

Praising Howard for his exceptional play at season's end, Phillies manager Charlie Manuel told Ken Mandel of MLB.com, "He did some unbelievable things for our team out of the six-hole [in the lineup]. I don't know where we would have been without him. He has no fear about being up in a big spot. He's going to be a special player."

Exhibiting supreme confidence in Howard's ability to handle the starting first base job, the Phillies traded Thome to the Chicago White Sox for center fielder Aaron Rowand during the subsequent offseason. Rewarding team management for the faith it placed in him, Howard responded by posting the following numbers over the course of the next four seasons:

YEAR	HR	RBI	RUNS	AVG	OBP	SLG	OPS
2006	58	149	104	.313	.425	.659	1.084
2007	47	136	94	.268	.392	.584	.976
2008	48	146	105	.251	.339	.543	.881
2009	45	141	105	.279	.360	.571	.931

In addition to leading the NL in home runs twice and RBIs three times, Howard finished second in each of those categories once and placed third in homers the other year. He also consistently ranked among the league leaders in slugging percentage and OPS, finishing second in each category once. Unfortunately, Howard also finished either first or second in the league in strikeouts all four years, with his 199 whiffs in 2007 establishing a new single-season major-league record. An All-Star in both 2006 and 2009, Howard also earned four straight top-five finishes in the NL MVP voting, winning the award in 2006. More importantly, the Phillies won three division titles, two pennants, and one World Series during that four-year stretch, claiming just their second world championship in 2008.

Standing 6'4" and weighing 250 pounds, Howard possessed long arms, quick wrists, and tremendous power that enabled him to drive the ball out of any part of the park. Like most left-handed home-run hitters, Howard tended to hammer pitches down in the strike zone. But he differed from others of his ilk in the way he used the entire ballpark, as Houston Astros veteran infielder Ty Wigginton noted when he said, "What really stands out about him is his ability to drive the ball the other way. You see a lot of power hitters who are pretty much pull only, but this guy is hitting them foul pole to foul pole."

Howard's immense power to all fields also elicited high praise from Hall of Famer and 1987 NL MVP Andre Dawson, who marveled, "I've never seen anyone like him. I came up with the Stargells, the Murrays, and the Parkers, but this kid is in a class by himself. They could hit homers down the line, but they didn't go from line to line like this guy."

Howard also made an extremely favorable impression on a pair of former Phillies sluggers, with Mike Schmidt commenting, "I've never seen anyone in the major leagues who is treating the game almost like an over-sized kid in the Little League World Series. Ryan actually is transcending the game. People are making him out to be America's hitter, the 'Mr. Clean' of home run hitting. . . . Right at this moment in time, he might be more dangerous than Barry Bonds ever was in his prime."

Meanwhile, Dick Allen said, "I'm really proud of him. He can swing that thing, can't he? He's very good. The ball inside, he's learning to attack that thing. He'll learn as he goes, and he's very good right now."

Somewhat less proficient in the field, Howard led all NL first basemen in errors four times and finished second on three other occasions, committing a career-high 19 miscues in 2008. Nevertheless, he proved to be surprisingly nimble for a man his size, displaying quick feet and soft hands around the bag.

Howard also gradually developed into one of the Phillies' team leaders, earning the respect of the other members of the ballclub with his strong work ethic and team-first mentality that he exhibited when he said, "Home runs are fine and dandy, but, as long as you're putting up RBIs . . . that's what helps your team win."

Howard helped lead the Phillies to two more division titles in 2010 and 2011, earning his final All-Star selection and a 10th-place finish in the NL MVP voting in the first of those campaigns by hitting 31 homers, driving in 108 runs, scoring 87 times, and batting .276, before reaching the seats 33 times, finishing third in the league with 116 RBIs, scoring 81 runs, and batting .253 the following year. But after suffering a torn Achilles on the final play of the 2011 NLDS, Howard never again performed at an elite level, spending the final five seasons of his career being plagued by knee, foot, and ankle problems.

Appearing in a total of only 151 games the next two years, Howard hit just 25 homers, knocked in only 99 runs, and posted batting averages of just .219 and .266. Although Howard proved to be somewhat more productive over the course of the next three seasons, totaling 71 homers and 231 RBIs from 2014 to 2016, he batted just .223, .229, and .196, prompting the Phillies to decline the $23 million option on his contract at the end of 2016.

Upon learning of his former teammate's impending departure from Philadelphia, Chase Utley said, "Ryan, on countless occasions, put us on his back and carried us to the finish line. He was such an important part of our success, and I hope Philadelphia recognizes that."

Subsequently unable to earn a roster spot with either the Atlanta Braves or Colorado Rockies after signing as a free agent with both clubs, Howard never appeared in another major-league game, ending his career with 382 homers, 1,194 RBIs, 848 runs scored, 1,475 hits, 277 doubles, 21 triples, a .258 batting average, a .343 on-base percentage, and a .515 slugging percentage. Officially announcing his retirement by publishing an article entitled, "Thank You, Philly," that appeared on the *Players' Tribune* on September 4, 2018, Howard reminisced about some of his most memorable moments during his 13 seasons in Philadelphia, called his career "a wild ride," and stated, "I'm glad that I got to stay on it for as long as I did. Which I guess has really also kind of become my overall perspective on things: How, when it's come to these last 14 years of mine—nothing has ever been easy for long, and nothing has ever been perfect for long. But I wouldn't have it any other way."

After retiring as an active player, Howard joined ESPN as an analyst for *Baseball Tonight* and became a partner at SeventySix Capital and chairman of the Athlete Venture Group, where he helps connect entrepreneurial athletes with emerging startups.

CAREER HIGHLIGHTS

Best Season

Howard posted monstrous power numbers for the Phillies from 2007 to 2009, averaging 47 homers and 141 RBIs during that three-year stretch. Nevertheless, Howard's MVP campaign of 2006 would have to be considered his finest season since, in addition to scoring 104 runs, he established career-high marks with 58 homers, 149 RBIs, 383 total bases, 182 hits, 108 walks, a .313 batting average, and an OPS of 1.084, leading the league in each of the first three categories.

Memorable Moments/Greatest Performances

Howard gave the Phillies a 5–4 win over the Dodgers on July 19, 2005, when he homered off Yhency Brazobán with one man aboard in the bottom of the 10th inning.

Howard again provided the big blow in a victory over the Dodgers on August 10, 2005, when he homered with the bases loaded in the top of the ninth inning during a 9–5 Phillies win.

Howard came up big in the clutch for the Phillies on September 21, 2005, giving them a 10–6 win over the Braves by hitting a grand slam homer in the top of the 10th inning.

Howard continued to display his penchant for delivering big hits on May 14, 2006, when, after tying the game in the top of the eighth inning with a solo homer off starter Brandon Claussen, he gave the Phillies a 2–1 win over the Reds by hitting a solo shot off reliever Chris Hammond in the 12th.

Although the Phillies lost to the Yankees 9–7 on June 20, 2006, Howard homered twice, tripled, and drove in a career-high seven runs.

Howard led the Phillies to an 8–7 win over the Braves on September 3, 2006, by going 4-for-4, with three home runs and four RBIs, hitting all three homers off Tim Hudson.

Howard drove in all three runs the Phillies scored during a 3–2 win over the Florida Marlins on September 8, 2006, with a pair of homers.

Howard helped lead the Phillies to a 13–11 victory over the Cardinals on September 17, 2007, by homering twice and knocking in five runs, with his sixth-inning grand slam proving to be the game's big blow.

Howard led the Phillies to a 10–2 win over Tampa Bay in Game 4 of the 2008 World Series by driving in five runs with a pair of homers.

Howard helped lead the Phillies to a 9–6 victory over the Washington Nationals on May 30, 2009, by homering twice and driving in five runs, with his mammoth third-inning grand slam off Shairon Martis landing in the third deck in right field at Citizens Bank Park.

Howard contributed to a 10–3 win over the Mets on April 29, 2011, by hitting two homers and knocking in six runs, with his sixth-inning grand slam putting the game out of reach.

Howard gave the Phillies a 6–3 victory over the Colorado Rockies on May 28, 2014, when he hit a three-run homer with two men out in the bottom of the ninth inning.

Howard again delivered the big blow in a 6–5 win over the Astros on August 7, 2014, putting the Phillies ahead to stay with a grand slam homer in the bottom of the eighth inning.

Notable Achievements

- Hit more than 20 home runs 10 times, topping 30 homers six times, 40 homers four times, and 50 homers once.
- Knocked in more than 100 runs six times, topping 130 RBIs on four occasions.

- Scored more than 100 runs three times.
- Batted over .300 once.
- Surpassed 30 doubles twice.
- Walked more than 100 times twice.
- Compiled on-base percentage over .400 once.
- Posted slugging percentage over .500 seven times, finishing with mark over .600 once.
- Compiled OPS over .900 four times, finishing with mark over 1.000 once.
- Hit three home runs in one game vs. Atlanta Braves on September 3, 2006.
- Led NL in home runs twice, RBIs three times, total bases once, and games played once.
- Finished second in NL in home runs once, RBIs once, extra-base hits twice, slugging percentage once, OPS once, intentional bases on balls twice, and games played once.
- Finished third in NL in home runs once, RBIs once, and total bases once.
- Led NL first basemen in putouts twice.
- Holds Phillies single-season records for most home runs (58 in 2006) and most intentional bases on balls (37 in 2006).
- Ranks among Phillies career leaders in home runs (2nd), RBIs (3rd), doubles (10th), extra-base hits (4th), total bases (5th), bases on balls (7th), intentional bases on balls (2nd), slugging percentage (7th), sacrifice flies (3rd), games played (7th), plate appearances (8th), and at-bats (10th).
- Five-time division champion (2007, 2008, 2009, 2010, and 2011).
- Two-time NL champion (2008 and 2009).
- 2008 world champion.
- Six-time NL Player of the Week.
- Four-time NL Player of the Month.
- 2005 NL Rookie of the Year.
- 2006 Silver Slugger Award winner.
- 2006 *Sporting News* Major League Player of the Year.
- 2006 NL MVP.
- Finished in top 10 in NL MVP voting five other times, placing second once and third once.
- 2009 NLCS MVP.
- 2006 *Sporting News* NL All-Star selection.
- Three-time NL All-Star (2006, 2009, and 2010).

10

DICK ALLEN

The most controversial player of his era, Dick Allen spent six tumultuous years in Philadelphia at the beginning of his career, establishing himself during that time as one of the most feared hitters in baseball. Supremely talented, Allen surpassed 30 homers three times, knocked in more than 100 runs once, and batted over .300 on four occasions, with his outstanding offensive production earning him three All-Star selections and two top-10 finishes in the NL MVP voting.

Nevertheless, Allen, the first Black superstar in franchise history, experienced a considerable amount of turmoil, sharing a rocky relationship with the hometown fans and media, and even some of his own teammates. Labeled a malingerer, a malcontent, and a locker-room cancer due to his unwillingness to adhere to the norms of the day, Allen reacted to the criticism he received by rebelling against the organization and its fans, finally forcing his way out of Philadelphia. Dealt to the St. Louis Cardinals following the conclusion of the 1969 campaign, Allen subsequently spent the next five seasons continuing to perform at an elite level for three different teams, before returning to the City of Brotherly Love for a second tour of duty during the latter stages of his career. In all, Allen spent eight full seasons with the Phillies, performing so well during that time that he eventually had his #15 retired by the team and gained induction into the Philadelphia Baseball Wall of Fame and the Philadelphia Sports Hall of Fame.

Born in Wampum, Pennsylvania, on March 8, 1942, Richard Anthony Allen grew up with his eight siblings in nearby Chewton, a village located some 45 miles northwest of Pittsburgh's Forbes Field. Raised mostly by his mother, who took a job working as a domestic after her husband abandoned the family shortly after Dick turned 15 years of age, Allen developed a love of baseball at an early age, spending much of his childhood batting stones in imaginary games he held near his home, with his mom recalling years later, "I was always paying for new windowpanes all over the neighborhood. The neighbors wouldn't even bother to ask the kids who was responsible. They would just come and tell me it was Dickie again. I knew they were right, too, because there were no baseball fields in all of Chewton or Wampum that could hold a stone if Dickie hit it good."

Eventually emerging as a star athlete at Wampum High School, Allen excelled in multiple sports, earning All-State honors in both baseball and basketball. In fact, many observers believed that Allen, who led the school's basketball team to the Division B State Championship as a senior in 1960, possessed the talent to pursue a career in the NBA,

Dick Allen possessed as much natural ability as any player in franchise history.
Courtesy of MearsonlineAuctions.com

with his exceptional scoring and leaping ability garnering him a considerable amount of interest from college scouts.

After receiving scholarship offers from several universities, Allen chose to sign with the Phillies, beginning his pro career with Elmira of the NY-Penn League in 1960. Although Allen struggled defensively at Elmira, committing 48 errors in 88 games at shortstop, he performed well at the plate, batting .281 and collecting 37 extra-base hits in 320 official at-bats. Promoted to Twin Falls of the Pioneer League in 1961 and Williamsport of the Eastern League the following year, Allen posted excellent offensive numbers at both stops and improved his work in the field as well, while splitting his time between second base and left field.

Moved to left field full-time after he joined the Triple-A Arkansas Travelers in 1963, Allen continued to produce at the plate, batting .289 and leading the International League with 33 home runs, 97 RBIs, and 12 triples. But, as the first African American to play pro baseball in the state, the shy and introverted Allen, who never experienced much racism while growing up in western Pennsylvania, encountered the harsh realities of life for the first time, receiving countless death threats and often being stopped by police for no reason. Recalling years later how he reacted to the shabby treatment he received, Allen said, "I didn't want to be a crusader. I kept thinking, 'Why me? Why do I have to be the first black ballplayer in Little Rock?'"

After nearly quitting the game, Allen decided to stay the course and ended up earning a promotion to the parent club in early September. Appearing in 10 games with the Phillies over the final three weeks of the 1963 campaign, Allen batted .292, collecting seven hits in 24 official at-bats. Allen became a regular member of the Phillies' lineup the following year, starting all 162 games for them at third base—a position he had never played before. Performing erratically in the field, Allen committed a league-leading 41 errors, although he managed to amass the second-most putouts and third-most assists of any NL third sacker. Proving to be far more consistent at the plate, Allen earned NL Rookie of the Year honors and a seventh-place finish in the league MVP voting by driving in 91 runs; ranking among the league leaders with 29 homers, 201 hits, 38 doubles, a .318 batting average, a .382 on-base percentage, and a .557 slugging percentage; and topping the circuit with 125 runs scored, 13 triples, and 352 total bases.

Yet, even though Allen received a considerable amount of notoriety for his outstanding play, he remained dissatisfied with the nickname "Richie" that the Phillies organization and the city's scribes bestowed upon him, once complaining, "To be truthful with you, I'd like to be called Dick. I don't know how the Richie started. My name is Richard, and they called me Dick in the minor leagues. . . . It makes me sound like I'm 10 years old. I'm 22. . . . Anyone who knows me well calls me Dick. I don't know why as soon as I put on a uniform it's Richie."

Allen, though, became far more disenchanted in early September 1964, when three days of race riots in Philadelphia caused the city's fans to turn on him. Jeered every time he stepped into the batter's box or fielded a ball at third base during a 4–3 victory over the Houston Astros on the first of the month, Allen found himself being vilified merely for being Black, with *Sport* magazine journalist Arnold Hano writing, "Although he quite obviously played no role in the riot himself and had been, up to that point, silent when it came to the city's racial politics and dynamics, Dick Allen, through the color of his skin and the way he spoke his mind, had become the symbolic face that unleashed white anxiety and discontent with the changing complexion of the city in the wake of the riot."

Things got even worse for Allen after he got into an altercation with veteran slugger Frank Thomas midway through the 1965 campaign. A white teammate with a mean sense of humor, Thomas often amused himself at the expense of the team's Black players, deriving special pleasure from offering them a soul handshake and then bending their thumbs backward. Focusing his attention on Johnny Briggs one day, Thomas called the young outfielder "boy" on several occasions, prompting Allen to later confront him during batting practice. The two men ultimately came to blows, forcing five team-mates to pull them apart. Although Allen and Thomas later shook hands, the fight became the talk of the town after the Phillies announced that very night that Thomas had been released.

Prohibited from talking about the incident afterward, Allen and his teammates never revealed to the public the events that transpired. But, with Thomas no longer a member of the team, he claimed that he had tried to apologize to Allen, who, he said, "cost me my job." Subsequently depicted as the villain by the local media, which continued to portray him as a bad teammate and a clubhouse cancer for the next five seasons, Allen spent his remaining time in Philadelphia being booed unmercifully by the hometown fans, with *Philadelphia Daily News* writer Bill Conlin later telling filmmaker Mike Tollin, "The Phillies let two million people come up with their own version of what happened. It was a catastrophic event in Allen's career and in the history of the ball club."

Meanwhile, as the *Philadelphia Inquirer* reported in July 2015, Thomas once told Tollin, "Richie Allen could have been the greatest player that ever played the game. . . . The incident that happened . . . was just an unfortunate thing. . . . The fans of Philadelphia crucified him because they liked me."

Yet, through it all, Allen continued to post outstanding numbers year after year, earning All-Star honors three straight times from 1965 to 1967. After hitting 20 homers, knocking in 85 runs, scoring 93 times, batting .302, and finishing second in the NL with 14 triples in the first of those campaigns, Allen had arguably the finest season of his career in 1966, when, despite missing three weeks due to a shoulder injury, he finished in the league's top five in 10 different offensive categories, including home runs (40), RBIs (110), runs scored (112), batting average (.317), on-base percentage (.396), and slugging percentage (.632), while splitting his time between third base and left field. Back at third base full-time again in 1967, Allen hit 23 homers, knocked in 77 runs, scored 89 times, batted .307, and topped the senior circuit with a .404 on-base percentage and an OPS of .970, even though his season ended one month early after he cut his right hand and wrist while tinkering with his automobile, severing in the process two tendons and his ulnar nerve.

Blessed with as much natural ability as anyone in the game, the right-handed-hitting Allen, who stood 5'11" and weighed 190 pounds, possessed a powerful physique that included broad shoulders, a thin waist, massive forearms, and a sprinter's legs. Capable of driving the ball out of any part of any ballpark, Allen wielded an enormous 42-ounce bat that helped propel multiple baseballs to tape-measure distances, with Willie Mays saying, "Dick could hit the ball farther than anybody that I've seen."

Hank Aaron also praised Allen for his prodigious power at the plate, stating, "Dick was a fine ball player. He did some great things and hit the ball much further than I did."

In discussing Allen's all-around hitting ability, Ken Harrelson revealed, "[Don] Drysdale thought Stan Musial was the best hitter he ever faced, but he said Richie Allen was in the top five. Coming from Drysdale, that shows that Richie was just a wonderful player."

An outstanding baserunner as well, Allen rarely received the credit he deserved for his excellence in that area. Displaying his insight into that particular aspect of the game on one occasion, Allen, who stole a career-high 20 bases for the Phillies in 1967, said, "Baserunning is an art and a skill. If I'm on second, one ball on the batter, I'm going to try and get a big lead to distract the pitcher. My job is to help get ball two. Now the pitcher's got to throw a strike. Batter knows that. I know that. He's in a position to get good wood on the ball. He gets a single, I score. That's good baserunning."

Bill White, who spent three seasons playing alongside Allen in Philadelphia, discussed the impression that his former teammate made on him during their time together when he stated, "I had the opportunity and pleasure to play with Hall of Famers Willie Mays, Willie McCovey, Orlando Cepeda, Juan Marichal, and many other excellent players. Dick Allen, in my opinion, ranks with these great players. I never saw a player hustle as much as Dick Allen."

And, even though the media suggested otherwise, Allen took his job seriously, as former Chicago White Sox teammate Rich Gossage said in the book *Pen Men*, claiming, "He studied the game intently. I can remember being in the dugout at times when some of the White Sox players would be horsing around. . . . Dick would suddenly pipe up with, 'Cut the crap and get your heads in the game. Watch the pitcher. Learn something.' . . . Allen played to win. . . . If I were to pick an 'All-Teammate Team' from my career, I'd put Dick Allen at first base."

Gossage added, "I have played on some great teams and played with some of the best players in baseball history. But I'll tell you this—the best player I ever played with was in a league of his own, and that's Dick Allen. Nobody else is even close. I played with him in 1972 in Chicago when he was the MVP. I saw him do the most incredible things with the bat, the glove. He hit more balls hard. I could take you to any ballpark we played and show you balls that he hit so hard, balls that looked like rockets. . . . You kinda listen to stories about the old guys, but it doesn't sink in because you don't have any recollection of them at all. You can't imagine how good they were: Mays, Mantle, and Maris . . . but I saw Dick Allen—he was the best. Just unbelievable."

Allen remained in Philadelphia for two more years, hitting 33 homers, driving in 90 runs, scoring 87 times, and batting .263 while manning left field in 1968, before homering 32 times, knocking in 89 runs, scoring 79 others, and batting .288 after moving to first base the following season, despite taking an unexplained one-month leave of absence after being suspended multiple times by new Phillies skipper Bob Skinner for missing games. Yet even though Allen remained one of the National League's foremost sluggers, his situation grew increasingly worse, especially after his rebellious behavior that included consistently showing up at the ballpark with beer on his breath helped lead to the firing of manager Gene Mauch less than halfway through the 1968 campaign. Treated with disdain by the hometown fans, who showered him with insults and racial epithets, before progressing to coins, bolts, and batteries, Allen began wearing a batting helmet whenever he took the field. Continuing to incur the wrath of the Philly Faithful after Skinner replaced Mauch at the helm, Allen became even more rebellious, prompting Skinner to finally hand in his resignation. In explaining his decision, Skinner said, "Now I know what Gene Mauch went through. You can fine Allen, and he just laughs at you. He negotiates with the front office, makes his own private agreement, and it's like handing the money right back to him. I don't want to go on managing this club under the circumstances."

With Allen having asked to be traded several times, the Phillies finally granted his request when they included him in a multiplayer deal that they completed with the Cardinals on October 7, 1969, that sent him, infielder Cookie Rojas, and pitcher Jerry Johnson to St. Louis in exchange for outfielder Curt Flood, catcher Tim McCarver, outfielder Byron Browne, and pitcher Joe Hoerner. Allen subsequently spent just one year in St. Louis, earning All-Star honors in 1970 by hitting 34 homers, driving in 101 runs, and batting .279, before being dealt to the Dodgers for two players at season's end. After hitting 23 homers, knocking in 90 runs, and batting .295 for L.A. in 1971, Allen headed to Chicago when the Dodgers traded him to the White Sox for pitcher Tommy John prior to the start of the ensuing campaign. Finding the AL very much to his liking, Allen earned league MVP honors his first year in the Windy City by batting .308 and topping the junior circuit in six different offensive categories, including home runs (37), RBIs (113), on-base percentage (.420), and slugging percentage (.603). Allen spent two more years in Chicago, leading the AL with 32 homers in 1974, before an ailing shoulder and an aching back prompted him to announce his retirement during the latter stages of the campaign.

Despite Allen's announcement, the White Sox traded him to the Atlanta Braves in December 1974. But, after Allen informed the Braves that he had no desire to play for them, they dealt him to the Phillies for a pair of minor-league players. Having experienced a change of heart after speaking with Mike Schmidt, Dave Cash, and longtime friend Tony Taylor, Allen welcomed a return to Philadelphia and gladly accepted the deal.

Allen spent the next two seasons serving the Phillies as a part-time player, contributing to their successful run to the 1976 division title by hitting 15 homers and driving in 49 runs in just 85 games and 298 official at-bats. Released by the Phillies on November 5, 1976, Allen subsequently signed with the Oakland Athletics, for whom he assumed a part-time role in 1977, before retiring for good with career totals of 351 home runs, 1,119 RBIs, 1,099 runs scored, 1,848 hits, 320 doubles, 79 triples, and 133 stolen bases, a .292 batting average, a .378 on-base percentage, and a .534 slugging percentage. During his two tours of duty with the Phillies, Allen hit 204 homers, knocked in 655 runs, scored 697 times, stole 86 bases, batted .290, compiled an on-base percentage of .371, posted a slugging percentage of .530, and collected 1,143 hits, 204 doubles, and 64 triples.

Following his playing days, Allen endured many personal tragedies and significant financial loss until he straightened out his life by returning to the game he loved. After working briefly for the Texas Rangers as a spring training coach in 1982, Allen served as hitting instructor for the White Sox and Phillies, before becoming a community fan representative for the Phils in 1994.

Meanwhile, Allen's reputation as someone who upset team chemistry continued to haunt him, proving to be a major factor in his inability to gain admission to the National Baseball Hall of Fame. However, Mike Schmidt stated in his book, *Clearing the Bases*, that he considered Allen to be his mentor and an excellent teammate, adding, "The baseball writers used to claim that Dick would divide the clubhouse along racial lines. That was a lie. The truth is that Dick never divided any clubhouse."

Other notable baseball personalities came to Allen's defense as well, with Pittsburgh Pirates Hall of Famer Willie Stargell saying: "Dick Allen played the game in the most conservative era in baseball history. It was a time of change and protest in the country, and baseball reacted against all that. They saw it as a threat to the game. The sportswriters were reactionary too. They didn't like seeing a man of such extraordinary skills doing it his way. It made them nervous. Dick Allen was ahead of his time. His views and way of doing things would go unnoticed today. If I had been manager of the Phillies back when he was playing, I would have found a way to make Dick Allen comfortable. I would have told him to blow off the writers. It was my observation that, when Dick Allen was happy, balls left the park."

And, in examining Allen's career, legendary *Philadelphia Inquirer* sportswriter Stan Hochman, who remained an ardent supporter of the Phillies slugger through the years, once wrote, "Dick Allen led the entire cockeyed world of baseball in OPS-plus for 10 years from 1964 to 1973. His number was 165, higher than Hank Aaron, higher than Willie McCovey, higher than Frank Robinson, Harmon Killebrew, Willie Stargell, Roberto Clemente, and Willie Mays. Dominate any phase of the game for 10 years, pitching or hitting or slugging, and you oughta be in the Hall of Fame. Allen is not in the Hall of Fame. The other seven guys are."

Unfortunately, if Allen is ever going to be admitted to Cooperstown, the honor will come to him posthumously, since he died at his home in Wampum at the age of 78, on December 7, 2020. Reflecting back on the life and career of his former teammate and good friend upon learning of his passing, Mike Schmidt said, "Dick was a sensitive Black man who refused to be treated as a second-class citizen. He played in front of home fans that were products of that racist era, with racist teammates and different rules for whites and Blacks. Fans threw stuff at him and, thus, Dick wore a batting helmet throughout the whole game. They yelled degrading racial slurs. They dumped trash in his front yard at his home. In general, he was tormented, and it came from all directions. And Dick rebelled."

PHILLIES CAREER HIGHLIGHTS

Best Season

Although Allen collected more hits (201) and scored more runs (125) during his brilliant rookie campaign of 1964, he compiled his best overall numbers as a member of the Phillies in 1966, earning a fourth-place finish in the NL MVP voting by ranking among the league leaders with 40 homers, 110 RBIs, 112 runs scored, 10 triples, 331 total bases, a batting average of .317, and an on-base percentage of .396, while also topping the circuit with a slugging percentage of .632 and an OPS of 1.027.

Memorable Moments/Greatest Performances

Allen led the Phillies to a 4–2 win over the Reds on April 28, 1964, by going 4-for-5, with a homer, triple, and two RBIs.

Allen contributed to a 9–3 victory over the Pirates on August 23, 1964, by homering twice and knocking in four runs.

Allen hit several tape-measure home runs during his time in Philadelphia, with perhaps the longest of those coming in the first inning of a 4–2 home win over the Cubs on May 29, 1965, when he drove a ball over the roof in left-center field into a tree that stood some 510 feet from home plate. Allen's blast is believed to be one of the longest ever hit at Connie Mack Stadium, with Phillies manager Gene Mauch later saying, "I've seen Allen hit balls harder and look better doing it, but that has to be his most impressive homer."

Allen drove in all four runs the Phillies scored during a 4–2 win over the Giants on July 8, 1965, when he homered off Jack Sanford with the bases loaded in the first inning.

Allen helped lead the Phillies to a 12–9 victory over the Cubs on July 2, 1966, by going 4-for-5, with two homers, three RBIs, and three runs scored.

Allen gave the Phillies a 6–5 win over the Astros on August 1, 1966, when he led off the bottom of the 10th inning with an inside-the-park home run.

Allen delivered another walkoff homer on August 19, 1966, with his mammoth two-out solo shot that cleared the first advertising sign atop the left field roof at Connie Mack Stadium giving the Phillies a 5–4, 10-inning win over the Mets.

Allen proved to be the difference in a 4–3 victory over the Cardinals on September 25, 1966, going 4-for-6, with a homer and three RBIs, with his two-out single to center field in the bottom of the 13th inning driving in the game-winning run.

Allen hit another of his patented tape-measure home runs during a 4–3, 10-inning win over the Cardinals at Connie Mack Stadium on July 9, 1967. In discussing Allen's eighth-inning blast, which traveled some 500 feet, Allen Lewis of the *Philadelphia Inquirer* wrote, "The ball cleared the centerfield fence about halfway between the flagpole and the light tower. . . . Allen's ball left the park at a height of at least 40 feet and is the first ball hit out of the park to the left of the light tower since the fence height was raised (to 32 feet)."

Allen gave the Phillies a 5–2 win over the Cubs on August 17, 1967, when he homered to the opposite field with two men on base in the bottom of the 12th inning.

Allen defeated the Cubs almost single-handedly on September 13, 1968, homering twice and knocking in three runs during a 3–1 Phillies win, with his two-run blast in the bottom of the eighth inning providing the margin of victory.

Allen led the Phillies to a 10–3 win over the Mets on September 29, 1968, by hitting three homers and driving in seven runs, putting the game out of reach with a ninth-inning grand slam.

Notable Achievements

- Surpassed 20 home runs six times, topping 30 homers three times and 40 homers once.
- Knocked in more than 100 runs once.
- Scored more than 100 runs twice.
- Batted over .300 four times.
- Surpassed 200 hits once.
- Finished in double digits in triples four times.
- Surpassed 30 doubles three times.
- Stole 20 bases once.
- Compiled on-base percentage over .400 once.
- Posted slugging percentage over .500 five times, topping .600-mark once.
- Compiled OPS over .900 four times, finishing with mark over 1.000 once.
- Hit three home runs in one game vs. New York Mets on September 29, 1968.
- Led NL in runs scored once, triples once, extra-base hits twice, total bases once, on-base percentage once, slugging percentage once, and OPS twice.
- Finished second in NL in home runs twice, triples once, slugging percentage twice, OPS once, games played once, and plate appearances once.
- Finished third in NL in RBIs once, runs scored once, hits once, total bases once, on-base percentage once, slugging percentage twice.
- Led NL third basemen in double plays once.
- Led NL left fielders in fielding percentage once.

- Ranks among Phillies career leaders in home runs (10th), triples (tied for 11th), slugging percentage (4th), OPS (10th), and intentional bases on balls (5th).
- 1976 division champion.
- 1964 NL Rookie of the Year.
- Finished in top 10 in NL MVP voting twice, placing as high as fourth in 1966.
- Three-time NL All-Star (1965, 1966, and 1967).
- Member of Philadelphia Baseball Wall of Fame.
- Member of Philadelphia Sports Hall of Fame.
- #15 retired by Phillies.

11
JIMMY ROLLINS

The emotional leader of Phillies teams that won five division titles, two pennants, and one World Series, Jimmy Rollins spent parts of 15 seasons in Philadelphia, starting at shortstop in 14 of those. An excellent table-setter at the top of the Phillies' lineup, the switch-hitting Rollins batted over .300 once and scored at least 100 runs six times, while also collecting at least 10 triples five times and surpassing 20 homers on four separate occasions. A superb baserunner and outstanding fielder as well, Rollins stole more than 30 bases 10 times and led all players at his position in fielding percentage four times, with his exceptional glove work earning him four Gold Gloves. A three-time NL All-Star and one-time league MVP, Rollins ended his lengthy stint in the City of Brotherly Love as one of the franchise's all-time leaders in virtually every major offensive category.

Born in Oakland, California, on November 27, 1978, James Calvin Rollins Jr. grew up in the Buena Vista section of Alameda, where he displayed an affinity for sports at an early age. The son of a man who wrestled, lifted weights, and ran track in high school, and a woman who starred as an infielder in the fast-pitch softball leagues of Northern California, young Jimmy absorbed a tremendous amount of baseball knowledge from his mother, who also passed on to him her strong, compact physique.

Developing his swagger and athletic skills on the local playgrounds, Rollins, who grew up rooting for the San Francisco 49ers and Oakland Athletics, excelled in multiple sports during his formative years, starring on both sides of the ball in Pop Warner football, while also displaying a considerable amount of ability on the diamond, where he tried to emulate his favorite player, Rickey Henderson.

Choosing to focus exclusively on baseball after he enrolled at nearby Encinal High School, Rollins eventually emerged as one of the region's most highly touted players. Ending his four-year career at Encinal High with 10 school records, including most stolen bases (99) and highest batting average (.484), Rollins earned All-USA High School Baseball Team honors

Jimmy Rollins holds franchise records
for most hits, doubles, and at-bats.
Courtesy of Keith Allison and All-Pro Reels

from *USA Today* and gained recognition from *Baseball America* as a Second-Team All-American and the top infielder in Northern California. Offered an athletic scholarship to Arizona State University, Rollins initially committed to playing college baseball, before changing his mind when the Phillies selected him in the second round of the 1996 MLB Draft.

Rollins subsequently spent most of the next five seasons in the minor leagues, displaying a good bat, solid glove, excellent speed, and superb instincts at five different levels of the Phillies' farm system, before being called up to the parent club during the latter stages of the 2000 campaign after batting .274, stealing 24 bases, and leading the International League with 11 triples with Triple-A Scranton. Acquitting himself extremely well over the final two weeks of the regular season, Rollins batted .321, knocked in five runs, and stole three bases in 14 games and 53 at-bats with the Phillies.

Handed the starting shortstop job the following year, Rollins performed exceptionally well in his first full big-league season, earning All-Star honors and a third-place finish in the NL Rookie of the Year voting by hitting 14 homers, driving in 54 runs, scoring 97 times, batting .274, and leading the league with 12 triples and 46 stolen bases, while hitting primarily out of the leadoff spot in the batting order. Although Rollins gained All-Star recognition once again in 2002, he proved to be somewhat less productive on offense, concluding the campaign with 11 homers, 60 RBIs, 82 runs scored, 31 stolen bases, a .245 batting average, and an on-base percentage of just .306.

After posting similar numbers the following year, Rollins, who, despite his smallish 5'7", 175-pound frame, spent most of his first three seasons swinging from his heels, altered his approach somewhat heading into 2004. Instructed by Hall of Famer Tony Gwynn, with whom he worked extensively during the offseason, to use more of the field, hit more ground balls, and display greater patience at the plate, Rollins developed into more of a complete hitter. Although he continued to swing early in the count and occasionally chase high pitches, Rollins reduced his strikeout total from 113 to 73 and increased his batting average from .263 to .289. Rollins also hit 14 homers; knocked in 73 runs; stole 30 bases; ranked among the league leaders with 119 runs scored, 190 hits, and 43 doubles; and topped the circuit with 12 triples. Rollins followed that up with three more outstanding seasons, posting the following numbers from 2005 to 2007:

YEAR	HR	RBI	RUNS	2B	3B	SB	AVG	OBP	SLG
2005	12	54	115	38	11	41	.290	.338	.431
2006	25	83	127	45	9	36	.277	.334	.478
2007	30	94	**139**	38	**20**	41	.296	.344	.531

Ranking among the league leaders in runs scored, hits, triples, and stolen bases all three years, Rollins gained All-Star recognition and finished 10th in the NL MVP voting in the first of those campaigns, which he concluded with a 36-game hitting streak that established a new franchise record (which he extended to 38 games the following year). Two years later, after making headlines during the previous offseason by telling reporters that the Phillies would be the team to beat in the NL East, Rollins earned NL MVP honors by leading them to the division title for the first of five straight times.

Commenting on Rollins's bold prediction, which he made prior to the start of spring training, on January 23, 2007, *USA Today* columnist Hal Bodley wrote, "The Phillies have needed someone to light a fire, especially in April. Rollins' bold, if not arrogant, prediction might just do that."

Having clearly established himself as the Phillies' leader, both on and off the field, Rollins drew praise from Hall of Famer Ernie Banks, who said, "Jimmy Rollins is one of the premier athletes in baseball today. His leadership and ability to produce offensively and play solid defense makes him one of the most exciting and valuable players in either league."

Serving as the Phillies' offensive catalyst from his leadoff spot in the batting order, Rollins fully understood his role, saying, "My role is to set everything in motion."

Claiming that Rollins did his job extremely well, Florida Marlins manager Jack McKeon suggested, "He's absolutely the key to that offense."

Yet even though Rollins provided the Phillies with speed, power, and outstanding run production from the top of the lineup, his aggressive approach at the plate made him something less than the ideal leadoff hitter, a fact he admitted when he said, "I'm not the prototypical leadoff man. I'm not the prototypical anything. I just try to be the prototypical Jimmy Rollins."

Stressing Rollins's importance to the success of the team, Phillies GM Ed Wade stated, "We know what this guy is all about, and what he means to our ball club."

An excellent fielder as well, Rollins possessed good range, soft hands, and a strong and accurate throwing arm, with a 2011 season preview in *Lindy's Sports* identifying him as an upper-echelon shortstop "with soft hands, excellent agility, and plus range left and right."

Expressing his admiration for the totality of Rollins's game, former All-Star shortstop Maury Wills said, "He's kind of a throwback for me, to the type of ballplayer from when I played. He's totally confident on the field—the kind of guy that would want the ball at the end of the game when the game is on the line."

Rollins also received high praise from two of his Phillies teammates, with Aaron Rowand stating, "Jimmy is incredible because it seems like he hits every ball hard."

Meanwhile, Rollins's double-play partner, Chase Utley, said, "We definitely feed off each other. It's a lot easier playing second with Jimmy over there. I always know where he's going to be."

Plagued by an injured ankle that forced him to miss nearly a month of action in 2008, Rollins posted slightly subpar numbers, finishing the season with 11 homers, 59 RBIs, 76 runs scored, and a .277 batting average, although he still managed to rank among the league leaders with 47 stolen bases and earn Gold Glove honors for the second of three straight times. Healthy again in 2009, Rollins hit 21 homers, knocked in 77 runs, scored 100 times, batted .250, placed near the top of the league rankings with 43 doubles and 31 stolen bases, and committed only six errors in the field, en route to leading all NL shortstops with a career-best .990 fielding percentage. Rollins subsequently suffered through an injury-marred 2010 campaign during which he appeared in only 88 games, before leading the Phillies to their fifth consecutive division title the following year by hitting 16 homers, driving in 63 runs, scoring 87 times, stealing 30 bases, and batting .268. A free agent at the end of 2011, Rollins signed a new four-year deal with the Phillies, saying at the time, "I could have gone out there and possibly gotten more money. But that's not where my heart was. My heart was here in Philly."

Rollins posted solid numbers once again in 2012, finishing the year with 23 homers, 68 RBIs, 102 runs scored, 30 steals, and a .250 batting average, before experiencing a precipitous decline in offensive production the next two seasons. After Rollins scored only 78 runs and batted just .243 in 2014, the Phillies traded him to the Dodgers for minor-league pitchers Tom Windle and Zach Eflin at the end of the year. Rollins, who left Philadelphia with career totals of 216 home runs, 887 RBIs, 1,325 runs scored, 2,306 hits, 479 doubles, 111 triples, and 453 stolen bases, a batting average of .267, an on-base percentage of .327, and a slugging percentage of .424, subsequently spent just one year in Los Angeles, scoring 71 runs and batting just .224 for the Dodgers in 2015, before retiring following the conclusion of the ensuing campaign after being released by the Chicago White Sox at midseason. Over parts of 17 big-league seasons, Rollins hit 231 homers, knocked in 936 runs, scored 1,421 times, stole 470 bases, batted .264, compiled an on-base percentage of .324, posted a slugging percentage of .418, and collected 2,455 hits, 511 doubles, and 115 triples.

After remaining away from the game for two years, Rollins returned to the Phillies in two separate capacities in 2019, taking on the role of special advisor for the club, while also serving as an on-air commentator for their television broadcasts. Rollins is also an investor for esports team NRG Esports and remains dedicated to The Johari & Jimmy Rollins Center for Animal Rehabilitation that he and his wife founded during his playing days.

With Rollins's name soon to be added to the Hall of Fame ballot, current Phillies manager Joe Girardi assessed his Hall of Fame credentials, stating, "He was a difference maker, Jimmy. He was a guy that could do a lot of different things . . . he was a switch-hitter . . . he could steal bases . . . play very good shortstop. I don't really have the numbers in front of me—like how many hits he amassed and all that—but I will tell you that during his time period he was one of the best shortstops in the game. And that's kind of what you look at is how you played during your era. And Jimmy was a difference maker."

Meanwhile, Rollins said, "If you're talented enough and play long enough, and put up numbers, you'll get to the Hall of Fame. That doesn't make you a World Series winner. . . . Ultimately, it's about being a champion."

PHILLIES CAREER HIGHLIGHTS

Best Season

Rollins played his best ball for the Phillies from 2004 to 2007, a period during which he scored well over 100 runs four straight times and hit more than 20 homers, stole more than 40 bases, and batted over .290 twice each. Although Rollins performed exceptionally well throughout the period, he had his finest season in 2007, when he earned NL MVP honors by establishing career-high marks with 30 homers, 94 RBIs, 139 runs scored, 212 hits, 20 triples, a .296 batting average, and an OPS of .875, accomplishing the rare feat of accumulating at least 20 home runs, 20 triples, 20 doubles, and 20 stolen bases in the same season by also amassing 38 doubles and stealing 41 bases.

Memorable Moments/Greatest Performances

Rollins led the Phillies to a 6–3 win over the Dodgers on August 11, 2002, by going 5-for-5, with two stolen bases, one RBI, and one run scored.

Rollins contributed to a 16–1 thrashing of the Pirates on April 5, 2003, by going 5-for-6, with three doubles, three RBIs, and four runs scored.

Rollins again hit safely in 5 of his 6 trips to the plate during a 3–2, 13-inning win over the Seattle Mariners on June 16, 2005, finishing the game with a triple, double, three singles, and two runs scored.

Rollins established a franchise record by hitting safely in 38 consecutive games from August 23, 2005, to the first two contests of the ensuing campaign. Batting .379 over the final 36 games of the 2005 season, Rollins hit three homers, amassed four triples and nineteen doubles, knocked in 22 runs, and scored 35 times during that stretch.

Rollins helped lead the Phillies to a convincing 16–8 victory over the Cardinals on August 2, 2006, by going 3-for-5, with two homers, four RBIs, and a career-high five runs scored.

Rollins punctuated a three-hit, four-RBI performance by delivering a two-out, two-run triple in the top of the 14th inning that gave the Phillies an 8–7 win over the Nationals on September 27, 2006.

Rollins again came through in the clutch on June 28, 2007, giving the Phillies an 8–7 victory over the Reds by driving in the winning run from second base with his fourth hit of the game with one man out in the bottom of the 10th inning.

Rollins led the Phillies to an 8–7, 13-inning win over the Mets on August 26, 2008, by going 5-for-7, with a homer, double, three stolen bases, and three RBIs.

Rollins delivered the big blow in a 14–6 win over the Cardinals on July 25, 2009, when he homered with the bases loaded in the bottom of the sixth inning.

Rollins gave the Phillies a 5–4 victory over the Dodgers in Game 4 of the 2009 NLCS when he knocked in the tying and winning runs with a two-run double to right-center with two men out in the bottom of the ninth inning.

Rollins turned a 6–5 deficit into a 7–6 Phillies win on June 23, 2010, when he homered off Cleveland Indians right-hander Kerry Wood with one man aboard in the bottom of the ninth inning.

Rollins gave the Phillies a 5–4 win over the Marlins on April 12, 2014, when he hit a solo homer with two men out in the bottom of the 10th inning.

Rollins contributed to a 9–1 win over the Cubs on July 20, 2011, by homering twice, knocking in three runs, and scoring four times.

Notable Achievements

- Batted over .300 once.
- Surpassed 20 home runs four times, hitting 30 homers once.
- Scored at least 100 runs six times.
- Surpassed 200 hits once.
- Finished in double digits in triples five times, amassing 20 three-baggers once.
- Surpassed 30 doubles 10 times, amassing more than 40-two baggers on four occasions.
- Stole at least 20 bases 13 times, topping 30 thefts 10 times and 40 thefts on four occasions.
- Posted slugging percentage over .500 once.
- Led NL in runs scored once, triples four times, stolen bases once, games played once, plate appearances three times, and at-bats four times.
- Finished second in NL in runs scored once, hits once, extra-base hits once, total bases once, plate appearances three times, and at-bats twice.
- Finished third in NL in runs scored twice, hits once, triples once, stolen bases once, plate appearances twice, and at-bats three times.
- Led NL shortstops in fielding percentage four times.

- Holds Phillies career records for most at-bats (8,628), hits (2,306), and doubles (479).
- Ranks among Phillies career leaders in runs scored (3rd), RBIs (8th), home runs (9th), triples (3rd), extra-base hits (2nd), total bases (2nd), stolen bases (2nd), walks (6th), sacrifice flies (tied for 6th), games played (2nd), and plate appearances (2nd).
- Five-time division champion (2007, 2008, 2009, 2010, and 2011).
- Two-time NL champion (2008 and 2009).
- 2008 world champion.
- Two-time NL Player of the Week.
- 2007 NL MVP.
- 2007 Silver Slugger Award winner.
- Four-time Gold Glove Award winner (2007, 2008, 2009, and 2012).
- 2014 Roberto Clemente Award winner.
- Three-time NL All-Star (2001, 2002, and 2005).

12
CY WILLIAMS

The first National League player to hit more than 200 home runs, Cy Williams proved to be one of the senior circuit's top sluggers for more than a decade, leading the league in homers four times between 1916 and 1927. Accomplishing the feat three times as a member of the Phillies, who acquired him from the Chicago Cubs prior to the start of the 1918 season in one of the greatest trades in franchise history, Williams hit as many as 30 home runs twice, becoming in 1923 just the second NL player ever to reach the 40-homer plateau. An outstanding all-around athlete who excelled in other aspects of the game as well, Williams also batted over .300 six times and did a superb job of patrolling center field for the Phillies, annually ranking among the top players at his position in putouts and fielding percentage. One of the Phillies' few bright spots for much of the 1920s, Williams accomplished all he did as a member of the team even though he arrived in Philadelphia at the rather advanced age of 30.

Born in the tiny town of Wadena, Indiana, on December 21, 1887, Fred Williams grew up on a farm, where he had very little exposure to organized sports, with *Baseball Magazine* reporting years later, "Williams never played even half a dozen games of baseball in his life before he went to Notre Dame, and those games were of the scrubbiest kind."

Finally given an opportunity to display his superior athletic ability after he enrolled at the University of Notre Dame in 1908, Williams excelled in multiple sports for the Fighting Irish, starring in baseball, football, and track, where he posted a personal-best time of 15.6 seconds in the 120-yard high-hurdles and leaped 22'3" in the broad jump. Acquiring the nickname "Cy" (a moniker often applied to rural-looking youngsters of the day) while at South Bend, Williams soon caught the attention of a Chicago Cubs scout, who wanted to sign him immediately. However, wishing to retain his amateur status, Williams turned down the offer, recalling years later, "I asked him if he thought I was able to go up to high company and make good right away. The scout said no. I told him, 'That is what I thought.

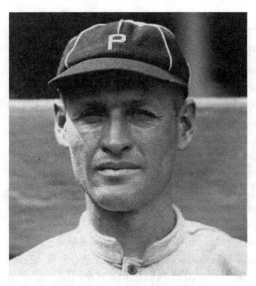

Cy Williams led the NL in home runs three times while playing for the Phillies.
Courtesy of RMYAuctions.com

Now, if I sign a contract, it will make me ineligible for college athletics, and I should like to compete in them as long as I am here.'"

Revealing that the scout accepted his answer but asked for his word that he would give the Cubs first choice if he ever considered turning pro, Williams stated, "I promised, and I kept my promise, even though somewhat unusual circumstances arose after that. The scout left the employ of [Cubs president Charles] Murphy and joined the Cleveland club. While there, he visited me again and wanted me to sign for Cleveland. But I told him I had agreed to give Murphy first choice and I would keep my word."

Signing with Chicago shortly after he graduated in 1912, the 24-year-old Williams bypassed the minor leagues completely and reported directly to the Cubs, turning down an opportunity to compete in that year's Stockholm Olympics as a hurdler and broad jumper. Used sparingly over the course of the next three seasons, Williams appeared in a total of just 132 games, hitting only four home runs and never batting any higher than .242. However, the left-handed-hitting Williams began to display his ability to deliver the long ball after he laid claim to the starting center field job in Chicago in 1915, finishing second in the NL with 13 homers, while also batting .257. Williams followed that up by batting .279 and leading the league with 12 home runs in 1916, prompting Ward Mason to describe him in an article entitled "The Greatest Outfielder in the National League" that appeared in the September 1916 issue of *Baseball Magazine* as "a great all 'round talent with a wealth of sheer natural ability which is unrivaled in the older circuit." Mason then added, "In all this, there isn't so much an appreciation of what Williams has already accomplished as a vague but definite impression of what he may do when he gets good and ready."

Also making an extremely favorable impression on Cubs player-manager Joe Tinker, Williams drew praise from the future Hall of Famer, who later called him "the greatest natural outfielder I ever saw."

Nevertheless, after hitting just five homers and batting only .241 in 1917, Williams found himself headed to Philadelphia for veteran outfielder Dode Paskert amidst rumors of dissension between himself and Cubs manager Fred Mitchell. Commenting on the trade shortly thereafter, the Chicago correspondent to the *Sporting News* wrote: "Williams was about the best fly catcher in the league and a fairly good batsman, but he had a fatal weakness: He possessed a poor throwing arm. A great throwing outfield is one of the pet hobbies of Mitchell, and it was a source of regret on his part that he couldn't boast such a combination last season."

Meanwhile, the Philadelphia correspondent to that same publication wrote, "[Phillies manager Pat] Moran expects to develop Williams into a hitting star. Certainly, the Broad and Huntingdon grounds here will help hike Williams' batting averages. He always hit a million when he came here. Cy is one of the fastest outfielders in the country, and he is expected to more than make good here. Williams is 29 and Paskert is 36, so about the only way the Phils can get the worst of the exchange is for the Army to draft tall Cy."

Williams posted relatively modest numbers his first two seasons in Philadelphia, hitting six homers, driving in 39 runs, and batting .276 during the war-shortened 1918 campaign, before reaching the seats nine times, knocking in another 39 runs, and batting .278 in 109 games the following year. But Williams finally began to live up to his enormous potential in 1920, when, in addition to leading the NL with 15 homers, he knocked in 72 runs, stole 18 bases, and ranked among the league leaders with 36 doubles, 192 hits, 88 runs scored, a .325 batting average, a .497 slugging percentage, and an OPS of .861. Williams had another solid season in 1921, hitting 18 homers, driving in 75 runs, and batting .320, before beginning an exceptional three-year run during which he posted the following numbers:

YEAR	HR	RBI	RUNS	AVG	OBP	SLG	OPS
1922	26	92	98	.308	.392	.514	.905
1923	**41**	114	98	.293	.371	.576	.947
1924	24	93	101	.328	.403	.552	.955

Establishing himself as one of the NL's most dangerous batsmen, Williams ranked among the league leaders in home runs, RBIs, total bases, slugging percentage, and OPS all three years, with his total of 91 homers representing the highest mark of any player in the senior circuit. Taking full advantage of his home ballpark's short right field fence, Williams, who stood 6'2" and weighed just 180 pounds, proved to be a perfect fit for the Baker Bowl. A dead-pull hitter, Williams hit almost everything to the right side of the field, once admitting, "I couldn't hit a ball to left if my life depended on it." As a result, National League managers soon began positioning their fielders deep and around toward right, in an early version of the "Williams Shift" that Cleveland player-manager Lou Boudreau employed against Cy's namesake, Ted, some 20 years later. Meanwhile, as Williams rose to elite status among NL hitters, he also emerged as one of the league's top defensive outfielders, with his outstanding speed enabling him to finish second among players at his position in putouts three times. And, even though Williams lacked a strong throwing arm, he managed to lead all NL center fielders in assists twice, throwing out as many as 20 runners on the basepaths on four separate occasions.

Although Williams missed a significant amount of playing time in each of the next three seasons due to age and injury, he continued to post outstanding offensive numbers. After batting .331, hitting 13 homers, and driving in 60 runs in just 107 games in 1925, Williams hit 18 homers, batted .345, and led the NL with a .568 slugging percentage and an OPS of .986 the following year, even though he once again appeared in only 107 contests. Williams then knocked in 98 runs and topped the senior circuit with 30 homers in 1927, before spending his final three seasons in Philadelphia serving as a part-time player and pinch-hitter deluxe. Choosing to announce his retirement following the conclusion of the 1930 campaign, Williams ended his major-league career with 251 home runs, 1,005 RBIs, 1,024 runs scored, 1,981 hits, 306 doubles, 74 triples, 115 stolen bases, a .292 batting average, a .365 on-base percentage, and a .470 slugging percentage. As a member of the Phillies, he hit 217 homers, knocked in 795 runs, scored 825 times, stole 77 bases, batted .306, compiled an on-base percentage of .380, posted a slugging percentage of .500, and collected 1,553 hits, 237 doubles, and 49 triples.

After leaving the majors, Williams spent one year serving as player-manager for Richmond in the Eastern League, before retiring to his dairy farm in Wisconsin, where he started a construction business and worked as an architect, eventually designing some of the finest buildings currently situated on Wisconsin's Upper Peninsula. Williams, who enjoyed hunting and fishing in his spare time, lived until April 23, 1974, when he passed away in Eagle River, Wisconsin, at the age of 86.

PHILLIES CAREER HIGHLIGHTS

Best Season

Williams had an excellent year for the Phillies in 1923, leading the NL with a career-high 41 home runs, while also finishing second in the league with 114 RBIs and 308 total bases, scoring 98 runs, batting .293, and compiling an OPS of .947. Particularly outstanding during the month of May, Williams knocked in 44 runs in 30 games. But even though Williams hit far fewer homers (24) and knocked in fewer runs (93) the following year, he posted equally impressive overall numbers, once again amassing 308 total bases, scoring 101 runs, recording a career-high 11 triples, batting .328, and compiling an OPS of .955. It's an extremely close call, but since Williams finished in the league's top five in eight different offensive categories in 1924, we'll identify that as his finest season.

Memorable Moments/Greatest Performances

Williams contributed to an 11–3 victory over the Brooklyn Robins on September 5, 1922, by homering twice and knocking in five runs.

Williams again feasted on Brooklyn pitching on April 20, 1923, going 4-for-5, with a homer, triple, and four RBIs during an 8–7 Phillies win.

Williams led the Phillies to a 20–14 victory over the St. Louis Cardinals on May 11, 1923, by hitting three homers and knocking in a career-high seven runs, reaching the seats once against southpaw Bill Sherdel and twice against right-hander Lou North.

Williams proved to be the difference in a 6–4 win over Brooklyn on September 30, 1923, homering twice off Dazzy Vance, with his two-run shot off the Hall of Fame right-hander in the top of the 12th inning providing the margin of victory.

Williams gave the Phillies a 7–6 victory over the Reds on June 11, 1924, by driving in the tying and winning runs with a two-out single in the bottom of the 13th inning.

Williams provided further heroics on September 4, 1924, when he gave the Phillies a 10–6 win over the Giants by hitting a walkoff grand slam in the bottom of the 10th inning.

Although the Phillies lost to the Giants two days later 16–14, Williams had the only five-hit game of his career, going 5-for-5, with five singles, two RBIs, and four runs scored.

Williams gave the Phillies a dramatic 8–4 victory over the Boston Braves on April 15, 1926, when he hit a pinch-hit grand slam home run with one man out in the bottom of the ninth inning.

Williams again came through in the clutch on September 8, 1926, giving the Phillies an 8–4 win over Brooklyn by homering with the bases loaded with two men out in the bottom of the ninth inning.

Williams led the Phillies to a 15–2 rout of the Reds on May 20, 1927, by driving in seven runs with a three-run homer in the bottom of the third and a sixth-inning grand slam.

Williams accomplished the rare feat of hitting for the cycle on August 5, 1927, going 4-for-4, with six RBIs and three runs scored during a 9–7 win over the Pirates in Pittsburgh.

Notable Achievements

- Hit more than 20 home runs four times, topping 30 homers twice and 40 homers once.
- Knocked in more than 100 runs once.
- Scored more than 100 runs once.
- Batted over .300 six times, topping the .320 mark on five occasions.
- Finished in double digits in triples twice.
- Surpassed 30 doubles three times.
- Compiled on-base percentage over .400 five times.
- Posted slugging percentage over .500 seven times.
- Compiled OPS over .900 six times.
- Hit three home runs in one game vs. St. Louis Cardinals on May 11, 1923.
- Hit for cycle vs. Pittsburgh Pirates on August 5, 1927.
- Led NL in home runs three times, slugging percentage once, and OPS once.
- Finished second in NL in home runs twice, RBIs once, doubles once, total bases twice, on-base percentage once, and slugging percentage twice.
- Finished third in NL in home runs four times, total bases once, extra-base hits twice, on-base percentage once, slugging percentage once, and OPS once.
- Led NL outfielders in assists once.
- Led NL center fielders in assists twice and fielding percentage once.
- Led NL right fielders in assists once and double plays once.
- Ranks among Phillies career leaders in home runs (8th), hits (10th), extra-base hits (12th), and total bases (9th).
- Member of Philadelphia Baseball Wall of Fame.

13

BOBBY ABREU

Hailed as "probably the most natural hitter I've ever seen" by former Phillies teammate Ron Gant, Bobby Abreu proved to be one of the National League's most outstanding offensive performers during his nine-year stint in Philadelphia that began in 1998. Blessed with a smooth left-handed swing, a keen batting eye, and excellent speed on the basepaths, Abreu hit at least 20 homers seven times, knocked in more than 100 runs four times, batted over .300 and scored more than 100 runs six times each, drew more than 100 bases on balls seven times, and stole at least 20 bases on eight separate occasions, en route to establishing himself as one of the franchise's all-time leaders in virtually every major offensive category. Meanwhile, although Abreu displayed an aversion to outfield walls that did not sit particularly well with the Philly Faithful, he also did a solid job in right field, leading all players at his position in putouts once and assists twice, with his strong all-around play earning him two All-Star nominations and a place in the Philadelphia Baseball Wall of Fame.

Born in Aragua, Venezuela, on March 11, 1974, Bob Kelly Abreu grew up with his five siblings in a part of the country where jungles, beaches, and flat plains come together. Developing a love for baseball at an early age, Bobby learned the game from his father, Nelson, who worked out regularly with his four sons until he lost the use of his legs in a car accident. After starting out as a second baseman, Bobby moved to the outfield to take better advantage of his speed, instincts, and strong throwing arm.

Discovered at the age of 14 by Houston Astros scout Andres Reimer while competing in a national tournament, Abreu spent two years attending classes at Aragua High School, while also honing his skills at Houston's burgeoning baseball academy in nearby Valencia. After signing with the Astros as an amateur free agent shortly after he celebrated his 16th birthday in 1990, Abreu began his pro career at Houston's Venezuelan academy, before joining the team's rookie-level squad in the Gulf Coast League the following year. Although Abreu performed well at Kissimmee, batting .301

Bobby Abreu ranks among the Phillies'
career leaders in virtually every major
offensive category.
Courtesy of Bryan Green

and stealing 10 bases in 56 games, he briefly considered giving up baseball when he learned that his father had died on the operating table while undergoing surgery to restore his mobility.

Continuing his ascent through Houston's farm system, Abreu excelled at every stop he made over the course of the next five seasons, before finally joining the Astros during the latter stages of the 1996 campaign after being named the organization's Minor League Player of the Year. But, after earning a roster spot during 1997 spring training, Abreu ended up spending most of the season back in the minors rehabbing an injury he sustained early in the year. Subsequently left unprotected in the 1997 MLB Expansion Draft, Abreu briefly became a member of the Tampa Bay Devil Rays, before the Phillies acquired him just hours later for shortstop Kevin Stocker.

Joining a Phillies team in transition, Abreu immediately laid claim to the starting right field job upon his arrival in Philadelphia, after which he went on to hit 17 homers, drive in 74 runs, score 68 times, steal 19 bases, bat .312, compile an on-base percentage of .409, and lead all players at his position with 17 assists in his first full big-league season. Continuing to perform extremely well the next seven years, Abreu posted the following numbers from 1999 to 2005:

YEAR	HR	RBI	RUNS	2B	AVG	OBP	SLG	OPS
1999	20	93	118	35	.335	.446	.549	.995
2000	25	79	103	42	.316	.416	.554	.970
2001	31	110	118	48	.289	.393	.543	.936
2002	20	85	102	**50**	.308	.413	.521	.934
2003	20	101	99	35	.300	.409	.468	.877
2004	30	105	118	47	.301	.428	.544	.971
2005	24	102	104	37	.286	.405	.474	.879

In addition to leading the NL with 50 doubles in 2002, Abreu topped the circuit with 11 triples in 1999, finished third in the league with a .335 batting average that same year, and consistently placed near the top of the league rankings in runs scored, on-base percentage, and walks. By homering 31 times and stealing 36 bases in 2001, Abreu became the first player in franchise history to top 30 homers and 30 steals in the same season. And when Abreu reached the seats 30 times and swiped 40 bags three years later, he became the team's first member of the 30-40 club. An NL All-Star in both 2004 and 2005, Abreu also won a Silver Slugger in the first of those campaigns, before being awarded the only Gold Glove of his career the following year. Extremely durable, Abreu missed just 29 games over the course of those seven seasons.

Although Abreu struck out frequently, regularly fanning well over 100 times, he proved to be a dependable clutch hitter who altered his approach at the plate depending on the situation and the opposing pitcher. Against lefties, the 6-foot, 220-pound Abreu typically drove the ball to left field and center. But, when facing a right-hander, Abreu looked to pull the ball more to right field. And, even though Abreu had the ability to hit the long ball, once winning the Home Run Derby at the All-Star Game, he never considered himself to be a home-run hitter, stating in the June 2002 edition of *Baseball Digest*, "I pride myself on average, not home runs. I'm never going to try to hit home runs because that's just not me."

In describing Abreu as a hitter, former Phillies batting coach Hal McRae said, "To me, Bobby's Tony Gwynn with power."

One of the game's most patient and disciplined hitters, Abreu did an exceptional job of wearing down opposing pitchers, as former Phillies manager Larry Bowa acknowledged when he suggested, "Bobby was way ahead of his time with regards to working pitchers. In an era when guys were swinging for the fences, Bobby never strayed from his game. Because of his speed, a walk would turn into a double. He was cool under pressure and always in control of his at-bats. He was the best combination of power, speed, and patience at the plate."

Abreu also received high praise from Phillies teammates Jim Thome and Curt Schilling, with Thome stating, "He's been one of the best players I've been around. He's a difference-maker." Meanwhile, Schilling proclaimed, "He's one of the top five or six hitters in the game."

Nevertheless, Abreu had his flaws, which included the reputation for moodiness he developed during the early stages of his career that caused him to frequently clash with his first manager in Philadelphia, Terry Francona. Yet even though Abreu's questionable attitude and chronic tardiness angered Francona, the Phillies skipper spoke highly of his star right fielder when he said, "Bobby is a wonderful kid. . . . I'll tell you this—Bobby Abreu is very, very good."

Abreu also found his toughness and commitment to winning being questioned by the hometown fans, who objected to his practice of shying away from outfield walls and extreme selectivity at the plate, which they mistook for passivity. Yet, once again, one of Abreu's managers came to his defense, with Larry Bowa later saying, "Bobby is not the reason the Phillies didn't win. I was there with him for four years, and we came in second three of the four —and it sure wasn't Bobby Abreu's fault."

With the Phillies well out of contention and Abreu having homered eight times, driven in 65 runs, and batted .277 through the first four months of the 2006 campaign, GM Pat Gillick completed a trade with the Yankees on July 31 that sent the 32-year-old outfielder and pitcher Cory Lidle to New York for four mid-level minor leaguers, none of whom ever amounted to anything. Abreu, who left the Phillies having hit 195 homers, knocked in 814 runs, scored 891 times, batted .303, compiled an on-base percentage of .416, posted a slugging percentage of .513, and collected 1,474 hits, 348 doubles, 42 triples, and 254 stolen bases as a member of the team, subsequently helped lead the Yankees to the AL East title by performing exceptionally well over the season's final 58 games, before spending two more successful years in New York. A free agent at the end of 2008, Abreu signed with the Los Angeles Angels of Anaheim, with whom he spent the next three seasons, having the last big year of his career in 2009, when he hit 15 homers, knocked in 103 runs, scored 96 times, and batted .293. After being released by the Angels early in 2012, Abreu signed with the Dodgers, appearing in 92 games with them, before sitting out the entire 2013 campaign after failing to receive an offer from any team. Returning to the majors in 2014 as a backup with the New York Mets, Abreu appeared in a total of 78 games, before announcing his retirement at season's end with career totals of 288 home runs, 1,363 RBIs, 1,453 runs scored, 2,470 hits, 574 doubles, 59 triples, and 400 stolen bases, a lifetime batting average of .291, a .395 on-base percentage, and a .475 slugging percentage.

Since retiring as an active player, Abreu, who during his time in Philadelphia founded "Abreu's Amigos," which purchased for children $10,000 worth of tickets to most Friday night home games, has continued his philanthropic work through the American Red Cross Blood Drive. Looking back favorably on the time he spent in the City of Brotherly Love, Abreu says, "I played in Philly for eight years, and I liked the city. The fans made me feel good over there."

PHILLIES CAREER HIGHLIGHTS

Best Season

Abreu had some fabulous seasons for the Phillies, with the 1999, 2000, and 2001 campaigns ranking among his finest. Nevertheless, I chose to go with 2004, a season in which Abreu placed in the league's top 10 in eight different offensive categories, finishing the year with 30 home runs, 105 RBIs, 118 runs scored, 47 doubles, 312 total bases, a career-high 40 stolen bases, a batting average of .301, and an OPS of .971.

Memorable Moments/Greatest Performances

Abreu gave the Phillies a 7–6 victory over the Colorado Rockies on May 6, 1998, by delivering a two-out bases loaded single in the bottom of the 10th inning, finishing the contest with four hits, three RBIs, and two runs scored.

Abreu contributed to a 12–1 win over the Florida Marlins on July 29, 1999, by going 4-for-4, with a homer, two doubles, two RBIs, and four runs scored.

Abreu starred in defeat on August 8, 1999, going 5-for-5, with a double and two RBIs during a 7–4 loss to the Arizona Diamondbacks.

Abreu homered twice and knocked in six runs during an 18–2 rout of the San Diego Padres on August 24, 1999.

Abreu hit another two homers during a 9–7 win over Houston on May 24, 2000, with his two-run shot off Billy Wagner in the top of the ninth inning giving the Phillies their first lead of the game.

After homering earlier in the contest, Abreu gave the Phillies a 2–1 victory over the Giants on August 27, 2000, by leading off the bottom of the 10th inning with an inside-the-park home run.

Abreu led the Phillies to an 8–6 win over the Montreal Expos on April 23, 2004, by going 4-for-5, with a homer, three doubles, five RBIs, and two runs scored.

Abreu gave the Phillies a dramatic 5–4 victory over the Mets on July 8, 2004, by leading off the bottom of the ninth inning with a home run off John Franco, putting the finishing touches on an outstanding 4-for-5, three-RBI effort.

Notable Achievements

- Hit at least 20 home runs seven times, surpassing 30 homers twice.
- Knocked in more than 100 runs four times.
- Scored more than 100 runs six times.
- Batted .300 or better six times, topping the .330 mark once.
- Finished in double digits in triples twice.
- Surpassed 30 doubles seven times, amassing more than 40 two-baggers on four occasions.
- Stole at least 20 bases eight times, topping 30 thefts on four occasions.
- Surpassed 100 bases on balls seven times.
- Compiled on-base percentage over .400 eight times.
- Posted slugging percentage over .500 five times.
- Compiled OPS over .900 six times.
- Led NL in triples once, doubles once, and games played twice.
- Finished second in NL in walks twice.
- Finished third in NL in batting average once, walks once, stolen bases once, on-base percentage once, and plate appearances once.
- Led NL right fielders in putouts once, assists twice, and double plays once.
- Ranks among Phillies career leaders in home runs (11th), RBIs (11th), runs scored (tied for 10th), doubles (4th), extra-base hits (8th), total bases (10th), walks (2nd), intentional walks (3rd), stolen bases (7th), sacrifice flies (4th), on-base percentage (4th), slugging percentage (8th), and OPS (3rd).
- Three-time NL Player of the Week.
- May 2005 NL Player of the Month.
- 2004 Silver Slugger Award winner.
- 2005 Gold Glove Award winner.
- Two-time NL All-Star (2004 and 2005).
- Member of Philadelphia Baseball Wall of Fame.

14

SHERRY MAGEE

One of baseball's first five-tool players, Sherry Magee excelled in every aspect of the game, displaying an ability to hit, hit with power, run, throw, and field his position well. Serving as the Phillies' starting left fielder and cleanup hitter from 1904 to 1914, Magee left a lasting impression on everyone who watched him play, being called at different times "one of the greatest and most neglected of sluggers," "a born dynamiter with the bat," and "a genuine murderer of the pill." Blessed with outstanding power, Magee consistently ranked among the NL leaders in home runs, RBIs, doubles, triples, and slugging percentage. An excellent hitter and baserunner, Magee also regularly placed near the top of the league rankings in batting average, runs scored, and stolen bases, with his 23 thefts of home representing one of the highest totals in major-league history. Meanwhile, Magee's speed, strong throwing arm, and overall fielding ability enabled him to annually place among the top players at his position in putouts and assists. Yet, despite his many accomplishments, it is for his 1911 attack on umpire Bill Finneran that Magee is largely remembered today.

Born in the tiny Warren County borough of Clarendon, Pennsylvania, on August 6, 1884, Sherwood Robert Magee grew up some 140 miles northeast of Pittsburgh, where he received his introduction to the national pastime. Discovered by a Phillies scout while competing in a sandlot game near Harrisburg, Pennsylvania, in 1904, Magee signed with the team immediately without ever having played a day in the minor leagues or in college. Arriving in Philadelphia just two days later, Magee made his big-league debut at the tender age of 19 on June 29, 1904, after which he went on to bat .277, hit three homers, drive in 57 runs, score 51 times, collect 12 triples, and steal 11 bases over the season's final three months. Starting every game in left field for the Phillies the following year, Magee developed into a star, batting .299, ranking among the league leaders with five home runs, 98 RBIs, 100 runs scored, 17 triples, 180 hits, and 48 stolen bases, amassing 19 outfield assists, and leading all players at his position with 341 putouts.

Magee continued his outstanding play in each of the next four seasons, performing especially well in 1906 and 1907. After hitting six homers, driving in 67 runs, batting .282, and finishing second in the NL with 36 doubles and 55 stolen bases in the first of those campaigns, Magee topped the circuit with 85 RBIs the following year, while also placing second in the league in seven other offensive categories, including batting average (.328), on-base percentage (.396), slugging percentage (.455), and stolen bases (46).

Sherry Magee starred in left field for the Phillies for 11 seasons.

Yet, even as he rose to prominence, Magee developed a reputation as a troublemaker who played primarily for himself, with the *Philadelphia Times* stating after the 1908 season, "On the ball field, Magee is so fussy most of the time that people who do not know him naturally form the opinion from his actions that he is a born grouch. That he is one of the most hot-headed players in either big league is admitted; it couldn't be denied, because the records, showing how often he has been suspended for scrapping with the umpires, speak for themselves."

Known to criticize his teammates for making bad plays, Magee often felt the wrath of Phillies captain Kid Gleason, who kept an old leather belt in his locker that he used on young players who misbehaved.

A completely different person off the playing field, Magee drew praise from one Philadelphia reporter, who called him "as gentle and good-natured as an old woman. You couldn't find a more sociable and companionable fellow anywhere." Still, another writer described him as "a man for whom it is easy to conceive a great liking or a passionate hatred."

Unbeknownst to virtually everyone, though, Magee, who stood 5'11" and weighed 179 pounds, suffered from epilepsy, with an unattributed clipping in his file at the National Baseball Library reading, "Poor soul! Little did they know that the fellow was an epileptic. I knew this and found it out one day while playing against Philadelphia. He fell into a fit and I called one of the Philadelphia players to help me revive him. It was this player who told me the secret. Magee, himself, would never admit that he was an epileptic, and was sensitive about that fact."

Despite his malady and volatile temperament, Magee put together arguably his finest all-around season in 1910, when he led the NL in eight different offensive categories and finished second in two others, concluding the campaign with six home runs, 123 RBIs, 110 runs scored, 17 triples, 39 doubles, 49 stolen bases, 94 walks, a batting average of .331, and an OPS of .952. Magee followed that up with another outstanding year, batting .288 and ranking among the league leaders with 15 homers, 94 RBIs, 32 doubles, and an OPS of .849 in 1911, despite being suspended for a month of the season for his actions during a July 10 meeting with the St. Louis Cardinals. Recalling the events that transpired that day, Phillies infielder Hans Lobert later told Lawrence S. Ritter in *The Glory of Their Times*: "We didn't play Sunday baseball in those days in Philadelphia. Monday, when we got back, was a beastly hot day, and Sherry Magee had been drinking and had a hangover. We played St. Louis that day and Bill Finneran was umpiring behind the plate. He called a bad strike on Sherry, and we could all see that Magee was about to go into a fit. He started frothing at the mouth and he went at Finneran like a crazy man. Finneran had his mask off, and Sherry hit him in the mouth and knocked him down before we could get out there and stop him. Sherry was suspended 30 days for that."

Magee's inappropriate behavior helped to further his reputation as a malcontent who lacked any sort of self-control. As a result, Magee remained mostly unpopular with the hometown fans, with one Philadelphia reporter writing a few years later, "For five years, prior to 1914, the local fans have roasted Sherwood Magee. They cheered his long swats as all fans do, but they still shouted for his release. . . . It is a cinch that no ball player ever played as brilliantly on the home field under such adverse circumstances."

John J. Ward of *Baseball Magazine* expressed similar sentiments, attributing Magee's lack of popularity to the widely held belief that he was "a man who played for his own personal record and not for the good of the team."

However, the perception that others held toward Magee began to change in 1914 after the Phillies named him their team captain, with one veteran teammate later saying, "When he was given the captaincy, everyone looked at affairs from a different viewpoint. Now he could talk all he liked and there would be no resentment, for that was all a part of his job. And it gave the added stimulus to Magee that made him the greatest team-worker we had."

Magee also posted some of the best numbers of his career in 1914, when, after hitting 11 homers, driving in 70 runs, scoring 92 others, and batting .306 the previous year, he placed at, or near, the top of the league rankings with 15 home runs, 103 RBIs, 96 runs scored, 11 triples, 39 doubles, 171 hits, a batting average of .314, and an OPS of .509, prompting one Philadelphia writer to call him "probably the best all-around ball player in the National League." Meanwhile, Jack Ryder of the *Cincinnati Enquirer* wrote, "To my mind, Sherwood Magee is one of the best all-around players the game has ever seen." John J. Ward of *Baseball Magazine* agreed, calling Magee "a greater slugger than [Ty] Cobb, [Shoeless Joe] Jackson, [Napoleon] Lajoie, or any of a score of stars whose names are a synonym for Hit."

Nevertheless, with the Phillies finishing sixth in the eight-team NL in 1914 with a record of 74-80, they decided to trade their controversial star to the world-champion Boston Braves at the end of the year for cash and two players to be named later, one of whom turned out to be hustling outfielder Possum Whitted, who ended up starting for them in left field the next few seasons. Upon learning of the deal, Phillies fans expressed mixed emotions, with some rejoicing at his impending departure. However, one hometown reporter conveyed the feelings of others when he wrote, "Just when Magee becomes popular with the fans and is playing the game of his life, the club makes another mistake by permitting him to go to a rival club."

Leaving Philadelphia with career totals of 75 home runs, 886 RBIs, 898 runs scored, 1,647 hits, 337 doubles, 127 triples, and 387 stolen bases, a .299 batting average, an on-base percentage of .371, and a slugging percentage of .447, Magee continues to rank among the franchise's all-time leaders in several of those categories more than 100 years later. One of just three men in team annals to swipe second, third, and home in the same inning, Magee remains the only Phillies player to steal home twice in the same game.

Although still only 30 years old when he arrived in Boston, Magee found himself unable to attain the same level of success that he reached in Philadelphia due to an unfortunate mishap that occurred during his first spring training with the Braves. While chasing a flyball, Magee stepped into a hole, fell, and broke his collarbone, limiting his effectiveness for the remainder of his career. After batting .280, driving in 87 runs, and scoring 72 times as Boston's starting left fielder in 1915, Magee assumed a part-time role the next four seasons, which he split between the Braves and Cincinnati Reds. Released by Cincinnati following the conclusion of the 1919 campaign, Magee never again played in the majors, ending his big-league career with 83 home runs, 1,176 RBIs, 1,112 runs scored, 2,169 hits, 425 doubles, 166 triples, 441 stolen bases, a .291 batting average, a .364 on-base percentage, and a .427 slugging percentage.

Following his release by the Reds, Magee spent seven years playing in the minor leagues, before finally announcing his retirement at age 42 after serving as player/manager of Jack Dunn's Baltimore Orioles in 1926. Ironically, Magee subsequently became an umpire, performing his duties so well at the minor-league level in 1927 that the NL offered him a job the following year. Unfortunately, Magee's umpiring career lasted just one season. After complaining of a headache and fever in early March 1929, Magee died of pneumonia just a few days later, passing away on March 13, 1929, at only 44 years of age.

PHILLIES CAREER HIGHLIGHTS

Best Season

Magee had a tremendous year for the Phillies in 1914, ranking among the NL leaders with a .314 batting average, 15 homers, 11 triples, and 96 runs scored, while also topping the circuit with 103 RBIs, 39 doubles, 171 hits, 277 total bases, and an OPS of .509. However, he proved to be slightly more dominant in 1910, when, in addition to placing in the league's top five with six home runs, 17 triples, 39 doubles, 172 hits, 49 stolen bases, and 94 walks, he led the NL with 123 RBIs, 110 runs scored, 62 extra-base hits, 263 total bases, a .331 batting average, an on-base percentage of .445, a slugging percentage of .507, and an OPS of .952 that exceeded his nearest rival's mark by 81 points.

Memorable Moments/Greatest Performances

Magee led the Phillies to a 10–7 win over the Boston Beaneaters on May 29, 1905, by knocking in five runs with a homer and single.

Magee became the first Phillies player to steal second, third, and home in the same inning when he accomplished the feat during a 7–6 loss to the St. Louis Cardinals on July 12, 1906.

Magee had a big day at the plate against the Boston Doves on May 7, 1907, going 4-for-5, with a triple and three RBIs during a 3–1 Phillies win, with his two-run single in the top of the 10th inning providing the margin of victory.

Magee had the only five-hit game of his career on October 5, 1907, going 5-for-5, with a triple and two RBIs during a 7–3 win over the Giants.

Magee helped lead the Phillies to a 7–5 win over the Cardinals on August 27, 1912, by going 3-for-4, with two homers, a triple, four RBIs, and three runs scored.

Magee touched up Hall of Fame southpaw Rube Marquard for two homers and four RBIs during a 6–3 win over the Giants on May 5, 1913.

Magee again reached the seats twice against Marquard during a 10–1 win over the Giants on April 14, 1914, finishing the game with a career-high six runs batted in.

Magee matched that total on September 9, 1914, going 4-for-5 with six RBIs during a 10–3 win over the Boston Braves.

Notable Achievements

- Hit 15 home runs twice.
- Knocked in more than 100 runs twice.
- Scored at least 100 runs twice.
- Batted over .300 five times, surpassing the .320 mark twice.
- Finished in double digits in triples seven times.
- Surpassed 30 doubles seven times.
- Stole at least 30 bases seven times, topping 40 thefts on five occasions.
- Compiled on-base percentage over .400 once.
- Posted slugging percentage over .500 twice.
- Compiled OPS over .900 once.
- Led NL in batting average once, RBIs three times, runs scored once, doubles once, hits once, extra-base hits three times, total bases twice, on-base percentage once, slugging percentage twice, OPS once, and games played once.
- Finished second in NL in batting average once, RBIs once, runs scored once, triples four times, doubles five times, extra-base hits three times, on-base percentage once, slugging percentage once, OPS twice, stolen bases twice, and games played once.
- Finished third in NL in home runs twice, triples once, doubles once, hits once, total bases once, slugging percentage once, and walks once.
- Led NL outfielders in fielding percentage once.
- Led NL left fielders in putouts twice, assists once, fielding percentage twice, and double plays twice.
- Ranks among Phillies career leaders in RBIs (9th), runs scored (9th), triples (2nd), doubles (6th), hits (8th), extra-base hits (9th), total bases (11th), stolen bases (4th), sacrifice hits (2nd), games played (10th), plate appearances (10th), and at-bats (11th).
- Finished seventh in 1914 NL MVP voting.
- Member of Philadelphia Baseball Wall of Fame.

15

GAVVY CRAVATH

The National League's preeminent home run hitter for much of the Dead Ball Era, Gavvy Cravath spent nine seasons in Philadelphia, serving as the Phillies' starting right fielder in eight of those. Topping the senior circuit in homers six times, Cravath retired in 1920 with more long balls to his credit than any other player in major-league history. More than just a slugger, Cravath also batted over .300 twice and consistently ranked among the league leaders in on-base percentage, compiling a mark over .400 on three separate occasions. Meanwhile, despite his lack of speed, Cravath proved to be more than adequate in the field, leading all NL outfielders in assists three times, with his strong all-around play helping to lead the Phillies to one pennant and three second-place finishes. Cravath accomplished all he did even though he did not arrive in Philadelphia until shortly after he celebrated his 31st birthday.

Born in Escondido, California, on March 23, 1881, Clifford Carlton Cravath starred in multiple sports while attending Escondido High School, serving as captain of the school's football team, while also excelling as a catcher in baseball. After assuming numerous odd jobs following his graduation, including fumigator and telegraph operator, Cravath began playing semipro baseball in San Diego and Santa Ana, where his family had relocated after the turn of the century. While competing at the semipro level, Cravath acquired the nickname "Gavvy," when, after inadvertently killing a seagull with a vicious line drive during a game in Mexico, he found himself being hailed as "gaviota" (the Spanish word for "seagull") every time he stepped to the plate throughout the rest of the series.

Finally turning pro in 1903, Cravath joined the Los Angeles Angels of the Pacific Coast League, with whom he spent five seasons starring in right field and at first base, contributing greatly to teams that won four pennants by hitting a total of 45 home runs and batting over .300 once. Sold to the Boston Red Sox following the conclusion of the 1907 campaign, Cravath subsequently assumed a part-time role in Boston in 1908, batting .256, hitting one homer, collecting 11 triples, and driving in 34 runs in 94 games and 277 official at-bats. But, with team management believing that the stocky 5'10", 190-pound Cravath lacked the foot speed to play the outfield full-time, the Red Sox sold him to the Chicago White Sox at the end of the year. Chicago then dealt Cravath to the Washington Senators during the early stages of the 1909 campaign, after which he spent most of the next three seasons playing for the Minneapolis Millers, a minor-league affiliate of the Senators.

Cravath's time in Minneapolis ended up having a huge impact on his career since, like the Baker Bowl, Nicollet Park, the home stadium of the Millers, featured a short porch in right

Gavvy Cravath led the NL in home runs six times.

field to which the right-handed-hitting Cravath soon learned to tailor his swing. Developing into the Millers' best player before long, Cravath hit 14 home runs and batted .327 in 1910, before leading the American Association with 29 homers and a .363 batting average the following year.

Unfortunately for Cravath, the draft rules of the day bound him to the Millers, forcing him to remain in Minneapolis until the organization inadvertently left out the word "not" in a telegram to Pittsburgh after the 1911 season. With the National Commission subsequently ruling that the clerical error prohibited the Millers from retaining Cravath's services, the 31-year-old slugger received his second chance to play in the major leagues when the Phillies purchased his rights for $9,000.

Making the most of his opportunity, Cravath laid claim to the starting right field job in Philadelphia shortly after he joined the Phillies in 1912, finishing his first full big-league season with 11 home runs, 70 RBIs, 63 runs scored, nine triples, 30 doubles, a .284 batting average, an OPS of .828, and a league-leading 26 outfield assists. Cravath then began an extremely productive three-year run during which he posted the following numbers:

YEAR	HR	RBI	RUNS	AVG	OBP	SLG	OPS
1913	19	128	78	.341	.407	.568	.974
1914	19	100	76	.299	.402	.499	.901
1915	24	115	89	.285	.393	.510	.902

Clearly establishing himself as the senior circuit's top slugger, Cravath led the NL in home runs and OPS all three years, while also placing at, or near, the top of the league rankings in RBIs, total bases, walks, on-base percentage, and slugging percentage each season. Cravath's 24 home runs in 1915 set a 20th-century single-season major-league record that stood until Babe Ruth homered 29 times four years later. And his 128 RBIs in 1913 established a new NL record that remained the benchmark for players in the circuit until Rogers Hornsby knocked in 152 runs for the Cardinals in 1922. Meanwhile, Cravath's .341 batting average in 1913 ranked as the second-highest mark in the league, helping him to earn a runner-up finish in the NL MVP voting. And two years later, Cravath's outstanding performance helped the Phillies capture their first National League pennant.

Cravath certainly benefited greatly from playing his home games at the Baker Bowl. Taking full advantage of the ballpark's short left field power alley and inviting right field fence that stood less than 300 feet from home plate, Cravath hit 78 percent of his career long balls at home. Nevertheless, Cravath bristled at the notion that he owed his impressive home-run totals entirely to the Baker Bowl's dimensions, once telling F. C. Lane of *Baseball Magazine*, "That right-field fence was never any farther away than it was when I joined the club. And, while we are on the subject, let me make a point. That fence isn't always a friend to the home-run slugger. I have hit that fence a good many times with a long drive that would have kept right on for a triple or a home run if the fence hadn't been there. There are always two sides to every fence."

Extremely proud of his ability to deliver the long ball, Cravath stated on another occasion, "Short singles are like left-hand jabs in the boxing ring, but a home run is a knockout punch. It is the clean-up man of the club that does the heavy scoring work even if he is wide in the shoulders and slow on his feet. There is no advice I can give in batting, except to hammer the ball."

Believing that his power at the plate compensated for his relative lack of foot speed, Cravath added, "They call me wooden shoes and piano legs and a few other pet names. I do not claim to be the fastest man in the world, but I can get around the bases with a fair wind and all sails set. And so long as I am busting the old apple on the seam, I am not worrying a great deal about my legs."

Yet even though Cravath lacked elite running speed, he proved to be an extremely competent outfielder whose strong and accurate throwing arm enabled him to consistently rank among the top players at his position in assists, with his career-high 34 outfield assists in 1914 making him the league-leader in that category for one of three times.

Despite missing 17 games due to injury in 1916, Cravath had another solid year, batting .283; ranking among the league leaders with 11 homers, 70 RBIs, and a .440 slugging percentage; and topping the circuit with a .379 on-base percentage. Although Cravath missed a significant number of games in each of the next three seasons as well, he led the league in home runs each year, performing especially well in 1919, when, while serving as player-manager, he batted .341, hit 12 homers, and knocked in 45 runs in only 83 games and 214 official at-bats. The 39-year-old Cravath continued to function in that dual role in 1920, batting .289, hitting one homer, and driving in 11 runs in only 54 plate appearances, before being released by the Phillies at the end of the year. Choosing to announce his retirement, Cravath ended his playing career with 119 home runs, 719 RBIs, 575 runs scored, 1,134 hits, 232 doubles, 83 triples, 89 stolen bases, a batting average of .287, an on-base percentage of .380, and a slugging percentage of .478. In his nine years with the Phillies, Cravath hit 117 homers, knocked in 676 runs, scored 525 times, stole 80 bases, batted .291, compiled an on-base percentage of .381, posted a slugging percentage of .489, and collected 1,054 hits, 222 doubles, and 72 triples.

After retiring as an active player, Cravath spent one year managing the Salt Lake City Bees of the Pacific Coast League and another scouting for the Minneapolis Millers, before returning home to Laguna Beach, California, where he became active in the real estate business. Although Cravath lacked any formal legal training, he was elected judge in 1927, later claiming that he based his decisions on the principles of sportsmanship he had learned during his playing career. Cravath remained in that position for 36 years, until May 23, 1963, when he died at the age of 82.

PHILLIES CAREER HIGHLIGHTS

Best Season

Cravath helped lead the Phillies to the pennant in 1915 by batting .285 and topping the senior circuit in eight different offensive categories, including home runs (24), RBIs (115), runs scored (89), total bases (266), and OPS (.902). But he posted slightly better overall numbers in 1913, earning a runner-up finish in the NL MVP voting by leading the league with 19 homers, 128 RBIs, 179 hits, 298 total bases, a slugging percentage of .568, and an OPS of .974, while also finishing second with a .341 batting average and a .407 on-base percentage.

Memorable Moments/Greatest Performances

Cravath led the Phillies to a 6–2 win over the Brooklyn Superbas on June 20, 1912, by driving in four runs with a pair of homers.

Cravath homered twice, doubled, and knocked in six runs during a 13–11 win over the Braves on July 6, 2012, with his two-run homer in the top of the 13th inning providing the margin of victory.

Cravath collected five hits in one game for the only time in his career during a 12–0 rout of the Reds on May 21, 1913, going a perfect 5-for-5, with a triple, six RBIs, and two runs scored.

Cravath helped lead the Phillies to an 8–7, 11-inning win over the Braves on May 30, 1914, by going 4-for-5, with three doubles, two RBIs, and three runs scored.

Cravath led the Phillies to a doubleheader sweep of the Brooklyn Robins on September 7, 1914, by driving in five runs with a homer and single during a 7–4 win in Game 1, before going 3-for-4, with a homer, double, two RBIs, and two runs scored during a 7–6 Game 2 victory.

Cravath contributed to a 9–4 victory over the Cubs on September 23, 1914, by homering twice, driving in five runs, and scoring three times.

Cravath had another big day against the Cubs on August 23, 1915, going 4-for-5, with a homer, double, five RBIs, and three runs scored during a 13–5 Phillies win.

Cravath delivered the decisive blow in a 7–3 win over the Giants on September 10, 1915, when he homered with the bases loaded in the bottom of the eighth inning.

Cravath led the Phillies to a 6–0 victory over the Cubs on September 16, 1916, by driving in five runs with a pair of homers.

Cravath gave the Phillies a 2–1 win over the Cardinals on June 14, 1918, when he led off the bottom of the 10th inning by hitting the 100th homer of his career off St. Louis starter Bill Doak.

Cravath drove in the only runs of a 3–0 win over the Giants at New York's Polo Grounds on April 20, 1920, when he hit a pinch-hit three-run homer in the top of the eighth inning, reaching the seats for the 119th and final time in his career.

Notable Achievements

- Surpassed 20 home runs once, hitting 19 homers two other times.
- Knocked in more than 100 runs three times.
- Batted over .300 twice, finishing with mark of .341 both times.
- Finished in double digits in triples twice.
- Surpassed 30 doubles three times.
- Compiled on-base percentage over .400 three times.
- Posted slugging percentage over .500 three times.
- Compiled OPS over .900 four times, finishing with mark above 1.000 once.
- Amassed at least 20 outfield assists four times.
- Led NL in home runs six times, RBIs twice, runs scored once, hits once, extra-base hits four times, total bases twice, walks once, on-base percentage twice, slugging percentage twice, and OPS three times.
- Finished second in NL in RBIs once, batting average once, doubles once, triples once, extra-base hits once, total bases once, on-base percentage once, slugging percentage twice, and OPS once.
- Finished third in NL in home runs twice, RBIs once, on-base percentage once, and walks twice.
- Led NL outfielders in assists three times.
- Led NL right fielders in assists twice.
- Ranks eighth in franchise history with 72 triples.
- 1915 NL champion.
- Finished second in 1913 NL MVP voting.
- Member of Philadelphia Baseball Wall of Fame.
- Member of Philadelphia Sports Hall of Fame.

16
GREG LUZINSKI

Nicknamed "The Bull" for his massive frame and prodigious power at the plate, Greg Luzinski spent parts of 11 seasons in Philadelphia, combining with Mike Schmidt to give the Phillies the most dynamic pair of sluggers in all of baseball for much of the 1970s. Known for his ability to deliver the long ball and drive in huge sums of runs, Luzinski topped 30 homers and 100 RBIs three times each from 1975 to 1978, earning in the process four consecutive All-Star selections and four straight top-10 finishes in the NL MVP voting. A solid all-around hitter, Luzinski also batted .300 or better four times, with his outstanding offensive production helping the Phillies capture four division titles and one world championship. A member of both the Philadelphia Baseball Wall of Fame and the Philadelphia Sports Hall of Fame, Luzinski continues to rank among the franchise's all-time leaders in home runs and RBIs more than 40 years after he donned a Phillies uniform for the last time.

Born in Chicago, Illinois, on November 22, 1950, Gregory Michael Luzinski grew up within five miles of Wrigley Field, before moving with his family to the Chicago suburb of Prospect Heights at the age of 10. Starring in multiple sports at Notre Dame High, Luzinski led the school's baseball team to three successive undefeated seasons as a slugging catcher/first baseman, while also earning All-America honors on the gridiron with his exceptional play at fullback and linebacker. Given the opportunity to attend either the University of Notre Dame or the University of Kansas on a football scholarship, Luzinski instead chose to sign with the Phillies, who selected him with the 11th overall pick of the 1968 Amateur Draft after learning of his enormous potential through Mike Vukovich, the neighbor of Notre Dame High's baseball coach and a close friend of Phillies owner Bob Carpenter.

Beginning his pro career at only 17 years of age, Luzinksi performed well for the short-season Single-A Huron (South Dakota) Phillies in 1968, leading the Northern League with 13 home runs and 43 RBIs. Impressed with Luzinski's outstanding play, Huron (and future Phillies) manager Dallas Green called him "one of the best hitting prospects I ever saw."

Ascending rapidly through the Phillies' farm system, Luzinski gained All-Star recognition at three different stops, causing him to be labeled a "can't miss" prospect. Making a particularly strong impression at Reading in 1970, the right-handed-swinging Luzinski earned a September callup to Philadelphia by hitting 33 homers, driving in 120 runs, and batting .325. Displaying his tremendous

Greg Luzinski earned two runner-up finishes in the NL MVP voting.

power at the plate on several occasions, Luzinski drove a ball more than 500 feet over an advertising sign atop the scoreboard in left-center field during a 7–3 win over the Manchester Yankees on May 2, before homering in three straight games a few weeks later. Nevertheless, after Luzinski batted just .167 in eight games and 15 plate appearances during his brief stint in Philadelphia, the Phillies returned him to the minors for more seasoning.

Continuing his prolific hitting with the Triple-A Eugene (Oregon) Emeralds in 1971, Luzinski hit 36 homers, drove in 114 runs, and batted .312, prompting the Phillies to summon him to the big leagues once again in September. Faring much better with the parent club this time, Luzinski hit three homers, knocked in 15 runs, and batted .300 in his 27 starts at first base.

Converted into an outfielder by the Phillies the following spring, Luzinski had a solid rookie season after moving to left field, concluding the 1972 campaign with 18 home runs, 68 RBIs, 66 runs scored, and a .281 batting average. Improving upon those numbers the following year, Luzinski ranked among the league leaders with 29 homers, knocked in 97 runs, scored 76 times, and batted .285. Hampered by injuries to his right hand and knee in 1974, Luzinski appeared in only 85 games, limiting him to just seven homers and 48 RBIs. Commenting on what the absence of Luzinski for much of the season meant to the Phillies, who ended up finishing eight games off the pace in the NL East, teammate Mike Schmidt said, "There is no way of estimating what the loss of Luzinski has cost the Phillies. That bat in the lineup probably would have meant five extra wins—and I'm being conservative."

Fully healthy by the start of the 1975 season, Luzinski emerged as one of the National League's most potent batsmen, beginning an outstanding four-year run during which he posted the following numbers:

YEAR	HR	RBI	RUNS	2B	AVG	OBP	SLG	OPS
1975	34	120	85	35	.300	.394	.540	.934
1976	21	95	74	28	.304	.369	.478	.847
1977	39	130	99	35	.309	.394	.594	.988
1978	35	101	85	32	.265	.388	.526	.914

In addition to topping the senior circuit with 120 runs batted in and 322 total bases in 1975, Luzinski ranked among the NL leaders in home runs, RBIs, slugging percentage, and OPS all four years, finishing in the league's top three in homers on three separate occasions. And even though Luzinski batted just .265 in 1978, he walked 100 times, allowing him to compile an on-base percentage of .388 that placed him fourth in the league rankings. Luzinski's outstanding offensive production earned him four consecutive top-10 finishes in the NL MVP voting, including a second-place finish in both 1975 and 1977. More importantly, the Phillies captured the NL East title in each of the last three seasons.

One of the most feared sluggers in the game, the 6'1" Luzinski, who spent most of his career playing at close to 250 pounds, had the ability to hit the ball as far as any player in either league, delivering several tape-measure home runs over the course of his career. First exhibiting his tremendous power to his Phillies teammates during a 3–2 loss to the Mets on September 12, 1971, Luzinski drove a ball some 480 feet over the second bullpen in left field at Shea Stadium. Luzinski flexed his muscles again during an 8–1 home loss to the Cubs on May 16, 1972, when he hit a ball that caromed off Veterans Stadium's replica Liberty Bell that stood beyond the center field fence, some 475 feet from home plate. Three months later, he became the first player to homer off the stadium scoreboard. In 1977, Luzinski reached the yellow seats in Houston's Astrodome, becoming in the process just the fourth player to accomplish the feat. And a year later, he became just the third player to homer into the left field loge sector at Dodger Stadium.

Commenting on Luzinski's awesome power, another well-known Phillies slugger, Dick Allen, stated in 1976, "Greg Luzinski is the most dangerous hitter in the game. . . . And he's only starting to reach his potential. Wait until two or three years from now. They're going to have to order more baseballs."

Meanwhile, Johnny Bench described Luzinski's power display during batting practice prior to the 1977 All-Star Game at Yankee Stadium thusly: "We were all kidding around, putting on a show. Joe Morgan hit a couple into the right field seats, Steve Garvey hit a couple into the bullpen. . . . Then Luzinski stepped up and made it look like he was driving golf balls. Everything he hit went out of sight. . . . It was awesome."

In addition to his contributions to the Phillies on the playing field, Luzinski proved to be a solid citizen who took an interest in the community. After signing a five-year, $1.5 million contract during the winter of 1976, Luzinski purchased a block of 126 loge seats in left field at Veterans Stadium that became known as "The Bull Ring." He then gave all the tickets to youngsters from organizations such as the Salvation Army and the Big Brothers Association. Luzinski also provided autographed pictures of himself to every youngster in "The Bull Ring" and donated $100 to the organization in that section any night a Phillies home run landed there. When asked about his philanthropic gesture, Luzinski told the *Sporting News*, "There are many children who have never had box seats, and I want to give some of them a chance to sit there and see how much fun it can be just to go to a baseball game at the Vet."

Unfortunately, the love affair that Luzinski shared with the fans of Philadelphia eventually came to an end. Although Luzinski posted outstanding home-run totals year after year, his propensity for striking out caused him to often incur the wrath of the Philly Faithful, who objected to the fact that he annually ranked among the league leaders in whiffs. Furthermore, the slow-footed Luzinski proved to be far less effective in the field than at the plate, once admitting, "I don't think I'll ever get paid for being a glover." Even though he had a decent arm and relatively good hands, leading all NL left fielders in assists and fielding percentage once each, Luzinski lacked the speed and dexterity possessed by most good outfielders, something that became quite evident when he misplayed a ball hit by Manny Mota in the ninth inning of Game 3 of the 1977 NLCS that opened the floodgates to a three-run Dodger rally that led to a Phillies defeat and an eventual series win by Los Angeles.

Subsequently booed by Phillies fans during the early stages of the 1978 campaign, Luzinski continued to draw their ire when he got off to a slow start at the plate. Although Luzinski eventually rebounded to hit 35 homers and drive in 101 runs, his situation grew increasingly worse when he homered just 37 times and knocked in only 137 runs over the course of the next two seasons. Particularly ineffective after he injured his knee sliding into second base during a 6–1 loss to the Cardinals on July 6, 1980, Luzinski ended up missing 45 games, finishing the season with just 19 homers, 56 RBIs, and a batting average of .228.

With manager Dallas Green questioning Luzinski's ability to contribute to the team moving forward, the Phillies sold the 30-year-old slugger to the Chicago White Sox on March 30, 1981. Luzinski, who left Philadelphia with career totals of 223 home runs, 811 RBIs, 618 runs scored, 1,299 hits, 253 doubles, and 21 triples, a lifetime batting average of .281, a .363 on-base percentage, and a .489 slugging percentage, spent the next four seasons serving the White Sox almost exclusively as a DH, winning the Outstanding Designated Hitter Award in both 1981 and 1983. Yet, Luzinski posted his best overall numbers as a member of the White Sox in 1982, when he hit 18 homers, knocked in 102 runs, scored 87 times, batted .292, and collected 37 doubles. Choosing to announce his retirement after he hit only 13 home runs and batted just .238 in 1984, Luzinski ended his 15-year major-league career with 307 home runs, 1,128 RBIs, 880 runs scored, 1,795 hits, 344 doubles, 24 triples, 37 stolen bases, a .276 batting average, an on-base percentage of .363, and a slugging percentage of .478.

Following his playing days, Luzinski began a career in coaching, first serving as both the baseball and football coach at his children's high school, Holy Cross High in Deltran, New Jersey, before spending the 1993 and 1994 campaigns serving as batting coach for the Oakland A's under his former White Sox manager Tony LaRussa. After coaching A's hitters for two years, Luzinski began a three-year stint fulfilling the same role for the Kansas City Royals under former Phillies teammate Bob Boone. Luzinski, who invested in an indoor tennis and racquetball complex in New Jersey while still playing for the Phillies, also became a successful businessman, eventually opening Bull's BBQ at the eastern end of Ashburn Alley in Citizens Bank Park, which sports a plaque honoring his accomplishments during his time in Philadelphia.

PHILLIES CAREER HIGHLIGHTS

Best Season

Luzinski earned a pair of runner-up finishes in the NL MVP voting, placing second in the balloting to Joe Morgan in 1975 after batting .300, leading the league with 120 RBIs and 322 total bases, and ranking among the leaders with 34 homers, 35 doubles, a .540 slugging percentage, and an OPS of .934 during the regular season. But Luzinski performed even better in 1977, finishing behind only George Foster in the MVP balloting after establishing career-high marks with 39 homers, 130 RBIs, 99 runs scored, 329 total bases, a .309 batting average, a .594 slugging percentage, and an OPS of .988.

Memorable Moments/Greatest Performances

Luzinski came up big for the Phillies during the latter stages of a 5–4, 11-inning win over the Pittsburgh Pirates on April 23, 1972, tying the game in the bottom of the ninth with a solo homer, before crossing the plate with the winning run two innings later on an RBI single by Tom Hutton after tripling to right field with two men out.

Luzinski powered the Phillies to a 6–5 win over the Atlanta Braves on July 11, 1973, by hitting a solo home run in the bottom of the sixth inning and reaching the seats again with one man on base in the ensuing frame.

Luzinski proved to be the difference in a 4–3 victory over the Expos on May 25, 1974, driving in all four Phillies runs with a sixth-inning double and a three-run homer in the bottom of the eighth.

Luzinski led the Phillies to a 2–1 win over the Houston Astros on July 11, 1975, by going 4-for-4, with his leadoff homer in the top of the sixth inning providing the margin of victory.

Luzinski drove in all three runs the Phillies scored during a 3–0 win over the San Diego Padres on July 11, 1976, when he doubled with the bases loaded in the bottom of the sixth inning.

Luzinski helped lead the Phillies to a 13–10 victory over the Braves on June 11, 1977, by going 3-for-4, with a homer, two doubles, and a career-high seven RBIs, four of which came on a first-inning grand slam.

Luzinski provided most of the offensive firepower during a 5–2 win over the Cardinals on July 13, 1977, driving in all five Phillies runs with a pair of homers off St. Louis starter Tom Underwood. Commenting on Luzinski's outstanding performance following the game, Underwood told the Associated Press, "Luzinski is the best two-out hitter in baseball. He never misses a down-and-in pitch. I'm not the first guy he's going to hit home runs off and certainly not the last. I made two bad pitches and I paid for it."

Luzinski gave the Phillies a 7–6 victory over the Giants on June 6, 1978, when he knocked in the tying and winning runs with a two-out bases loaded single to center field in the bottom of the ninth inning.

Luzinski helped the Phillies clinch the NL East title on the next-to-last day of the 1978 regular season by hitting a three-run homer in the top of the sixth inning of a 10–8 win over the Pirates, later calling the blast, which put his team ahead to stay, "the biggest thrill of my life."

Notable Achievements

- Hit more than 30 home runs three times, topping 20 homers on two other occasions.
- Knocked in more than 100 runs three times.
- Batted .300 or better four times.
- Surpassed 30 doubles four times.
- Walked 100 times once.
- Posted slugging percentage over .500 three times.
- Compiled OPS over .900 three times.
- Led NL in RBIs once, total bases once, and intentional bases on balls once.
- Finished second in NL in home runs once, RBIs once, slugging percentage twice, OPS once, extra-base hits twice, and sacrifice flies once.
- Finished third in NL in home runs twice, total bases once, OPS once, and games played once.
- Led NL outfielders in fielding percentage once.
- Led NL left fielders in assists once, fielding percentage once, and double plays twice.
- Ranks among Phillies career leaders in home runs (7th), RBIs (12th), intentional bases on balls (tied for 7th), and sacrifice flies (5th).
- Four-time division champion (1976, 1977, 1978, and 1980).
- 1980 NL champion.
- 1980 world champion.
- Two-time NL Player of the Week.
- Two-time NL Player of the Month.
- Finished in top 10 in NL MVP voting four times, placing second twice (1975 and 1977).
- 1978 Roberto Clemente Award winner.
- Two-time *Sporting News* NL All-Star selection (1975 and 1977).
- Four-time NL All-Star (1975, 1976, 1977, and 1978).
- Member of Philadelphia Baseball Wall of Fame.
- Member of Philadelphia Sports Hall of Fame.

17

JIM BUNNING

lthough Jim Bunning gained even greater fame following his playing days as a member of the US House of Representatives and US Senate, he initially made a name for himself as one of major-league baseball's most consistent and durable pitchers. During a 17-year big-league career spent primarily with the Phillies and Tigers, Bunning won 224 games and struck out 2,855 batters, becoming in the process just the second pitcher in baseball history to record more than 100 victories and 1,000 strikeouts in each league. After winning a total of 118 games for the Tigers from 1955 to 1963, Bunning performed even better for the Phillies over the course of the next four seasons, posting 74 victories, while also compiling an ERA under 3.00 and registering more than 200 strikeouts each year. Ranking among the NL leaders in virtually every major pitching category four straight times from 1964 to 1967, Bunning earned two All-Star selections and one runner-up finish in the Cy Young voting, with his superb pitching in 1964 nearly leading the Phillies to the NL pennant. Although the Phillies traded Bunning to Pittsburgh following the conclusion of the 1967 campaign, the hard-throwing right-hander returned to Philadelphia for a second tour of duty with the club in 1970, spending his final two seasons in the City of Brotherly Love, before retiring and subsequently entering the world of politics.

Born in Southgate, Kentucky, on October 23, 1931, James Paul David Bunning spent his youth enjoying the outdoors and all athletic pursuits, developing his trademark sidearm delivery skipping stones in the lake near his hometown. Attending school in Cincinnati, just across the Ohio River, Bunning starred in baseball, basketball, and track at St. Xavier High School, with his excellence in all three sports earning him an athletic scholarship to Xavier University. Although Bunning continued to compete in multiple sports during his first two years of college, he chose to focus exclusively on baseball after the Detroit Tigers persuaded him to pursue a career in pro ball at the end of his sophomore year.

After signing with the Tigers as an amateur free agent in 1950, Bunning spent six long years toiling in the minor leagues, during which time he continued his education, receiving his bachelor's degree in economics in 1953. Finally called up to Detroit during the second half of the 1955 campaign, Bunning failed to impress, going just 3-5 with an ERA of 6.35. Unhappy with his poor performance, Bunning spent the ensuing offseason playing in the Cuban Winter League, where he learned how to throw the slider, which eventually became his signature pitch. Working on his new offering while splitting the 1956 season between the Tigers and their top farm club, Bunning arrived in Detroit in 1957 ready to assume a regular spot in the starting rotation.

Jim Bunning finished second in the 1967 NL Cy Young voting.
Courtesy of MearsonlineAuctions.com

Employing his full arsenal of pitches and a sweeping sidearm delivery that caused his knuckles to nearly scrape the ground on his follow-through, Bunning quickly developed into one of the junior circuit's top hurlers, earning his first All-Star selection and a ninth-place finish in the AL MVP voting by leading the league with 20 wins and 267 1/3 innings pitched, while also placing among the leaders with a 2.69 ERA, 182 strikeouts, and 14 complete games. Though not nearly as effective in any of the next three seasons, Bunning still managed to compile an overall mark of 42-39, finish second in the league in ERA once, place near the top of the league rankings in innings pitched twice, and lead all AL hurlers in strikeouts twice.

Returning to top form in 1961, Bunning earned All-Star honors for the first of four straight times by going 17-11 with a 3.19 ERA, before compiling a record of 19-10 and an ERA of 3.59 the following year. However, after Bunning finished just 12-13 with an ERA of 3.88 in 1963, the Tigers included him in a multiplayer trade they completed with the Phillies on December 5, 1963, that sent him and veteran catcher Gus Triandos to Philadelphia for outfielder Don Demeter and pitcher Jack Hamilton. Bunning, who compiled a record of 118-87 and an ERA of 3.45 during his time in Detroit, subsequently took his game up a notch following his arrival in Philadelphia, posting the following numbers over the course of the next four seasons:

YEAR	W-L	ERA	SO	SHO	CG	IP	WHIP
1964	19-8	2.63	219	5	13	284.1	1.034
1965	19-9	2.60	268	7	15	291	1.082
1966	19-14	2.41	252	5	16	314	1.003
1967	17-15	2.29	253	6	16	302.1	1.039

Establishing himself as one of the senior circuit's finest pitchers, Bunning ranked among the league leaders in each of those categories all four years, earning in the process two All-Star nominations and a second-place finish in the NL Cy Young voting in 1967, when, despite going just 17-15, he led all NL hurlers in three categories and finished second in two others.

Although the 6'3", 200-pound Bunning proved to be particularly tough on right-handed hitters due to his exaggerated sidearm motion, he also caused problems for left-handed batters, with the lefty-swinging Jesse Gonder saying, "He would get two strikes on you, and you didn't want to be caught looking, so you swung."

Revealing the confidence that the other members of Philadelphia's starting rotation had in Bunning, fellow Phillies pitcher Dennis Bennett said, "He's the leader of the staff. When he loses, we are shocked."

In discussing the ace of his team's pitching staff, Phillies manager Gene Mauch stated, "He's 200 pounds of pride. He takes care of himself, likes money, loves his family, has a great arm and a great delivery."

Allen Lewis, a 1981 Ford C. Frick Award winner who covered Bunning while writing for the *Philadelphia Inquirer*, spoke of the right-hander's sense of purpose on the mound when he claimed, "He's the only pitcher I ever saw who never threw a pitch that he didn't know exactly what he was trying to do with it. He had purpose with every pitch."

Bunning also made an extremely favorable impression on former Phillies manager Frank Lucchesi, who said, "He was one of the best competitors I ever managed. He was a jewel to manage. He never alibied. It was always, 'Just give me the ball.'"

Meanwhile, J. G. Taylor Spink Award winner Joe Falls praised Bunning for the advanced approach he took to his craft, stating, "Jim Bunning was a computer guy before they had computers. He was an agent before they had agents. And he was an aerobics guy before they had aerobics. He was the first guy I ever saw in baseball who kept a book on the hitters. And he kept track of everything he did. I always felt he got more out of his talent than anybody."

Despite the success that Bunning experienced the previous four seasons, the Phillies found themselves in a rebuilding mode at the end of 1967, prompting them to trade him to the Pittsburgh Pirates during the ensuing offseason for a package of four players that included pitcher Woodie Fryman and infielder Don Money. Bunning subsequently spent most of the next two seasons in Pittsburgh, going just 14-23 for the Pirates, before being dealt to the Dodgers during the latter stages of the 1969 campaign. Released by the Dodgers on October 22, 1969, Bunning signed with the Phillies one week later, after which he compiled an overall record of 15-27 for them over the course of the next two seasons, before announcing his retirement with an overall record of 89-73, an ERA of 2.93, a WHIP of 1.111, 1,197 strikeouts, 65 complete games, 23 shutouts, and 1,520 2/3 innings pitched as a member of the team. Over the course of 17 major-league seasons, Bunning compiled a record of 224-184, an ERA of 3.27, and a WHIP of 1.179; recorded 2,855 strikeouts; and threw 151 complete games, 40 shutouts, and 3,760 1/3 innings, ranking second all-time only to Walter Johnson in strikeouts at the time of his retirement. Bunning also joined the legendary Cy Young as the only pitchers in history, to that point, to post more than 100 victories and strike out more than 1,000 batters in each league.

Despite his other accomplishments, Bunning's tremendous consistency is the thing that made him most proud, as he revealed years later when he said, "I am most proud of the fact I went through nearly 11 years without missing a start. They wrote my name down, and I went to the post."

After retiring as an active player, Bunning spent five years managing in the Phillies farm system. However, after failing to earn a promotion to the big leagues, Bunning returned to his home state of Kentucky, where he began his career in politics as a Kentucky state representative. Elected to the US House of Representatives in 1986, Bunning continued to serve in the House for the next 12 years, during which time he gained induction into the Baseball Hall of Fame via the Veterans Committee. Elected to the US Senate in 1998, Bunning served two terms, before announcing his decision not to run for re-election. Bunning lived until May 26, 2017, when he passed away at the age of 85 after suffering a stroke some seven months earlier.

PHILLIES CAREER HIGHLIGHTS

Best Season

Despite going just 17-15 in 1967, Bunning had an outstanding year, ranking among the NL leaders with a 2.29 ERA, a WHIP of 1.039, and 16 complete games, while also topping the circuit with 253 strikeouts, six shutouts, and 302 1/3 innings pitched. But Bunning made a greater overall impact in 1964, when he helped the Phillies finish a close second in the NL standings by placing near the top of the league rankings with 19 wins, 219 strikeouts, five shutouts, 13 complete games, 284 1/3 innings pitched, an ERA of 2.63, and a WHIP of 1.034.

Memorable Moments/Greatest Performances

Bunning excelled in his first start as a member of the Phillies, recording 11 strikeouts and allowing seven hits during a complete-game 4–1 win over the Mets on April 15, 1964.

Bunning tossed a six-hit shutout nine days later, striking out nine batters, while also going 3-for-4 at the plate during a 10–0 win over the Cubs on April 24, 1964.

Bunning allowed just two men to reach base during a 4–0 shutout of the Houston Colt .45s on May 18, 1964, hitting Nellie Fox with a pitch and yielding a fifth-inning single to Jim Wynn.

Bunning achieved perfection on June 21, 1964, when he retired 27 consecutive batters and recorded 10 strikeouts during a 6–0 win over the Mets.

Bunning dominated the Mets again on May 5, 1965, surrendering just four hits to them during a 1–0 shutout and accounting for the game's only run with a sixth-inning homer off Warren Spahn.

Bunning allowed just a pair of hits to outfielder Johnny Lewis during a 5–1 win over the Mets on July 24, 1965, with Lewis reaching him for a two-out homer in the bottom of the fourth inning.

Bunning tossed a five-hit shutout against the hard-hitting Pittsburgh Pirates on August 6, 1965, issuing no walks and recording 12 strikeouts, with Hall of Fame outfielders Roberto Clemente and Willie Stargell going a combined 0-for-8, with five strikeouts.

Bunning hurled another gem on September 14, 1965, allowing just a second-inning double to Jesse Gonder and a seventh-inning double to Eddie Mathews during a 2–0 shutout of the Milwaukee Braves.

Bunning ended the 1965 campaign in style, allowing just one walk and a pair of harmless singles by Ron Hunt and Bud Harrelson during a 6–0 shutout of the Mets in the regular-season finale.

Bunning yielded just three hits during a complete-game 5–1 victory over the Cincinnati Reds on June 7, 1966, recording a career-high 14 strikeouts in the process.

Bunning worked eight strong innings during a 3–2 win over the Reds on May 17, 1971, allowing two runs on five hits, and accounting for the Phillies' second run of the game with a sixth-inning homer off Jim Merritt.

Notable Achievements

- Won 19 games three times, posting 17 victories on another occasion.
- Posted winning percentage over .600 twice.
- Compiled ERA under 3.00 four times, finishing with mark below 2.50 twice.
- Struck out more than 200 batters four times.
- Threw more than 300 innings twice, tossing more than 250 frames two other times.
- Threw perfect game vs. New York Mets on June 21, 1964.
- Led NL pitchers in strikeouts once, innings pitched once, shutouts twice, strikeouts-to-walks ratio once, putouts once, and starts twice.
- Finished second among NL pitchers in ERA once, strikeouts once, innings pitched once, shutouts once, WHIP once, and starts once.
- Finished third among NL pitchers in wins once, shutouts once, WHIP once, and strikeouts-to-walks ratio three times.
- Ranks among Phillies career leaders in strikeouts (7th), innings pitched (11th), shutouts (5th), WHIP (4th), strikeouts-to-walks ratio (6th), and starts (9th).
- June 1964 NL Player of the Month.
- Finished second in 1967 NL Cy Young voting.
- 1964 *Sporting News* NL All-Star selection.
- Two-time NL All-Star (1964 and 1966).
- #14 retired by Phillies.
- Member of Philadelphia Baseball Wall of Fame.
- Elected to Baseball Hall of Fame by members of Veterans Committee in 1996.

18

SCOTT ROLEN

One of the best all-around third basemen ever to play the game, Scott Rolen spent 17 years in the big leagues excelling at the hot corner for four different teams. Having many of his finest seasons for the Phillies from 1996 to 2002, Rolen starred both at the bat and in the field, hitting more than 20 homers five times, knocking in more than 100 runs twice, winning four Gold Gloves, and earning one All-Star selection, before differences with team management led to his departure from Philadelphia. Continuing to perform at an elite level after leaving the City of Brotherly Love, Rolen won four more Gold Gloves and gained All-Star recognition another six times over the course of the next 10 seasons, giving him an extremely impressive list of credentials that may one day earn him a place in Cooperstown.

Born in Evansville, Indiana, on April 4, 1975, Scott Bruce Rolen lived in nearby Ft. Branch until the age of three, when his family moved some 45 miles northeast to Jasper, a farming town of about 10,000 people located approximately one hour outside Evansville. Rolen, whose parents both served as teachers in the Indiana school system, learned as a youngster the importance of putting in a hard day's work and remaining humble about one's accomplishments, recalling years later that his father often told him, "If you do something well, you don't have to tell anyone. They'll know."

An outstanding all-around athlete, Rolen starred in baseball and basketball at Jasper High School, being named Indiana's "Mr. Baseball" his senior year, while also finishing third in the voting for "Mr. Basketball." Following a recruiting frenzy that included scholarship offers from the University of Georgia, Oklahoma State, and the University of Alabama, Rolen committed to play basketball for the Georgia Bulldogs. However, the Phillies ultimately convinced him to sign with them after they selected him in the second round of the 1993 MLB Amateur Draft. Rolen subsequently spent most of the next four years playing in the minors, excelling at four different levels of the Phillies' farm system, before earning a promotion to the parent club in August 1996. Starting 37 games at third base for the Phillies before a pitch from Chicago's Steve Trachsel broke his arm, Rolen acquitted himself extremely well in his first stint in the majors, batting .254, hitting four homers, and driving in 18 runs, while committing only four errors in the field.

Handed the starting third base job by new Phillies skipper Terry Francona in the spring of 1997, Rolen went on to have an excellent year, earning NL Rookie of the Year honors by hitting 21 homers, knocking in 92 runs,

Scott Rolen won one Silver Slugger and four Gold Gloves while playing for the Phillies.
Courtesy of MearsonlineAuctions.com

scoring 93 times, batting .283, and stealing 16 bases, while also leading all NL third basemen in putouts and finishing second among players at his position in assists and double plays turned, despite playing a month with what turned out to be a broken hand. Signed to a four-year, $10 million contract by the Phillies at season's end, Rolen drew praise from the team's general manager, Ed Wade, who called his young third baseman "the most mature and levelheaded young player I've ever been around."

Rewarding Wade for the faith he placed in him, Rolen had another outstanding year in 1998, hitting 31 homers, driving in 110 runs, batting .290, compiling an OPS of .923, and ranking among the league leaders with 45 doubles and 120 runs scored, while also winning the first Gold Glove of his career for his excellent work at the hot corner. Hampered by a bad back in 1999, Rolen appeared in only 112 games. Nevertheless, he still managed to hit 26 homers, drive in 77 runs, score 74 times, bat .268, compile an on-base percentage of .368, and post a slugging percentage of .525. Although limited by ankle and back problems to 128 games the following year, Rolen once again posted solid numbers, finishing the season with 26 homers, 89 RBIs, 88 runs scored, a .298 batting average, a .370 on-base percentage, and a .551 slugging percentage.

Standing 6'4" and weighing 245 pounds, the right-handed-hitting Rolen presented an imposing figure at the plate. Blessed with a lightning-quick bat, Rolen drove fierce line drives to all parts of the ballpark, many of which cleared the outfield fences. And, despite his size, Rolen proved to be an outstanding baserunner who displayed aggressiveness, excellent instincts, surprising speed, and good decision-making on the basepaths. Meanwhile, Rolen's powerful throwing arm and exceptional range at third that both Mike Schmidt and Brooks Robinson claimed ranked with the best they ever saw made him the most complete third baseman of his time. Moving to his right better than most shortstops, Rolen completely shut down the third base line. Rolen also moved so well to his left that he allowed his shortstop to cheat toward second base, with former Cardinal teammate Edgar Renteria stating, "He could cover third base AND shortstop."

Commenting on the totality of Rolen's game, former Phillies manager Larry Bowa, who shared a tempestuous relationship with his star third baseman during their time together in Philadelphia, said, "He does a lot of things that other guys don't. He gets from first to third. He hustles every time he hits the ball. He probably saves 75 to 100 runs a year."

Curt Schilling also expressed his admiration for the determination his teammate exhibited on the playing field when he stated, "Not a lot of players play the game the way he does. But a lot more should."

Meanwhile, Rico Brogna spoke of Rolen's selfless attitude and outstanding leadership ability when he said, "When I first saw him play, it was easy to tell he was not only a special player, but a special person."

Former Phillies All-Star Dick Allen also addressed Rolen's team-first mentality when he suggested, "He's not caught up in individual stuff. He's a team guy, and that's what baseball is all about."

Eager to sign Rolen to a long-term contract extension prior to the start of the 2001 campaign, the Phillies offered him a new deal. But, with Rolen openly questioning the front office's commitment to winning, he chose to delay negotiations until the end of the year. Upset with Rolen's decision, new Phillies manager Larry Bowa spent much of the season finding fault with his play, at one point blaming him for the team's sluggish start. Following an argument between the two men, Rolen found himself being booed by the hometown fans, who sided with the feisty Bowa. Meanwhile, Phillies senior advisor Dallas Green added more fuel to the fire in August when he called Rolen a "so-so" player and suggested that his personality would likely prevent him from becoming a superstar. Yet, despite the many distractions, Rolen ended up having an excellent year, earning MVP consideration by hitting 25 homers, driving in 107 runs, scoring 96 times, and batting .289.

Having vowed to himself that he would not re-sign with the Phillies unless the conditions within the organization changed, Rolen turned down a seven-year deal worth $90 million during the subsequent offseason. In explaining his decision to enter free agency following the conclusion of the 2002 campaign, Rolen stated that, even though the Phillies operated in baseball's fourth-largest market, team management failed to spend like a big-market team. He then went on to say, "I did what I thought was right. I made the decision based upon principle and with my heart, and if that makes me a bad person, I don't want to be a bad person. I let my heart and principles guide my decision. If that is wrong, I will get what I deserve."

Rolen created more waves on the first day of spring training when he spent 45 minutes detailing to the media every flaw in the Philadelphia organization, prompting Bowa to confront him a few days later. Following another heated discussion, the Phillies manager demanded that GM Ed Wade trade him to another team.

Although Rolen remained in Philadelphia for another four months, Bowa eventually got his wish when the Phillies dealt the beleaguered third baseman to the St. Louis Cardinals for infielder Plácido Polanco and pitchers Mike Timlin and Bud Smith just prior to the trade deadline. Commenting on the decision to part ways with arguably the club's best player, Ed Wade, who one year earlier called Rolen "the best third baseman in the game," said that the 27-year-old infielder changed over his time with the Phillies and that the team and the player were no longer a good fit.

Rolen, who up to that point had homered 17 times, driven in 66 runs, and batted .259 in 2002, ended up finishing the season with 31 home runs, 110 RBIs, and a .266 batting average. Posting even better overall numbers the next two years, Rolen gained All-Star recognition in both 2003 and 2004 by hitting 28 homers, driving in 104 runs, scoring 98 times, and batting .286 in the first of those campaigns, before earning a fourth-place finish in the NL MVP voting the following season by hitting 34 homers, knocking in 124 runs, scoring 109 times, and batting .314 for the pennant-winning Cardinals.

Despite battling back problems the next three seasons, Rolen continued to perform well for the Cardinals whenever he found himself able to take the field, with his 22 homers, 95 RBIs, 94 runs scored, 48 doubles, and .296 batting average in 2006 earning him All-Star honors for the fourth straight time. Meanwhile, Rolen remained the league's top defensive third baseman, winning another three Gold Gloves, with his exceptional work in the field prompting Cardinal teammate Jason Isringhausen to say, "When Mike Schmidt says you're the best third baseman he's ever seen, that's pretty good."

Traded to the Toronto Blue Jays at the end of 2007, Rolen split the next five seasons between the Blue Jays and Cincinnati Reds, before announcing his retirement following the conclusion of the 2012 campaign with career totals of 316 home runs, 1,287 RBIs, 1,211 runs scored, 2,077 hits, 517 doubles, 43 triples, and 118 stolen bases, a lifetime batting average of .281, a .364 on-base percentage, and a .490 slugging percentage. Over parts of seven seasons in Philadelphia, Rolen hit 150 homers, knocked in 559 runs, scored 533 times, stole 71 bases, batted .282, compiled an on-base percentage of .373, posted a slugging percentage of .504, and collected 880 hits, 207 doubles, and 19 triples.

Since retiring as an active player, Rolen, who during his playing days started a children's charity with his brother, sister, and wife, has continued his philanthropic work, creating a 40-acre recreation site with horses, golf courses, canoes, and baseball fields that houses the families of sick children. Hired as the director of player development for Indiana University baseball on July 18, 2018, Rolen currently works with the coaching staff to recruit players on campus and gives advice to players on lifestyle choices and making decisions about their careers in baseball.

PHILLIES CAREER HIGHLIGHTS

Best Season

Although Rolen also posted outstanding numbers in 2000 and 2001, he had his finest all-around season for the Phillies in 1998, when he batted .290 and led the team with 31 homers, 110 RBIs, 120 runs scored, 45 doubles, 93 walks, and an OPS of .923.

Memorable Moments/Greatest Performances

Rolen led the Phillies to a 6–0 win over the Dodgers on August 21, 1996, by driving in three runs with a pair of homers.

Rolen knocked in five of the runs the Phillies scored during a 9–3 win over the Florida Marlins on June 23, 1997, with a homer and double.

Rolen continued his assault on Marlin pitching on July 11, 1997, going 3-for-4, with a homer, five RBIs, and three runs scored during a 13–3 Phillies win.

After homering with one man on earlier in the game, Rolen gave the Phillies an 8–7 win over the Marlins on September 27, 1997, by hitting a solo homer in the bottom of the ninth inning.

Rolen hit a pair of solo homers during a 3–2 win over the Tampa Bay Devil Rays on July 18, 1999, with his eighth-inning blast off Albie Lopez providing the margin of victory.

Rolen followed that up by going 3-for-5, with two homers, a double, four RBIs, and three runs scored during a 16–3 rout of the Devil Rays the very next day.

Rolen led the Phillies to a 5–2 victory over the Atlanta Braves on September 17, 2001, by hitting a pair of homers off Hall of Fame right-hander Greg Maddux.

Rolen contributed to an 11–1 pasting of the Detroit Tigers on June 7, 2002, by going 4-for-4, with a homer, double, and five RBIs.

Notable Achievements

- Hit more than 30 home runs twice, topping 20 homers four other times.
- Knocked in more than 100 runs twice.
- Scored more than 100 runs once.
- Surpassed 30 doubles four times, amassing more than 40 two-baggers once.
- Posted slugging percentage over .500 three times.
- Compiled OPS over .900 twice.
- Finished second in NL in triples once and sacrifice flies once.
- Led NL third basemen in putouts twice and assists once.
- Ranks 13th in franchise history with .504 slugging percentage.
- August 12, 2001, NL Player of the Week.
- 1997 NL Rookie of the Year.
- 2002 Silver Slugger Award winner.
- 2002 *Sporting News* NL All-Star selection.
- Four-time Gold Glove Award winner (1998, 2000, 2001, and 2002).
- 2002 NL All-Star.

19

CURT SCHILLING

An exceptional big-game pitcher who helped lead two different teams to the world championship, Curt Schilling spent parts of nine seasons in Philadelphia, serving as the ace of the Phillies' starting rotation much of that time. Despite playing for mostly mediocre Phillies teams, Schilling surpassed 15 victories on four separate occasions, en route to posting the seventh most wins in franchise history. One of only two Phillies pitchers to record as many as 300 strikeouts in a season, Schilling accomplished the feat twice, with his 319 Ks in 1997 representing the highest single-season total in team annals. A member of the Phillies' 1993 pennant-winning ballclub, Schilling earned three All-Star selections during his nine years in the City of Brotherly Love, before being further honored following the conclusion of his playing career by being inducted into both the Philadelphia Sports Hall of Fame and the Philadelphia Baseball Wall of Fame.

Born in Anchorage, Alaska, on November 14, 1966, Curtis Montague Schilling received his introduction to baseball at a very early age, with a biographical entry on ESPN stating, "When Curt was brought home from the hospital, there was a baseball glove in the crib that Cliff [his father] had placed there."

The son of a master sergeant in the US Army who served in the military for 22 years, young Curt eventually moved with his family to Kentucky, then Illinois, before finally settling in Phoenix, Arizona, where he attended Shadow Mountain High School. After playing baseball his senior year at Shadow Mountain, Schilling enrolled at Yavapai Junior College in Prescott, Arizona. However, he chose to leave school early after the Boston Red Sox selected him in the second round of the 1986 MLB Amateur Draft. Schilling subsequently spent the next two-and-a-half years advancing through Boston's farm system, during which time his father died of brain cancer. Later commenting on the loss of his father, Schilling, who rarely spoke to his mother and older sister, said, "My father was the glue that held us together. When he died, I kind of lost my family."

Curt Schilling's total of 319 strikeouts in 1997 represents a single-season franchise record. Courtesy of MearsonlineAuctions.com

Traded to the Baltimore Orioles on July 29, 1988, without ever having appeared in a game with the Red Sox, Schilling worked almost exclusively out of the Baltimore bullpen for the next two-and-a-half years, failing to distinguish himself during that time. Dealt to the Houston Astros prior to the start of the 1991 campaign, Schilling continued to struggle on the mound, going just 3-5 with a 3.81 ERA and eight saves in 56 relief appearances.

With the 25-year-old Schilling having failed to live up to his enormous potential his first few years in the big leagues, he received a lecture from his idol, Roger Clemens, during the 1991 offseason that prompted him to rededicate himself to his profession. After being accused by Clemens of failing to take the game seriously and not putting to good use his wide assortment of pitches that included an overpowering fastball, an exceptional split-finger fastball, and an above-average changeup, Schilling arrived in Philadelphia with new motivation after the Phillies acquired him just prior to the start of the 1992 season for fellow right-handed pitcher Jason Grimsley. Emerging as the ace of the Phillies' pitching staff after being inserted into the starting rotation during the early stages of the campaign, Schilling compiled a record of 14-11, recorded 147 strikeouts, led all NL hurlers with a WHIP of 0.990, and ranked among the league leaders with an ERA of 2.35, 10 complete games, and four shutouts. Although Schilling concluded the 1993 campaign with a far less impressive ERA of 4.02, he helped lead the Phillies to a playoff berth by going 16-7 with 186 strikeouts during the regular season, before earning NLCS MVP honors by posting an ERA of 1.69, striking out 19 batters, and allowing just 11 hits in 16 innings of work in two starts as Philadelphia defeated Atlanta to win the NL pennant.

Yet, despite his outstanding performance against the Braves in the NLCS, Schilling drew a considerable amount of criticism from several of his teammates, most notably pitchers Mitch Williams, Larry Andersen, and Danny Jackson, at the end of the year for the manner with which he conducted himself during the Phillies' six-game loss to the Toronto Blue Jays in the World Series. Fully aware of the many cameras being used throughout the ballpark to record the players' reactions to the events transpiring on the field, the self-absorbed Schilling, who reveled in the attention of others, repeatedly hid his face with a towel while sitting in the dugout every time the unpredictable Williams sought to extricate himself from a sticky situation on the mound. Although Schilling attempted to defend his boorish behavior by blaming it on World Series pressure, his teammates accused him of being disrespectful.

Hampered at different times by a torn labrum and bone spurs in his right elbow, Schilling posted an overall record of just 18-23 from 1994 to 1996, although he managed to record 182 strikeouts and lead the NL with eight complete games in the last of those campaigns. Fully healthy by the start of the 1997 season, Schilling earned a fourth-place finish in the NL Cy Young voting and All-Star honors for the first of three straight times by going 17-11 with a 2.97 ERA, leading the league with 319 strikeouts, and ranking among the leaders with seven complete games, 254 1/3 innings pitched, and a WHIP of 1.046. Schilling followed that up with two more outstanding seasons, compiling a record of 15-14, posting an ERA of 3.25, and leading the league with 300 strikeouts, 15 complete games, and 268 2/3 innings pitched in 1998, before going 15-6 with a 3.54 ERA, 152 strikeouts, and eight complete games in 1999, despite missing more than a month of action with right biceps and shoulder issues.

Although the 6'5", 220-pound Schilling possessed an outstanding four-seam fastball that consistently registered somewhere between 94 and 98 mph on the radar gun, his signature pitch proved to be his patented split-finger fastball, which he generally located beneath the strike zone. Schilling also threw an above-average changeup, an effective slider, and an occasional curveball. Blessed with exceptional command of all his pitches, Schilling annually ranked among the league leaders in strikeout-to-walk ratio, with his career mark of 4.383 representing the eighth-best figure in MLB history. In discussing his approach to pitching and the success he experienced over the course of his career, Schilling said, "It's command. Control is the ability to throw strikes. In the big leagues, everybody has control. Command is the ability to throw quality strikes. And, when you add preparation to command, good things will happen."

Schilling pitched somewhat less effectively during the first four months of the 2000 season, going 6-6 with a 3.91 ERA, before his outspoken nature and criticism of Philadelphia's front office prompted the Phillies to trade him to the Arizona Diamondbacks in late July for a package of four players that included first baseman–outfielder Travis Lee and pitchers Omar Daal, Nelson Figueroa, and Vicente Padilla. Schilling left the Phillies having compiled an overall record of 101-78, an ERA of 3.35, and a WHIP of 1.120 as a member of the team. He also registered 1,554 strikeouts, tossed 14 shutouts, and threw 61 complete games and 1,659 1/3 innings during his time in Philadelphia.

After compiling a record of 5-6 and an ERA of 3.69 for the Diamondbacks the rest of the year, Schilling reached the apex of his career the next two seasons, earning a pair of runner-up finishes in the NL Cy Young voting and top-10 finishes in the league MVP balloting by going 22-6, with a 2.98 ERA, 293 strikeouts, and a league-leading 256 2/3 innings pitched for Arizona's World Series championship team in 2001, before compiling a record of 23-7, an ERA of 3.23, and a WHIP of 0.968 in 2002, while also striking out 316 batters and throwing 259 1/3 innings. Particularly outstanding during the 2001 postseason, Schilling went a perfect 4-0, with an ERA of 1.12 and 56 strikeouts in 48 1/3 innings of work. Schilling spent one more year in Arizona, before signing with the Boston Red Sox as a free agent following the conclusion of the 2003 campaign. Continuing to excel on the mound for the Red Sox, Schilling compiled a record of 21-6 and an ERA of 3.26 during the 2004 regular season, before helping to end the "Curse of the Bambino" by winning three of his four decisions during Boston's successful postseason run to the world championship.

Schilling ended up spending three more years in Beantown, before arm problems forced him to officially announce his retirement on March 23, 2009. Over parts of 20 big-league seasons, Schilling compiled an overall record of 216-146, an ERA of 3.46, and a WHIP of 1.137, struck out 3,116 batters in 3,261 innings of work, and threw 83 complete games and 20 shutouts. Perhaps the finest big-game pitcher of his generation, Schilling also posted a career record of 11-2 and an ERA of 2.23 in postseason play.

After retiring as an active player, Schilling spent six years working as a studio analyst at ESPN, before his controversial political views forced the network to relieve him of his duties. After Schilling compared Muslim extremists to Nazis in Germany in an August 2015 tweet, ESPN removed him from its telecasts of that year's Little League World Series and all remaining 2015 *Sunday Night Baseball* games. Then, after Schilling shared an anti-transgender post on Facebook in April 2016, the network handed him his walking papers.

Following his release by ESPN, Schilling, who overcame a bout with throat cancer in 2014 that he claimed resulted from using smokeless tobacco for 30 years, joined Breitbart News, a conservative opinion and news organization, where he hosts his own show. Schilling also continues his charitable work for victims of amyotrophic lateral sclerosis that he began during his playing career.

PHILLIES CAREER HIGHLIGHTS

Best Season

Although Schilling finished just 14-11 in 1992, he had one of his finest seasons for the Phillies, leading the league with a WHIP of 0.990, while also ranking among the leaders with an ERA of 2.35, 10 complete games, and four shutouts. However, Schilling proved to be somewhat more dominant in 1997, earning his first All-Star selection and a fourth-place finish in the NL Cy Young voting by going 17-11, with a 2.97 ERA, WHIP of 1.046, 254 1/3 innings pitched, and league-leading and career-high 319 strikeouts.

Memorable Moments/Greatest Performances

Schilling turned in an outstanding all-around effort on June 8, 1992, surrendering just three hits during a 7–0 shutout of the Pirates and driving in a pair of runs with a second-inning double.

Schilling dominated the Mets on September 9, 1992, yielding just one hit and striking out eight batters during a 2–1 Phillies win, with Bobby Bonilla's fifth-inning homer serving as the only blemish on his record.

Schilling proved to be almost as dominant on June 7, 1995, surrendering just two hits and recording eight strikeouts during a 7–1 win over the San Diego Padres, who scored their only run of the game on a seventh-inning homer by third baseman Ken Caminiti.

Schilling limited the Dodgers to just two hits during a 6–0 Phillies win on August 21, 1996, yielding just a pair of harmless singles to outfielders Wayne Kirby and Raúl Mondesí.

Schilling tossed a three-hit shutout against the Cardinals on August 10, 1997, issuing just one walk and striking out eight batters during an 8–0 Phillies win.

Schilling turned in a dominant performance against the Yankees on September 1, 1997, recording 16 strikeouts over the first eight innings of a 5–1 Phillies win.

Schilling won a 2–1 pitchers' duel with Greg Maddux on April 5, 1998, throwing a complete-game five-hitter against the Braves during which he struck out 15 batters, with Atlanta's only run coming on a first-inning homer by Chipper Jones.

Schilling outdueled Maddux again just five days later, winning a 1–0 decision during which he recorded 10 strikeouts and allowed just two hits and one walk.

Schilling tossed another complete-game two-hitter on June 17, 1998, allowing just two safeties and one walk during a 3–1 win over the Pittsburgh Pirates.

Schilling hurled a pair of gems against the Diamondbacks in August 1998, yielding just three hits during a 3–0 shutout of his future team on the 10th of the month, before allowing just four hits and recording 14 strikeouts during a complete-game 11–1 victory 10 days later.

Notable Achievements

- Won at least 15 games four times.
- Posted winning percentage over .600 three times.
- Compiled ERA under 3.00 twice, finishing with mark below 2.50 once.
- Struck out more than 300 batters twice.
- Threw 15 complete games in 1998.
- Threw more than 250 innings twice.
- Posted WHIP under 1.000 once.
- Led NL pitchers in strikeouts twice, complete games three times, innings pitched once, WHIP once, and starts twice.
- Finished second in NL in complete games three times, shutouts once, and strikeouts-to-walks ratio once.
- Finished third in NL in complete games once, innings pitched once, shutouts three times, and WHIP once.
- Holds Phillies single-season record for most strikeouts (319 in 1997).
- Ranks among Phillies career leaders in wins (7th), strikeouts (5th), innings pitched (9th), shutouts (tied-11th), WHIP (7th), strikeouts-to-walks ratio (5th), strikeouts per nine innings pitched (5th), and starts (7th).
- 1993 division champion.
- 1993 NL champion.
- May 1999 NL Pitcher of the Month.
- 1993 NLCS MVP.
- 1995 Lou Gehrig Memorial Award winner.
- Three-time NL All-Star (1997, 1998, and 1999).
- Member of Philadelphia Baseball Wall of Fame.
- Member of Philadelphia Sports Hall of Fame.

20

ROY THOMAS

The National League's premier leadoff hitter for most of the first decade of the 20th century, Roy Thomas spent parts of 12 seasons in Philadelphia, serving as the Phillies' everyday center fielder in nine of those. Starting in center for the Phillies from 1899 to 1907, Thomas, who specialized in fouling off pitches and drawing walks, possessed virtually no power at the plate, hitting just seven homers and driving in only 299 runs over the course of his 13-year major-league career. Nevertheless, the slightly built Thomas used his speed, tremendous bat control, and patience at the plate to bat over .300 five times, score more than 100 runs four times, and draw more than 100 bases on balls seven times, topping the senior circuit in the last category on seven separate occasions. An excellent outfielder as well, Thomas did an outstanding job of patrolling center field for the Phillies, regularly ranking among the top players at his position in putouts, assists, and fielding percentage.

Born in Norristown, Pennsylvania, on March 24, 1874, Roy Allen Thomas grew up in nearby Sheetz's Mill and attended Norristown High School, where he honed his baseball skills before enrolling at the University of Pennsylvania. After starring in the Quakers outfield during his time in college, Thomas spent four years playing semipro ball for the Orange Athletic Club, whose roster included several former collegians.

Finally turning pro in 1899, Thomas signed with the Phillies, who immediately made him their starting center fielder and leadoff hitter. Performing exceptionally well as a rookie, the 25-year-old Thomas batted .325, stole 42 bases, and finished among the NL leaders with 137 runs scored, 115 walks, and an on-base percentage of .457. Thomas followed that up by batting .316, stealing 37 bases, placing second in the league with a .451 on-base percentage, and topping the circuit with 132 runs scored and 115 bases on balls in 1900, before batting .309, swiping 27 bases, scoring 102 runs, and leading the NL with 100 walks in 1901. Thomas continued to excel as a table-setter in each of the next three seasons, leading the league in walks three straight times and on-base percentage twice, while also batting over .300 once and scoring no fewer than 88 runs. Particularly effective in 1903, Thomas batted a career-high .327 and topped the circuit with 107 bases on balls and an on-base percentage of .453.

A left-handed slap hitter and bunter extraordinaire, the 5'11", 150-pound Thomas, who crouched down in his stance and held the bat low, made good use of his speed and ability to handle the bat, reportedly averaging approximately 200 bunt attempts a season. And, even though opposing teams knew that Thomas hit the ball almost exclusively to left field, he managed to finish in the league's top 10 in batting average on three separate occasions, with Chicago Cubs pitcher Ed Reulbach later marveling at Thomas's success at the plate, saying:

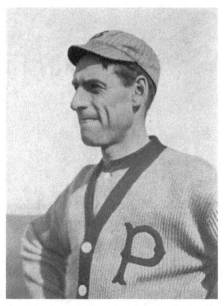

Roy Thomas proved to be arguably the National League's finest leadoff hitter of his time.

> He not only hit almost all the time to left field, but he was a short-field hitter as well. This tendency handicapped him tremendously. With Thomas at bat, the left fielder moved close to the foul line and came well in. The center fielder shifted a way over toward left and at the same time advanced close up behind short and second. The third baseman moved over nearly to the foul line, and the shortstop followed him to a point at least 15 feet beyond his natural position. Thomas naturally realized the force of the conspiracy against him. But if he tried to pull the ball to the other field, the nearest he could come to that aim would be perhaps to loop it over the pitcher's box. But the second baseman was also in the conspiracy. When the shortstop moved over, the second baseman followed, so that, instead of being considerably to the right of second base, he was literally in line with the bag, so he was waiting ready for the ball if Thomas "pulled" it. The sole defense against such a conspiracy

is the ability to hit hard. Thomas, however, unfortunately for him, did not possess this ability.

Indeed, Thomas lacked the ability to drive the ball deep into the outfield, collecting a total of only 160 extra-base hits over the course of his career, with all seven of his home runs being of the inside-the-park variety. Yet, Thomas presented a tremendous challenge to opposing pitchers due to his ability to recognize pitches and foul off the ones he did not like. Frequently turning lengthy at-bats into bases on balls, Thomas reportedly once fouled off as many as 27 pitches in a single at-bat, with his peskiness at the plate contributing greatly to the implementation of a new rule that went into effect in 1901. Prior to that year, foul balls were not counted as strikes. But, with Thomas infuriating opposing hurlers with his ability to foul off good pitches while taking the bad ones in order to earn a walk, the National League passed a rule that counted foul balls as strikes early in the count. The American League followed suit two years later, giving us the foul-strike rule that has governed the game for the past 120 years.

In addition to being the top leadoff hitter of his time, Thomas proved to be an excellent outfielder and outstanding baserunner. Blessed with sure hands, exceptional range, and a good throwing arm, Thomas led all NL center fielders in putouts three times, assists twice, and fielding percentage three times, compiling as many as 27 assists one year. Possessing marvelous instincts on the basepaths as well, Thomas stole more than 20 bases six times and consistently ranked among the NL leaders in runs scored.

Thomas remained a top offensive performer for one more year, batting .317, compiling an on-base percentage of .417, scoring 118 runs, and drawing 93 bases on balls in 1905, before his skills began to fade. Although Thomas led the NL in walks in each of the next two seasons, he scored a total of only 151 runs and batted just .254 and .243, prompting the Phillies to release him during the early stages of the 1908 campaign. Thomas subsequently signed with the Pittsburgh Pirates, for whom he batted .256 in 102 games, before assuming a part-time role with the Boston Doves the following year. Thomas then returned to Philadelphia, where he served as a backup with the Phillies in 1910 and 1911, before announcing his retirement. In addition to his seven home runs and 299 RBIs, Thomas ended his playing career with 1,011 runs scored, 1,537 hits, 100 doubles, 53 triples, 244 stolen bases, 1,042 walks, a .290 batting average, a .413 on-base percentage, and a .333 slugging percentage. During his time in Philadelphia, Thomas hit six homers, knocked in 264 runs, scored 923 times, batted .295, compiled an on-base percentage of .421, posted a slugging percentage of .334, and collected 1,364 hits, 80 doubles, 42 triples, and 228 stolen bases. At the time of his retirement, Thomas held NL records for the highest fielding percentage by any player and the most putouts by a center fielder.

Following his playing days, Thomas worked for a Philadelphia-based coal company as a sales representative and remained close to the game by coaching at the collegiate and minor-league levels from 1909 to 1933, serving as head man at his alma mater, the University of Pennsylvania, for 11 years. After retiring from coaching, Thomas remained in the Philadelphia area, where the city continued to view him as a link to its baseball heritage until he died at his home on the corner of Haws Avenue and Airy Street in Norristown on November 20, 1959, at 85 years of age.

PHILLIES CAREER HIGHLIGHTS

Best Season

Thomas had an outstanding year for the Phillies in 1903, batting .327, scoring 88 runs, stealing 17 bases, and leading the NL with 107 bases on balls and a .453 on-base percentage, while also recording more putouts than any other outfielder in the league for the first of three straight times. Nevertheless, Thomas's rookie campaign of 1899 proved to be his finest, since, in addition to batting .325, he established career-high marks with 47 RBIs, 137 runs scored, 178 hits, 42 stolen bases, 115 walks, and an OPS of .819.

Memorable Moments/Greatest Performances

Thomas provided much of the impetus for a 6–2 victory over the Cincinnati Reds on October 1, 1901, by leading off the bottom of the first inning with a home run.

Thomas helped lead the Phillies to a 9–2 win over the St. Louis Cardinals on July 14, 1902, by going 5-for-5, with two stolen bases, an RBI, and three runs scored.

Thomas contributed to a 12–1 rout of the Giants on April 21, 1904, by going 4-for-6, with a homer and four runs scored.

Thomas led the Phillies to a 15–7 victory over the Pirates on May 6, 2004, by going 4-for-4, with two RBIs and three runs scored.

Thomas sparked the Phillies to an 8–7 win over the Boston Beaneaters on July 26, 1904, by going a perfect 5-for-5, with a double, a stolen base, and two runs scored.

Thomas gave the Phillies a 4–3 victory over the Reds on August 4, 1904, by driving in the winning run with his fourth single of the game in the bottom of the ninth inning.

Thomas helped lead the Phillies to a 6–1 win over the Cardinals on August 17, 1907, by scoring three times and knocking in two runs with a homer and single.

Notable Achievements

- Batted over .300 five times, topping .the 320 mark twice.
- Scored more than 100 runs four times.
- Stole more than 20 bases six times, topping 30 thefts twice.
- Drew more than 100 bases on balls seven times.
- Compiled on-base percentage over .400 seven times.
- Led NL in walks seven times, runs scored once, on-base percentage twice, and plate appearances once.
- Finished second in NL in runs scored once, on-base percentage three times, walks once, and plate appearances twice.
- Finished third in NL in runs scored once and walks once.
- Led NL outfielders in putouts three times, assists once, fielding percentage once, and double plays once.
- Led NL center fielders in putouts twice, assists twice, fielding percentage three times, and double plays once.
- Ranks among Phillies career leaders in on-base percentage (2nd), walks (tied-3rd), runs scored (8th), stolen bases (9th), and sacrifice hits (4th).

21

JOHNNY CALLISON

Once referred to as "the next Mickey Mantle," Johnny Callison displayed Hall of Fame talent during the early stages of his career, with Phillies manager Gene Mauch saying of his star right fielder, "He can run, throw, field, and hit with power. There's nothing he can't do well on the ball field." The team's most popular player from 1962 to 1966, Callison surpassed 30 homers, knocked in more than 100 runs, and scored more than 100 runs twice each over the course of those five seasons, while also amassing more putouts and assists than any other player at his position, with his exceptional all-around play earning him three All-Star selections and a runner-up finish in the 1964 NL MVP voting. Yet, oddly enough, Callison experienced a precipitous decline in offensive production after 1966, never again hitting as many as 20 homers, driving in more than 68 runs, or scoring more than 66 times in his final seven big-league seasons, which he split between the Phillies, Chicago Cubs, and New York Yankees. Nevertheless, Callison accomplished enough during his 10 years with the Phillies to gain induction into the Philadelphia Baseball Wall of Fame and the Philadelphia Sports Hall of Fame.

Born in Qualls, Oklahoma, on March 12, 1939, John Wesley Callison grew up in poverty, with his father working odd jobs in and around Qualls in the dying days of the Great Depression, before joining the Army during World War II. Relocating with his mother and three siblings to Bakersfield, California, following the enlistment of his father, the quiet and shy Callison developed into a star athlete at Bakersfield High School, proving to be particularly proficient in baseball, which became his sanctuary. Revealing years later that his favorite sport provided an emotional release from his poor upbringing and lack of self-confidence, Callison said, "I found my refuge in baseball because only on the ball field did I feel worthy of measuring up."

Pursued by major-league scouts while still in high school, Callison eventually signed with the Chicago White Sox for $10,000, after which he began his professional career in 1957 with the Bakersfield Bears of the Class

Johnny Callison finished second in the 1964 NL MVP voting.

C California League. Excelling in his first year of pro ball, the 18-year-old Callison batted .340 and stole 31 bases in just 86 games, earning him a promotion to the Triple-A Indianapolis Indians of the American Association in 1958. Continuing to perform at an elite level at Indianapolis, Callison topped the circuit with 29 homers, knocked in 93 runs, and batted .283, prompting the White Sox to call him up during the latter stages of the campaign. Acquitting himself extremely well in 18 games with the parent club during the month of September, Callison batted .297, drove in 12 runs, and hit his first big-league homer.

However, after earning a spot on the White Sox roster the following spring, Callison experienced adversity for the first time in his young career, hitting only three homers and batting just .173 in 49 games, before being sent back down to the minors. After spending the rest of the year at Indianapolis, Callison found himself heading to Philadelphia when the White Sox traded him to the Phillies for veteran third baseman Gene Freese on December 9, 1959.

Still only 21 years old when he arrived in the City of Brotherly Love, Callison spent his first year with the Phillies assuming the role of a fourth outfielder, hitting nine homers, driving in 30 runs, scoring 36 times, and batting .260 in 99 games, while splitting his time between right field and left. Although Callison continued to see action at both positions again in 1961, he became a regular member of the starting lineup during the early stages of the campaign, after which he went on to hit nine homers, drive in 47 runs, score 74 times, bat .266, and finish second in the league with 11 triples.

Despite posting relatively modest numbers his first two seasons in Philadelphia, Callison gradually developed into a solid all-around hitter, with the help of manager Gene Mauch, who made him his pet project. In addition to working with the 5'10", 175-pound Callison on smoothing out his left-handed swing, Mauch encouraged him to hit to left field and suggested that he make better use of his exceptional running speed by occasionally bunting the ball to the right side of the infield. Having learned his lessons well, Callison subsequently began an outstanding four-year run during which he compiled the following numbers:

YEAR	HR	RBI	RUNS	3B	AVG	OBP	SLG	OPS
1962	23	83	107	10	.300	.363	.491	.854
1963	26	78	96	11	.284	.339	.502	.840
1964	31	104	101	10	.274	.316	.492	.809
1965	32	101	93	16	.262	.328	.509	.836

In addition to leading the NL in triples twice, Callison ranked among the leaders in that category two other times and placed near the top of the league rankings in RBIs twice, homers three times, and runs scored and total bases all four years. Although the 34-foot-high right field wall at Connie Mack Stadium likely cost the pull-hitting Callison several homers, he increased his home-run total each year, with his 32 long balls in 1965 representing the highest single-season total by any left-handed batter in the ballpark's history. Meanwhile, after being moved to right field full-time prior to the start of the 1962 campaign, Callison led all players at that position in fielding percentage twice and putouts and assists all four years, throwing out a total of 91 runners on the basepaths, with his exceptional all-around play earning him three All-Star nominations and a runner-up finish in the NL MVP voting in 1964, when he nearly led the Phillies to the pennant.

Commenting on the totality of Callison's game, Tim McCarver, who caught for the St. Louis Cardinals in those days, later said, "Cannon for an arm. Compact power. Just a superb ballplayer. He was the whole package. While I didn't know him well personally, I had enormous respect for him as a player. Particularly the 1964 season with the Phillies, when he was such a clutch performer for that very, very good ballclub."

Callison posted solid numbers again in 1966, batting .276, scoring 93 runs, and leading the league with 40 doubles. However, he hit only 11 homers and knocked in just 55 runs, beginning a trend that lasted for the remainder of his career. His days as a power hitter and major run producer over at the age of 27, Callison totaled just 44 home runs, 168 RBIs, and 174 runs scored over the course of the next three seasons, while failing to hit any higher than .265.

Although Callison later attributed his diminishing numbers to a series of nagging injuries and health issues that included problems with his legs and vision, speculation arose in baseball circles that a loss of self-confidence ultimately led to his fall from elite status, with Callison himself admitting in an article that appeared in a 1964 edition of *Sport* magazine that he was "the biggest worrier around."

Frustrated with Callison's lack of offensive production, the Phillies chose to include him in a trade they completed with the Cubs on November 17, 1969, that sent him and pitcher Larry Colton to Chicago for pitcher Dick Selma and outfielder Oscar Gamble. During his 10 years in Philadelphia, Callison hit 185 homers, knocked in 666 runs, scored 774 times, stole 60 bases, batted .271, compiled an on-base percentage of .338, posted a slugging percentage of .457, and collected 1,438 hits, 265 doubles, and 84 triples.

After leaving the Phillies, Callison put up decent numbers his first year in Chicago, hitting 19 homers, driving in 68 runs, scoring 65 times, and batting .264. But he often found himself clashing with outspoken and dictatorial Cubs manager Leo Durocher, who he later claimed almost drove him out of baseball. After one more year in Chicago, during which he served the Cubs as a part-time player, Callison spent his final two seasons assuming a similar role in New York with the Yankees, who eventually released him on August 18, 1973, bringing his playing career to an end. Callison, who retired with 226 home runs, 840 RBIs, 926 runs scored, 1,757 hits, 321 doubles, and 89 triples, a batting average of .264, an on-base percentage of .331, and a slugging percentage of .441, subsequently worked in a variety of unfulfilling jobs, including car salesman and bartender, before a series of ulcers and a heart attack forced him to retire to private life. Callison spent his remaining time living in the Philadelphia suburb of Glenside, where he died from cancer at the age of 67, on October 12, 2006.

Upon learning of his former teammate's passing, Jim Bunning said, "He had all the tools that a great player needs. He did an unbelievable job playing right field and knocking in a lot of key runs."

Dick Allen also had fond memories of Callison, recalling, "Johnny was more than a teammate to me, he was a close friend. He was a terrific player with a great arm from right field. He also had a funny, dry sense of humor."

And Rubén Amaro Sr., who spent six seasons playing with Callison in Philadelphia, remembered, "I had some of the greatest times of my life and my career with Johnny. We grew up in baseball together. We were part of the Phillies that couldn't win a game in 1961, and he was really one of our big guns in 1964, when we should have won. My heart goes out to his wife and daughters."

PHILLIES CAREER HIGHLIGHTS

Best Season

Callison played his best ball for the Phillies from 1962 to 1965, hitting more than 20 homers four straight times, while also driving in more than 100 runs and scoring more than 100 runs twice each. The 1962 campaign would certainly have to be considered one of Callison's finest, since, in addition to hitting 23 homers and knocking in 83 runs, he led the NL with 10 triples and established career-high marks with 181 hits, 107 runs scored, a .300 batting average, and an OPS of .854. But Callison made his greatest overall impact in 1964, when he earned a runner-up finish to Ken Boyer in the NL MVP voting by batting .274, compiling an OPS of .809, and ranking among the league leaders with 31 homers, 104 RBIs, 101 runs scored, 10 triples, and 322 total bases, while also leading all NL right fielders in putouts and assists for the third straight time.

Memorable Moments/Greatest Performances

Callison gave the Phillies a dramatic 6–5 victory over the Giants on August 3, 1960, when he hit a pinch-hit two-run homer in the bottom of the ninth inning.

Callison provided further heroics on June 9, 1963, when, after homering earlier in the contest against Reds starter Bob Purkey, he capped off a five-run rally by the Phillies in the bottom of the ninth inning by hitting a two-out, two-run game-tying inside-the-park home run off Bill Henry. The Phillies pushed across another run in the ensuing frame on an RBI single by Bobby Wine, giving them an 8–7, 10-inning win.

Callison led the Phillies to a 13–4 rout of the Pittsburgh Pirates on June 27, 1963, by hitting for the cycle, going 4-for-5, with four RBIs and two runs scored.

Callison contributed to a 10–2 victory over the Dodgers on July 16, 1963, by going 4-for-4, with a pair of homers, three RBIs, and three runs scored.

Callison had the only five-hit game of his career on May 20, 1964, going 5-for-5, with a homer, three RBIs, and two runs scored during a 7–2 win over the Giants.

Callison helped lead the Phillies to a lopsided 13–5 victory over the Cubs on August 11, 1964, by scoring four times and knocking in four runs with a homer and a pair of doubles, picking up all four RBIs on a sixth-inning grand slam off Dick Ellsworth.

Callison hit three home runs in one game twice, accomplishing the feat for the first time during a 13–8 loss to the Milwaukee Braves on September 27, 1964, and again during a 10–9 win over the Cubs on June 6, 1965, finishing the second contest with four hits and four RBIs.

Yet, Callison will always be remembered most for giving the NL a 7–4 victory over the AL in the 1964 All-Star Game by hitting a game-winning three-run homer off Dick Radatz in the bottom of the ninth inning. Recalling his feelings at the time, Callison said years later, "That homer was the greatest thrill of my life, but I remember thinking that it was only the beginning. It was going to be the Phillies' year. We had everything going our way. Everything."

Notable Achievements

- Hit more than 30 home runs twice, topping 20 homers two other times.
- Knocked in more than 100 runs twice.
- Scored more than 100 runs twice.
- Batted .300 once.
- Finished in double digits in triples five times.
- Surpassed 30 doubles four times, amassing 40 two-baggers once.
- Posted slugging percentage over .500 twice.
- Amassed more than 20 outfield assists three times.
- Hit three home runs in one game twice (vs. Milwaukee Braves on September 27, 1964, and vs. Chicago Cubs on June 6, 1965).
- Hit for cycle vs. Pittsburgh Pirates on June 27, 1963.
- Led NL in triples twice and doubles once.
- Finished second in NL in triples once, sacrifice hits once, games played once, and at-bats once.
- Finished third in NL in home runs once, triples once, doubles once, and extra-base hits twice.
- Led NL outfielders in assists four times, fielding percentage once, and double plays once.
- Led NL right fielders in putouts five times, assists four times, fielding percentage twice, and double plays twice.
- Ranks among Phillies career leaders in home runs (12th), triples (6th), total bases (12th), and extra-base hits (10th).

- 1964 All-Star Game MVP.
- Finished second in 1964 NL MVP voting.
- Three-time NL All-Star.
- Member of Philadelphia Baseball Wall of Fame.
- Member of Philadelphia Sports Hall of Fame.

22

GARRY MADDOX

Dubbed the "Secretary of Defense" by *Philadelphia Daily News* columnist Bill Conlin in 1976, Garry Maddox proved to be the finest defensive center fielder of his time, winning eight consecutive Gold Gloves while manning that post for the Phillies for parts of 12 seasons. After beginning his career with the San Francisco Giants, Maddox helped lead the Phillies to five division titles, two pennants, and one world championship by doing a masterful job of patrolling center field at Veterans Stadium, while also performing well both at the plate and on the basepaths. Compiling a batting average of .284 and stealing 189 bases as a member of the Phillies, Maddox batted over .300 once and swiped more than 20 bags six times, with his stellar all-around play earning him one top-five finish in the NL MVP voting and a place in the Philadelphia Sports Hall of Fame following his retirement.

Born in Cincinnati, Ohio, on September 1, 1949, Garry Lee Maddox moved with his parents and eight siblings at an early age to the Los Angeles, California, suburb of San Pedro, where he spent his youth rooting for the San Francisco Giants and his favorite player, Willie Mays. The son of a former Negro League pitcher, Maddox grew up in poverty, recalling years later, "We were very poor . . . I remember doing without things other kids take for granted . . . getting one toy for all nine kids to play with at Christmas."

Maddox continued, "I ran with a rough crowd, kids who got into almost every kind of trouble you could get into, but, somehow, I stayed out of trouble."

An outstanding all-around athlete, Maddox starred in baseball, basketball, and football at San Pedro High School, with his outfield play drawing the attention of Giants superscout George Genovese, who remembered, "I saw tremendous speed. He would run down absolutely everything hit anywhere near him in the outfield."

Selected by the Giants in the second round of the January 1968 MLB draft, Maddox began his minor-league career in Salt Lake City, where he played center field and batted .252 in 58 games, before finishing the season with the Class A Fresno Giants. However, after discovering that the $1,500 signing bonus he received from the Giants fell far short of the amount typically offered to a second-round pick, Maddox grew increasingly disenchanted, causing him to enlist in the US Army at the end of the year. Recalling his feelings at the time, Maddox said, "I played that one season and then I quit, and I joined the Army. I was bitter. I didn't like the hassle. My family needed the money."

After completing basic training, Maddox volunteered for service in Vietnam, where he ended up spending one year serving as a perimeter guard, avoiding the worst of the conflict, but wit-

Garry Maddox won eight Gold Gloves during his time in Philadelphia.
Courtesy of MearsonlineAuctions.com

nessing the aftermath of a friend's suicide and a considerable amount of racial conflict within his own camp. Later calling the experience "pure hell," Maddox, who turned to religion as a way of coping with the brutality that surrounded him, stated, "The scene over there was going to change you one way or another."

Although Maddox had originally enlisted for four years, he applied for a hardship discharge early in 1970 to help support his family after his father suffered multiple heart attacks. Forced to swallow his pride, Maddox reached out to the Giants, recalling, "In order to get out on a hardship discharge, you have to have a job. And the only thing I had done was, right after high school, played a little bit of baseball."

Following his return to the States, Maddox spent the fall of 1970 playing in the Arizona Instructional League, before rejoining the Fresno Giants, for whom he hit 30 homers, knocked in 106 runs, and scored 105 times in 1971. Maddox then began the 1972 campaign at Triple-A Phoenix. However, after getting off to a fast start with the Giants' top minor-league affiliate, Maddox found himself heading to San Francisco, with Phoenix GM Rosy Ryan saying of the 22-year-old outfielder, "This is an exceptional prospect. There isn't a thing he can't do. In centerfield, he catches everything. He swings smooth, and he's got wrists like Henry Aaron."

Laying claim to the Giants' starting center field job after team owner Horace Stoneham traded the aging Willie Mays to the Mets on May 11, 1972, Maddox had a solid rookie season, batting .266, hitting 12 homers, driving in 58 runs, and scoring 62 times, in just under 500 plate appearances. Improving upon those numbers the following year, Maddox hit 11 homers, knocked in 76 runs, scored 81 times, collected a career-high 187 hits, and finished third in the league with a .319 batting average. Although Maddox posted a less-impressive stat-line in 1974, he had another solid season. But, after slumping during the early stages of the 1975 campaign, the right-handed-hitting Maddox found himself being platooned with the lefty-swinging Von Joshua, prompting him to request a trade to another team. The Giants obliged, dealing him to the Phillies on May 4, 1975, for first baseman Willie Montañez.

Despite missing nearly a month of action with an injured knee shortly after he joined the Phillies, Maddox performed well the rest of the year, batting .291, scoring 50 runs, and stealing 24 bases in just 99 games, while earning Gold Glove honors for the first of eight straight times. Nevertheless, Phillies Hall of Fame outfielder-turned-broadcaster Richie Ashburn questioned Maddox's ability to contribute consistently to the team on offense, stating during spring training in 1976, "I wonder if he's ever really going to hit. He says he can't pick up the spin on the ball, and I never heard of a really good hitter who couldn't do that. It's awfully hard to hit the breaking ball if you can't recognize that it IS a breaking ball."

Maddox himself admitted, "I don't pick up the spin on anything. I never tell myself 'This is a curveball; this is a slider.' I see the ball and I swing, that's it."

Maddox's simplistic approach to hitting worked well for him in 1976, when he earned a fifth-place finish in the NL MVP voting by driving in 68 runs, scoring 75 times, and finishing third in the league with a .330 batting average and 37 doubles for a Phillies team that captured the division title for the first of three straight times. Maddox followed that up by hitting 14 homers, knocking in 74 runs, scoring 85 times, batting .292, and stealing 22 bases in 1977, before reaching the seats 11 times, driving in 68 runs, collecting 34 doubles, swiping 33 bags, and batting .288 the following year.

Built very much like a greyhound, the 6'3", 175-pound Maddox employed a wide stance in the batter's box that prevented him from overstriding. Predominantly a pull hitter who tended to drive the ball hard to left field, Maddox lacked consistent home-run power, although he finished in double digits in homers six times during his career, including four times as a member of the Phillies. Somewhat impatient at the plate, Maddox rarely walked, never drawing more than 42 bases on balls in any single season. Explaining his approach to hitting prior to the start of the 1977 campaign, Maddox, who usually batted sixth for the Phillies, said, "I don't want to go up there taking or waiting. I like to just go up there and swing."

But, while Maddox had his strengths and weaknesses as a hitter, he had few peers as an outfielder. Altering his defensive philosophy somewhat following his arrival in Philadelphia, Maddox, who spent his time in San Francisco battling the glare, sun, and wind at Candlestick Park, found that the relative tranquility of Veterans Stadium enabled him to play an extremely shallow center field, claiming, "Most of the balls hit over my head in this park are either against the wall or over it." And even though Maddox did not possess a particularly strong throwing arm, he learned that "by playing in close and charging the ball, I can prevent a runner from taking the extra base."

Better positioning himself by reviewing hitters' spray charts and discussing pitching plans with catcher Bob Boone, Maddox got an excellent jump on the ball and used his tremendous speed to run down drives that other center fielders lacked the ability to reach, prompting noted sportswriter Ray Didinger to claim in the September 1978 issue of *Baseball Digest*, "Two thirds of the Earth are covered by water. The other one third by Garry Maddox," a quote also occasionally attributed to Phillies broadcaster Harry Kalas and Mets broadcaster Ralph Kiner.

Yet, despite his defensive brilliance, Maddox committed the occasional error, one of which came at a most inopportune time in the 1978 NLCS. With the Phillies trailing the Dodgers 2–1 in the series and the score tied at 3–3 in the bottom of the 10th inning of Game 4, Phillies closer Tug McGraw issued a two-out walk to Ron Cey. Maddox then dropped a routine line drive hit by Dusty Baker that would have ended the inning, allowing Bill Russell to subsequently drive in Cey with the winning run from second base with an RBI single. Accepting full culpability for his miscue after the game, Maddox said, "I didn't think it was a tough play at all. It was very routine. It was a line drive right at me that should have been caught. I missed it." Maddox then added, "I've had other crises in my life. This is just another one."

Eventually forgiven by Phillies fans, who appreciated him for all he gave them, both on and off the field, Maddox came to fully embrace the city of Philadelphia, stating in August 1977, "Now, for the first time in my career, I'm having a lot of fun." Displaying his love for his new home, Maddox spent the 1977 offseason raising money for the Child Guidance Clinic, which served the mental health and family therapy needs of Philadelphia's children. In discussing his philanthropic gesture, Maddox said, "I saw this as just a good way to get involved in the community that has treated me so well. But once I visited a few times and saw first-hand the job the clinic does, it became an interest instead of a supposed duty. I don't just represent the clinic. I support it and care about it."

Maddox continued to perform well for the Phillies in 1979 and 1980, hitting 13 homers, driving in 61 runs, scoring 70 times, stealing 26 bases, and batting .281 in the first of those campaigns, before homering 11 times, knocking in 73 runs, swiping 25 bags, and batting .259 the following year. But injuries and a platoon system put in place by new Phillies manager Pat Corrales began to cut into Maddox's playing time shortly thereafter, reducing his offensive output the next few seasons as trade rumors surrounding him abounded. Although Maddox batted over .280 twice more for the Phillies from 1982 to 1985, he never again appeared in more than 119 games, knocked in more than 61 runs, or scored more than 39 times.

Yet, through it all, Maddox remained a true professional, with one local sportswriter commenting midway through the 1984 season, "He has quietly gone about his job with dignity and class after being shopped all over baseball for months."

After undergoing back surgery in December 1984, Maddox assumed a backup role the following year, starting only 44 games in center field. Although Maddox returned to the Phillies in 1986, he chose to announce his retirement on May 7, two weeks after his ailing back prevented him from running down three balls in center in his first start of the season.

In explaining his decision at the time, Maddox said, "It was a very difficult decision in many ways. I felt it was in my best interest and my family's. I'm gonna have a lot of years left after baseball, and I'd like to spend them with my family, and in good health. I was not sure that, by continuing to play baseball, I would be able to do that. You see and read stories about people who played that one game too many, or the boxer who fought one fight too many. I didn't want to risk that."

Over the course of 15 big-league seasons, Maddox hit 117 homers, knocked in 754 runs, scored 777 times, stole 248 bases, batted .285, compiled an on-base percentage of .320, posted a slugging percentage of .413, and collected 1,802 hits, 337 doubles, and 62 triples. As a member of the Phillies, Maddox hit 85 homers, drove in 566 runs, scored 556 times, stole 189 bases, batted .284, compiled an on-base percentage of .320, posted a slugging percentage of .409, and amassed 1,333 hits, 249 doubles, and 42 triples.

After retiring as an active player, Maddox attended Temple University, before becoming CEO of an office furniture company in Philadelphia and, later, a director of the Philadelphia Reserve Bank for four years. Maddox also worked as a spring training instructor for the Phillies and as a color analyst for Phillies games on Philadelphia's now-defunct cable-sports network PRISM from 1987 to 1995. Continuing to contribute to the community, Maddox founded the Urban Youth Golf Association, which is dedicated to linking academics to sports for inner-city children. He also launched Compete 360, which helps train teachers and facilitates student-led projects that explore problems in the classroom and the community.

PHILLIES CAREER HIGHLIGHTS

Best Season

Maddox had an outstanding year in 1977, hitting a career-high 14 homers, driving in 74 runs, scoring 85 times, batting .292, and collecting 10 triples, while doing his usual splendid job of patrolling center field. But he performed even better the previous season, earning a fifth-place finish in the 1976 NL MVP voting by hitting six homers; knocking in 68 runs; scoring 75 others; stealing 29 bases; ranking among the league leaders with 175 hits, 37 doubles, and a .330 batting average; and leading all NL outfielders with 441 putouts, which represented the second-highest total of his career.

Memorable Moments/Greatest Performances

Maddox contributed to a 13–5 win over the Cubs on August 5, 1975, by going 3-for-5, with a homer, four RBIs, and two runs scored.

Maddox gave the Phillies a 4–3 victory over the Mets on September 26, 1975, by knocking in the game-winning run in the bottom of the 12th inning with a two-out bases loaded single to center.

Maddox helped lead the Phillies to a 4–3, 14-inning win over the Pirates on May 29, 1978, by going 4-for-5, with a walk, RBI, and career-high four stolen bases.

Maddox continued to be a thorn in the side of Pittsburgh pitchers on April 17, 1979, going 4-for-5, with a homer, four RBIs, and three runs scored during a 13–2 Phillies win, with his fifth-inning grand slam proving to be the game's big blow.

Maddox played a big role in an 8–7 victory over the Houston Astros in Game 5 of the 1980 NLCS that clinched the pennant for the Phillies, driving in what proved to be the game-winning run with an RBI double in the top of the 10th inning, before making the catch for the final out in the bottom of the frame.

Maddox delivered the big blow in a 5–4 victory over the Astros on June 10, 1981, when he capped a five-run Phillies' rally in the bottom of the eighth inning by hitting a two-out, three-run homer.

Maddox led the Phillies to a 10–5 win over the Montreal Expos on September 8, 1981, by driving in five runs with a homer and single.

Although the Phillies ended up losing the 1983 World Series to the Baltimore Orioles in five games, Maddox gave them a 2–1 win in Game 1 when he led off the top of the eighth inning with a home run off starter Scott McGregor.

Maddox collected five hits in one game for the only time as a member of the Phillies when he went 5-for-6 during an 11–9, 10-inning win over the Atlanta Braves on August 25, 1982.

Notable Achievements

- Batted over .300 once.
- Finished in double digits in triples once.
- Surpassed 30 doubles three times.
- Stole more than 20 bases six times, topping 30 thefts once.
- Led NL with eight sacrifice flies in 1981.
- Finished third in NL with .330 batting average and 37 doubles in 1976.
- Led NL outfielders in putouts twice, fielding percentage once, and double plays once.
- Led NL centerfielders in putouts twice, assists twice, fielding percentage once, and double plays three times.
- Five-time division champion (1976, 1977, 1978, 1980, and 1983).
- Two-time NL champion (1980 and 1983).
- 1980 world champion.
- May 28, 1978, NL Player of the Week.
- Finished fifth in 1976 NL MVP voting.
- 1986 Roberto Clemente Award winner.
- Eight-time Gold Glove Award winner (1975, 1976, 1977, 1978, 1979, 1980, 1981, and 1982).
- Member of Philadelphia Baseball Wall of Fame.
- Member of Philadelphia Sports Hall of Fame.
- Named to Phillies Centennial Team in 1983.

23

CHRIS SHORT

One of the preeminent left-handers in the game during the mid-1960s, Chris Short combined with Jim Bunning to give the Phillies a dynamic tandem at the top of their starting rotation. After struggling during the early stages of his career, Short posted a total of 83 victories from 1964 to 1968, winning at least 17 games on four separate occasions. Consistently ranking among the NL leaders in ERA, strikeouts, and innings pitched as well, Short compiled an ERA under 3.00 five times, recorded more than 200 strikeouts twice, and threw more than 250 innings three times, earning in the process two All-Star selections. A member of the Phillies for 14 seasons, Short continues to rank among the franchise's all-time leaders in several categories nearly 50 years after he threw his last pitch, with his many contributions to the team eventually gaining him induction into the Philadelphia Sports Hall of Fame and landing him a spot on the Philadelphia Baseball Wall of Fame.

Born in Milford, Delaware, on September 19, 1937, J. Christopher Short grew up in a largely rural area some 70 miles north, in the city of Wilmington, where he got his start in organized baseball at Sunny Hills School. Nearly giving up the sport in the 10th grade after he beaned and knocked out a batter while pitching for Lewes High School, Short recalled years later, "I was real wild then. I nearly broke out in tears. I didn't want to pitch anymore. But my high school coach urged me not to give up, said it wasn't my fault."

Heeding the advice of his coach, Short continued to pitch for Lewes High for two more years, before enrolling at Bordentown Military Academy in Bordentown, New Jersey, for his senior year. Developing into a top prospect at Bordentown, Short struck out 147 batters in just 83 innings, enabling him to run his overall high school record to 30-6. Pursued by several major-league clubs, Short ultimately chose to sign with his favorite team, the Phillies, inking his first professional contract with scout John "Jocko" Collins.

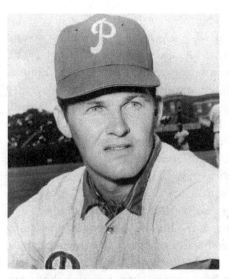

Chris Short ranks fourth in team annals in wins, innings pitched, strikeouts, and shutouts.

Beginning his pro career with the Johnson City Phillies of the Class D Appalachian League, Short went 9-2 with a 3.45 ERA in 1957, earning him a promotion to Class B High Point-Thomasville the following year. After winning 13 of his 26 decisions at Thomasville, the 21-year-old Short began the 1959 campaign in Philadelphia. However, he performed poorly in his only two starts in April, prompting the Phillies to send him down to Triple-A Buffalo for the rest of the year.

Arriving in Philadelphia to stay in 1960, Short subsequently spent his first three major-league seasons working as both a starter and a reliever as he struggled to gain a better command of the strike zone. After going 6-9 and compiling an ERA of 3.94 for a Phillies team that finished last in the NL with a record of 59-95 in 1960, Short regressed somewhat the following year, compiling a record of 6-12 and an ERA of 5.94, while issuing 71 bases on balls in 127 innings of work. However, after developing a slider to go with his live fastball, the 6'4", 205-pound Short began to show signs of maturing in 1962, going 11-9 with an ERA of 3.42, and walking 56 batters in 142 innings pitched, while still spending much of his time working out of the bullpen. Performing especially well down the stretch, Short won six of his last eight decisions and compiled an ERA of 2.59 from August 15 to the end of the year, earning in the process the trust of Phillies manager Gene Mauch, who, during his earlier struggles, quipped that he would trade the southpaw "for a bale of hay."

Coming off his strong finish the previous season, Short assumed a regular spot in the starting rotation in 1963. However, he got off to a slow start, winning just one of his first nine decisions, before straightening himself out during a one-month stint in the bullpen. Returning to the rotation in late July, Short performed exceptionally well the rest of the year, going 8-4, to finish the season with a record of 9-12, while also compiling an ERA of 2.95 and recording 160 strikeouts. Emerging as one of the best pitchers in the senior circuit the following year, Short earned All-Star honors for the first time by posting a record of 17-9, registering 181 strikeouts, and finishing third in the league with an ERA of 2.20 and a WHIP of 1.020. Unfortunately, the season ended on a sour note for Short and the Phillies, since, after holding a 6 1/2-game lead with just 12 games left to play, they lost 10 straight contests, relegating them to a close second-place finish in the NL standings. Manager Gene Mauch subsequently received much of the blame for the team's collapse since he insisted on starting his two best pitchers, Short and Jim Bunning, in eight of the final 12 games. But Short pitched respectably despite the heavy workload, surrendering just six earned runs in 18 innings of work over his final three starts.

Short had another outstanding year in 1965, establishing himself as a legitimate rival to Bunning as the ace of the Phillies' pitching staff by going 18-11, with a 2.82 ERA, 237 strikeouts, five shutouts, 15 complete games, and 297 1/3 innings pitched. Short then became the first Phillies left-hander in 50 years to reach the 20-win plateau in 1966, finishing the season with a record of 20-10, an ERA of 3.54, 177 strikeouts, four shutouts, 19 complete games, and 272 innings pitched.

Yet, despite the success that Short experienced on the mound, his team-mates viewed him as something of an oddity due to his many eccentricities that included frequently taking just an extra shirt, a hairbrush, and a tooth-brush with him on road trips and washing his underwear every night and hanging it out to dry. Just a country boy at heart, Short, said former Phillies teammate Doug Clemens, was "a very unique guy, probably a bit naïve." Meanwhile, *Baseball Digest* once referred to him as "the left-handedest left-hander the Phillies own, as consistent as a three-dollar watch."

Nevertheless, beneath Short's kooky exterior lay the heart of a true competitor who expected to win every time he took the mound, once say-ing, "I feel I'm a better pitcher than the batter is a hitter."

Despite missing six weeks in 1967 with a knee injury he suffered in a collision with a teammate during batting practice, Short earned his second All-Star nomination by finishing third in the league with a 2.39 ERA. Fully recovered by the start of the 1968 season, Short posted some of the best numbers of his career, going 19-13, with a 2.94 ERA, 202 strikeouts, and 269 2/3 innings pitched. However, an injury to his back he sustained during the early stages of the 1969 campaign prevented Short from ever again being a top-flight starter. After undergoing season-ending surgery in June to remove a herniated disk, Short spent three more years in Philadelphia, compiling an overall record of just 17-31 during that time, before being released by the Phillies following the conclusion of the 1972 campaign. Short then signed with the Milwaukee Brewers, for whom he went 3-5 in 1973 while working primarily in relief, before announcing his retirement at the end of the year. Over parts of 14 seasons with the Phillies, Short compiled a record of 132-127, an ERA of 3.38, and a WHIP of 1.283; recorded 1,585 strikeouts; threw 88 complete games, 24 shutouts, and 2,253 innings; and collected 16 saves.

After retiring as an active player, Short returned to Delaware, where he entered the insurance business and continued to pitch in local beer leagues for several more years. Eventually diagnosed with diabetes, Short collapsed at his office in Wilmington, Delaware, on October 20, 1988, the victim of a ruptured brain aneurysm. Found in a semiconscious state by a coworker several hours later, Short subsequently lapsed into a coma, after which he spent 13 months at nearby Christiana Hospital, before ending up in a Wilmington convalescent home. As Short's medical expenses increased, his former Phillies teammates came to his aid, with Art Mahaffey organizing a yearly celebrity golf tournament, the proceeds of which went toward the care of his onetime roommate. Having never regained consciousness, Short died on August 1, 1991, passing away at only 53 years of age.

PHILLIES CAREER HIGHLIGHTS

Best Season

Although Short won 20 games for the only time in his career in 1966, he pitched his best ball for the Phillies two years earlier, earning one of his two All-Star selections in 1964 by going 17-9, with 181 strikeouts, 220 2/3 innings pitched, and a career-best 2.20 ERA and 1.020 WHIP.

Memorable Moments/Greatest Performances

Short defeated the eventual world champion Los Angeles Dodgers 3–2 on September 13, 1963, working all nine innings and allowing just four hits, while recording 14 strikeouts.

Short tossed a pair of complete-game shutouts against the Houston Astros in 1965, surrendering just four hits and striking out 11 batters during a 2–0 Phillies win on April 12, before yielding five hits and recording 13 strikeouts during a 5–0 win on June 13.

Short emerged victorious in a 1–0 pitchers' duel with Pittsburgh's Bob Friend on July 7, 1964, allowing just three hits and striking out seven batters, in going the distance.

Although Short failed to earn a victory in a game called after 18 innings due to time constraints, he worked the first 15 innings of a 0–0 tie with the Mets on October 2, 1965, surrendering nine hits and recording a career-high 18 strikeouts.

Short yielded just three hits during a 12–0 shutout of the Cubs on April 30, 1966, allowing just a double by Ron Santo and a pair of singles by Don Kessinger.

Short hurled another gem on July 17, 1966, surrendering just a sixth-inning single to catcher Jeff Torborg and a seventh-inning single to second baseman Nate Oliver during a 3–0, two-hit shutout of the Dodgers.

Short dominated the Dodgers again on April 10, 1968, yielding just four hits and recording 10 strikeouts during a 2–0 Phillies win.

Short threw a complete-game two-hitter against the Cubs on September 13, 1968, allowing just a fifth-inning double to Ernie Banks and a ninth-inning homer to Glenn Beckert during a 3–1 win.

Short shut out the hard-hitting Pirates on just four hits on May 19, 1970, issuing no walks and striking out 10 batters during a 2–0 Phillies win.

Notable Achievements

- Won 20 games once, surpassing 17 victories three other times.
- Posted winning percentage over .600 three times.
- Compiled ERA under 3.00 five times, finishing with mark below 2.50 twice.
- Struck out more than 200 batters twice.
- Threw 19 complete games in 1966.
- Threw more than 250 innings three times.
- Finished third among NL pitchers in ERA twice, WHIP once, and starts once.
- Ranks among Phillies career leaders in wins (4th), innings pitched (4th), strikeouts (4th), shutouts (4th), pitching appearances (5th), and starts (3rd).
- Two-time NL All-Star (1964 and 1967).
- Member of Philadelphia Baseball Wall of Fame.
- Member of Philadelphia Sports Hall of Fame.

24

LARRY BOWA

Atremendous competitor whose positive attitude and extraordinary work ethic enabled him to overcome his physical limitations, Larry Bowa carved out an extremely successful 16-year major-league career that began in Philadelphia in 1970. The Phillies' starting shortstop for 12 seasons, Bowa used his outstanding speed, soft hands, and accurate throwing arm to establish himself as one of the finest defenders in the game, setting several fielding records for players who manned his position, en route to winning two Gold Glove Awards. A member of Phillies teams that won four division titles and one World Series, Bowa proved to be a solid offensive performer as well, batting over .300 once, scoring more than 90 runs twice, and stealing at least 20 bases nine times, with his excellent all-around play earning him five All-Star selections and one top-five finish in the NL MVP voting. And following the conclusion of his playing career, Bowa returned to Philadelphia, where he spent another 17 seasons serving the Phillies at different times as a coach and manager.

Born in Sacramento, California, on December 6, 1945, Lawrence Robert Bowa had baseball in his blood, with his father, Paul, having played and managed in the St. Louis Cardinals farm system. Recalling the love that her son developed for the game at an early age, Bowa's mother, Mary, said, "Larry first had a baseball in his hand when he was 18 months old. It was always baseball."

Yet, despite the passion he exhibited for the national pastime, Bowa found himself being discouraged from pursuing a career in his favorite sport, with his father advising him, "Don't be a baseball bum. Go to college." Meanwhile, Bowa's baseball coach at McClatchy High School, who cut him from the team three times, told him flatly, "You're not good enough."

Nevertheless, Bowa's stubborn and persistent nature did not allow him to give up his dream of one day playing in the major leagues. After being cut from his high school team for the third time, Bowa honed his skills playing

American Legion ball until he began competing for Sacramento City College when no major-league club selected him in the Amateur Draft. While playing for Sacramento City, Bowa caught the attention of Phillies scout Eddie Bockman, who submitted the following report after watching him get ejected from both ends of a doubleheader: "Have always liked his potential, but his attitude will make you throw up at times. A definite major league prospect if he can keep the bugs out of his head."

Larry Bowa led all NL shortstops in fielding percentage five times.

And years later, Bockman recalled, "I caught him as he was going over to the bus. He was still upset. You know him—throwing helmets, trashing bats. I told him, 'I'll be back to see you. You'll be a pretty good player if you can stay in the game.' He asked me who I was. When I told him, that pretty much quieted him down."

In attempting to explain his unseemly behavior many years later, Bowa said, "People have always thought that I lost my cool because I was cocky. The truth is that I battled hard because I always doubted my ability. Instead of forgetting about my disappointments, I would dwell on them. I was afraid that I was blowing my chance for acceptance or recognition. Now I have a more positive attitude."

Eventually signing with the Phillies for $2,000, Bowa began his pro career with Single-A Spartanburg (South Carolina) in 1966, faring well during spring training before experiencing a major setback in the regular-season opener that he later recounted: "The first bleepin' game, we're playing in Greenville against the New York Mets team. I had a really good spring training, and I felt like a stud. The line on me was, 'This guy from nowhere, he got $2,000, he's a prospect.' First game, we faced Nolan Ryan. Four punchouts. I had no prayer. I figured if this is what professional ball was going to be, I had no chance."

Gathering himself after his inauspicious start, Bowa went on to bat .312 and steal 23 bases for Spartanburg in 1966, before missing most of the ensuing campaign while serving in the military. Bowa then spent the entire 1968 season at Reading, where he batted just .242, prompting manager Frank Lucchesi to later say, "He tends to get sour on himself. He was hitting something like .140 in June and was afraid he was going to be sent out. I sat him down and told him the things that were going to get him to the big leagues were his legs, his glove, his arm, and his hustle. I told him he was my shortstop for the season, no matter what he hit."

With Bob Skinner having replaced Gene Mauch as manager in Philadelphia during the 1968 season, he toyed with the idea of promoting Bowa to the majors the following spring, saying in late March 1969, "He's got the arm, the glove, and the speed. He's our fastest runner, and I wouldn't be afraid to play him in centerfield if the situation arose. I know he'll go after the ball. We feel he'll have excellent utility value to the ball club, and, in the meantime, we'll see if we can get him straightened out at the plate."

However, Bowa told Skinner on the last day of spring training that he preferred to remain in the minor leagues for one more year, later explaining, "I didn't want to make the ball club that soon. They wanted me there as a utility player. I wanted to play every day."

Sent to Triple-A Eugene, Bowa, a natural right-handed batter, learned to switch-hit on the advice of Skinner, who told him that doing so would give him his best chance of making the major leagues as a regular. Reunited with Lucchesi at Eugene, Bowa worked feverishly on developing his skills from the left side of the plate, recalling, "We went out every day and hit, hit, hit. All of a sudden, toward the middle of the year, I started getting into a groove."

Bowa ended up leading Eugene to the PCL Southern Division championship by batting .287 and stealing 48 bases, prompting Lucchesi to say, "I've never seen a kid turn to switch-hitting and do the job he did this past season. Two or three years ago, anybody could knock the bat right out of his hands, but no more. Of course, his speed helps, but he made tremendous improvement from both sides of the plate. He keeps improving as a base-runner too."

With Lucchesi being promoted to manager of the Phillies prior to the start of the 1970 season, he took Bowa with him to Philadelphia, immediately making him the team's starting shortstop. But, when Bowa started the season slowly, he began to doubt his abilities, later saying, "I got to the point where I wondered if I could play up here."

Once again, though, Lucchesi came to the rescue, later revealing the contents of a conversation he had with Bowa when he called him into his office one day: "He had his head down because he thought he was being shipped out. I was sitting down behind my desk. I stood up, walked over to him, put my hand on his shoulder, and I said, 'Larry, forget what's in the paper. You're my shortstop tonight, you're my shortstop tomorrow, and you're my shortstop next week. You're going to be my shortstop all year. Someday, you're going to prove me right that you're going to be one hell of a shortstop. Just remember that. Now get out of here.'"

His confidence restored, Bowa went on to have a decent offensive season, batting .250, scoring 50 runs, and stealing 24 bases, while also committing only 13 errors in the field, with his solid all-around play earning him a third-place finish in the NL Rookie of the Year voting. Although Bowa showed little improvement on offense the following year, batting .249, scoring 74 runs, and swiping 28 bags, he performed exceptionally well in the field, leading all NL shortstops in assists and fielding percentage, at one point going 47 straight games without committing an error.

After batting .250, scoring 67 runs, leading the league with 13 triples, and winning the first Gold Glove of his career in 1972, Bowa missed a month of the ensuing campaign after fracturing a bone above his left ankle trying to steal second base, finishing the year with just 42 runs scored and a batting average of .211. But he rebounded in a big way in 1974, earning his first All-Star selection by batting .275, scoring 97 runs, collecting 184 hits and 10 triples, and stealing a career-high 39 bases. Bowa followed that up with another outstanding season, earning his second consecutive All-Star selection by batting a career-best .305, scoring 79 runs, and stealing 23 bases, despite missing 26 games due to injury.

Although the 5'10", 160-pound Bowa possessed virtually no power at the plate, hitting a total of just 15 home runs over the course of his career, he gradually developed into a solid offensive player by making good use of his excellent speed and taking full advantage of Veterans Stadium's artificial turf by slapping down on the ball. In addition to stealing more than 20 bases nine times, Bowa collected more than 175 hits on four separate occasions and struck out more than 50 times in a season just three times. In describing Bowa's style of play, Joe Torre stated, "He was a terrific player. He made himself a hitter. He was pesky. He made contact, he could run like hell, and he was very reliable at shortstop."

Feisty and combative, Bowa also drew praise from Buck Martinez for the many intangible qualities he possessed, with Martinez saying, "Here's a guy who made himself into a hell of a player—a little, skinny kid who just believed he could play, and he wasn't going to have anybody tell him he couldn't. He is the epitome of a self-made player. He understood he wanted to be a ballplayer, and he played his ass off to become a good player."

While Bowa improved himself dramatically as a hitter following his arrival in Philadelphia, he excelled from the very beginning at shortstop, once saying, "When I came up, people told me that, considering the way I play defense, I could hit .220 and still be in the majors for 10 or 15 years. But that's not the way I am. I'm always trying to improve."

In discussing the keys to playing shortstop, Bowa stated, "Y'know, everybody says I have good hands and everything, but the thing that makes a good shortstop is the footwork involved. If you have good footwork, if you can get to the ball, you can set up and get your body out of the way so you can make the throw. I think that's the most important thing."

Though not particularly fluid in his movements, Bowa had excellent range, rarely bobbled the ball, and possessed a strong and accurate throwing arm, with former Mets shortstop Bud Harrelson saying of his new teammate after he joined the Phillies as a reserve in 1978, "He's the best every-day shortstop I've ever seen. He makes routine plays out of balls I'd have to dive for. If the ball goes in his direction, you know the runner's going to be out."

Despite leading NL shortstops in fielding percentage five times as a member of the Phillies, Bowa finished first among players at his position in assists just once, attributing that fact to the defensive skills of the other players around him when he said, "Schmidt is able to cut off a lot of balls hit to my right, and Maddox plays so shallow that he takes anything over my head."

Although Bowa had something of an off year in 1976, batting just .248 and scoring only 71 runs, he earned his third consecutive All-Star selection by ranking among the top players at his position in assists and fielding percentage, with his consistently excellent play in the field helping the Phillies capture the NL East title for the first of three straight times. Bowa followed that up with two of his finest offensive seasons, batting .280, scoring 93 runs, and stealing 32 bases in 1977, before earning a third-place finish in the NL MVP balloting in 1978 by batting .294, scoring 78 runs, swiping 27 bags, and ranking among the league leaders with 192 hits. Though far less productive at the plate in 1979 (he batted just .241 and scored only 74 runs), Bowa proved to be virtually flawless in the field, committing just six errors, en route to setting a then–major-league record for shortstops with a .991 fielding percentage.

Bowa remained the Phillies' starting shortstop for two more years, batting .267 and scoring 57 runs in 1980, before batting .283 and scoring 34 runs during the strike-shortened 1981 campaign. But his time in Philadelphia came to an end shortly after the Carpenter family, which had owned the Phillies since 1943, sold the team to a group headed by Phils' executive vice president Bill Giles in November 1981. With Bowa having verbally agreed on a new three-year contract with Ruly Carpenter at season's end, he reacted harshly when Giles refused to honor the terms of that agreement and instead offered him just a one-year deal. The feud between the two men eventually became public, with Bowa calling Giles a liar in the media. Forced to intervene, Phillies GM Paul Owens contacted the Chicago Cubs, who agreed to trade their starting shortstop, Iván DeJesús, to the Phillies for Bowa and a minor-league infielder named Ryne Sandberg, in what turned out to be one of the worst swaps the Phils ever made.

Bowa, who in his 12 years with the Phillies hit 13 homers, knocked in 421 runs, scored 816 times, stole 288 bases, batted .264, compiled an on-base percentage of .301, posted a slugging percentage of .324, and collected 1,798 hits, 206 doubles, and 81 triples, spent the next three-and-a-half seasons starting at shortstop for the Cubs, before ending his playing career late in 1985 as a backup with the New York Mets. In addition to his 15 home runs, Bowa retired with 525 RBIs, 987 runs scored, 2,191 hits, 262 doubles, 99 triples, 318 stolen bases, a lifetime batting average of .260, an on-base percentage of .300, a slugging percentage of .320, and then-NL records for most games played (2,222) and highest fielding percentage (.980) by a shortstop.

Following his playing days, Bowa began a lengthy career in coaching that included stints with the Phillies (1988–1996 and 2014–2017), Angels (1997–1999), Mariners (2000), Yankees (2006–2007), and Dodgers (2008–2010). He also managed the Padres from 1987 to 1988 and the Phillies from 2001 to 2004, guiding his former team to two second-place finishes and a pair of third-place finishes. Bowa also worked as an in-studio analyst for ESPN, cohosted a show on Sirius XM radio, and served as an analyst for the MLB Network at various times. Bowa currently is the senior advisor to Phillies GM Sam Fuld.

PHILLIES CAREER HIGHLIGHTS

Best Season

Bowa posted some of the best numbers of his career in 1977, when he hit four homers, knocked in 41 runs, scored 93 times, collected 175 hits, stole 32 bases, and batted .280. But he had his finest all-around season the following year, earning a third-place finish in the 1978 NL MVP voting by hitting three homers, driving in 43 runs, scoring 78 times, batting .294, stealing 27 bases, and establishing career-high marks with 31 doubles and 192 hits, while also leading all NL shortstops in fielding percentage.

Memorable Moments/Greatest Performances

Bowa contributed to a 10–4 win over the Cubs on July 11, 1970, by going 4-for-5, with a triple, three RBIs, and one run scored.

Bowa led the Phillies to a 3–2 victory over the Cardinals on May 3, 1971, by going 4-for-5, with a double, stolen base, and two RBIs, which came on a game-winning bases loaded single in the bottom of the eighth inning.

Bowa collected another four hits during a 4–0 win over the Houston Astros on June 5, 1973, going a perfect 4-for-4, with a double, two stolen bases, and three runs scored.

Bowa keyed a 4–3 victory over the Mets on September 26, 1975, by going 3-for-6 with two triples and scoring the winning run in the bottom of the 12th inning on a single by Garry Maddox.

Bowa helped lead the Phillies to a 15–9 win over the Reds on June 22, 1977, by going 4-for-4, with four RBIs and four runs scored, delivering the game's big blow in the bottom of the seventh inning, when he homered with the bases loaded off southpaw reliever Joe Hoerner.

Bowa helped the Phillies earn a doubleheader sweep of the Mets on September 23, 1978, by going 5-for-5, with a triple, double, three singles, and three RBIs during a 6–3 win in Game 2.

Bowa again hit safely five times during a 23–22, 10-inning win over the Cubs on May 17, 1979, going 5-for-8, with two doubles, a stolen base, and four runs scored.

In addition to performing flawlessly in the field during the 1980 World Series, Bowa excelled for the Phillies on offense, going 9-for-24 (.375), with two RBIs, three runs scored, and three stolen bases.

Notable Achievements

- Batted over .300 once.
- Finished in double digits in triples three times.
- Surpassed 30 doubles once.
- Stole at least 20 bases nine times, topping 30 thefts on three occasions.
- Led NL in triples once, sacrifice hits once, assists once, and at-bats once.

- Led NL shortstops in assists once, fielding percentage five times, and double plays turned once.
- Ranks among Phillies career leaders in hits (6th), triples (7th), stolen bases (6th), sacrifice hits (7th), games played (4th), plate appearances (4th), and at-bats (4th).
- Four-time division champion (1976, 1977, 1978, and 1980).
- 1980 NL champion.
- 1980 world champion.
- May 18, 1975, NL Player of the Week.
- Finished third in 1978 NL MVP voting.
- Two-time Gold Glove Award winner (1972 and 1978).
- Two-time *Sporting News* NL All-Star selection (1975 and 1978).
- Five-time NL All-Star (1974, 1975, 1976, 1978, and 1979).
- Member of Philadelphia Baseball Wall of Fame.
- Member of Philadelphia Sports Hall of Fame.
- Named to Phillies Centennial Team in 1983.

25

CURT SIMMONS

One of the original "Bonus Babies," Curt Simmons arrived in Philadelphia at the tender age of 18, after which he went on to establish himself as one of the National League's top left-handers over the course of the next several seasons. Combining with Robin Roberts to give the Phillies a formidable one-two punch at the top of their starting rotation for much of the 1950s, Simmons won at least 14 games five times and posted a winning percentage over .600 on three separate occasions despite pitching for mostly mediocre teams. A three-time NL All-Star, Simmons also compiled an ERA under 3.00 twice and threw more than 20 complete games once, before arm problems began to limit his effectiveness. A member of both the Philadelphia Baseball Wall of Fame and the Philadelphia Sports Hall of Fame, Simmons continues to rank extremely high in team annals in several pitching categories more than 60 years after he donned a Phillies uniform for the last time.

Born in Egypt, Pennsylvania, on May 19, 1929, Curtis Thomas Simmons grew up during the Great Depression, before the inception of Little League baseball, recalling years later, "We would play pickup games on open fields and behind the schools until we were old enough for American Legion ball. Some kids had bats, we used tire-tap balls, or some kid had a real ball. I remember us walking four miles to play another town. We didn't have coaching then—my father was working in a cement mill and didn't have time for baseball. Times were different. A lot of my stuff comes natural to me."

Evolving into a star athlete at nearby Whitehall High School, Simmons excelled in baseball, football, and basketball, although he chose to focus primarily on further developing his skills on the diamond in his final season. Later crediting much of his success to head coach Bud Nevins, who had previously been a catcher in the farm system of the St. Louis Cardinals, Simmons emerged as a high school phenom by leading his team to three straight Lehigh Valley championships. Particularly outstanding his senior year, Simmons struck out 102 batters and surrendered just 12 hits in 43 innings of work, while also hitting two home runs and batting .465. Excelling in American Legion ball as well, Simmons struck out seven of the nine batters he faced in the Pennsylvania American Legion All-Star Game and earned MVP honors at the East-West All-Star Game, played at the old Polo Grounds in New York.

Curt Simmons led all NL pitchers with six shutouts in 1952.

Pursued heavily by several major-league teams as graduation neared, Simmons eventually narrowed his choices down to the Phillies, Detroit Tigers, and Boston Red Sox, before ultimately deciding to sign with the Phillies on June 16, 1947, making him one of the first of the postwar "bonus babies." Initially assigned to the Wilmington Blue Rocks of the Class B Interstate League, Simmons performed exceptionally well at his first pro stop, compiling a record of 13-5 that earned him a late-season callup. After going the distance in a 3–1 victory over the New York Giants in the final game of the 1947 regular season, Simmons joined the Phillies for good the following year due to a rule in place at the time that permitted "bonus babies" to spend just one year in the minor leagues before being assigned to the major-league roster.

Struggling in his first two full seasons in Philadelphia, Simmons compiled an overall record of just 11-23 and a composite ERA of 4.75 after pitching coach George Earnshaw tried to change his cross-body delivery to help protect his shoulder. However, Simmons began to flourish after he returned to his original pitching motion in 1950, posting a record of 17-8 and an ERA of 3.40, before the nation's involvement in the Korean War resulted in the activation of his National Guard unit in early September. Forced to miss the remainder of the year, Simmons could only watch as the Yankees swept the Phillies in the World Series. With Simmons unable to compete in 1951 as well, the Phillies slipped to fifth place in the NL, prompting manager Eddie Sawyer to later say, "Not having Curt Simmons all year really hurt us in 1951."

Returning from the military in 1952, Simmons earned the first of his three All-Star selections by going 14-8, with a 2.82 ERA, 15 complete games, 141 strikeouts, and a league-leading six shutouts. Despite missing a month of the ensuing campaign after cutting off part of his left big toe while mowing his lawn, Simmons earned All-Star honors once again by compiling a record of 16-13 and an ERA of 3.21, throwing 19 complete games and 238 innings, striking out 138 batters, and tossing four shutouts. Although Simmons subsequently finished just 14-15 in 1954, he performed extremely well once again, ranking among the league leaders with a 2.81 ERA, 125 strikeouts, 21 complete games, and 253 innings pitched.

Simmons, who stood 5'11" and weighed 175 pounds, did not throw particularly hard, depending mostly on offspeed pitches, a tricky fastball, and his deceptive delivery to keep opposing hitters off balance. Nevertheless, the right-handed-hitting Hank Aaron, who hit 6 of his 755 career home runs off Simmons, considered the southpaw to be one of the toughest pitchers he faced, once telling a sportswriter, "Speed had nothing to do with it. It was that motion of his. He would turn his body, give me a view of his backside, then he would throw, and I wouldn't see the ball until a split second before he would let it go . . . then it came floating in like plastic." After suffering through a subpar 1955 campaign during which he went just 8-8 with a 4.92 ERA, Simmons returned to top form the following year, compiling a record of 15-10 and an ERA of 3.36. Simmons then earned his final All-Star nomination in 1957 by going 12-11 with a 3.44 ERA, before his practice of throwing across his body began to catch up with him. Troubled by a sore shoulder and an aching elbow in 1958, Simmons finished 7-14 with a 4.38 ERA, before undergoing elbow surgery during the subsequent offseason. After missing virtually all of the ensuing campaign, Simmons returned to the Phillies in 1960, only to be released in mid-May. Over parts of 13 seasons in Philadelphia, Simmons compiled a record of 115-110, an ERA of 3.66, and a WHIP of 1.332; threw 109 complete games and 18 shutouts; and struck out 1,052 batters in 1,939 2/3 innings of work.

Following his release by the Phillies, Simmons signed with the St. Louis Cardinals, with whom he spent parts of the next seven seasons, performing especially well for them in 1963 and 1964. After going 15-9 with a career-low 2.48 ERA in the first of those campaigns, Simmons contributed to the Cardinals' 1964 World Series championship team by compiling a record of 18-9 and an ERA of 3.43 during the regular season. Simmons remained in St. Louis until June 1966, when the Cardinals sold him to the Chicago Cubs. He subsequently split the next year-and-a-half between the Cubs and the California Angels, before retiring following the conclusion of the 1967 campaign with a career record of 193-183, an ERA of 3.54, a WHIP of 1.307, 163 complete games, 36 shutouts, and 1,697 strikeouts in 3,348 1/3 innings pitched.

Although Simmons briefly returned to the Phillies as part of their minor-league instructional staff in March 1970, he spent most of his post-playing career managing the golf course near Ambler, Pennsylvania, that he and Robin Roberts purchased during their time together in Philadelphia, before retiring to private life. Now 92 years of age, Simmons remains one of baseball's oldest living players.

PHILLIES CAREER HIGHLIGHTS

Best Season

Simmons contributed greatly to the Phillies' unlikely pennant run in 1950 by going 17-8, with a 3.40 ERA, 11 complete games, 214 2/3 innings pitched, and a WHIP of 1.239. But he performed better in two or three other years, with the 1952 campaign standing out as his finest as a member of the Phillies. In addition to compiling a record of 14-8 and leading all NL hurlers with six shutouts, Simmons ranked among the league leaders with a 2.82 ERA, 15 complete games, and a WHIP of 1.192, earning in the process All-Star honors for the first of three times.

Memorable Moments/Greatest Performances

Simmons made his major-league debut a memorable one, surrendering just five hits and recording nine strikeouts during a complete-game 3–1 victory over the New York Giants in the final game of the 1947 regular season.

Although Simmons performed well on the mound during a 9–3 win over the Pirates on June 23, 1949, working all nine innings and allowing six hits, he excelled even more at the plate, going 4-for-5, with a double and an RBI.

Simmons recorded a career-high 12 strikeouts and allowed just two walks and two hits during a 6–0 shutout of the Cubs on May 13, 1952.

Simmons hurled another gem on May 22, 1952, shutting out the Pirates, 6–0, on just three hits, while also driving in three runs with the only home run of his career.

Simmons tossed another three-hit shutout on June 27, 1952, allowing two walks and striking out five during a 6–0 win over the Giants.

Simmons earned a 1–0 victory over the Dodgers on September 23, 1952, by allowing just five hits and recording eight strikeouts over 11 scoreless innings, before giving way to reliever Kent Peterson after the Phillies scored the game's only run in the top of the 12th on an RBI double by Johnny Wyrostek.

Simmons turned in the most dominant pitching performance of his career against the Milwaukee Braves on May 16, 1953, striking out 10 batters and allowing just a leadoff single to Bill Bruton in the top of the first inning, before retiring the next 27 men he faced during a 3–0 Phillies win.

Simmons dominated the Braves again some three months later, surrendering just five hits and recording 10 strikeouts during a 4–1 Phillies win on August 2, 1953.

Notable Achievements

- Won at least 15 games three times.
- Posted winning percentage of at least .600 three times.
- Compiled ERA under 3.00 twice.
- Threw 21 complete games in 1954.
- Threw more than 250 innings once.
- Led NL pitchers with six shutouts in 1952.
- Finished third in NL in ERA once and complete games twice.
- Ranks among Phillies career leaders in wins (5th), innings pitched (5th), strikeouts (9th), shutouts (tied for 6th), and starts (6th).
- 1950 NL champion.
- Three-time NL All-Star (1952, 1953, and 1957).
- Member of Philadelphia Baseball Wall of Fame.
- Member of Philadelphia Sports Hall of Fame.

26

PINKY WHITNEY

One of the finest all-around third basemen of his time, Arthur "Pinky" Whitney spent parts of 10 seasons in Philadelphia, excelling for the Phillies both at the bat and in the field during his two tours of duty with the club. An outstanding hitter, Whitney batted over .300 and knocked in more than 100 runs four times each, while also amassing more than 200 hits, 40 doubles, and 10 triples twice each. An elite defender as well, Whitney led all NL third sackers in fielding percentage twice and topped all players at his position in putouts, assists, and double plays three times each, with his excellent all-around play earning him one All-Star selection and MVP consideration on three separate occasions.

Born in San Antonio, Texas, on January 2, 1905, Arthur Carter Whitney attended local Brackenridge Grammar School, before enrolling at Brackenridge High School. Nicknamed "Pinky" after a popular comic-strip character of the day, Whitney starred in multiple sports at Brackenridge High, excelling in basketball, while also serving as captain of the school's baseball and football teams.

After spending his teenage years idolizing hometown hero and future Hall of Fame outfielder Ross Youngs of the New York Giants, Whitney chose to turn pro himself in 1924 when a scout for the Cleveland Indians offered him $2,500 to sign with the club after watching him play shortstop for a team representing the Alamo-Peck Furniture Company of San Antonio. Electing to forgo a scholarship from the University of Texas because his family needed the money, Whitney soon joined the Decatur Commodores of the Illinois-Indiana-Iowa League, for whom he batted .326 in 1925 and .286 in 1926 while splitting his time between shortstop and third base. Moved to third full-time after he became a member of the Southern Association's New Orleans Pelicans in 1927, Whitney helped his new team win the pennant by batting .336. Yet, despite Whitney's exceptional play at those two stops, the Indians showed no interest in promoting him to the majors, enabling the Phillies to acquire him in the minor-league draft.

In addition to batting over .300 and knocking in more than 100 runs four times each, Pinky Whitney led all NL third basemen in putouts, assists, and double plays three times.
Courtesy of MearsonlineAuctions.com

Joining the Phillies in 1928, the 23-year-old Whitney had an outstanding rookie season, hitting 10 homers, driving in 103 runs, scoring 73 times, collecting 35 doubles, and batting .301. Impressed with Whitney's strong play and serious demeanor, sportswriter Tommy Holmes wrote, "The best all-around star of the Philadelphia infield is Arthur Whitney, called 'Pinky' for the boyish mildness which he does not possess. Whitney wears his cap low over a pair of piercing black eyes and carries his underslung chin thrust outward like a heavyweight pugilist. He is a good hitter and a bear at bat with men on base. And there are few better third basemen anywhere than Pinky Whitney."

Performing even better his second year in the league, Whitney hit eight homers, knocked in 115 runs, scored 89 others, collected 200 hits, batted .327, compiled an on-base percentage of .390 and a slugging percentage of .482, and ranked among the league leaders with 43 doubles and 14 triples. Equally impressive in the field, Whitney led all NL third basemen in putouts, assists, and double plays. Continuing his outstanding play in 1930, Whitney homered eight times, drove in 117 runs, scored 87 others, collected 207 hits, 41 doubles, and five triples, batted .342, compiled an OPS of .849, and once again led all NL third sackers in putouts, assists, and double plays, prompting the recently retired Grover Cleveland Alexander, who ended his Hall of Fame career with the Phillies that year, to proclaim, "Pinky Whitney is the greatest third baseman in baseball. It's a shame he couldn't have gotten with a winning club. That boy is a wonderful fielder and one of the most dangerous hitters in the game."

Hampered by injuries in 1931, Whitney batted just .287 and drove in only 74 runs. But he returned to top form the following year, when, after being named team captain, he hit 13 homers, finished third in the league with 124 RBIs, scored 93 runs, batted .298, and led all players at his position in putouts, assists, double plays, and fielding percentage.

Listed generously by Baseball-reference at 5'10" and 165 pounds, Whitney likely stood closer to 5'8". A right-handed batter who drove the ball well to all fields, Whitney possessed a keen batting eye, rarely going after bad pitches and striking out more than 50 times just twice his entire career. In addressing Whitney's ability to hit the ball with authority, fellow third baseman Pie Traynor stated, "He can belt your brains out with his slashing drives."

An outstanding curveball hitter who excelled at hitting behind the runner on the hit-and-run play, Whitney proved to be especially tough with men on base, with Cardinals catcher and former Phillies teammate Jimmie Wilson saying, "He won't help you any by going after bad balls. And he's twice as mean with runners on the cushions."

Meanwhile, the *Charleston Daily Mail* in West Virginia extolled Whitney's fielding ability, claiming, "He can dive full length over the bag for a drive down the foul line, bound back to his feet and throw the runner out. He can slip like a goose in front of the shortstop, spear the ball in his glove and throw in almost one motion. And he has scarcely an equal at coming in for the slow ones, taking them in his bare hands and shooting them to the bag."

And, although Whitney remained quiet, reserved, and soft-spoken off the playing field, he proved to be a fierce competitor who got everything possible out of his somewhat limited natural ability.

Plagued by an ailing back that he injured during spring training, Whitney got off to a slow start in 1933, batting just .264 through mid-June, before being dealt to the Boston Braves for two players and an undisclosed amount of cash believed to be somewhere between $50,000 and $75,000 on June 15. Whitney subsequently spent the next two-and-a-half years in Boston, failing to achieve the same level of success he attained with the Phillies, although he did lead all NL third basemen with 12 home runs, 79 RBIs, and a .968 fielding percentage in 1934.

Traded back to the Phillies for utility infielder Mickey Haslin during the early stages of the 1936 campaign, Whitney performed well over the season's final five months, earning his lone All-Star selection by batting .294, hitting six homers, and driving in 59 runs. He followed that up by hitting eight homers, knocking in 79 runs, and ranking among the league leaders with a .341 batting average in 1937, with his strong play earning him a top-15 finish in the NL MVP voting. After Whitney spent the next two seasons as a part-time player, the Phillies released him in December 1939. Whitney subsequently spent one year playing in the minor leagues for the Toledo Mud Hens, before retiring from professional baseball. Ending his big-league career with 93 home runs, 927 RBIs, 696 runs scored, 1,701 hits, 303 doubles, 56 triples, a .295 batting average, a 343 on-base percentage, and a .415 slugging percentage, Whitney hit 69 homers, knocked in

734 runs, scored 554 times, batted .307, compiled an on-base percentage of .357, posted a slugging percentage of .432, and collected 1,329 hits, 237 doubles, and 48 triples during his time in Philadelphia. Meanwhile, in 8 of his 12 years in the majors, Whitney ranked either first or second among NL third basemen in fielding percentage.

Following his playing days, Whitney returned to his native San Antonio, where he operated a bowling alley, managed an amateur baseball team, and worked for the San Antonio Spurs. Yet, even though Whitney spent his remaining years living in San Antonio, he continued to hold the city of Philadelphia and its fans close to his heart until he died from cancer at the age of 82 on September 1, 1987, once recalling, "Old Philly, lowly Philly, it had the worst water, best ice cream and most loyal fans in the game. They'd really fight for you. They'd ride the umpires and the visiting ball players. We'd get beat 14–0, 14–2 in a doubleheader, and they'd still be cheering for us."

PHILLIES CAREER HIGHLIGHTS

Best Season

Although the National League's use of a livelier ball in 1929 and 1930 enabled Whitney to compile the most impressive offensive numbers of his career those two seasons, he played his best ball for the Phillies in 1932, when, in addition to batting .298 and ranking among the league leaders with 11 triples, he established career-high marks with 13 homers, 124 RBIs, and 93 runs scored. Particularly outstanding during the month of July, Whitney set a club record for third basemen by driving in 38 runs in 30 games.

Memorable Moments/Greatest Performances

Whitney helped lead the Phillies to a 10–7 win over the Reds on June 16, 1928, by going 4-for-5, with three RBIs and two runs scored.

Whitney did most of the damage against Hall of Fame right-hander Dazzy Vance during a 4–3, 13-inning win over the Dodgers on June 30, 1928, hitting a solo homer off him in the top of the seventh inning, before driving in a pair of runs with a bases loaded single in the 13th.

Whitney gave the Phillies a 2–1 victory over the Cubs on May 6, 1929, when he drove in the winning run from third base with a one-out, bases loaded single in the bottom of the ninth inning.

Whitney fell a single short of hitting for the cycle when he homered, doubled, tripled twice, knocked in two runs, and scored three times during a 13–5 rout of the Pirates on July 30, 1929.

After hitting a game-tying two-out, two-run homer off Dazzy Vance in the top of the ninth inning, Whitney gave the Phillies a 4–3 victory over the Dodgers on July 3, 1932, when he delivered the winning run two innings later with an RBI single off Vance.

Whitney helped the Phillies complete a doubleheader sweep of the Pirates on July 30, 1932, by going 4-for-5, with four RBIs and three runs scored during a 13–3 win in Game 2.

Although the Phillies lost to the Cardinals 11–6 on May 18, 1936, Whitney hit two home runs in one game for the only time in his career, finishing the contest with five RBIs.

Whitney set the tone for a 15–0 thrashing of the Giants on May 22, 1936, by hitting a grand slam home run off Freddie Fitzsimmons in the top of the first inning.

After hitting a three-run homer one inning earlier, Whitney gave the Phillies a 9–8 victory over the Pirates on July 17, 1937, by delivering a game-winning RBI double in the bottom of the ninth.

Whitney contributed to a 13–11 victory over the Reds on July 24, 1937, by going 4-for-5, with two doubles, four RBIs, and two runs scored.

Whitney picked up the last RBI of his career on June 6, 1939, when he gave the Phillies a 9–8 victory over the Cubs by driving in the winning run from third base with a pinch-hit single to center field in the bottom of the ninth inning.

Notable Achievements

- Batted over .300 four times, topping the .340 mark twice.
- Knocked in more than 100 runs four times.
- Surpassed 200 hits twice.
- Finished in double digits in triples twice.
- Surpassed 30 doubles five times, amassing more than 40 two-baggers twice.
- Led NL in games played once.
- Finished third in NL with 124 RBIs in 1932.
- Led NL third basemen in putouts three times, assists three times, fielding percentage twice, and double plays three times.
- Ranks ninth in franchise history with 117 sacrifice hits.
- 1936 NL All-Star.

27

PAT BURRELL

elected by the Phillies with the first overall pick of the 1998 MLB Amateur Draft, Pat Burrell arrived in Philadelphia two years later with huge expectations surrounding him. Although the man who became known as "Pat the Bat" for his outstanding power at the plate subsequently proved to be something of a disappointment to many Phillies fans, who often voiced their displeasure over his penchant for striking out, he nevertheless established himself as a top slugger during his nine-year stint in the City of Brotherly Love, surpassing 30 homers four times and 100 RBIs twice, while also posting a slugging percentage over .500 five times and an OPS in excess of .900 twice. A solid outfielder as well, Burrell led all NL left fielders in putouts once and assists twice, with his strong all-around play and outstanding leadership ability making him a key contributor to Phillies teams that won two division titles, one pennant, and one World Series.

Born in Eureka Springs, Arkansas, on October 10, 1976, Patrick Brian Burrell grew up in a blue-collar family that moved to Boulder Creek, California, during his youth. A sports enthusiast from an early age, Pat played football, basketball, and baseball as a child, with the Burrells' backyard serving as the backdrop for year-round contests.

Continuing to compete in all three sports at San Lorenzo Valley High School, Burrell starred at quarterback on the gridiron, center on the hardwood, and pitcher and third base on the diamond his freshman year. However, prior to the start of his sophomore season, Burrell, who aspired to one day play baseball in the major leagues, transferred to Bellarmine College Preparatory, an all-boys Jesuit high school in San Jose that competed in the more visible West Coast Athletic League.

After spending his first two years at Bellarmine serving as a member of the school's baseball, basketball, and football teams, Burrell decided to focus exclusively on his favorite sport his senior year. Developing a reputation as an elite slugger in his final season at Bellarmine, Burrell earned California Coaches 1995 Player of the Year honors by hitting 11 homers, driving in

29 runs, and batting .369. Subsequently recruited by several
major colleges, Burrell ultimately
elected to enroll at the University
of Miami after rejecting a contract
tendered him by the Boston Red
Sox, who selected him in the 43rd
round of the 1995 MLB Draft.

Continuing his exceptional
play at Miami, Burrell won the
Golden Spikes Award as the best
player in college baseball at the
end of his junior year and gained
First-Team All-America recognition three straight times by hitting
a total of 61 homers, driving in
187 runs, and drawing 170 bases

Pat Burrell hit more than 30 home runs
for the Phillies four times. **Courtesy of
Scott Ableman**

on balls in just 162 games, prompting Miami batting coach Turtle Thomas
to say of his protégé, "He's a pretty natural hitter. He understands hitting,
and he can fix himself. He's got a very good thought process at the plate.
He's just a guy who sees it and hits it."

Burrell also drew high praise from Hurricanes head baseball coach Jim
Morris after the Phillies selected him with the very first pick of the 1998
MLB Draft, with Morris saying at the time, "I've seen some great players.
I've seen some first picks, but I'll tell you, I've never seen anyone hit the ball
as hard as he does consistently. It was really a dream to get the opportunity
to coach him."

A third baseman in college, Burrell moved across the diamond to first
base after being assigned to the Class A Clearwater Phillies, for whom he
batted .303 with seven homers and 30 RBIs in 37 games in 1998. Advancing rapidly through the Phillies farm system, Burrell finished the ensuing
campaign with the Triple-A Scranton/Wilkes-Barre Red Barons after establishing himself as the organization's top minor-league prospect by hitting
29 home runs and batting .320. Struggling somewhat in the field, though,
Burrell switched positions once again, this time moving from first base to
left field.

Promoted to the parent club in May 2000, Burrell ended up appearing
in 111 games with the Phillies, earning a fourth-place finish in the NL
Rookie of the Year voting by hitting 18 homers, driving in 79 runs, and
batting .260, despite striking out 139 times. Impressed with the youngster's

strong play, Ron Gant, whom Burrell replaced as the Phillies' starting left fielder, stated, "Pat's going to be here for a long time. He's going to be the man here."

Phillies manager Terry Francona also sang Burrell's praises, saying, "He's a big, strong kid with a quick bat, and he's a better athlete than we were ready to give him credit for coming in. He didn't get outworked by anybody. He was quiet, he listened, he blended in, he did a good job."

In discussing the skill set of his new teammate, Bobby Abreu gushed, "He is awesome. He is young, and he really has power and speed."

Curt Schilling added, "Pat has big, big pop. But what he shows more of than any young player I've ever seen is deep-count discipline."

Burrell followed up his solid rookie season by hitting 27 homers, knocking in 89 runs, scoring 70 times, batting .258, and leading all NL outfielders with 18 assists in 2001, although he also finished third in the league with 162 strikeouts. Emerging as one of the senior circuit's foremost sluggers in 2002, Burrell batted .282, scored 96 runs, and ranked among the league leaders with 37 home runs and 116 RBIs, prompting the Phillies to sign him to a six-year, $50 million contract at season's end. But with Burrell putting too much pressure on himself to live up to the terms of his new deal, he suffered through a horrific 2003 campaign during which he hit just 21 homers, knocked in only 64 runs, and batted just .209, with his poor performance drawing him a considerable amount of criticism from Phillies fans and the local media.

Rebounding somewhat in 2004, Burrell hit 24 homers, drove in 84 runs, and batted .257, despite being slowed by a wrist injury that forced him to miss 35 games. After undergoing surgery during the subsequent offseason, Burrell returned to top form in 2005, earning a seventh-place finish in the NL MVP voting by hitting 32 home runs, finishing second in the league with a career-high 117 RBIs, scoring 78 times, batting .281, and compiling an on-base percentage of .389 and a slugging percentage of .504.

Although the right-handed-hitting Burrell, who stood 6'4" and weighed 235 pounds, built his reputation primarily on his ability to deliver the long ball, he proved to be surprisingly nimble for a man his size, displaying good speed both on the bases and in the outfield. Eventually turning himself into a solid outfielder, Burrell got a good jump on the ball and possessed an above-average throwing arm. Extremely popular with his teammates as well, Burrell set an example for the other players on the ballclub with his extraordinary work ethic, with Phillies coach Gary Varsho stating, "Let's put it this way: Pat's one of those kids who maybe doesn't have to listen, but he gets in the cage and works as hard as anybody I've ever seen. He doesn't just want to be a big-leaguer, but a superstar—a front-line, all-star, major-league player. He has those types of aspirations."

And when discussing his longtime teammate years later, Jimmy Rollins said, "He definitely worked hard. You don't get the nickname 'The Machine' by not working hard. You don't get that big, billboard chest hanging out without working hard."

Meanwhile, former Phillies manager Charlie Manuel spoke of Burrell's engaging personality and leadership ability when he stated, "Pat Burrell, he has tremendous personality. He'd always come in there and talk smack with [pitching coach] Dubee and me, he'd pick at you, he'd bring his bulldog and let him come underneath my desk. But he was always at the ballpark, and he wanted to win. I'd say it started around 2007 when he really got involved more with the team. I think when we changed our team, Pat got into our team more. All of our guys came together, and he was definitely a leader on our team. . . . He was a determined player."

Burrell followed up his outstanding 2005 season with another solid year, hitting 29 homers, driving in 95 runs, scoring 80 times, batting .258, and compiling an on-base percentage of .388 and a slugging percentage of .502 in 2006. Then, after posting extremely similar numbers in 2007, he helped lead the Phillies to the pennant the following year by homering 33 times, knocking in 86 runs, scoring 74 others, batting .250, and compiling an on-base percentage of .367 and a slugging percentage of .507. Although Burrell subsequently collected just one hit in 14 official at-bats during the Phillies' five-game victory over the Tampa Bay Rays in the World Series, it proved to be a big one, with his leadoff double in the seventh inning of the series clincher igniting the game-winning rally.

Ironically, the double that Burrell delivered in the 2008 World Series finale proved to be his last hit as a member of the Phillies. After haggling with the veteran outfielder over a new contract during the subsequent off-season, the Phillies decided to sign Raúl Ibáñez instead and let Burrell leave via free agency. Inking a two-year deal with Tampa Bay, Burrell left Philadelphia with career totals of 251 home runs, 827 RBIs, 655 runs scored, 1,166 hits, 253 doubles, and 14 triples, a lifetime batting average of .257, an on-base percentage of .367, and a slugging percentage of .485.

Burrell ended up spending only one full season in Tampa Bay, hitting just 14 homers, driving in only 64 runs, and batting just .221 in 2009, before joining the eventual world champion San Francisco Giants during the early stages of the ensuing campaign. After one more year in San Francisco, Burrell announced his retirement, ending his career with 292 home runs, 976 RBIs, 767 runs scored, 1,393 hits, 299 doubles, 16 triples, a

.253 batting average, a .361 on-base percentage, and a .472 slugging percentage. After retiring as an active player, Burrell became a scout for the Giants, before eventually accepting a position as an in-studio analyst for NBC Sports. Remaining at that post for just one year, Burrell returned to the Giants in 2020 as hitting coach for the team's Class A affiliate in the California League.

PHILLIES CAREER HIGHLIGHTS

Best Season

Although Burrell earned his only top-10 finish in the NL MVP voting in 2005 by hitting 32 homers, finishing second in the league with 117 RBIs, scoring 78 times, batting .281, and compiling an OPS of .892, he posted slightly better overall numbers in 2002, when, in addition to placing third in the league with 116 RBIs, he established career-high marks with 37 home runs, 96 runs scored, 39 doubles, a batting average of .282, and an OPS of .920.

Memorable Moments/Greatest Performances

Burrell led the Phillies to a 10–5 win over the Mets on June 21, 2000, by homering twice in one game for the first time in his career, reaching the seats against Al Leiter with no one on base in the top of the sixth inning, before taking Armando Benítez deep with the bases loaded in the ninth.

Burrell contributed to a 10–4 victory over the Padres on August 8, 2000, by driving in five runs with a pair of homers, with his eighth-inning grand slam off Kevin Walker breaking the game open.

Burrell delivered the key blow in a 5–3 win over the Mets on May 28, 2001, when he homered against Armando Benítez with one man aboard in the top of the 10th inning.

Burrell gave the Phillies a 3–2 win over the Florida Marlins on April 7, 2002, when he led off the bottom of the 11th inning with a home run off Braden Looper.

Burrell provided further heroics three days later when his two-run homer in the bottom of the 11th inning gave the Phillies a 7–5 victory over the Atlanta Braves.

Burrell helped lead the Phillies to a 16–2 rout of the Braves on April 9, 2003, by driving in five runs against Greg Maddux with a pair of homers.

After tying the score with a solo homer two innings earlier, Burrell gave the Phillies an 8–6 win over the Giants on August 9, 2003, by reaching the seats with one man on in the top of the 10th.

Burrell turned in an outstanding all-around effort during a 7–3 win over the Cardinals on April 27, 2004, going 4-for-4 with two doubles and three RBIs at the plate, while also robbing former Phillies teammate Scott Rolen of a home run with a leaping catch against the left field wall and throwing out Albert Pujols at third base following a single by Édgar Rentería.

Less than one week later, on May 2, 2004, Burrell delivered a big two-out, two-run pinch-hit homer off Matt Mantei of the Arizona Diamond-backs in the bottom of the ninth inning that tied the score at 4–4. The Phillies eventually won the game, 6–5, in 14 innings.

Burrell led the Phillies to a 10–4 win over the Cardinals on April 9, 2005, by going 4-for-5, with a homer, double, and five RBIs.

Burrell drove in all the runs the Phillies scored during a 4–3 win over the Astros on September 15, 2006, when he homered off Roger Clemens in the first inning with the bases loaded.

Burrell proved to be the difference in a 7–2 victory over the Cubs on May 11, 2007, driving in five runs with a pair of homers.

Burrell gave the Phillies a dramatic 6–5 win over the Giants on May 2, 2008, when he homered off closer Brian Wilson with one on and two out in the bottom of the 10th inning.

Burrell helped lead the Phillies to a 6–2 win over the Milwaukee Brewers in Game 4 of the 2008 NLDS by going 3-for-4, with two homers and four RBIs.

Notable Achievements

- Hit more than 30 home runs four times, topping 20 homers on four other occasions.
- Knocked in more than 100 runs twice.
- Surpassed 30 doubles three times.
- Walked more than 100 times twice.
- Compiled on-base percentage of .400 once.
- Posted slugging percentage over .500 five times.
- Compiled OPS over .900 twice.
- Finished second in NL with 117 RBIs in 2005.
- Finished third in NL in RBIs once and bases on balls twice.
- Led NL outfielders with 18 assists in 2001.

- Led NL left fielders in putouts once and assists twice.
- Ranks among Phillies career leaders in home runs (4th), RBIs (10th), bases on balls (5th), extra-base hits (11th), and sacrifice flies (11th).
- Two-time division champion (2007 and 2008).
- 2008 NL champion.
- 2008 world champion.
- Two-time NL Player of the Week.
- Finished seventh in 2005 NL MVP voting.
- Member of Philadelphia Baseball Wall of Fame.

28

COLE HAMELS

O nce called "the best lefthander in the National League" by Atlanta Braves Hall of Fame third baseman Chipper Jones, Cole Hamels spent parts of 10 seasons in Philadelphia, amassing the sixth-most wins and the third-most strikeouts in franchise history during that time. Consistently ranking among the NL leaders in wins, strikeouts, and ERA, Hamels surpassed 15 victories twice, recorded more than 200 strikeouts three times, and compiled an ERA under 3.00 twice, earning in the process three All-Star selections and Cy Young consideration on four separate occasions. Nevertheless, Hamels, who contributed significantly to Phillies teams that won five division titles, two pennants, and one World Series, will always be remembered most fondly in the City of Brotherly Love for his brilliant pitching during the 2008 postseason that led the Phillies to their second world championship.

Born in San Diego, California, on December 27, 1983, Colbert Michael Hamels grew up some 25 miles north, in the town of Rancho Bernardo, where he spent his youth rooting for Tony Gwynn, Trevor Hoffman, and the rest of the San Diego Padres. Yet, despite his allegiance to his hometown team, Hamels idolized Atlanta Braves pitcher Tom Glavine, after who he hoped to one day pattern his own career.

After attending Meadowbrook Middle School, Hamels enrolled at Rancho Bernardo High School, where, in addition to excelling in the classroom (he scored a 1510 out of 1600 on the SAT), he developed into a top pitching prospect, leading the Broncos to three straight division championships. Garnering the attention of scouts with his 94-mph fastball, Hamels recalled, "Where I grew up in San Diego, at my high school games there were like 30 or 40 scouts a game . . . the kids in the Midwest, in farm towns, they might get one."

Hamels, though, experienced a setback prior to the start of his junior year, when, after fracturing his left arm in a pickup football game earlier in the day, he took the mound against a local rival. Recalling the events that

Cole Hamels's superb pitching during the 2008 postseason led the Phillies to their second world championship.
Courtesy of Keith Allison

subsequently transpired, Broncos pitching coach Mark Furtak, whom Hamels failed to inform of his injury, later told the *San Diego Union-Tribune*, "He threw a pitch, and it went to the top of the backstop. You could hear it [his arm] pop. . . . It's a sound I never heard before, and I never want to hear again."

After missing the entire season, Hamels showed no ill effects from his injury the following year, winning 10 games, compiling an ERA of 0.39, and recording 130 strikeouts in 71 innings of work, with his fabulous performance prompting the Phillies to select him with the 17th overall pick of the 2002 MLB Draft.

Hamels spent the next three years advancing through the Phillies' farm system, although he sustained injuries in 2004 and 2005 that slowed his progression somewhat. After missing several starts in 2004 with a strained left elbow, Hamels sat out the first two months of the ensuing campaign while recovering from a broken bone in his hand he suffered during a barroom fight with a local patron. Shortly after Hamels returned to action, he had to be shut down again when he began experiencing severe spasms in his lower back caused by a balky disk pressing against his spine.

Finally promoted to the Phillies early in 2006 after he surrendered just one run and recorded 36 strikeouts in his three starts at Triple-A Scranton/Wilkes-Barre, Hamels made his major-league debut on May 12, 2006, allowing just one hit, issuing five walks, and striking out seven batters over the first five innings of an 8–4 win over the Cincinnati Reds. Although Hamels later spent three weeks on the disabled list with a sprained left shoulder, he ended up having a solid rookie season, finishing the year with a record of 9-8, an ERA of 4.08, and 145 strikeouts in 132 1/3 innings of work. Particularly effective after the Phillies acquired Jamie Moyer in mid-August, Hamels went 7-3 with a 2.70 ERA in his last 12 starts, soaking in as much information as possible from the veteran southpaw, who shared with him his knowledge of pitching and opposing batters.

Continuing to heed the advice of Moyer and Phillies pitching coach Rich Dubee in 2007, Hamels developed into one of the league's top starters, earning All-Star honors and a sixth-place finish in the NL Cy Young voting by going 15-5, with a 3.39 ERA, a WHIP of 1.124, and 177 strikeouts in 183 1/3 innings pitched, despite missing a handful of starts with a tender elbow.

Commenting on the tremendous strides that Hamels made his second year in the league, Moyer said, "He's a great kid. He's learned a lot. . . . I think he's well on his way to becoming a great pitcher."

Expressing similar sentiments, Phillies backup catcher Chris Coste stated, "He really doesn't have a ceiling. . . . I'm not going to predict that he's a Hall of Famer or anything like that. But he's going to be an ace of a pitching staff for a long time."

Meanwhile, Hamels's childhood idol, Tom Glavine, said, "He's impressive. He's made the progression to throwing more strikes and being more aggressive with all his pitches."

Hamels performed extremely well once again in 2008, helping to lead the Phillies to their second straight division title by compiling a record of 14-10 and an ERA of 3.09, recording 196 strikeouts, finishing second in the league with 227 1/3 innings pitched, and leading all NL hurlers with a WHIP of 1.082. Even better in the postseason, Hamels went a perfect 4-0, earning NLCS MVP honors by winning both his starts against the Dodgers, before also being named World Series MVP after he started two games and won his lone decision against Tampa Bay.

Expressing his admiration for Hamels following the conclusion of the Fall Classic, Rays All-Star third baseman Evan Longoria commented, "We knew he was good, but I didn't know he was that good."

Also impressed with Hamels's exceptional mound work, Rays manager Joe Maddon claimed, "Hamels has probably the best change-up—one of the best change-ups—in all of baseball."

Although the 6'4", 205-pound Hamels relied heavily on his changeup to navigate his way through opposing lineups, his arsenal also included a four-seam fastball that consistently clocked in the low- to mid-90s, a cut fastball that typically registered somewhere between 87 and 89 miles per hour on the radar gun, and a sharp-breaking curveball that approached the plate at somewhere between 73 and 77 mph. In discussing the problems that Hamels presented to opposing hitters with his vast array of offerings, Chipper Jones said, "You have to respect his fastball, and his change-up is devastating. If you're guessing fastball and you get change-up, you're way out in front of it. His change-up is a soft sinker that just falls down."

In addition to his superior "stuff," Hamels possessed tremendous poise and self-confidence, with fellow Phillies pitcher Rhéal Cormier saying, "He doesn't seem to get rattled."

Phillies teammate David Dellucci commented, "The way he handles himself on the mound and in the clubhouse . . . that's what superstars are made of."

Revealing the confidence that he placed in the ace of his pitching staff, Phillies manager Charlie Manuel stated, "When I send Cole Hamels to the mound, I expect to look good."

Hamels also received high praise from teammate Chase Utley, who said, "He's obviously a great pitcher, and he's done a lot for this organization. He has the advantage of being left-handed; he has the advantage of being tall. He throws 91–95 miles per hour. He has a great change-up, curveball, and cut fastball. He wants to succeed."

Hamels had something of an off year in 2009, finishing just 10-11 with a 4.32 ERA, before pitching some of the best ball of his career over the course of the next three seasons. After going 12-11 with an ERA of 3.06 and 211 strikeouts in 2010, Hamels earned All-Star honors the following year by compiling a record of 14-9, striking out 194 batters in 216 innings of work, and ranking among the league leaders with an ERA of 2.79 and a WHIP of 0.986. Hamels gained All-Star recognition once again in 2012, when, after undergoing elbow and hernia surgeries during the offseason, he finished third in the league with 216 strikeouts and compiled a record of 17-6, an ERA of 3.05, and a WHIP of 1.124.

Yet even though Hamels performed extremely well on the mound for the Phillies, he never truly felt at home in the City of Brotherly Love, due primarily to the disconnect he felt with the hometown fans, who found fault with the immature manner with which he conducted himself during the early stages of his career. Hamels first drew negative attention to himself when, after struggling on the mound against Colorado in the opening game of the 2007 NLDS, he blamed his troubles on a long-sleeve shirt that he claimed made him sweat profusely, thereby hindering his ability to grip the baseball. Then, after whining about being underpaid in 2008, Hamels pouted on the mound during the 2009 NLCS as a way of showing his displeasure with the defensive play of some of his teammates. Public disdain for Hamels subsequently peaked during the 2009 World Series, when, following a Game 3 loss to the Yankees, he told reporters, "I can't wait for it [the season] to end. It's been mentally draining. It's one of those things where, a year in, you just can't wait for a fresh start."

To his credit, though, Hamels later accepted full culpability for his lack of popularity with the Philly Faithful, admitting, "I wasn't relatable earlier on. I was just this young guy from Southern California, and I had to learn and grow up."

Hampered by poor run support in 2013 and 2014, Hamels posted a combined record of just 17-23, although he struck out close to 200 batters each year and ranked among the league leaders with a 2.46 ERA in the second of those campaigns. But after going just 6-7 with a 3.64 ERA through the first four months of the 2015 season, Hamels found himself heading to Texas when the Phillies traded him to the Rangers for six minor leaguers on July 31. Hamels left Philadelphia with a career record of 114-90, an ERA of 3.30, a WHIP of 1.145, 14 complete games, seven shutouts, and 1,844 strikeouts in 1,930 innings pitched.

Performing well for the Rangers following his arrival in Texas, Hamels helped lead them to consecutive division titles by going 7-1 over the final two months of the 2015 season, before earning All-Star honors the following year by compiling a record of 15-5 and an ERA of 3.32, while also registering 200 strikeouts in 200 innings of work. After splitting the next three seasons between the Rangers and Chicago Cubs, Hamels signed with the Atlanta Braves when he became a free agent at the end of 2019. However, he ended up appearing in only one game for them, before being shut down for the season after suffering a shoulder injury. Hamels's shoulder troubles continued into 2021, when he signed with the Dodgers in August but did not throw a single pitch.

Hamels currently boasts a career record of 163-122, an ERA of 3.43, a WHIP of 1.183, 17 complete games, seven shutouts, and 2,560 strikeouts in 2,698 innings pitched.

If Hamels is unable to resume his big-league career, he will likely continue to keep himself busy with the Hamels Foundation, an organization he created with his wife, Heidi, during his time in Philadelphia that provides at-risk schools in the area with playground equipment and other educational supplies. Hamels also coaches a yearly all-star hitting and pitching clinic for athletes, ages 12–17, and gives back to American troops for their service through Operation 35, which provides military veterans and their guests tickets to home games.

PHILLIES CAREER HIGHLIGHTS

Best Season

A strong case could certainly be made for identifying the 2008 campaign as the finest of Hamel's career since, after going 14-10, with 196 strikeouts, a 3.09 ERA, and a league-leading 1.082 WHIP during the regular season, he led the Phillies to the world championship by compiling a perfect 4-0 record in the postseason, earning in the process NLCS and World Series MVP honors. It could also be argued that Hamels pitched his best ball for the Phillies in 2011, when he earned a fifth-place finish in the NL Cy Young voting by going 14-9, with a 2.79 ERA, 194 strikeouts, and a career-best WHIP of 0.986. Nevertheless, I opted to go with 2012, a season in which Hamels finished 17-6, with a 3.05 ERA, 216 strikeouts, and a WHIP of 1.124.

Memorable Moments/Greatest Performances

In addition to allowing just five hits during a 4–1 complete-game win over the Reds on April 21, 2007, Hamels recorded a career-high 15 strikeouts.

Hamels nearly matched that total on September 28, 2007, striking out 13 batters in eight innings of work during a 6–0 win over the Washington Nationals.

Hamels turned in an outstanding all-around effort on May 15, 2008, surrendering just four hits and going 2-for-4 at the plate during a 5–0 shut-out of the Atlanta Braves.

Hamels baffled the Cincinnati lineup on June 5, 2008, allowing just three hits and issuing three walks during a 5–0 shutout of the Reds.

Hamels performed magnificently in Game 1 of the 2008 NLDS, allow-ing just two hits, issuing one walk, and recording nine strikeouts in eight innings of work during a 3–1 win over the Brewers. Commenting on his effort afterward, Hamels said, "I knew the importance of the game. And it's something where, because of last year, I learned what it really takes in trying to . . . kind of mellow out, not to have that sort of excitement where you can't really control everything."

Hamels followed that up by going 2-0 with a 1.93 ERA against the Dodgers in the NLCS, before compiling a record of 1-0 and an ERA of 2.77 during the Phillies' five-game win over Tampa Bay in the World Series, with his fabulous pitching earning him MVP honors of both series. Later praising Hamels for his brilliant mound work in his book *Worth the Wait: Tales of the 2008 Phillies*, noted baseball writer Jayson Stark wrote: "The names on the list are the names who have carved their legends in the month of October. . . . We know their names because October was their kind of month, and they belong on that list because they once did something very few pitchers have ever done. They all won four starts in the same postsea-son. And now they have company . . . a 24-year-old left-hander named Cole Hamels. And with every time the Phillies handed him the baseball in

October 2009, it became more apparent that he is one of the sport's most special talents."

Hamels surrendered just two hits and one walk during a 1–0 shutout of the Giants on September 1, 2009, with San Francisco's only hits coming on a second-inning double by first baseman Ryan Garko and a ninth-inning pinch-hit single by Rich Aurilia.

Hamels dominated the Reds in Game 3 of the 2010 NLDS, allowing just five hits and recording nine strikeouts during a 2–0 shutout.

Although the Phillies ultimately lost 2–1 to the Pirates in 12 innings on June 3, 2011, Hamels performed magnificently over the first eight innings, allowing just one run on one hit, while also going 2-for-3 at the plate.

Hamels struggled on the mound against San Francisco on July 21, 2012, allowing five runs and 10 hits over the first 7 2/3 innings of a game the Phillies ended up losing 6–5 in 10 innings. Nevertheless, Hamels experienced a surreal moment in the third inning when he hit the first home run of his career against Giants starter Matt Cain.

After throwing the first six innings of a combined no-hitter the previous year, Hamels tossed a no-hitter against the Cubs on July 25, 2015, issuing just two walks and striking out 13 batters during a 5–0 Phillies win that proved to be Hamels's last appearance as a member of the team.

Notable Achievements

- Won at least 15 games twice.
- Posted winning percentage over .600 three times.
- Compiled ERA under 3.00 twice, finishing with mark under 2.50 once.
- Struck out more than 200 batters three times.
- Threw more than 200 innings six times.
- Posted WHIP under 1.000 once.
- Threw no-hitter vs. Chicago Cubs on July 25, 2015.
- Led NL pitchers in shutouts once, WHIP once, and fielding percentage twice.
- Finished second in NL in innings pitched once, shutouts once, WHIP once, and starts once.
- Finished third in NL in winning percentage once, strikeouts once, shutouts once, and WHIP once.
- Ranks among Phillies career leaders in wins (6th), strikeouts (3rd), innings pitched (6th), WHIP (9th), strikeouts per nine innings pitched (4th), strikeouts-to-walks ratio (4th), and starts (4th).

- Five-time division champion (2007, 2008, 2009, 2010, and 2011).
- Two-time NL champion (2008 and 2009).
- 2008 world champion.
- Two-time NL Player of the Week.
- 2008 NLCS MVP.
- 2008 World Series MVP.
- Three-time NL All-Star (2007, 2011, and 2012).

29

DON HURST

The major-league career of Don Hurst lasted just seven seasons, making the slugging first baseman a mere afterthought in the minds of even the most knowledgeable baseball historians. Nevertheless, the sturdily built Hurst established himself as one of the NL's most feared batsmen during the late-1920s and early-1930s, consistently ranking among the league leaders in home runs, RBIs, and bases on balls. One of the senior circuit's foremost sluggers and run producers from 1929 to 1932, Hurst, who spent virtually his entire career in Philadelphia, hit more than 30 homers once and knocked in more than 100 runs twice, with his 143 RBIs in 1932 leading the league. A solid all-around hitter who batted over .300 four times and compiled an on-base percentage in excess of .400 twice, Hurst also excelled in the field, leading all players at his position in assists twice and fielding percentage once. Yet, oddly enough, Hurst never appeared in a major-league game after he turned 30 years of age.

Born in Maysville, Kentucky, on August 12, 1905, Frank O'Donnell Hurst grew up with his mother and three older siblings some 60 miles northwest, in the Cincinnati suburb of Norwood, Ohio. The product of a failed marriage, Hurst hardly knew his father, who divorced his mother when he was still quite young.

After receiving his introduction to organized sports on the sandlots of Norwood, Hurst enrolled at The Ohio State University, where he played freshman football, before dropping out of school in the spring of 1924 to pursue a career in professional baseball. Hurst subsequently spent two seasons serving as an outfielder and part-time pitcher for the Paris (Kentucky) Bourbons of the Class D Blue Grass League, hitting 20 home runs and batting .382 one year, with his exceptional play earning him a promotion to the International League. Continuing to perform at an elite level after being converted into a first baseman by Syracuse Stars manager Burt Shotton, Hurst batted well over .300 in both 1926 and 1927. But, with Syracuse becoming a minor-league affiliate of the St. Louis Cardinals in 1927 and

Don Hurst led the National League with 143 RBIs in 1932.
Courtesy of RMYAuctions.com

future Hall of Famer Jim Bottomley holding down the first base job in St. Louis, the Cardinals completed a trade with the Phillies on May 11, 1928, that sent Hurst, catcher Spud Davis, and outfielder Homer Peel to Philadelphia for catcher Jimmie Wilson, pitcher Art Decatur, and journeyman first baseman Bill Kelly.

Joining the Phillies immediately, Hurst spent the remainder of 1928 in Philadelphia, batting .285, hitting 19 homers, driving in 64 runs, and scoring 73 times, in 107 games and 396 official at-bats. Emerging as a star the following year, Hurst concluded the 1929 campaign with 31 home runs, 125 RBIs, 100 runs scored, a batting average of .304, and an OPS of .914, placing among the league leaders in each of the first two categories. Although plagued by injuries in each of the next two seasons, Hurst hit 17 homers, drove in 78 runs, and batted .327 in 1930, before reaching the seats 11 times, knocking in 91 runs, and batting .305 the following year. Hurst subsequently posted the most impressive stat-line of his career in 1932, when he finished in the league's top 10 in 12 different offensive categories, including home runs (24), RBIs (143), runs scored (109), hits (196), doubles (41), total bases (317), batting average (.339), on-base percentage (.412), and slugging percentage (.547).

Reaching the major leagues at the perfect time, the 6-foot, 215-pound Hurst joined the Phillies just as the NL began experimenting with a livelier ball, contributing greatly to the lofty numbers he posted his first few seasons in Philadelphia. Furthermore, the left-handed-swinging Hurst benefited greatly from playing his home games at the bandbox known as the Baker Bowl. However, it should also be noted that Hurst's outstanding performance in 1932 came after the senior circuit discontinued its use of a livelier baseball. And Hurst's seventh-place finish in the NL MVP voting that year reflects the high regard with which others held him.

Unfortunately, Hurst never again reached the heights he attained in 1932. After holding out for more money the following offseason, Hurst slumped badly during the early stages of the 1933 campaign, causing him to fall out of favor with team management. Although Hurst finished the season with decent numbers, hitting eight homers, driving in 76 runs, and batting .267, the Phillies decided to trade him to the Chicago Cubs for fellow first baseman Dolph Camilli in June 1934 after he began that campaign in similar fashion. Leaving Philadelphia with career totals of 112 home runs, 598 RBIs, 497 runs scored, 946 hits, 185 doubles, and 28 triples, a batting average of .303, an on-base percentage of .382, and a slugging percentage of .488, Hurst subsequently hit just three homers and batted only .199 in 51 games with the Cubs in 1934, before being sold to his original team, the St. Louis Cardinals, on January 4, 1935. Assigned by the Cardinals to their American Association affiliate, the Columbus Red Birds, Hurst never played in the major leagues again, making his final big-league appearance as a member of the Cubs less than two months after he celebrated his 29th birthday. After one season in Columbus, Hurst spent two years playing first base for the Los Angeles Angels in the Pacific Coast League, before ending his career in baseball as a player-manager with the Hamilton Red Wings of the Class D Pennsylvania-Ontario-New York League in 1939.

Following his playing days, Hurst spent several years working as a manager at Veterans Memorial Auditorium in Culver City, California. Stricken with cancer early in 1952, Hurst died en route to a Los Angeles hospital on December 6, 1952, at only 47 years of age.

PHILLIES CAREER HIGHLIGHTS

Best Season

Hurst had a big year for the Phillies in 1929, hitting a career-high 31 homers, driving in 125 runs, scoring 100 times, batting .304, and compiling an OPS of .914. But he performed even better in 1932, earning a seventh-place finish in the NL MVP voting by leading the league with 143 RBIs and ranking among the leaders with 24 homers, 109 runs scored, 196 hits, 41 doubles, a .339 batting average, and an OPS of .959.

Memorable Moments/Greatest Performances

Hurst helped lead the Phillies to an 11–6 win over the Pirates on May 11, 1929, by going 4-for-5, with two homers, a double, and four RBIs.

Hurst starred in defeat on June 19, 1929, going 4-for-7, with a homer, five RBIs, and three runs scored during a 15–14, 11-inning loss to the Giants.

Although the Phillies lost to the Chicago Cubs 12–10 on July 29, 1929, Hurst had another big game, driving in five runs with a pair of homers, with his sixth-inning grand slam tying the score at 9–9.

Hurst contributed to a 2–0 victory over the Pirates on August 2, 1929, by hitting a solo home run in the top of the ninth inning, giving him at least one homer in five of the last six games.

Hurst drove in what proved to be the game-winning run of a 4–3 victory over the Giants on September 2, 1929, when he singled home Chuck Klein from second base with two men out in the top of the 12th inning.

Hurst came up big in the clutch again on September 25, 1929, when he gave the Phillies a 10–9 win over the Brooklyn Robins by hitting a walkoff homer in the bottom of the ninth inning.

Hurst contributed to a 15–7 win over the Cincinnati Reds on September 11, 1930, by hitting a pair of homers, knocking in five runs, and scoring three times.

Hurst led the Phillies to a 5–4 victory over the Reds on June 18, 1931, by driving in all five runs with a homer, two singles, and a game-winning bases loaded walk in the bottom of the ninth inning.

Hurst delivered the game-winning blow of a 7–6 win over the Giants on April 15, 1932, when he homered off Carl Hubbell with the bases loaded in the top of the eighth inning.

Hurst victimized the Giants again on May 24, 1932, going 4-for-5, with four RBIs and three runs scored during an 11–8 Phillies win.

Hurst led the Phillies to a doubleheader sweep of the Dodgers on July 23, 1932, by collecting five hits, homering three times, and driving in a total of eight runs. After homering once during the Phillies' 10–2 Game 1 victory, Hurst reached the seats another two times and knocked in a career-high six runs, in leading them to a 16–5 rout of the Dodgers in Game 2.

Hurst accounted for both runs the Phillies scored during a 2–1 win over the Giants at New York's Polo Grounds on August 13, 1933, by hitting a pair of solo homers off Carl Hubbell.

Hurst contributed to a 16–4 thrashing of the Pittsburgh Pirates on May 20, 1934, by going 5-for-6, with two RBIs and two runs scored.

Notable Achievements

- Hit more than 20 home runs twice, topping 30 homers once.
- Knocked in more than 100 runs twice.

- Scored more than 100 runs twice.
- Batted over .300 four times, topping the .320 mark twice.
- Surpassed 30 doubles twice, amassing more than 40 two-baggers once.
- Compiled on-base percentage over .400 twice.
- Posted slugging percentage over .500 four times.
- Compiled OPS over .900 three times.
- Led NL with 143 RBIs in 1932.
- Finished second in NL in bases on balls once and games played once.
- Finished third in NL in on-base percentage once.
- Led NL first basemen in assists twice, fielding percentage once, and double plays once.
- Finished seventh in 1932 NL MVP voting.

30
LEFTY O'DOUL

Although Frank "Lefty" O'Doul spent just two short years in Philadelphia, the brilliance he displayed at the plate during his brief stay in the City of Brotherly Love ended up earning him a spot on this list. Combining with Chuck Klein in 1929 and 1930 to give the Phillies arguably the most dynamic hitting tandem in the senior circuit, O'Doul batted over .380, compiled an OPS in excess of 1.000, and surpassed 200 hits twice each, with his 254 safeties in 1929 setting a single-season National League record that only New York Giants Hall of Fame first baseman Bill Terry later equaled. A two-time NL batting champion, O'Doul won his first title as a member of the Phillies in 1929, compiling an average of .398 that represents the franchise's highest single-season mark of the so-called modern era that began in 1900. Continuing to excel as a hitter for the Brooklyn Dodgers and New York Giants after leaving Philadelphia, O'Doul retired with a lifetime batting average of .349 that ranks as the fourth-best in MLB history, posting that lofty mark after beginning his professional career as a pitcher.

Born in San Francisco, California, on March 4, 1897, Francis Joseph O'Doul grew up in an Irish neighborhood in the city's meat-packing district then known as Butchertown (the area is now known as Bayview–Hunters Point). The son of a German mother and a French and Irish father who worked as a butcher in a slaughterhouse, O'Doul attended Bay View High School, where he first began to hone his baseball skills under the watchful eye of coach Rosie Stoltz, who O'Doul later said, "taught me the essential fundamentals of the game. She taught me to pitch, field, and hit."

After helping Bay View capture the city championship in 1912, O'Doul quit school at the age of 16 to join his father in the slaughterhouse. He then spent the next four years working six days a week and playing baseball on Sundays for amateur and semipro teams, eventually making a name for himself as one of the region's finest pitchers.

Plucked off the roster of a semipro club by his hometown San Francisco Seals of the Pacific Coast League in 1917, O'Doul split the next two seasons between San Francisco and Des Moines of the Western League, compiling an overall record of 20-14, before being drafted by the New York Yankees on September 21, 1918. Although O'Doul remained with the Yankees in 1919 and 1920, he saw extremely limited duty, working a total of just 8 2/3 innings in relief and garnering only 30 plate appearances, with most of those coming as a pinch-hitter.

Lefty O'Doul batted over .380, hit more than 20 homers, and amassed more than 200 hits in each of his two seasons with the Phillies.

Returned to San Francisco in 1921, O'Doul had an outstanding year for the Seals, going 25-9 with an ERA of 2.39, and batting .338 in 74 games, prompting the Yankees to exercise their option on him at season's end. O'Doul subsequently spent the entire 1922 campaign in New York, once again receiving very little playing time, before being included in a multi-player deal the Yankees completed with the Red Sox. After spending most of 1923 sitting on the bench in Boston, O'Doul returned to the Pacific Coast League, where he batted .392 and posted a record of 7-9 for Salt Lake City in 1924, before arm problems forced him to become a full-time outfielder. Establishing himself as the PCL's finest hitter the next three seasons, O'Doul posted batting averages of .375, .338, and .378 for Salt Lake City, Hollywood, and San Francisco, respectively, while also totaling 810 hits and 77 home runs, with his extraordinary offensive production prompting the New York Giants to draft him on October 4, 1927.

Beginning his major-league career in earnest at the rather advanced age of 31, O'Doul laid claim to the starting left field job immediately upon his arrival in New York. However, after breaking his ankle during the early stages of the campaign, O'Doul ended up missing six weeks, limiting him to just eight home runs and 46 RBIs, although he managed to bat a very respectable .319. Choosing to move on from O'Doul, the Giants completed a trade with the Phillies on October 29, 1928, that sent him to Philadelphia for outfielder Freddy Leach, who had hit 13 homers, driven in 96 runs, and batted .304 the previous season.

Dwarfing those numbers his first year in Philly, O'Doul hit 32 homers, knocked in 122 runs, and led the NL with a .398 batting average. Taking full advantage of the Baker Bowl's short right field fence, the lefty-swinging O'Doul, who stood 6-foot and weighed close to 185 pounds, also amassed 35 doubles, topped the circuit with 254 hits and a .465 on-base percentage, and ranked among the league leaders with 397 total bases, 152 runs scored, a slugging percentage of .622, and an OPS of 1.087. Doing an excellent job in left field as well, O'Doul led all players at his position in putouts and assists, throwing out 14 runners on the basepaths. O'Doul followed that up with another outstanding year, concluding the 1930 campaign with 22 homers, 97 RBIs, 122 runs scored, 202 hits, 37 doubles, a .383 batting average, and an OPS of 1.057, before inexplicably being traded to the Dodgers at season's end for cash and a package of three players that included outfielder Hal Lee and pitchers Clise Dudley and Jumbo Elliott. In his two years with the Phillies, O'Doul hit 54 homers, knocked in 219 runs, scored 274 times, batted .391, compiled an on-base percentage of .460, posted a slugging percentage of .614, and collected 456 hits, 72 doubles, and 13 triples.

Continuing to perform at an elite level the next two seasons in Brooklyn, O'Doul batted .336 for the Dodgers in 1931, before leading the NL with a .368 batting average, driving in 90 runs, and ranking among the league leaders with 21 homers, 120 runs scored, 219 hits, and an OPS of .978 the following year. After O'Doul got off to a slow start in 1933, the Dodgers traded him to the Giants, with whom he spent the final year-and-a-half of his career, before announcing his retirement with career totals of 113 home runs, 542 RBIs, 624 runs scored, 1,140 hits, 175 doubles, and 41 triples, a .349 batting average, an on-base percentage of .413, and a slugging percentage of .532. Extremely difficult to strike out, O'Doul also fanned just 122 times in 3,660 total plate appearances.

Following his playing career, O'Doul returned to the West Coast, where he managed the San Francisco Seals from 1935 to 1951, leading them to several Pacific Coast League championships during that time. O'Doul also later managed San Diego, Oakland, Seattle, and Vancouver in the PCL, developing a reputation wherever he went as an excellent manager and an outstanding batting instructor. Perhaps his most noted pupil, Ted Williams, who grew up in the San Diego area, recalled the first time that he ever saw O'Doul hit during the latter's playing days in the PCL, telling the *Sporting News* in 1994: "A kid copies what is good. I remember the first time I saw Lefty O'Doul, and he was as far away as those palms. And I saw the guy come to bat in batting practice. I was looking through a knothole, and I said, 'Geez, does that guy look good!' And it was Lefty O'Doul, one of the greatest hitters ever."

While managing in the PCL, O'Doul also became an ambassador of sorts, proving to be extremely instrumental in spreading baseball's growth and popularity in Japan by organizing trips there. Credited with being one of the founders of the Nippon Baseball League, O'Doul remains a legendary figure in Japan, gaining induction into the Japanese Baseball Hall of Fame in 2002.

After retiring from managing in 1957, O'Doul opened a restaurant in San Francisco that bore his name. It became a popular hangout and operated continuously for six decades until closing in 2017. O'Doul lived until December 7, 1969, when he died of a massive coronary at the age of 72 after suffering a stroke three weeks earlier.

PHILLIES CAREER HIGHLIGHTS

Best Season

O'Doul posted prolific offensive numbers his two years in Philadelphia, performing especially well in 1929, when he earned a runner-up finish to Rogers Hornsby in the NL MVP voting by establishing career-high marks with 32 home runs, 122 RBIs, 152 runs scored, 254 hits, a batting average of .398, and an on-base percentage of .465, leading the league in each of the last three categories, with his 254 hits setting a single-season franchise record that still stands.

Memorable Moments/Greatest Performances

O'Doul led the Phillies to a 7–4 win over the Brooklyn Robins on May 16, 1929, by touching up Hall of Fame right-hander Dazzy Vance for two homers and four RBIs.

Although the Phillies suffered a 14–13 defeat at the hands of the Robins the following day, O'Doul continued his assault on Brooklyn's pitching staff, going 4-for-4, with a double, two walks, three RBIs, and four runs scored.

O'Doul helped lead the Phillies to an 8–6 victory over the St. Louis Cardinals on September 8, 1929, by going 3-for-4, with a homer, double, two RBIs, and four runs scored.

O'Doul contributed to a 9–3 win over the Cardinals the very next day by driving in four runs with a homer, triple, and single.

O'Doul starred during a 16–11 loss to the Cardinals on May 7, 1930, going 5-for-5, with three doubles, one RBI, and three runs scored.

O'Doul again hit safely in all five of his trips to the plate during a 13–3 win over the Cardinals on June 21, 1930, going a perfect 5-for-5, with two homers, a double, three RBIs, and three runs scored.

O'Doul delivered the big blow in a 7–5 win over the Cubs on September 13, 1930, when he came off the bench to hit a game-winning pinch-hit two-run homer in the bottom of the eighth inning.

Notable Achievements

- Batted more than .380 twice.
- Hit more than 20 home runs twice, topping 30 homers once.
- Knocked in more than 100 runs once.
- Scored more than 120 runs twice.
- Surpassed 200 hits twice.
- Surpassed 30 doubles twice.
- Compiled on-base percentage over .450 twice.
- Posted slugging percentage over .600 twice.
- Compiled OPS over 1.000 twice.
- Led NL in batting average once, hits once, on-base percentage once, and plate appearances once.
- Finished second in NL in runs scored once, OPS once, games played once, and at-bats once.
- Finished third in NL in total bases once.
- Led NL left fielders in putouts once, assists once, and double plays once.
- Holds share of NL record for most hits in a season (254 in 1929).
- Finished second in 1929 NL MVP voting.

31
PETE ROSE

Baseball's all-time hit king, Pete Rose arrived in Philadelphia in 1979 having already amassed 3,164 safeties, earned nine top-10 finishes in the NL MVP voting, and gained All-Star recognition 12 times as a member of the Cincinnati Reds. Continuing to perform at an elite level for most of the next five seasons, Rose batted over .320 twice, surpassed 200 hits once, and earned four more All-Star nominations, with his outstanding play helping the Phillies win two division titles, two pennants, and one World Series. Eventually returning to Cincinnati, where he spent his final three seasons serving the Reds as a player-manager, Rose ended his 24-year playing career with more hits, times on base, games played, plate appearances, and official at-bats than anyone else in the history of the game, earning in the process a number 25 ranking on the *Sporting News'* 1999 list of Baseball's 100 Greatest Players and a berth on Major League Baseball's All-Century Team. Nevertheless, the controversial Rose continues to be ostracized from the sport he loves due to the sins he committed while managing the Reds.

Born in Cincinnati, Ohio, on April 14, 1941, Peter Edward Rose grew up in the city's Anderson Ferry section, where his father, Harry, a semipro athlete who boxed and played baseball, softball, and football well into his 40s, passed on to him his fierce competitive spirit. Eventually emerging as a standout athlete at Western Hills High School, Rose excelled in baseball and football, although he failed to display a similar aptitude in the classroom, forcing him to repeat the ninth grade. Ineligible to compete on the diamond for Western Hills during his senior season because of his extra year of schooling, Rose instead played in a semipro league, where he attracted the attention of scouts. Signed by the Reds and his uncle, Buddy Bloebaum, on the day he graduated from Western Hills in 1960, Rose later recalled, "I don't remember ever wanting to be anything but a professional athlete, and it's a good thing I became one because I never prepared for anything else."

Rose subsequently spent the next three seasons advancing through the Reds' farm system, before joining the parent club prior to the start of the 1963 campaign. After laying claim to the starting second base job, the switch-hitting Rose went on to earn NL Rookie of the Year honors by batting .273, scoring 101 runs, and finishing second among players at his position with 360 putouts. Rose remained at second for the Reds for three more years, earning his first All-Star nomination in 1965 by batting .312, driving in 81 runs, scoring 117 times, and leading the league with 209 hits, before batting .313, hitting 16 homers, knocking in 70 runs, scoring 97 others, and finishing second in the league with 205 hits and 38 doubles the following year.

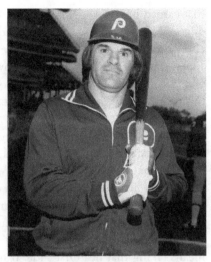

Pete Rose earned All-Star honors in four of his five seasons with the Phillies.
Courtesy of MearsonlineAuctions.com

Moved to the outfield in 1967, Rose spent the next eight seasons switching back and forth between left field and right, while also seeing some action in center. Performing well wherever the Reds put him, Rose gained All-Star recognition another seven times and won three batting titles, two Gold Gloves, and one league MVP trophy. Particularly outstanding in 1968, 1969, and 1973, Rose, who employed a short, compact swing from both sides of the plate that made him extremely difficult to strike out, earned a runner-up finish in the NL MVP balloting in the first of those campaigns by leading the league with 210 hits, a .335 batting average, and a .391 on-base percentage, while also finishing second in the circuit with 94 runs scored and 42 doubles. Rose finished fourth in the voting the following year after collecting 218 hits, driving in a career-high 82 runs, and leading the league with a .348 batting average and 120 runs scored. Rose then earned NL MVP honors in 1973 by leading the league with a .338 batting average and 230 hits, while also ranking among the leaders with 115 runs scored and a .401 on-base percentage.

In addition to establishing himself as one of the National League's premier players during his time in Cincinnati, Rose became known for his aggressive style of play, win-at-all-cost mentality, and tremendous hustle

that earned him the nickname "Charlie Hustle." Able to squeeze more production out of his somewhat limited natural ability than perhaps anyone
else who ever played the game, Rose possessed neither outstanding speed,
superior power at the plate, nor a powerful throwing arm in the field, once
admitting, "I didn't get to the majors on God-given ability. I got there on
hustle, and I have had to hustle to stay. That's the only way I know how to
play the game."

Further expounding upon the aggressive approach that he took to his
craft on another occasion, Rose said, "People say I don't have great tools.
They say that I can't throw like Ellis Valentine or run like Tim Raines or hit
with power like Mike Schmidt. Who can? I make up for it in other ways, by
putting out a little bit more. That's my theory, to go through life hustling.
In the big leagues, hustle usually means being in the right place at the right
time. It means backing up a base. It means backing up your teammate. It
means taking that headfirst slide. It means doing everything you can do to
win a baseball game."

Also known for his unbridled enthusiasm and obsession with winning,
Rose, said longtime teammate Joe Morgan, "played the game, always, for
keeps. Every game was the seventh game of the World Series. He had this
unbelievable capacity to literally roar through 162 games as if they were
each that one single game."

However, Rose's take-no-prisoners mentality and forceful personality
often rubbed opposing teams and their fans the wrong way, causing him to
also develop a reputation as someone who cared little about the welfare of
others. After seriously injuring Cleveland Indians promising young catcher
Ray Fosse in a collision at home plate in the 1970 All-Star Game, the 5'11",
200-pound Rose set off a bench-clearing brawl in the 1973 NLCS when
he picked a fight with slightly built Mets shortstop Bud Harrelson, causing
him to be viewed by many as something of a bully. Nevertheless, while
aggressive and combative on the playing field, Rose proved to be extremely
accommodating to reporters and fans, rarely refusing requests for interviews
or autographs. And, even though Rose often found himself being portrayed
as a selfish player who cared only about money, fame, and his statistics, he
always picked up the check at dinner, routinely invited teammates to live
with him, and agreed to change positions several times during his career to
help his team.

After moving to third base in 1975, Rose spent four years manning that
post for the Reds, earning four more All-Star selections and another two
top-10 finishes in the NL MVP voting by batting over .300 each season and
amassing more than 200 hits, 40 doubles, and 100 runs scored three times

each. But, after setting a modern NL record by hitting safely in 44 consecutive games in 1978, Rose chose to sign with the Phillies for four years and $3.2 million when his nasty divorce, hard lifestyle, and alleged associations with gamblers left the Reds feeling lukewarm about inking him to a long-term deal when he became a free agent at season's end.

Joining a Phillies team that had captured the NL East title in each of the previous three seasons, Rose, who had helped lead the Reds to five division titles, four pennants, and two world championships, believed that he represented the missing piece to the puzzle in Philadelphia, once telling Joe Morgan during their time together in Cincinnati, "That team's got talent. All they need is a leader."

Switching positions once again after he arrived in the City of Brotherly Love, Rose moved to first base, where he ended up having an outstanding season. Appearing in every game the Phillies played for the first of four straight times in 1979, the 38-year-old Rose earned the seventh of his 10 consecutive All-Star selections by scoring 90 runs, stealing a career-high 20 bases, collecting 208 hits, finishing second in the league with a .331 batting average, and topping the circuit with an on-base percentage of .418. Despite his exceptional performance, though, the Phillies finished well out of contention, placing fourth in the division with a record of 84-78.

Rebounding the following year, the Phillies captured the NL East title, before defeating the Houston Astros in the NLCS and the Kansas City Royals in the World Series, winning in the process their first world championship. A key contributor all year long, Rose batted .282, drove in 64 runs, scored 95 times, amassed 185 hits, led the league with 42 doubles, and finished first among players at his position in assists and fielding percentage. Particularly outstanding against Houston in the NLCS, Rose helped the Phillies overcome a 2–1 deficit in the best-of-five series by batting .400 and compiling an on-base percentage of .520, reaching base safely 13 times in 25 plate appearances, and scoring what proved to be the winning run in Game 4 when he scored all the way from first base on a double to left field by Greg Luzinski in the top of the 10th inning. Commenting on his former teammate's effort afterward, Astros second baseman Joe Morgan said, "I know Pete Rose. Pete Rose was never going to stop."

Rose subsequently performed extremely well during the strike-shortened 1981 campaign, finishing second in the league with 73 runs scored and a .325 batting average, while topping the circuit with 140 hits. But, after earning All-Star honors for the 16th time the following year by batting .271 and scoring 80 runs, the 42-year-old Rose finally began to show his age in 1983, batting just .245 and scoring only 52 times. Released by the Phillies at season's end, Rose left Philadelphia having hit eight homers, driven in 255 runs, scored 390 times, batted .291, compiled an on-base percentage of .365, posted a slugging percentage of .361, and amassed 826 hits, 139 doubles, 18 triples, and 51 stolen bases as a member of the team.

Later commenting on the impact that Rose made during his five-year stint in Philadelphia, Steve Carlton said, "Pete Rose came over to the Phillies in '79, and he became the catalyst that helped us to put it all together. His example on the field and his leadership helped to bring everybody's play up a notch."

After being released by the Phillies, Rose signed with the Montreal Expos, for whom he appeared in 95 games in 1984, before being traded back to the Reds on August 16 of that year. Rose subsequently spent the next two-plus seasons assuming the dual role of player-manager in Cincinnati, seeing a limited amount of action on the playing field, before unofficially retiring as a player after the Reds dropped him from their 40-man roster on November 11, 1986. In addition to ending his career with more hits (4,256), games played (3,562), plate appearances (15,890), at-bats (14,053), and times on base (5,929) than any other player in major-league history, Rose, who hit 160 homers, knocked in 1,314 runs, collected 135 triples, stole 198 bases, batted .303, compiled an on-base percentage of .375, and posted a slugging percentage of .409, ranks among baseball's all-time leaders with 2,165 runs scored, 746 doubles, and 5,752 total bases.

Following his retirement as an active player, Rose continued to manage the Reds until August 24, 1989, when he voluntarily accepted a permanent place on baseball's ineligible list after an investigation conducted by the commissioner's office determined that he had bet on the sport during his tenure as Reds skipper. Although Rose continued to deny the allegations made against him for the next 15 years, he finally admitted his guilt in his 2004 book entitled *My Prison without Bars*. Some 10 years later, on June 22, 2015, ESPN concluded its own investigation of Rose and determined that he had bet on baseball while still serving the Reds as a player-manager. The results of the investigation were made public and revealed the records of wagers that Rose had made on baseball that US federal authorities had seized from one of his associates. Long before that, though, in April 1990, Rose pleaded guilty to charges related to income-tax evasion and served five months in the federal penitentiary in Marion, Illinois.

Despite Rose's banishment from baseball and illicit behavior away from the playing field, Phillies fans voted for him to be inducted into the team's Wall of Fame in 2017. But the Phillies canceled their plans to honor him after a woman claimed that he had a sexual relationship with her when she was a minor many years earlier. Rose, who was in his mid-30s and married with two children at the time, acknowledged having a relationship with the woman, but claimed that it started when she was 16—the legal age of consent in Ohio.

Accepting the Phillies' decision to cancel the festivities planned for him, Rose issued a statement that read, "While I am truly honored that the Phillies fans voted for me to be this year's Wall of Fame inductee, I am concerned that other matters will overshadow the goodwill associated with Alumni Weekend, and I agree with the decision not to participate."

Rose added, "My baseball years in Philadelphia were amazing, not just because we won it all in 1980 and came close in 1983, but also because the fans welcomed me from day one."

PHILLIES CAREER HIGHLIGHTS

Best Season

Although Rose also performed exceptionally well in each of the next two seasons, the 1979 campaign proved to be his finest as a member of the Phillies. In addition to scoring 90 runs, stealing a career-high 20 bases, and leading the NL with a .418 on-base percentage, Rose placed near the top of the league rankings with a .331 batting average, 208 hits, 40 doubles, and 95 bases on balls, earning in the process All-Star honors for the 13th time in his career.

Memorable Moments/Greatest Performances

Rose played a huge role in a 9–8 win over the San Diego Padres on May 8, 1979, driving in two runs with a sixth-inning single, before knocking in what proved to be the game-winning runs in the top of the 12th with a two-run double.

Rose contributed to a 9–6 victory over the Mets on August 1, 1979, by going 4-for-4, with a walk and two runs scored.

Rose victimized the Mets again on September 13, 1979, collecting another four hits during a 2–1 Phillies win.

Rose accomplished the rare feat of stealing second, third, and home in the same inning during a 7–3 win over the Cincinnati Reds on May 11, 1980. After leading off the top of the seventh inning with a walk, Rose stole second and third and then crossed the plate on the back end of a double steal, with Mike Schmidt swiping second base with Mario Soto on the mound for Cincinnati and Greg Luzinski at the plate for the Phillies.

Rose helped lead the Phillies to a 7–2 win over the Cubs on July 11, 1980, by going 3-for-4, with three doubles, a walk, three RBIs, and one run scored.

Rose surpassed Stan Musial as the National League's all-time hits leader on August 10, 1981, when he singled to left field against right-hander Mark Littell in the bottom of the eighth inning of a 7–3 loss to the St. Louis Cardinals.

Rose, who amassed five hits in one game 10 times over the course of his career, accomplished the feat for the only time as a member of the Phillies on April 28, 1982, when he went 5-for-5, with a double, one RBI, and one run scored during a 9–3 win over the Dodgers.

Rose had another big day against the Dodgers on May 12, 1982, when he went 4-for-5, with two RBIs and two runs scored during an 11–3 Phillies win.

Notable Achievements

- Batted over .320 twice.
- Surpassed 200 hits once.
- Surpassed 40 doubles twice.
- Stole 20 bases once.
- Compiled on-base percentage over .400 once.
- Led NL in doubles once, hits once, on-base percentage once, and games played once.
- Finished second in NL in batting average twice, runs scored once, games played twice, and plate appearances four times.
- Finished third in NL in hits once and at-bats twice.
- Led NL first basemen in assists once and fielding percentage once.
- Holds MLB records for most hits (4,256), times on base (5,929), games played (3,562), plate appearances (15,890), and official at-bats (14,053).
- Ranks among MLB all-time leaders with 2,165 runs scored (6th), 746 doubles (2nd), and 5,752 total bases (9th).
- Two-time division champion (1980 and 1983).
- Two-time NL champion (1980 and 1983).
- 1980 world champion.
- Four-time NL Player of the Week.
- September 1979 NL Player of the Month.

- 1981 Silver Slugger Award winner.
- 1981 *Sporting News* NL All-Star selection.
- Four-time NL All-Star (1979, 1980, 1981, and 1982).
- Named to Phillies Centennial Team in 1983.
- Number 25 on the *Sporting News*' 1999 list of Baseball's 100 Greatest Players.
- Member of Major League Baseball's All-Century Team.

32

ROY HALLADAY

K nown for his extraordinary work ethic, tremendous intensity, and ability to go deep into ballgames, Roy Halladay arrived in Philadelphia in 2010 having already established himself as a likely Hall of Famer, previously winning one Cy Young Award, earning four other top-five finishes in the voting, and gaining All-Star recognition on six separate occasions as a member of the Toronto Blue Jays. Continuing to perform magnificently for the Phillies, the right-handed-throwing Halladay, who acquired the nickname "Doc" in deference to Wild West gunslinger Doc Holliday while pitching north of the border, won another Cy Young Award and earned two more All-Star selections over the course of the next four seasons by surpassing 19 victories, compiling an ERA under 2.50, and recording more than 200 strikeouts twice each. Also making history during his time in the City of Brotherly Love by throwing a perfect game and becoming just the second pitcher ever to toss a no-hitter in postseason play, Halladay helped lead the Phillies to two division titles, with his superb mound work earning him a place in the Philadelphia Baseball Wall of Fame. Sadly, though, Halladay spent his entire career being plagued by personal demons that ended up taking him from us far too soon.

Born in Denver, Colorado, on May 14, 1977, Harry Leroy Halladay III grew up in the Denver suburb of Arvada, where he developed into an outstanding all-around athlete with the help of his parents, who encouraged him to compete in sports at every level. Tall and graceful, Roy excelled in baseball and basketball as a teenager, starring in both sports while attending Arvada West High School. Particularly outstanding on the diamond, Halladay compiled an overall record of 25-2 and a miniscule ERA of 0.55 in his four years at Arvada High, earning in the process All-Conference and All-State honors three times each.

Offered an athletic scholarship to the University of Arizona, Halladay initially agreed to play baseball for the Wildcats, before changing his mind when the Toronto Blue Jays selected him in the first round of the

1995 MLB Draft, with the 17th overall pick. Halladay subsequently spent most of the next four seasons in the minor leagues, before joining the Blue Jays during the latter stages of the 1998 campaign. Remaining with the parent club the following year, Halladay performed relatively well in his first full big-league season, going 8-7 with a 3.92 ERA, while serving the Blue Jays as a spot-starter and middle-inning reliever. Halladay then suffered through a dismal 2000 campaign during which he pitched so poorly that the Blue Jays returned him to the minor leagues.

Roy Halladay earned NL Cy Young honors his first year in Philadelphia.
Courtesy of Dirk Hansen

Having lost all confidence in himself, Halladay briefly contemplated retirement, before consulting with a sports psychologist, who helped him regain his self-esteem and improve his mental approach to the game.

Returning to the Blue Jays midway through the 2001 season with a new attitude and a newly mastered split-finger fastball he used to complement his two-seamer and four-seamer, Halladay went 5-3 with a 3.16 ERA in his 16 starts, before emerging as one of the AL's best pitchers the following year, when he earned his first All-Star selection by compiling a record of 19-7, ranking among the league leaders with a 2.93 ERA and 168 strikeouts, and topping the circuit with 239 1/3 innings pitched. Halladay followed that up by going 22-7 with a 3.25 ERA and 204 strikeouts in 2003, while also leading the league with nine complete games, two shutouts, and 266 innings pitched, with his superb pitching earning him AL Cy Young honors and the admiration of Yankees shortstop Derek Jeter, who said, "Everyone talks about the great pitchers in the game. They need to start talking about Halladay because he's as good as they come."

Hampered by a sore shoulder in 2004, Halladay failed to perform at the same lofty level. But, after missing nearly half of the ensuing campaign with a broken left tibia he sustained when a line drive struck him in the shin, Halladay reestablished himself as one of the finest pitchers in all of baseball over the course of the next four seasons, earning three All-Star selections and four top-five finishes in the AL Cy Young voting by compiling an overall record of 69-33 and leading the league in complete games three times, shutouts twice, and innings pitched once.

The 6'6", 225-pound Halladay, whose repertoire included a curveball that typically approached the plate at just under 80 miles per hour and a hard two-seam sinking fastball, a four-seam fastball, and a cut fastball, all of which registered somewhere in the low 90s on the radar gun, possessed pinpoint control of all his pitches, annually ranking among the league leaders in strikeouts-to-walks ratio and fewest walks allowed per nine innings pitched. Employing a three-quarter arm delivery, Halladay had the ability to start his curveball at a right-handed batter's head and nip the outside corner of the plate. Yet he generally relied on either his two-seam fastball or cutter to retire opposing batters in crucial situations.

In addition to his varied arsenal, Halladay possessed an extremely competitive nature, a keen sense of his opponent's thought process, and the ability to block out any outside distractions. Prior to and during each start, he went into a complete "isolation mode," refusing to talk to anyone other than his manager or pitching coach.

In discussing his teammate's ability to focus on the task at hand, Toronto catcher Bengie Molina commented, "Roy is like a machine. He's the type of pitcher that doesn't care what happens around him. He still is going to get the batters out any way he can. That's what makes him a lot better than most."

Blue Jays manager John Gibbons added, "He never loses focus. That's the thing about him. He never loses his intensity or concentration."

Carlos Tosca, who also managed Halladay in Toronto, said, "He is—by far, and nobody comes close—the toughest, toughest individual mentally, and the most driven I've ever been associated with."

Former AL MVP Miguel Tejada also had high praise for Halladay, stating, "It's hard to say how good he is because, every time he pitches, he wins. He can take an aggressive hitter out of the game because he works so fast. What can I say? He's an ace."

Nevertheless, with the Blue Jays in a rebuilding mode, they elected to trade Halladay to the Phillies for minor-league prospects Travis d'Arnaud, Kyle Drabek, and Michael Taylor following the conclusion of the 2009 campaign. After completing the deal, Phillies general manager Rubén Amaro Jr. said in a statement, "Without question, Roy is one of the top pitchers in the game today. He has the talent, professionalism, and makeup that embody what we look for in players, and we're very happy to have him in a Phillies uniform for at least the next four seasons."

Phillies manager Charlie Manuel added, "Roy is known as the best pitcher in baseball and will have instant respect. He's a No. 1, a blue chipper, and I expect him to stabilize our pitching staff. Roy brings a great work ethic and tremendous character, and he'll have a big presence in our clubhouse."

Adapting extremely well to pitching in a new league in 2010, Halladay earned Cy Young and All-Star honors by compiling a record of 21-10; ranking among the NL leaders with an ERA of 2.44 ERA, a WHIP of 1.041, and 219 strikeouts; and topping the circuit with nine complete games, four shutouts, and 250 2/3 innings pitched. Halladay followed that up with another outstanding season, earning All-Star honors and a runner-up finish in the 2011 Cy Young balloting by posting a record of 19-6, leading all NL hurlers with eight complete games, and ranking among the leaders with an ERA of 2.35, a WHIP of 1.040, 220 strikeouts, and 233 2/3 innings pitched.

Later crediting much of the success that he experienced his first two seasons in Philadelphia to Phillies pitching coach Rich Dubee, who he claimed taught him a variation of the split-finger fastball, Halladay said, "My entire career, I had not been able to throw a changeup that was any kind of effective at all. Rich showed me a split-fingered grip, and it was like the best changeup I had in my life. It became a put-away pitch, a get-ahead pitch."

Halladay also found the environment at Citizens Bank Park very much to his liking, stating, "When the game would start, I would be in awe. I just could not believe that I was playing in a place that was that excited, that sold out. I would look around at the other guys on the team and think, 'Man, they expect this. They're used to this. They're almost spoiled.' So, it used to frustrate me when we'd lose games. I felt like, we gotta start going here, we gotta start doing better than this!"

Consequently, Halladay gave everything he had to the Phillies, with teammate Cole Hamels saying, "There's a reason he's done so well in his career, and it comes from his incredible work ethic and his desire to win."

Plagued by a bad back in 2012, Halladay started only 25 games, finishing the season just 11-8 with a 4.49 ERA, before missing much of the ensuing campaign as well due to a sore right shoulder that forced him to spend nearly four months on the disabled list. Choosing to announce his retirement in December 2013, Halladay later said, "At the time, to not really have a decision in how I wanted my career to end, I felt, 'How cruel is this?' Looking back on it, though, it might have been a blessing in disguise. Look at Peyton Manning and guys like that. I can't imagine how I would feel walking away from the sport and always questioning if I could have done more. It would have driven me up the wall."

Halladay, who retired with a career record of 203-105, an ERA of 3.38, a WHIP of 1.178, 67 complete games, 20 shutouts, and 2,117 strikeouts in 2,749 1/3 innings pitched, ended his four-year stint in Philadelphia with a record of 55-29, a 3.25 ERA, a WHIP of 1.119, 18 complete games, five shutouts, 622 strikeouts in 702 2/3 innings of work, and a strikeouts-to-walks ratio of 4.450 that ranks as the second-best mark in franchise history.

After spending the early days of his retirement focusing on his wife, sons, and favorite hobby of flying, Halladay began working as a guest instructor in the farm systems of the Phillies and Blue Jays. He also volunteered to coach baseball for his oldest son's team at Calvary Christian High School in Clearwater, Florida. But on November 7, 2017, just months after he purchased an ICON-A5 two-seat amphibious aircraft, the 40-year-old Halladay lost his life when his plane crashed into the Gulf of Mexico, off the Florida coast.

Upon learning of Halladay's passing, the Phillies released a statement that read: "We are numb over the very tragic news about Roy Halladay's untimely death. There are no words to describe the sadness that the entire Phillies family is feeling over the loss of one of the most respected human beings to ever play the game. It is with the heaviest of hearts that we pass along our condolences to Brandy, Ryan and Braden."

Remembering his former teammate, Cole Hamels said, "Behind everything he did, he had a purpose. I think you come to realize that you have very small, short moments in life to do something great, so you have to maximize it. You have to make the best of it. And he did. He made us push to a level that sometimes you didn't think you could actually reach. He made everybody better."

Some two months later, in January 2018, an autopsy report released by the Pinellas-Pasco Medical Examiner's Office revealed that Halladay's blood contained a dangerous combination of drugs that included an antidepressant, a muscle relaxant, and a sleep aid, with forensic pathologist Burr Hartman stating, "He had a drug combination similar to a speedball. He was impaired by these drugs. It was definitely not safe for him to fly an airplane."

Then, on April 15, 2020, the National Transportation Safety Board released a report stating that Halladay's erratic behavior also contributed greatly to his death, with witnesses claiming that they saw him executing aerobics that included steep climbs and turns that caused his plane to come dangerously close to the water.

Shortly thereafter, Halladay's widow, Brandy, hoping to prevent others from making similar errors in judgment, opened up about her husband's struggles with addiction and mental health issues in the ESPN documentary *Imperfect*. Revealing that injuries to his back and shoulder caused her husband to develop an addiction to painkillers, Halladay's widow also disclosed that the Hall of Fame pitcher struggled with anxiety so much that he regularly vomited before games and needed sleeping pills the night before he pitched. Suggesting that flying seemed to provide him with a therapeutic escape from his troubles, Brandy Halladay claimed that her husband guarded his image carefully, saying, "Most people knew him based on what he wanted them to think. Baseball is what he did. It's not who he was."

PHILLIES CAREER HIGHLIGHTS

Best Season

Halladay performed brilliantly in each of his first two seasons in Philadelphia, going 21-10, with an ERA of 2.44, a WHIP of 1.041, 219 strikeouts, and a league-leading 250 2/3 innings pitched, nine complete games, and four shutouts in 2010, before compiling a record of 19-6, an ERA of 2.35, a WHIP of 1.040, and 220 strikeouts the following year, while also throwing one shutout, 233 2/3 innings, and a league-leading eight complete games. While either of those seasons would make an excellent choice, the fact that Halladay led all NL pitchers in five different categories en route to earning Cy Young honors and a sixth-place finish in the league MVP voting in 2010 prompted me to identify that as his finest season as a member of the Phillies.

Memorable Moments/Greatest Performances

Halladay excelled in his first start for the Phillies, allowing just one run on six hits in seven innings of work during an 11–1 win over the Washington Nationals in the opening game of the 2010 regular season.

Halladay threw his first shutout as a member of the Phillies on April 21, 2010, allowing just five hits and one walk during a 2–0 win over the Braves in Atlanta.

Halladay shut out the Mets on just three hits on May 1, 2010, walking one batter and striking out six during a 10–0 Phillies win.

Halladay achieved perfection on May 29, 2010, when he recorded 11 strikeouts and retired all 27 batters that he faced during a 1–0 win over the Florida Marlins.

Halladay turned in another dominant performance on September 27, 2010, allowing just a third-inning single to catcher Wilson Ramos and an eighth-inning single to first baseman Adam Dunn during an 8–0 shutout of the Nationals,

Halladay became just the second pitcher in major-league history to throw a no-hitter in postseason play when he surrendered only a fifth-inning walk to Jay Bruce during a 4–0 win over the Cincinnati Reds in Game 1 of the 2010 NLDS.

Halladay worked 8 2/3 strong innings against San Diego on April 24, 2011, allowing just one run on five hits, while also recording a career-high 14 strikeouts during a 3–1 Phillies win.

Halladay helped the Phillies begin the 2012 season on a positive note by yielding just two hits and recording five strikeouts in eight innings of work during a 1–0 win over the Pirates on Opening Day.

Notable Achievements

- Surpassed 20 victories once, winning 19 games another time.
- Posted winning percentage over .600 twice.
- Compiled ERA under 2.50 twice.
- Struck out more than 200 batters twice.
- Threw more than 200 innings twice, surpassing 250 innings pitched once.
- Threw perfect game vs. Florida Marlins on May 29, 2010.
- Threw no-hitter vs. Cincinnati Reds in Game 1 of 2010 NLDS.
- Led NL pitchers in wins once, complete games twice, shutouts once, innings pitched once, and strikeouts-to-walks ratio twice.
- Finished second in NL in ERA once, winning percentage once, strikeouts once, innings pitched once, and WHIP once.
- Finished third in NL in wins once, ERA once, winning percentage once, and strikeouts once.
- Ranks among Phillies career leaders in winning percentage (2nd), WHIP (6th), bases on balls allowed per nine innings pitched (7th), strikeouts per nine innings pitched (6th), and strikeouts-to-walks ratio (2nd).

- Two-time division champion (2010 and 2011).
- Two-time NL Player of the Week.
- July 2010 NL Pitcher of the Month.
- 2010 *Sporting News* NL Pitcher of the Year.
- 2010 NL Cy Young Award winner.
- Finished second in 2011 NL Cy Young voting.
- Finished in top 10 in NL MVP voting twice (2010 and 2011).
- Two-time NL All-Star (2010 and 2011).
- Member of Philadelphia Baseball Wall of Fame.
- Elected to Baseball Hall of Fame by members of BBWAA in 2019.

33

CLIFF LEE

An outstanding left-handed pitcher who became known during his time in Philadelphia for his calm demeanor and ability to excel in big-game situations, Cliff Lee spent parts of five seasons with the Phillies, doing two tours of duty with the club. A two-time NL All-Star, Lee also earned consideration for the league's Cy Young Award on two separate occasions by winning 17 games once, compiling an ERA under 3.00 twice, and recording more than 200 strikeouts three times, with his excellent mound work helping the Phillies capture two division titles and one NL pennant. Lee accomplished all this after earlier surpassing 14 victories four times and winning the AL Cy Young Award as a member of the Cleveland Indians.

Born in the Little Rock suburb of Benton, Arkansas, on August 30, 1978, Clifton Phifer Lee spent most of his leisure time as a youngster playing sports with his cousins and friends, displaying at an early age a fierce competitive spirit that caused him to take defeats personally. Always believing that a career as a major-league pitcher awaited him, Lee starred in baseball at Benton High School, where he developed a reputation as an extremely confident pitcher who enjoyed showing up his opponent. Selected by the Florida Marlins in the eighth round of the 1997 MLB Draft following his senior year at Benton High, Lee elected to delay the start of his professional career and enroll at Meridian Community College in Mississippi, where he spent the next two years refining his skills, before accepting a scholarship offer from the University of Arkansas. After spending his junior year at Arkansas further sharpening his game, Lee decided to turn pro when the Montreal Expos selected him in the fourth round of the 2000 MLB Draft.

After signing with Montreal, Lee remained in the Expos' farm system until they included him in a six-player trade they completed with the Cleveland Indians on June 27, 2002. Lee then spent most of the next year-and-a-half in the minor leagues, although he also made brief appearances with the Indians in both 2002 and 2003, compiling an overall record of 3-4 and an ERA of 3.30 in a total of 11 starts, while recording 50 strikeouts and surrendering 47 hits in 62 2/3 innings of work.

Earning a regular spot in the Cleveland starting rotation in 2004, Lee got off to a tremendous start, winning 10 of his first 11 decisions, before slumping during the season's second half and finishing the year with a record of 14-8 and an ERA of 5.43. Regaining his earlier form in 2005, Lee earned a fourth-place finish in the AL Cy Young voting by going 18-5 with a 3.79 ERA. But, after winning 14 games the following year, Lee suffered through a horrendous 2007 campaign during which he performed so badly that

Cliff Lee gave the Phillies their only two wins over the Yankees in the 2009 World Series.
Courtesy of Keith Allison

the Indians demoted him to the minor leagues at one point. Left off Cleveland's playoff roster after finishing the regular season with a record of 5-8 and an ERA of 6.29, Lee later revealed that his most memorable game as a member of the Indians proved to be one in which he failed to make an appearance, recalling, "It was the postseason in 2007, when we were up on Boston, 3–1 [in the ALCS], and I didn't pitch in any of the games. I would have liked to have had a shot at one of those last three games, but we lost them all, and I didn't pitch in any of them. I'm not saying we would have won it if I had pitched in one of those games, but that was definitely motivation for me to get my career turned around."

After working extensively with Cleveland pitching coach Carl Willis during the subsequent offseason, Lee altered his approach on the mound somewhat, becoming more adept at mixing up his pitches and working the corners of the plate. Far more focused and relaxed than ever before, Lee emerged as the AL's best pitcher in 2008, earning Cy Young honors by leading the league with a record of 22-3 and an ERA of 2.54, while also ranking among the leaders with a WHIP of 1.110, 223 1/3 innings pitched, and 170 strikeouts. Commenting years later on the incredible improvement in his performance, Lee stated, "It was the low point and the high point of my career, from one year to the next. I went from being really bad to being really good, real quick."

However, with Lee scheduled to become a free agent following the conclusion of the 2010 campaign, the Indians dealt him and outfielder Ben Francisco to the Phillies on July 29, 2009, for a package of four players that included utility infielder Jason Donald, backup catcher Lou Marson, and minor-league pitchers Carlos Carrasco and Jason Knapp. Commenting on the trade years later, Lee stated, "I was somewhat surprised by the trade, but there were rumors floating around, and I knew that they [the Indians] traded C.C. [Sabathia] the year before, so, knowing all that, it wasn't that much of a surprise."

Lee, who had posted a record of 7-9 and an ERA of 3.14 through the first four months of the 2009 season, performed extremely well for the Phillies in August and September, going 7-4 with an ERA of 3.39, before compiling a perfect 4-0 record and a brilliant 1.56 ERA in the postseason, while also completing two of his five starts and defeating the Yankees twice in the World Series. But, with the Phillies sending a package of prospects to the Toronto Blue Jays for Roy Halladay after coming up short against the Yankees in the Fall Classic, they felt a need to replenish their farm system, prompting them to trade Lee to the Seattle Mariners on December 16, 2009, for minor leaguers J. C. Ramírez, Phillippe Aumont, and Tyson Gillies.

Expressing his surprise shortly after learning of the deal, Lee said, "At first, I didn't believe it. I thought we were working out an extension with the Phillies. I thought I'd be spending the rest of my career there. . . . I was under the impression they wanted to keep me there for a long time. In my mind, it was going to happen."

Lee subsequently split the 2010 campaign between the Mariners and Texas Rangers, earning his second All-Star nomination by compiling an overall record of 12-9 and a 3.18 ERA, before leading the Rangers to their first AL pennant by winning all three of his playoff starts. Making an extremely favorable impression on Texas manager Ron Washington during the season's second half, Lee drew praise from his skipper, who said, "He can move the ball around. He can change speeds. He can hit spots. He can do whatever he has to do."

Meanwhile, Hall of Fame pitcher and Rangers president and CEO Nolan Ryan stated, "He's the most consistent pitcher I've ever seen."

A free agent at the end of 2010, Lee fielded offers from several teams, with the Rangers and Yankees proving to be two of his most ardent suitors. Ultimately, though, Lee chose to return to Philadelphia when the Phillies offered him a five-year, $120 million contract that included a vesting option for a sixth season. After inking his deal with the Phillies on December 15, 2010, Lee told reporters, "I never wanted to leave this place in the first place. To get an opportunity to come back and be a part of this team and this pitching rotation is gonna be something that's historic, I believe. Can't wait to get to Spring Training and get this thing going."

Joining a starting rotation that also included Roy Halladay, Cole Hamels, and Roy Oswalt, Lee proved to be as good as any other member of Philadelphia's pitching staff in 2011, earning All-Star honors and a third-place finish in the NL Cy Young voting by compiling a record of 17-8, finishing second in the league with six complete games and a career-high 238 strikeouts, placing third in the circuit with an ERA of 2.40 and a WHIP of 1.027, and leading all NL hurlers with six shutouts.

Certainly, the 6'3", 205-pound Lee's superb pitching could be attributed in large part to his exceptional control (he walked only 42 batters in 232 2/3 innings) and his mastery of every pitch in his repertoire, which included a slider, curveball, and circle changeup; a four-seam fastball and a two-seam fastball, both of which registered somewhere between 90 and 93 mph on the radar gun; and an 85–88 mph cut fastball. In describing his approach to pitching, Lee suggested, "You've got to be able to pitch with your fastball. If you can't do that, if you can't locate your fastball and put it where you want to, the other pitches, what good are they? . . . Working ahead, mixing speeds, and staying out of the heart of the plate—that's what you need to do to be a successful pitcher."

However, sportswriter Sheldon Ocker also credited Lee's fabulous performance to his calm demeanor and confidence in his own abilities, noting, "Whether he is on the mound or in the clubhouse, Cliff Lee is the picture of serenity. Unfazed, unhurried, unflappable, unexcitable."

Former Phillies teammate Matt Stairs added, "He was just so cool. Nothing bothered him. He didn't panic."

Indeed, Lee's mound presence proved to be one of his greatest weapons. Thriving under pressure, Lee unnerved his opponents with his stoic nature and tremendous self-confidence that helped make him one of the finest postseason pitchers of his generation.

Hindered by poor run support in 2012, Lee proved to be somewhat less successful, finishing just 6-9, although he compiled a very respectable 3.16 ERA, led the league with a strikeouts-to-walks ratio of 7.393, and ranked among the leaders with 207 strikeouts and a WHIP of 1.114. Lee subsequently earned the last of his four All-Star selections and a sixth-place finish in the NL Cy Young voting in 2013 by compiling a record of 14-8, an ERA of 2.87, and a WHIP of 1.010, while also placing near the top of the league rankings with 222 strikeouts and 222 2/3 innings pitched. But, after straining his left elbow during the early stages of the 2014 campaign,

Lee ended up making only 13 starts, finishing the season with a record of 4-5 and an ERA of 3.65. Unable to appear in a single contest the following year after tearing his left common flexor tendon, Lee announced his retirement at season's end, ending his career with a record of 143-91, a 3.52 ERA, a WHIP of 1.196, 29 complete games, 12 shutouts, and 1,824 strikeouts in 2,156 2/3 innings of work. As a member of the Phillies, Lee compiled a record of 48-34, an ERA of 2.94, and a WHIP of 1.089; threw 12 complete games and eight shutouts; struck out 813 batters in 827 1/3 innings pitched; and posted a strikeouts-to-walks ratio of 6.556 that places him first in team annals. After leaving the game, Lee returned to his home state of Arkansas, where he now lives with his family.

PHILLIES CAREER HIGHLIGHTS

Best Season

Lee's first season with the Phillies following his return to Philadelphia in 2011 proved to be his finest as a member of the team. En route to earning a third-place finish in the NL Cy Young voting, Lee ranked among the league leaders with 17 wins, a 2.40 ERA, 238 strikeouts, 232 2/3 innings pitched, six complete games, and a WHIP of 1.027, while also topping the circuit with six shutouts.

Memorable Moments/Greatest Performances

Lee excelled in his first start as a member of the Phillies on July 31, 2009, giving them a 5–1 victory over the Giants by throwing a complete-game four-hitter.

Lee performed even better on August 19, 2009, going the distance, recording 11 strikeouts, and allowing just two hits and one unearned run during an 8–1 win over the Arizona Diamondbacks.

Lee tossed his first shutout for the Phillies on September 15, 2009, surrendering six hits and striking out nine batters during a 5–0 victory over the Washington Nationals.

Lee excelled on the mound for the Phillies in Game 3 of the 2009 NLCS, yielding just three hits and recording 10 strikeouts over the first eight innings of an 11–0 blowout of the Dodgers.

Lee subsequently dominated the Yankees in Game 1 of the 2009 World Series, recording 10 strikeouts and allowing just six hits and one unearned run during a complete-game 6–1 victory.

Lee turned in another dominant performance on April 14, 2011, shutting out the Nationals, 4–0, on just three hits and recording 12 strikeouts.

Although Lee surrendered three runs and nine hits during a 5–0 loss to the Braves on May 6, 2011, he recorded a career-high 16 strikeouts in his seven innings of work.

Lee put together a pair of impressive scoreless innings streaks during the 2011 campaign, keeping the opposition off the scoreboard for 34 1/3 straight frames from June 11 to July 3, before throwing another 32 consecutive scoreless innings from August 17 to September 10.

Lee shut out the Florida Marlins on just two hits on June 16, 2011, also contributing to the 3–0 victory by going 2-for-3 at the plate, with a double and one RBI.

Lee tossed another two-hit shutout on June 28, 2011, allowing just a sixth-inning single to shortstop Marco Scutaro and an eighth-inning double to left fielder Darnell McDonald during a 5–0 win over the Boston Red Sox.

Although the Phillies ultimately lost to the Braves in 11 innings 4–1 on July 9, 2011, Lee performed brilliantly over the first eight innings, allowing just one run on three hits, while also reaching the seats for the first home run of his career.

Lee turned in another exceptional all-around effort on August 9, 2011, earning a 2–1 victory over the Dodgers by surrendering just four hits over eight scoreless innings, striking out 10 batters, and taking Ted Lilly deep for the only other home run of his career.

Lee excelled both on the mound and in the batter's box once again on May 22, 2013, allowing just three hits and going 2-for-4 at the plate during a 3–0 shutout of the Miami Marlins.

Lee victimized the Marlins again on September 16, 2013, recording 14 strikeouts over the first eight innings of a 12–2 Phillies win, while also going 3-for-4 at the plate, with a triple and four RBIs.

Lee starred in defeat on September 27, 2013, surrendering just three hits and recording 13 strikeouts in eight innings of work during a 1–0 loss to the Braves.

Notable Achievements

- Won 17 games in 2011.
- Posted winning percentage over .600 three times.
- Compiled ERA under 3.00 twice, finishing with mark under 2.50 once.

- Struck out more than 200 batters three times.
- Threw more than 200 innings three times.
- Led NL pitchers in shutouts once and strikeouts-to-walks ratio twice.
- Finished second in NL in complete games once, strikeouts twice, and strikeouts-to-walks ratio once.
- Finished third in NL in ERA once, innings pitched once, and WHIP once.
- Holds Phillies single-season record for best strikeouts-to-walks ratio (7.393 in 2012).
- Holds Phillies career record for best strikeouts-to-walks ratio (6.557).
- Ranks among Phillies career leaders in strikeouts (12th), WHIP (3rd), bases on balls allowed per nine innings pitched (2nd), and strikeouts per nine innings pitched (3rd).
- Two-time division champion (2009 and 2011).
- 2009 NL champion.
- Two-time NL Pitcher of the Month.
- Finished third in 2011 NL Cy Young voting.
- Two-time NL All-Star (2011 and 2013).

34

DOLPH CAMILLI

Although he is perhaps more closely associated with the Brooklyn Dodgers, Dolph Camilli first made a name for himself as a member of the Phillies, for whom he starred at first base from 1934 to 1937. Developing into one of the senior circuit's foremost sluggers during his time in Philadelphia, Camilli ranked among the NL leaders in home runs in each of his final three seasons in the City of Brotherly Love, while also placing near the top of the league rankings in RBIs, runs scored, on-base percentage, and slugging percentage in both 1936 and 1937. Continuing his outstanding offensive production after he joined the Dodgers in 1938, Camilli ultimately finished in the league's top four in home runs eight straight times, knocked in more than 100 runs five times, scored more than 100 runs four times, and batted over .300 twice. A solid defender as well, Camilli led all NL first basemen in putouts twice, assists once, and fielding percentage once.

Born to first-generation Italian immigrant parents in San Francisco, California, on April 23, 1907, Adolph Louis Camilli grew up in fear, often being beaten by his alcoholic and abusive father. After his mother escaped her husband with her two daughters by leaving San Francisco, young Adolph ultimately discussed his situation with officials at his school, who gave him a cot to sleep on and a job as a janitor in one of their buildings.

Essentially on his own by the age of 13, Camilli attended local Sacred Heart Cathedral Preparatory High School, before beginning a lengthy eight-year minor-league career by splitting the 1926 campaign between the Class C Logan Collegians and the Pacific Coast League's San Francisco Seals. From San Francisco, Camilli moved on to Utah, where he batted .333 as a member of the Salt Lake City Bees in 1928. Camilli then spent the next five seasons playing first base for the Sacramento Solons in the PCL, during which time his older brother, who fought under the name Frankie Campbell, died of cerebral hemorrhaging following a match with future heavyweight boxing champion Max Baer.

Finally called up to the major leagues during the latter stages of the 1933 campaign after the Cubs purchased his contract from Sacramento, Camilli appeared in 16 games with Chicago, batting .224, homering twice, and driving in seven runs. Camilli then spent the first two months of the 1934 season sharing time at first base with Cubs player-manager Charlie Grimm, before being dealt to the Phillies for fellow first sacker Don Hurst on June 11, 1934. Initially unhappy over the prospect of joining the lowly Phillies, Camilli briefly considered quitting

Dolph Camilli established himself as one of the NL's top sluggers during his time in Philadelphia.
Courtesy of MearsonlineAuctions.com

baseball and returning home. However, a meeting with Phillies manager Jimmie Wilson, who informed him that he planned to play him every day, convinced Camilli to give Philadelphia a try.

Inserted into the starting lineup immediately upon his arrival in Philadelphia, Camilli hit 12 homers, knocked in 68 runs, scored 52 times, and batted .265 over the final four months of the campaign, giving him a batting average of .267 and totals of 16 home runs, 87 RBIs, and 69 runs scored in his first full season in the majors. Improving upon those numbers in 1935, Camilli finished third in the league with 25 homers, drove in 83 runs, scored 88 times, and batted .261, although he also established a new NL record by striking out 113 times.

The free-swinging Camilli, who led the NL in strikeouts four times during his career, developed into more of a complete hitter in 1936, ranking among the league leaders in virtually every major offensive category. In addition to finishing second in the circuit with 28 homers, 13 triples, 70 extra-base hits, 116 walks, a .577 slugging percentage, and an OPS of 1.018, Camilli batted .315 and placed near the top of the league rankings with 102 RBIs, 106 runs scored, and a .441 on-base percentage. Although limited by injuries to 131 games the following year, Camilli posted outstanding numbers once again, finishing the season with 27 homers, 80 RBIs, 101 runs scored, a .339 batting average, and a league-leading .446 on-base percentage.

Camilli's powerful left-handed bat proved to be a perfect fit for Philadelphia's Baker Bowl, with the muscular 5'10", 185-pound first baseman possessing a ferocious swing that often drove balls off and over the ballpark's high screen in right field. Recalling years later the impact that playing in the Baker Bowl had on him as a hitter, Camilli said, "We always faced tough pitching in that park. Other teams knew we had good hitting and they didn't pitch any humpty-dumpties against us, and often they were left-handers. As a result, I think I hit them better than right-handers. I hit the left-handers good and, the more I saw them, the better I hit them."

An excellent defensive first baseman as well, Camilli later drew praise from Duke Snider for the totality of his game, with the Hall of Fame outfielder stating, "Pee Wee Reese told me how good Dolph Camilli was. He said Camilli was an outstanding first baseman, the best the Dodgers had until Gil Hodges came along. I met Camilli after the Dodgers moved to Los Angeles. . . . I was struck by the fact that Dolph had so much power for such a little guy—only 5'10" and about 185 pounds—but he was strong."

Despite Camilli's outstanding all-around play, his repeated contract squabbles with team management convinced the Phillies to trade him to the Dodgers for a reported $75,000 in cash and an unknown outfielder named Eddie Morgan prior to the start of the 1938 campaign. Looking back at the difficulties he encountered when trying to negotiate a new contract with team brass, Camilli said, "No matter what kind of year you had, all they wanted to do was give you about a $1,000 raise."

Remaining one of the senior circuit's top sluggers following his arrival in Brooklyn, Camilli averaged 24 homers, 100 RBIs, and 101 runs scored from 1938 to 1940, before earning league MVP honors in 1941 by hitting 34 homers, driving in 120 runs, and batting .285 for the pennant-winning Dodgers. Camilli followed that up by hitting 26 homers and knocking in 109 runs in 1942, before a slow start in 1943 prompted new Brooklyn general manager Branch Rickey to trade him to the Giants in late July. Refusing to report to the Dodgers' bitter rivals, Camilli chose instead to spend most of the next two seasons managing the Pacific Coast League's Oakland Oaks, before joining the Boston Red Sox midway through the 1945 campaign. After batting just .212, with two homers and 19 RBIs in 63 games with the Red Sox, the 38-year-old Camilli announced his retirement, ending his career with 239 home runs, 950 RBIs, 936 runs scored, 1,482 hits, 261 doubles, 86 triples, 60 stolen bases, a .277 batting average, an on-base percentage of .388, and a slugging percentage of .492. In his four years with the Phillies, Camilli hit 92 homers, knocked in 333 runs, scored 347 times, stole 23 bases, batted .295, compiled an on-base percentage of .395, posted a slugging percentage of .510, and collected 585 hits, 95 doubles, and 28 triples.

Following his playing days, Camilli spent 25 years either managing in the minors or scouting for the Yankees, Phillies, Athletics, and Angels, before retiring from the game in 1971. Camilli lived until October 21, 1997, when he died in San Mateo, California, at the age of 90.

PHILLIES CAREER HIGHLIGHTS

Best Season

Camilli had an outstanding year for the Phillies in 1937, hitting 27 homers, driving in 80 runs, scoring 101 times, batting a career-high .339, finishing second in the NL with 90 walks and an OPS of 1.034, and leading the league with a .446 on-base percentage. But Camilli performed even better in 1936, when, in addition to batting .315, he placed near the top of the league rankings in 10 different offensive categories, including home runs (28), RBIs (102), runs scored (106), triples (13), total bases (306), walks (116), and OPS (1.018).

Memorable Moments/Greatest Performances

Camilli led the Phillies to a 10–9 win over the Dodgers on April 18, 1935, by hitting a pair of two-run homers off starter Dutch Leonard.

Camilli followed that up by hitting another two homers and knocking in a career-high seven runs during an 18–7 rout of the New York Giants on April 19, 1935.

Camilli contributed to an 11–6 home win over the Chicago Cubs on May 15, 1936, by going 4-for-4, with a homer, triple, and four runs batted in.

After hitting a solo homer earlier in the contest, Camilli gave the Phillies a 5–3 win over the Cubs on July 28, 1936, by homering with one man aboard with two men out in the bottom of the ninth inning.

Camilli helped lead the Phillies to a 9–6 win over the Cardinals on August 28, 1937, by hitting a pair of two-run homers.

In addition to scoring three times during a 9–5 win over the Reds on September 23, 1937, Camilli delivered the game's big blow in the third inning when he homered with the bases loaded.

Notable Achievements

- Hit more than 25 home runs three times.
- Batted over .300 twice, topping the .330 mark once.
- Knocked in more than 100 runs once.
- Scored more than 100 runs twice.
- Finished in double digits in triples once.
- Walked more than 100 times once.
- Compiled on-base percentage over .400 twice.
- Posted slugging percentage over .500 twice.
- Compiled OPS over 1.000 twice.
- Led NL in on-base percentage once and games played once.
- Finished second in NL in home runs once, triples once, extra-base hits once, walks twice, slugging percentage once, and OPS twice.
- Finished third in NL in home runs twice and slugging percentage once.
- Led NL first basemen in putouts twice and fielding percentage once.
- Ranks among Phillies career leaders in on-base percentage (8th), slugging percentage (9th), and OPS (9th).

35

JIM THOME

Already an established star by the time he arrived in Philadelphia in 2003, Jim Thome spent the previous 12 years terrorizing American League pitchers with his powerful left-handed bat as a member of the Cleveland Indians. Gaining general recognition as one of baseball's foremost sluggers during his time in Cleveland, Thome surpassed 30 homers seven times, knocked in more than 100 runs six times, and scored more than 100 runs on six separate occasions, earning in the process three All-Star selections and three top-10 finishes in the AL MVP voting. Continuing his prolific slugging after signing with the Phillies as a free agent, Thome topped 40 homers and 100 RBIs in each of his first two seasons in the City of Brotherly Love, before a subpar performance in 2005 brought on by back problems prompted the Phillies to trade him to the Chicago White Sox at the end of the year. Nevertheless, Thome, who ranks among the franchise's all-time leaders in on-base percentage, slugging percentage, and OPS, accomplished enough during his brief stay in Philadelphia to earn a spot on our list.

Born in Peoria, Illinois, on August 27, 1970, James Howard Thome learned how to play baseball from his father, Chuck, who, in addition to working long days helping to build bulldozers as a foreman at Caterpillar Industries, Inc., spent many years starring in the local fast-pitch softball leagues. Recalling that his son developed a love for the game at an early age, Chuck said, "The only thing the kid ever wanted to do was play baseball. He used to have a hard time getting kids to spend as much time on the field as he wanted to. Rain or shine, he'd take a bucket of rubber baseballs and hit them for hours."

Following in the footsteps of his two older brothers, both of whom starred on the diamond at Limestone Community High School in nearby Bartonville, Jim attended that same institution, where he earned All-State honors as a guard in basketball and a shortstop in baseball. After enrolling at Illinois Central College following his graduation in 1988, Thome

Jim Thome led the NL with 47 home runs his first year in Philadelphia.
Courtesy of Keith Allison

continued to compete in both sports, performing well enough in his one year of college ball to draw interest from the Cleveland Indians, who selected him in the 13th round of the 1989 MLB Draft. Recalling the impression that Thome made on him one afternoon, Indians scout Tom Couston said, "There were a bunch of scouts there, but they'd all come to see another player. Thome was playing shortstop, and he went 1-for-4, or maybe it was 0-for-4. But every ball he hit was a rocket. His swing was so quick and powerful that I was surprised he didn't kill somebody."

After signing with the Indians, Thome spent most of the next five seasons in the minor leagues, although he also appeared in a total of 114 games with the parent club from 1991 to 1993, hitting 10 homers and driving in 43 runs for the Tribe during that time.

Thome's lengthy stint in the minors could be attributed primarily to his subpar defense. Manning the hot corner while advancing through Cleveland's farm system, Thome later recalled, "There were times when I really needed to work, especially defensively. I had to put in a lot of extra work and hard times defensively to make myself an even adequate defensive player. Early on, I had a hard time defensively."

Thome also struggled at the plate during the early stages of his pro career, displaying a lack of patience as a hitter and often waving at curveballs and splitters in the dirt, particularly against southpaw pitching. However, things finally started to come together for Thome at Triple-A Scranton in 1993, when, with the help of future major-league manager Charlie Manuel, he earned International League MVP honors by hitting 25 home runs and batting .332. Crediting Manuel with his development as a hitter, Thome claims, "He was everything to me. Hands down. From confidence, to what he taught me, to the mental side of hitting. We didn't talk about mechanics a whole lot, but he got me in position when he put me on home plate with my back foot and opened me up. I really saw my power keep progressing."

Thome also revealed that he first began using the technique of pointing his bat toward the pitcher while awaiting his delivery at Manuel's behest, stating, "I did that in Scranton when Charlie Manuel had seen a clip of Roy Hobbs" (the protagonist in the movie *The Natural*). "Roy Hobbs would point his bat, and, when I got in the box, I was really tense. I was tight, and he wanted to create that relaxing feeling in the box, and it got my trigger ready to hit."

Thome's stellar performance in 1993 earned him a promotion to the Indians the following year, when, after laying claim to the starting third base job, he batted .268, hit 20 homers, and knocked in 52 runs, even though a players' strike shortened the season to just 113 games. Thome followed that up by hitting 25 homers, knocking in 73 runs, scoring 92 times, drawing 97 bases on balls, batting .314, and finishing third in the league with a .438 on-base percentage in 1995.

Emerging as a true offensive force in 1996, Thome began an exceptional seven-year run during which he averaged 40 home runs, 109 RBIs, and 103 runs scored for the Indians. Performing especially well in 1996, 2001, and 2002, Thome hit 38 homers, knocked in 116 runs, scored 122 times, and batted .311 in the first of those campaigns, prompting teammate Sandy Alomar Jr. to say, "He's a natural-born hitter. He's gotten better since he's been in the big leagues, and I think he can continue to improve." After moving across the diamond to first base the following year, Thome earned a pair of top-10 finishes in the AL MVP voting by hitting 49 homers, driving in 124 runs, scoring 101 times, and batting .291 in 2001, before batting .304, ranking among the league leaders with 52 homers, 118 RBIs, and a .445 on-base percentage, and topping the circuit with 122 walks, a .677 slugging percentage, and an OPS of 1.122 in 2002.

Thome, who stood 6'4" and weighed close to 250 pounds, proved to be a slugger in the truest sense of the word, intimidating opposing pitchers with his size, brute strength, and potent swing. Possessing tremendous power to all fields, Thome had the ability to drive the ball out of any part of the park, hitting many of his home runs to center and left-center field. Thome also gradually developed a keen batting eye and superior knowledge of the strike zone, enabling him to top the circuit in walks three times. However, he also struck out frequently, leading his league in strikeouts on three separate occasions.

In discussing his greatest flaw as a hitter, Thome stated, "The strikeouts were a part of my game that I didn't like, but I wasn't going to take away the aggressiveness. I think the biggest help to my game was the fact that I walked. I was a hitter that did strike out, but I also went through periods of good contact. I had the ability to take the ball the other way, I had power, but the strikeouts were a part of my game that I always tried to improve on, but it was just a part of my game. It was the way that I was constructed."

As Thome rose to stardom as a member of the Indians, he grew increasingly popular with the hometown fans, writers, and broadcasters, who very much appreciated his strong work ethic, old-fashioned values, and friendly demeanor. Extremely approachable, Thome never rejected autograph requests, once stating, "I sign every autograph I can for kids because I remember myself at that age. I think it's ridiculous that some guys won't sign for a kid."

Commenting on Thome's likable personality, Indians GM John Hart suggested, "He's got that 'aw gee, aw shucks' air about him. Jim is Huck Finn personified, and he really likes to play baseball."

Identifying former Indians first baseman Eddie Murray as his role model, Thome credited his calm demeanor to his onetime teammate, noting, "Eddie taught me to play the game exactly the same when you fail and when you succeed. Hit a home run, hey, enjoy the moment, but then let it go. If you strike out with the bases loaded, same thing, let it go. I don't smash helmets when I strike out, because it's not the helmet's fault, it's my fault."

Yet, despite his gentle nature, Thome possessed a fierce competitive spirit, with Richie Sexson saying of his former teammate, "He's an emotional player who likes to play for something. Every team has a guy who refuses to lose, a big-time player who pushes and pulls the rest of the team."

A free agent heading into the 2003 campaign, Thome hoped to remain in Cleveland. But, with the Indians offering him $60 million over five years, Thome elected to sign with the Phillies when they came calling with a six-year, $85 million offer. Quickly earning the respect of Phillies manager Larry Bowa during his first spring training with his new team, Thome drew praise from his new skipper, who said, "Jim Thome hasn't missed a road trip. I've given him the option. He says: 'I like to ride the bus. I get to bond with my players.' I've never heard that in my life."

Thome also made an extremely favorable impression on Bowa with his exceptional on-field performance in 2003, earning a fourth-place finish in the NL MVP voting by leading the league with 47 homers, driving in 131 runs, scoring 111 times, batting .266, compiling an on-base percentage of .385, and posting a slugging percentage of .573. Thome posted excellent numbers once again in 2004, gaining All-Star recognition by hitting 42 homers, knocking in 105 runs, scoring 97 others, batting .274, compiling a .396 on-base percentage, and posting a .581 slugging percentage, before suffering a terrible loss during the subsequent offseason when his mother died of cancer on January 5, 2005. In discussing his mom's passing, Thome said, "In a lot of different ways, she was my best friend. My mom was really the go-to lady in our family. She was the rock. She was the foundation. We all kind of fed off what she did."

Still reeling from the loss of his mother, Thome spent the entire 2005 season being plagued by back and elbow problems that limited him to just 59 games, seven homers, 30 RBIs, and a .207 batting average. Following Thome's poor performance and the emergence of NL Rookie of the Year Ryan Howard, the Phillies elected to trade the 35-year-old first baseman to the Chicago White Sox for outfielder Aaron Rowand and pitcher Gio González at season's end.

Thome subsequently spent most of the next four seasons with the White Sox, having his best year for them in 2006 when he earned All-Star honors for the fifth and final time by hitting 42 homers, driving in 109 runs, scoring 108 others, and batting .288. But, after being dealt to the Los Angeles Dodgers during the latter stages of the 2009 campaign, Thome never again performed at an elite level. Signed by the Minnesota Twins as a free agent prior to the start of the 2010 season, Thome split his last three years in the big leagues between four different teams, briefly returning to Cleveland and Philadelphia for second tours of duty with the Indians and Phillies, before announcing his retirement following the conclusion of the 2012 campaign with career totals of 612 home runs, 1,699 RBIs, 1,583 runs scored, 2,328 hits, 451 doubles, and 26 triples, a .276 batting average, a .402 on-base percentage, and a .554 slugging percentage. Over parts of four seasons in Philadelphia, Thome hit 101 homers, drove in 281 runs, scored 243 times, batted .260, compiled an on-base percentage of .384, posted a slugging percentage of .541, and collected 348 hits, 67 doubles, and four triples.

In discussing Thome's Hall of Fame prospects following his retirement, sportswriter Stephen Silver wrote in *Philadelphia* magazine:

"It's not just the numbers. Thanks to his gregarious personality, Thome is the rare athlete who played in several cities and was beloved everywhere he went. I saw the Twins and Phillies play each other in Philadelphia when Thome was with the Twins, and the same two teams in Minnesota two years later when Thome was a Phillie, and the opposing crowd cheered Thome both times, even when he hit home runs for the road team. Thome was similarly loved in his long stints in Cleveland and Chicago, as well as shorter runs in Los Angeles and Baltimore."

Expressing similar sentiments during Thome's second tour of duty in Philadelphia in 2012, Phillies GM Rubén Amaro Jr. said, "I can't think of anyone who could have had this impact. Ichiro wouldn't have been embraced like this guy. It's almost like they [the fans] feel he's a Philadelphian."

Thome, who gained induction into the Baseball Hall of Fame the first time his name appeared on the ballot in 2018, joined the White Sox organization as a special assistant to GM Rick Hahn following his playing days. He later accepted a part-time studio analyst position with MLB Network, with whom he currently works, while still fulfilling his role with the White Sox.

PHILLIES CAREER HIGHLIGHTS

Best Season

Although Thome also posted outstanding numbers the following year, the 2003 campaign proved to be his finest in Philadelphia. In addition to batting .266, compiling an OPS of .958, and leading the NL with 47 home runs, Thome ranked among the league leaders with 131 RBIs, 111 runs scored, 111 walks, and 331 total bases.

Memorable Moments/Greatest Performances

Thome contributed to a 16–2 rout of the Braves on April 9, 2003, by homering twice and knocking in five runs, connecting off Joey Dawley for a three-run homer in the seventh inning and a two-run blast in the eighth. Thome hit another two home runs during a 6–5, 13-inning win over the Red Sox on June 21, 2003, with his two-out solo shot in the bottom of the 12th inning tying the score at 3–3.

Thome helped lead the Phillies to an 11–4 win over the Brewers on August 13, 2003, by hitting a pair of homers and driving in four runs, reaching the seats against starter Ben Sheets with two men on base in the first inning, before homering with no one on off Mike DeJean in the bottom of the eighth.

Thome provided much of the offensive firepower during a 4–2 win over the Montreal Expos on April 16, 2004, going 4-for-4, with a homer and two runs scored.

Thome starred in defeat on June 8, 2004, driving in six runs with a pair of three-run homers during a 14–11 loss to the Chicago White Sox.

Thome again performed extremely well during an 8–2 win over the Kansas City Royals on June 20, 2004, going 3-for-3, with two homers, a double, a walk, and five RBIs.

Notable Achievements

- Hit more than 40 home runs twice.
- Knocked in more than 100 runs twice.
- Scored more than 100 runs once.
- Surpassed 30 doubles once.
- Walked more than 100 times twice.
- Posted slugging percentage over .500 twice.
- Compiled OPS over .900 twice.
- Led NL with 47 home runs in 2003.
- Finished second in NL with 111 bases on balls in 2003.
- Finished third in NL with 131 RBIs and 80 extra-base hits in 2003.
- Ranks among Phillies career leaders in on-base percentage (12th), slugging percentage (3rd), and OPS (5th).
- Two-time NL Player of the Week.
- Two-time NL Player of the Month.
- 2004 Lou Gehrig Memorial Award winner.
- Finished fourth in 2003 NL MVP voting.
- 2004 NL All-Star.
- Member of Philadelphia Baseball Wall of Fame.
- Elected to Baseball Hall of Fame by members of BBWAA in 2018.

36

SHANE VICTORINO

K nown for his bubbly personality, energetic style of play, and ability to perform well under pressure, Shane Victorino established himself as one of the Phillies' most popular players during his eight-year stint in the City of Brotherly Love that began in 2005. A solid hitter, excellent base-runner, and outstanding outfielder, Victorino batted over .280 four times, scored more than 100 runs twice, stole more than 30 bases three times, and won three Gold Gloves for his exceptional defensive work in center field. A two-time NL All-Star, Victorino proved to be a key contributor to Phillies teams that won five division titles, two pennants, and one World Series.

Born in Wailuku, Hawaii, on November 30, 1980, Shane Patrick Victorino grew up on the island playing baseball, basketball, football, and soccer, while also competing in track. Diagnosed with attention deficit hyperactivity disorder at an early age, Victorino, who is of Portuguese, Hawaiian, Japanese, and English descent, attended local St. Anthony High School, where he won state championships in the 100, 200, and 400 meters his senior year. After signing a letter of intent to play college baseball for the Hawaii Rainbow Warriors, Victorino instead chose to turn pro when the Los Angeles Dodgers selected him in the sixth round of the June 1999 MLB Amateur Draft.

Victorino subsequently spent the next four years in the minor leagues, making it as high as Double-A Jacksonville in 2002, before the San Diego Padres plucked him from the Dodgers' farm system in the Rule 5 Draft. Returned to the Dodgers after he batted just .151 in 36 games with the Padres, Victorino remained in the Los Angeles farm system for another two years, before the Phillies nabbed him in the 2004 Rule 5 Draft.

Finally establishing himself as a legitimate major-league prospect at Triple-A Scranton/Wilkes-Barre in 2005, Victorino earned International League MVP honors by batting .310 in 126 games, prompting the Phillies to summon him to the big leagues during the latter stages of the campaign. Appearing in 21 games with the parent club during the season's final month, Victorino homered twice, knocked in eight runs, and batted .294 in 17 official at-bats.

Victorino subsequently spent the first few months of the 2006 season serving the Phillies primarily as a fourth outfielder, before taking over in right field for Bobby Abreu when the team traded him to the Yankees just prior to the trade deadline. Despite garnering just 415 official at-bats over the course of the campaign, Victorino posted solid numbers, finishing the season with six homers, 46 RBIs, 70 runs scored, and a .287 batting average. Victorino remained in right field for one more year, hitting 12 homers, knocking in 46 runs, scoring 78 times, stealing 37 bases, and batting .281 in 2007, before replacing Aaron Rowand as the Phillies' full-time starter in center field the following season after the latter signed with the San Francisco Giants as a free agent. Developing into an outstanding all-around player in 2008, Victorino helped lead the eventual world champion Phillies to their first pennant in 15 years by hitting 14 homers, driving in 58 runs, scoring 102 times, stealing 36 bases, batting .293, and earning Gold Glove honors for the first of three straight times. An All-Star for the first time in his career the following season, Victorino homered 10 times, knocked in 62 runs, scored 102 others, stole 25 bases, collected a league-leading 13 triples, batted .292, and established career-high marks with 39 doubles and a .358 on-base percentage.

Shane Victorino helped lead the Phillies to two pennants and one world championship.
Courtesy of Keith Allison

Generally hitting either first or second in the Phillies lineup, the switch-hitting Victorino, who stood 5'9" and weighed 190 pounds, provided a spark at the top of the batting order, often using his speed, exceptional baserunning ability, and aggressive style of play to upset opposing defenses. Although not a power hitter, Victorino possessed the ability to deliver the long ball, finishing in double digits in homers for the Phillies five straight times. Meanwhile, Victorino often inspired his teammates with the tremendous hustle and enthusiasm he exhibited on the playing field.

Victorino continued to perform well for the Phillies in 2010 and 2011, hitting 18 homers, driving in 69 runs, scoring 84 times, stealing 34 bases, and batting .259 in the first of those campaigns, before reaching the seats 17 times, knocking in 61 runs, scoring 95 others, leading the league with 16 triples, batting .279, and posting a career-high .847 OPS the following year. But, with the Phillies in a rebuilding mode by 2012, they dealt Victorino to the Dodgers for three minor-league prospects just prior to the trade deadline, thereby ending his eight-year stay in Philadelphia.

Upon acquiring Victorino, Dodgers general manager Ned Colletti spoke of the many positive things he expected the 31-year-old outfielder to bring to his team when he said, "We're excited to add an All-Star caliber player with postseason experience. He plays the game with passion, gives us a top of the order bat from both sides of the plate, can steal bases, and is solid defensively in the outfield."

Victorino, who left the Phillies having hit 88 homers, driven in 390 runs, scored 582 times, stolen 179 bases, batted .279, compiled a .345 on-base percentage, posted a .439 slugging percentage, and collected 998 hits, 181 doubles, and 63 triples as a member of the team, finished out the year in Los Angeles, before signing with the Boston Red Sox as a free agent prior to the start of the ensuing campaign. After two-and-a-half years in Boston, one of which ended with a world championship for the Red Sox, Victorino returned to the Dodgers, who reacquired him just prior to the 2015 trade deadline. A free agent again at the end of the year, Victorino failed to garner significant interest from any team, forcing him to sit out the next two seasons, before officially announcing his retirement on July 3, 2018, with career totals of 108 home runs, 489 RBIs, 731 runs scored, 1,274 hits, 231 doubles, 70 triples, 231 stolen bases, a .275 batting average, a .340 on-base percentage, and a .425 slugging percentage.

Making his decision known to the public during an interview with NBC Philadelphia, Victorino said, "It's time to hang it up and call it a career. I think I've been blessed with that opportunity as a baseball player growing up in Maui, getting that opportunity to represent my state, represent my people. It's about that time, it's time for me to say . . . it's time for me to move on. It's time for me to enjoy retirement."

Victorino added, "It's nice to be known as a World Series champ, an All-Star, and a Gold Glover, but ultimately my biggest accomplishment in the game is when fans tell me that I play the game the right way. I think that hits home for me more than anything."

Victorino later signed a one-day contract with the Phillies that allowed him to officially retire as a member of the team, telling the fans in attendance at Citizens Bank Park during the Phillies' Alumni Weekend festivities, "I will always have you woven into the fabric of my life. This is not a goodbye. It's just the next chapter. Mahalo, Philly."

Victorino continued, "This city made me the person that I am. I was a 25-year-old kid bouncing all over the place just looking for an opportunity, and I got to come to a first-class organization with first-class people. . . . In 2005, I came to Philadelphia as a Rule 5 player. The city and me shared a DNA—an expectation for mediocrity. Well, this is far from what happened. Hard work, dedication and teamwork were the formula for success. Philadelphia, I can proudly look you all in the eye and say this: We succeeded. A World Series championship! We have rallied and today Philadelphia is respected—a booming city of winners. . . . I've been lucky. For the rest of my life, I'll forever be part of this organization."

Since retiring as an active player, Victorino, who, along with his wife, Melissa, generously donated $1 million to reconstruct a once dilapidated Boys and Girls Club in Nicetown, Philadelphia, during his playing days, has continued his charitable work through The Shane Victorino Foundation, which is working to build baseball and after-school facilities in Maui and runs an annual toy drive in Las Vegas.

PHILLIES CAREER HIGHLIGHTS

Best Season

It could be argued that Victorino made his greatest impact on the Phillies in 2008, when he helped lead them to the NL pennant and an eventual world championship by hitting 14 homers, driving in 58 runs, scoring 102 times, batting .293, stealing 36 bases, and compiling an OPS of .799. However, he posted slightly better overall numbers the following year, concluding the 2009 campaign with 10 homers, 62 RBIs, 102 runs scored, 25 stolen bases, a league-leading 13 triples, a career-high 39 doubles, a batting average of .292, and an OPS of .803.

Memorable Moments/Greatest Performances

Victorino gave the Phillies an 8–7 win over the Braves on September 3, 2006, by driving in the decisive run with an RBI single in the bottom of the ninth inning.

Victorino led the Phillies to a 14–2 rout of the Florida Marlins on September 29, 2006, by going 5-for-6, with a triple, two doubles, three RBIs, and three runs scored.

Victorino helped celebrate Shane Victorino Day at Citizens Bank Park on June 3, 2007, by hitting a solo homer in the bottom of the ninth inning that gave the Phillies a 9–8 victory over the Giants.

Victorino hit safely five times during a 15–3 win over the Dodgers on July 17, 2007, going 5-for-7, with a triple, two RBIs, and two runs scored.

Victorino starred during a 5–2 win over the Milwaukee Brewers in Game 2 of the 2008 NLDS, collecting three hits, homering once, and stealing two bases, with his second-inning grand slam off C. C. Sabathia giving the Phillies all the runs they needed.

Victorino experienced an emotional moment during a 9–8 win over the Washington Nationals on April 13, 2009, when, after hitting a solo homer in the top of the third inning, he pointed up to the broadcast booth as a way of honoring longtime Phillies play-by-play man Harry Kalas, who died of a heart attack just prior to the start of the game.

Victorino homered with the bases loaded during a 7–3 victory over the Florida Marlins on April 24, 2009, with his ninth-inning grand slam off reliever Matt Lindstrom turning a 3–2 deficit into a 6–3 Phillies lead.

Victorino led the Phillies to a 10–7 win over the Cardinals on May 5, 2009, by going 4-for-5, with a homer, double, three RBIs, and three runs scored.

Victorino contributed to a 22–1 thrashing of the Reds on July 6, 2009, by going 4-for-5, with a homer, two doubles, four RBIs, and career-high five runs scored.

Victorino had a huge game against the Washington Nationals on April 14, 2010, going 4-for-5, with a homer, triple, five RBIs, and three runs scored during a 14–7 Phillies win.

Victorino helped pace the Phillies to a 9–6 victory over the Baltimore Orioles on June 8, 2012, by driving in five runs with a homer, double, and single.

Notable Achievements

- Scored more than 100 runs twice.
- Finished in double digits in triples three times.
- Surpassed 30 doubles twice.
- Stole more than 20 bases five times, topping 30 thefts on three occasions.
- Led NL in triples twice.
- Finished third in NL in triples once and stolen bases once.
- Led NL outfielders in assists once, fielding percentage twice, and double plays once.

- Led NL center fielders in assists once and fielding percentage twice.
- Led NL right fielders in double plays once.
- Five-time division champion (2007, 2008, 2009, 2010, and 2011).
- Two-time NL champion (2008 and 2009).
- 2008 world champion.
- Three-time Gold Glove Award winner (2008, 2009, and 2010).
- 2008 Lou Gehrig Memorial Award winner.
- 2011 Branch Rickey Award winner.
- Two-time NL All-Star (2009 and 2011).

37

FRED LUDERUS

The Phillies' starting first baseman from 1911 to 1919, Fred Luderus spent parts of 11 seasons in Philadelphia, developing a reputation during that time for his power at the plate and tremendous durability. After establishing himself as one of the National League's top sluggers during the early stages of his career, Luderus eventually became known more for his strength and endurance by appearing in a then-record 533 consecutive games from 1916 to 1919. A solid all-around hitter, the left-handed-swinging, right-handed-throwing Luderus batted over .300 twice and annually placed near the top of the league rankings in home runs, doubles, RBIs, total bases, and slugging percentage, finishing second in the circuit in each of the first two categories twice each. Meanwhile, Luderus led all NL first sackers in putouts twice and assists five times, with his 1,597 putouts at first in 1917 establishing a single-season franchise record that still stands.

Born to German-immigrant parents in Milwaukee, Wisconsin, on September 12, 1885, Frederick William Luderus spent his teenage years developing his baseball skills on the sandlots of his hometown, where his strong play garnered him interest from pro scouts. After signing with Sault Ste. Marie of the Class D Copper County Soo League in 1905, Luderus spent the next three years competing in that circuit, before sitting out most of the 1908 campaign with diphtheria. Returning to action with Freeport (Illinois) of the Wisconsin-Illinois League in 1909, Luderus topped the circuit with a .321 batting average, prompting the Chicago Cubs to purchase his contract for $2,200. The 24-year-old Luderus subsequently appeared in 11 games with the Cubs over the final two weeks of the 1909 campaign, batting .297, hitting his first big-league homer, and driving in nine runs in just 37 official at-bats.

After seeing extremely limited duty with the Cubs during the first four months of the 1910 season, Luderus headed to Philadelphia when the Phillies acquired him in a July 29, 1910, trade for journeyman left-hander Bill Foxen. Although the Phillies initially intended to use Luderus as a temporary replacement at first base for the ailing Kitty Bransfield, they altered their plans when, after batting .294 and knocking in 14 runs down the stretch in 1910, Luderus made an extremely favorable impression on them the following spring. Choosing to release Bransfield, the Phillies handed the first base job to Luderus, who rewarded them for the faith they placed in him by batting .301, finishing second in the league with 16 home runs, and placing third in the circuit with 99 RBIs and 260 total bases. Although Luderus posted less impressive overall

Fred Luderus appeared in every game the Phillies played from 1917 to 1919.

numbers in 1912, hitting 10 homers, driving in 69 runs, and batting .257, he managed to score a career-high 77 runs. Luderus then returned to top form the following year, finishing second in the NL to teammate Gavvy Cravath with 18 homers, 57 extra-base hits, and 254 total bases, while also ranking among the league leaders with 86 runs batted in.

Benefiting greatly from playing his home games at the Baker Bowl, the thick-boned Luderus, who stood 5'11" and weighed 185 pounds, learned to take full advantage of the ballpark's dimensions, hitting 75 percent of his 84 career homers there. But Luderus, a dead fastball hitter who feasted on pitches high in the strike zone, proved to be much more than just a slugger during his time in Philadelphia, displaying his all-around hitting ability in 1915, when, after hitting 12 homers and batting just .248 the previous year, he helped lead the Phillies to their first pennant by finishing second in the NL with a career-high .315 batting average and 36 doubles. Impressed with Luderus's outstanding play, J. C. Kofoed referred to him in the July 1915 issue of *Baseball Magazine* as "the most underrated man in baseball today." An exceptional leader as well, Luderus served as captain of the Phillies during that championship campaign of 1915. And, even though accounts of Luderus's overall game describe him as being nothing more than an adequate defensive first baseman, he annually ranked among the top players at his position in putouts, assists, double plays turned, and fielding percentage.

Curiously, Luderus lost his ability to deliver the long ball after 1915, hitting just five home runs in each of the next four seasons. Yet, he remained a solid offensive performer from 1916 to 1919, batting over .280 three times, while also ranking among the league leaders in RBIs and doubles twice each. And, over the course of those four seasons, Luderus missed a total of just eight games, appearing in 533 consecutive contests from June 2, 1916, to the end of the 1919 campaign. By doing so, Luderus established a new major-league record, breaking the previous mark of 478 straight games played set by Hall of Fame second baseman Eddie Collins just one year earlier. To commemorate Luderus's accomplishment, the Phillies held a Fred Luderus Day at the Baker Bowl between games of a doubleheader on September 24, 1919, presenting him with a gold watch and diamond stickpin during the festivities.

Luderus's streak finally ended on Opening Day of the 1920 season, when an attack of lumbago forced him to the bench. Plagued by back problems the rest of the year, Luderus appeared in just 16 games before announcing his retirement with career totals of 84 home runs, 642 RBIs, 570 runs scored, 1,344 hits, 251 doubles, 54 triples, 55 stolen bases, a batting average of .277, an on-base percentage of .340, and a slugging percentage of .403, compiling virtually all those numbers as a member of the Phillies.

Following his playing days, Luderus began a career in managing, spending 10 of the next 13 years piloting clubs in the minor leagues, serving as a player-manager in some of those. In fact, Luderus batted .362 in part-time duty with Oklahoma City in 1923, while guiding the team to the Western League pennant. With the same club the following season, Luderus claimed to have taught a young Carl Hubbell how to throw a screwball.

Retiring from baseball altogether in 1933, Luderus returned to his home state of Wisconsin, where he briefly worked as the grounds' supervisor at the Milwaukee Yacht Club, before starting his own toy business. Luderus lived until January 5, 1961, when he suffered a fatal heart attack at his home in Three Lakes, Wisconsin, at the age of 75.

PHILLIES CAREER HIGHLIGHTS

Best Season

Luderus performed extremely well for the Phillies during the pennant-winning campaign of 1915, hitting seven homers, driving in 62 runs, and finishing second in the NL with 36 doubles, a .315 batting average, a .457 slugging percentage, and an .833 OPS. He also posted solid numbers in 1913, batting .262 and ranking among the league leaders with 18 home runs, 86 RBIs, and 32 doubles. But Luderus had his finest all-around season in 1911, when he placed near the top of the league rankings in seven different offensive categories, including home runs (16), RBIs (99), hits (166), triples (11), batting average (.301), and OPS (.825).

Memorable Moments/Greatest Performances

Luderus hit two home runs in one game for the first time in his career during a 7–5 win over the Giants on July 4, 1911.

Luderus starred in defeat two days later, hitting another two homers and knocking in five runs during a 13–9 loss to the Cardinals on July 6, with one of his homers coming with the bases loaded.

Luderus continued his home-run-hitting binge on July 15, 1911, leading the Phillies to a 2–1 win over the Pirates by becoming the first player in team history to hit two over-the-fence homers in a game, with his ninth-inning blast off Pittsburgh ace Babe Adams providing the margin of victory.

Luderus helped lead the Phillies to a 9–8 win over the Cubs on July 18, 1912, by driving in five runs, with his first-inning grand slam proving to be the game's big blow.

Luderus delivered the game-winning hit in a 3–2 victory over the Reds on June 10, 1913, when he bounced the ball into the right field stands at Redlands Field on one hop for a solo homer in the top of the ninth inning. In describing Luderus's blast, which landed in the stands more than 400 feet from home plate after initially hitting on the field, *Cincinnati Enquirer* reporter Jack Ryder wrote, "The feat was thought impossible. There is little chance of another hit like that of Luderus being made on this field for many seasons."

Luderus contributed to a 16–3 rout of the Cubs on August 8, 1913, by going 3-for-5, with two homers and five RBIs.

Luderus collected five hits in one game for the only time in his career on September 16, 1915, going 5-for-5, with a triple and two doubles during a 10–3 rout of the Reds in Cincinnati.

Although the Phillies lost the 1915 World Series to the Red Sox in five games, Luderus performed extremely well, going 7-for-16 (.438), with a homer, two doubles, and six RBIs.

Luderus led the Phillies to a 7–2 win over the Brooklyn Robins on April 23, 1918, by going 3-for-4, with a homer, double, four RBIs, and three runs scored.

Notable Achievements

- Batted over .300 twice.
- Finished in double digits in triples once.
- Surpassed 30 doubles four times.
- Played in 533 consecutive games from 1916 to 1919, appearing in every game for three straight seasons (1917 to 1919).
- Led NL in games played once.
- Finished second in NL in batting average once, home runs twice, doubles twice, total bases once, slugging percentage once, and OPS once.
- Finished third in NL in runs batted in twice, total bases once, and games played once.
- Led NL first basemen in putouts twice and assists five times.
- Holds Phillies single-season record for most putouts at first base (1,597 in 1917).
- 1915 NL champion.

38

JIM KONSTANTY

The only Phillies pitcher ever to earn NL MVP honors, Jim Konstanty accomplished the feat in 1950, when his brilliant work out of the bullpen helped lead Philadelphia's "Whiz Kids" to the second pennant in franchise history. Performing magnificently over the course of the campaign, Konstanty also gained recognition as the *Sporting News* NL Pitcher of the Year and the Associated Press Athlete of the Year by topping the senior circuit in pitching appearances, games finished, and saves. Although Konstanty never again reached such heights, he pitched effectively during most of his time in Philadelphia, winning at least 14 games twice and posting a winning percentage over .600 four times, ironically achieving success in the City of Brotherly Love with the help of an undertaker.

Born in Strykersville, New York, on March 2, 1917, Casimir James Konstanty moved with his family to Buffalo as an infant, before relocating once again to Delevan, New York, where his parents ran a small country hotel. Following the passing of his mother, who died when he was 11 years old, young Jim moved with his father, stepmother, and five siblings to a farm seven miles from Delevan, in Eagle, New York, where he learned the rigors of farm work.

Starring in multiple sports at Arcade High School, Konstanty excelled in baseball, basketball, and football, captaining all three teams his senior year, after leading the basketball squad to a league championship as a junior. Particularly proficient on the diamond, Konstanty pitched and played third base, earning team MVP honors twice with his outstanding all-around play. During his final two years of high school, Konstanty also played on the *Buffalo Evening News*–sponsored Arcade town team in the Suburban League.

Offered a partial athletic scholarship to Syracuse University, Konstanty ended up working his way through school by assuming numerous odd jobs, including waiting on tables in a girls' dorm. Meanwhile, Konstanty continued to display his superior athletic ability by lettering in baseball, basketball, soccer, and boxing. Playing mostly first base and third base for

Jim Konstanty's superb pitching in 1950 earned him NL MVP honors.

the school's baseball team, Konstanty later described himself as "a strong wild-armed third baseman with a big chest to knock balls down, a fair hitter, but very, very slow on foot."

After graduating from Syracuse with a degree in physical education, Konstanty spent nearly two years teaching Phys Ed in high school, before entering the world of professional baseball with Massena (NY) of the Northern League in the summer of 1940. Converted into a pitcher while at Massena, Konstanty subsequently split the next three years between two different minor-league teams, during which time he learned how to compensate for his mediocre fastball by changing speeds and using breaking pitches to fool opposing hitters.

Finally promoted to the big leagues at the age of 27 in June 1944 after beginning the year 8-6 for the Syracuse Chiefs of the International League, Konstanty ended up starting 12 games, throwing 112 2/3 innings, and compiling a record of 6-4 and an ERA of 2.80 for the Cincinnati Reds, before missing the entire 1945 campaign while serving in the Navy during World War II. Discharged from the military early in 1946, Konstanty then spent most of the next three seasons back in the minor leagues, where he experienced very little success until advice from an unlikely source helped him turn his career around.

Konstanty, who typically spent the offseason in Worcester, New York, one day invited a neighbor of his named Andy Skinner to accompany him on a trek up north. Although Skinner, who happened to be the local undertaker, had never played baseball, Konstanty found that his experience as a bowler gave him a considerable amount of insight into the manner with which a ball tends to twist and spin on its way to its ultimate destination. When Konstanty subsequently applied the same philosophy to throwing a baseball, he experienced immediate results, causing him to depend heavily on Skinner through the years to help him improve his slider and changeup, with the pitcher later calling his advisor his "bread and butter."

After Konstanty performed better with the Toronto Maple Leafs of the International League in 1947, Toronto manager Eddie Sawyer began using him more and more in relief the following year. And, with Konstanty thriving in his new role, Sawyer had the Phillies purchase his contract shortly after he became manager in Philadelphia during the latter stages of the 1948 campaign, saying at the time, "I have never seen him get hit really hard. He is murder to good hitters. . . . He gets even better as he tires. His pitches break more sharply as he goes along."

Excelling for the Phillies down the stretch, Konstanty appeared in six games and worked 9 2/3 innings, winning his lone decision, collecting two saves, and compiling an ERA of just 0.93. Emerging as the leader of the Phillies bullpen the following year, Konstanty threw 97 innings, compiled a record of 9-5, posted an ERA of 3.25, and finished second in the league with seven saves. Konstanty then reached the apex of his career in 1950, when he earned NL MVP honors and his lone All-Star selection by compiling a record of 16-7 and an ERA of 2.66, throwing 152 innings, and leading the league with 22 saves, 74 mound appearances, and 62 games finished.

Commenting on the qualities that enabled Konstanty to perform so brilliantly over the course of the campaign, *Baseball Magazine* columnist Ed Rumill wrote in the November 1950 edition of that publication, "Jim wins because he can control the ball, and he knows what he's doing. He uses his head. When he throws a fastball, he throws it where they can only look at it, not hit it. When they're swinging, they get a slider, screwball, palm ball, or curve—some kind of breaking stuff. He really has those hitters buffaloed."

Relying almost exclusively on offspeed pitches to retire opposing batters, the right-handed-throwing Konstanty, who stood 6'1" and weighed 202 pounds, possessed very little velocity on his fastball, with teammate Willie "Puddin' Head" Jones once saying that if they put the speed gun on Konstanty that had been used to measure Bob Feller's fastball, "I don't think it would work."

Hall of Fame manager Leo Durocher agreed, commenting, "He could hit you between the eyes with his best pitch and not give you a headache."

Konstanty himself later admitted that he survived in the major leagues with just two pitches, a slider and a changeup that was sometimes called a palm-ball, stating, "When I threw a fastball, I got killed."

An extremely intelligent pitcher, Konstanty, according to former teammate Bubba Church, kept a black book in which he recorded every pitch he threw to each batter, and where the ball ended up going. Konstanty also earned the respect and admiration of his teammates and manager with his dedication to his profession, his desire to take the ball every day, and his excellent conditioning, with Eddie Sawyer later calling him the team's best-conditioned athlete.

Nevertheless, Konstanty's age and way of thinking prevented him from truly being "one of the boys" on Philadelphia's 1950 NL pennant-winning team that included "Whiz Kid" members Richie Ashburn, Del Ennis, Granny Hamner, Robin Roberts, and Curt Simmons. In discussing his relationship with the bespectacled Konstanty, who didn't smoke or drink and didn't care much for teammates who did, Ashburn recalled years later, "We never agreed on much, but we talked a lot."

Konstanty followed up his banner year by going just 4-11, with a 4.05 ERA and only nine saves in 1951, later attributing his poor performance to his experimentation with a new pitch that he claimed fouled up his motion, causing him to lose the bite on his breaking pitches and his pinpoint control. Although Konstanty performed somewhat better the next two seasons, finishing 5-3 with a 3.94 ERA and six saves in 1952, before going 14-10 with a 4.43 ERA and five saves in 1953, he failed to regain his earlier form, prompting the Phillies to eventually place him on waivers on August 22, 1954. Ending his stint in Philadelphia with an overall record of 51-39, a .567 winning percentage, an ERA of 3.64, 54 saves, and a WHIP of 1.294, Konstanty subsequently joined the New York Yankees, for whom he pitched extremely well in 1955, going 7-2 with a 2.32 ERA and 12 saves, before retiring the following year after splitting the campaign between the Yankees and St. Louis Cardinals.

Konstanty, who ended his playing career with a record of 66-48, a winning percentage of .579, an ERA of 3.46, a WHIP of 1.296, and 76 saves, subsequently returned to Oneonta, New York, and his sporting goods store, which he originally opened in 1947. Konstanty also served as a minor-league pitching coach for the Yankees and Cardinals, before spending five years serving as the director of athletics at Hartwick College in Oneonta. Konstanty lived until June 11, 1976, when he died at the age of 59, some five months after being diagnosed with cancer of the liver.

PHILLIES CAREER HIGHLIGHTS

Best Season

Was there ever any doubt? Konstanty had easily the finest season of his career in 1950, when he led the Phillies to the pennant and earned NL

MVP honors by going 16-7, with an ERA of 2.66, a WHIP of 1.039, 152 innings pitched, and a league-leading 74 mound appearances and 22 saves, at one point tossing 22 1/3 consecutive scoreless innings.

Memorable Moments/Greatest Performances

Konstanty performed heroically in relief during an 18-inning, 4–3 win over the Pirates on June 9, 1949, earning the victory by allowing no runs and seven hits over the final nine frames.

Konstanty picked up another win in relief on May 28, 1950, allowing no runs and just one hit in five innings of work during a 5–2, 11-inning victory over the Giants at the Polo Grounds.

Konstanty proved to be the key figure in a 9–7, 15-inning win over the Pirates on August 25, 1950, allowing just one run and five hits over the final nine innings after entering the game in the seventh.

Although Konstanty lost a 1–0 pitchers' duel with Vic Raschi in Game 1 of the 1950 World Series, he performed magnificently, surrendering just one run on four hits in eight innings of work, with the Yankees scoring the game's only run in the top of the fourth inning on a sacrifice fly by second baseman Jerry Coleman.

Konstanty turned in a tremendous all-around effort during a 4–0 win over the Braves on August 31, 1952, not only tossing a three-hit shutout, but also driving in the first two runs of the game with an opposite field double in the top of the ninth inning.

Konstanty earned a pair of notable victories over the Giants in 1953, holding them to just one run on seven hits during a complete-game 5–1 win on July 3, and throwing 4 2/3 innings of two-hit shutout ball in relief during a 5–2 win on August 15.

Notable Achievements

- Won at least 14 games twice.
- Posted winning percentage over .600 four times.
- Compiled ERA under 3.00 twice.
- Saved more than 20 games once.
- Posted WHIP under 1.000 once.
- Led NL in saves once and pitching appearances once.
- Finished second in NL in saves once and pitching appearances once.
- 1950 NL champion.
- 1950 Associated Press Athlete of the Year.

- 1950 NL MVP.
- 1950 *Sporting News* NL Pitcher of the Year.
- 1950 *Sporting News* MLB All-Star selection.
- 1950 NL All-Star.
- Named to Phillies Centennial Team in 1983.

39
JOHN KRUK

One of the most colorful personalities in Phillies history, John Kruk spent parts of six seasons in Philadelphia, developing a reputation during that time for his carefree attitude, self-deprecating sense of humor, and ability to hit a baseball. Starting for the Phillies at first base and both corner outfield positions, Kruk did a solid job wherever he played in the field, although it was as a hitter that he truly excelled. An extremely consistent offensive performer, Kruk batted over .300 four times and compiled an on-base percentage in excess of .400 twice, while also hitting more than 20 homers, driving in more than 90 runs, and scoring 100 runs once each. A three-time NL All-Star who made significant contributions to the Phillies' 1993 pennant-winning team, Kruk later received the additional honor of being named to the Philadelphia Baseball Wall of Fame.

Born in Charleston, West Virginia, on February 9, 1961, John Martin Kruk moved with his family as an infant to New Jersey, where his father worked two shifts in a bottling company to ensure that his children played baseball. After his family moved back to West Virginia and settled in the city of Keyser some 10 years later, Kruk went on to establish himself as a star outfielder/first baseman at Keyser High School, before enrolling at Potomac State College and later transferring to Allegheny Community College in Maryland, where he played for Junior College Hall of Fame coach Steve Bazarnic. Originally drafted by the Pittsburgh Pirates in January 1981, Kruk chose to remain in school. However, while playing for New Market in the NCAA-sanctioned Shenandoah Valley League five months later, Kruk signed with the San Diego Padres after they selected him in the third round of the June 1981 Draft Secondary Phase.

Kruk subsequently spent five long years in the minor leagues, playing for four teams at three different levels, before finally being summoned to the majors by the Padres at the start of the 1986 campaign. Arriving in San Diego at the rather advanced age of 25, the lefty-swinging, lefty-throwing Kruk performed well for the Padres in a part-time role as a rookie, batting

.309 and compiling an on-base percentage of .403, although he hit just four homers and drove in only 38 runs in 278 official at-bats while platooning in left field with the righty-swinging Carmelo Martínez. Garnering more significant playing time the following year while seeing action both at first base and in left field, Kruk responded by hitting 20 homers, knocking in 91 runs, batting .313, and stealing a career-high 18 bases. But, after Kruk slumped to just nine home runs, 44 RBIs, and a .241 batting average in 1988 and began the ensuing campaign in similar fashion, he found himself heading to Philadelphia when the Padres traded him and utility man Randy Ready to the Phillies for outfielder Chris James on June 2, 1989.

John Kruk earned three straight All-Star nominations during his time in Philadelphia.
Courtesy of MearsonlineAuctions.com

Finding his new home very much to his liking, Kruk finished the 1989 season strong, hitting five homers, driving in 38 runs, and batting .331, in 81 games and 281 official at-bats, while serving as the Phillies' starting left fielder. Kruk posted solid numbers once again in 1990 while splitting his time between the outfield and first base, finishing his first full season in Philadelphia with seven homers, 67 RBIs, a .291 batting average, and a .386 on-base percentage. But he performed even better after the Phillies made him their primary first baseman in 1991, earning All-Star honors for the first of three straight times by hitting 21 homers, knocking in 92 runs, scoring 84 times, batting .294, and compiling an on-base percentage of .367. Kruk followed that up with two more excellent years, hitting 10 homers, driving in 70 runs, scoring 86 times, and placing near the top of the league rankings with a .323 batting average and a .423 on-base percentage in 1992, before reaching the seats 14 times, knocking in 85 runs, scoring 100 others, batting .316, drawing 111 bases on balls, and compiling an on-base percentage of .430 for the Phillies' 1993 pennant-winning team, which became known as "The Wild Bunch" due to the scruffy appearance and gruff demeanor of several of its members.

A line-drive hitter who hit the ball to all parts of the ballpark, Kruk possessed good gap-to-gap power, surpassing 30 doubles on two separate occasions, although he reached the 20-homer plateau just twice his entire career. Extremely patient at the plate, Kruk also displayed excellent knowledge of the strike zone, enabling him to consistently rank among the NL leaders in on-base percentage. And, despite his unathletic build, Kruk, who stood 5'10" and weighed more than 200 pounds, had soft hands and moved well in the field, committing a total of only 42 errors over the course of his career.

Kruk's many contributions to the Phillies on the playing field made him a fan favorite in Philadelphia. But, as much as the hometown fans came to appreciate Kruk for his consistently excellent play, they embraced him equally for his sense of humor and willingness to laugh at himself and his teammates. Once asked by David Letterman during the Phillies' dreadful 1992 campaign, "Are you optimistic for the rest of the season for your team's chances?" Kruk replied, "To finish the season?"

On another occasion, when asked if fans mistook him for a ballplayer, Kruk responded, "Me, no! John Goodman, maybe."

And, in his typically self-deprecating style, Kruk related a story in his book "*I Ain't an Athlete, Lady . . .*": "There's a story, a funny story, about me sitting in a restaurant. I'm eating this big meal and maybe having a couple of beers and smoking a cigarette. A woman comes by the table. She recognizes me and she's shocked because it seems like I should be in training or something. She's getting all over me, saying that a professional athlete should take better care of himself. I lean back and I say to her, 'I ain't an athlete, lady. I'm a baseball player.'"

Kruk's ability to poke fun at himself often caused his peers to respond in kind, with Pittsburgh Pirates outfielder Andy Van Slyke saying that the burly first baseman, "would be the one guy I'd pay for of any player in the big leagues to see, 'cause he'd be like the truck driver or delivery beer guy who somehow slipped past security and put a uniform on."

Meanwhile, during Kruk's appearance at the 1993 All-Star Game, Hall of Famer Reggie Jackson commented, "John Kruk's hitting .350, man. I don't care, don't matter what you look like, that boy can hit."

Hit in the groin with an errant pickoff throw made by Phillies pitcher Mitch Williams in 1993, Kruk subsequently underwent a medical examination the following spring that revealed the presence of testicular cancer. After having surgery to remove the affected testicle, Kruk ended up appearing in only 75 games during the strike-shortened 1994 campaign, finishing the year with five home runs, 38 RBIs, and a .302 batting average. A free agent at season's end, Kruk signed with the Chicago White Sox, leaving the Phillies having hit 62 homers, driven in 390 runs, scored 403 times, batted .309, compiled an on-base percentage of .400, posted a slugging percentage of .461, and collected 790 hits, 145 doubles, and 29 triples as a member of the team.

Although Kruk posted decent numbers for the White Sox as a part-time DH in 1995, knocking in 23 runs, batting .308, and compiling an on-base percentage of .399 through the first four months of the campaign, chronic knee soreness prompted him to abruptly announce his retirement on July 30, just hours after he removed himself from a game against the Baltimore Orioles. In explaining his decision, Kruk told the media, "The desire to compete at this level is gone. When that happens, it's time to go."

And, years later, Kruk admitted, "I hated baseball. I really didn't like baseball at all until someone decided they were going to pay me. Every year I played in the big leagues, the day the season ended, I called my buddies in West Virginia and said, 'I'll be home tomorrow.'"

Kruk, who retired with career totals of 100 homers, 592 RBIs, 582 runs scored, 1,170 hits, 199 doubles, 34 triples, and 58 stolen bases, a .300 batting average, an on-base percentage of .397, and a slugging percentage of .446, subsequently began a career in broadcasting, serving as an analyst and commentator for several stations, including Fox Sports and ESPN, where he remained from 2004 to 2016, before mutually parting ways with the network because he claimed their phone calls interrupted his golf games. Later amending that remark somewhat, Kruk stated, "The phone calls weren't that bad. It was having to listen to them that was painful." After leaving ESPN, Kruk joined the Phillies broadcast crew at Comcast, where he continued to entertain his audience with his unique perspective of the national pastime. In addition to his work as a broadcaster, Kruk has appeared in five motion pictures, with his screen credits including *The Fan, American Pastime, The Sandlot, Aqua Teen Hunger Force,* and *Ring the Bell.*

On a more personal note, Kruk, who has been married twice and currently resides in Naples, Florida, credits his second wife, Melissa, a former Miss New Jersey (1999), with helping him overcome his addiction to alcohol, saying, "I was a mess. She saved my life." Kruk, a steady drinker during his playing days who developed an even more serious problem in retirement, continued, "I was no angel when I played the game. . . . When I went out, I drank to get drunk because I wanted to be drunk—not because I couldn't go without it. And you don't stop doing something like that by taking a pill or getting some medicine. You stop when you realize that you're an idiot. I've heard all the talk about chemical imbalances and the other crap about some people being predisposed to addiction. Let me tell you all something: It still comes down to a choice. I never chose to have cancer, but I did choose to have a drink."

PHILLIES CAREER HIGHLIGHTS

Best Season

Although Kruk hit more homers (21) and drove in more runs (92) in 1991, he had his finest all-around season for the Phillies in 1993, when, in addition to hitting 14 homers, knocking in 85 runs, and batting .316, he established career-high marks with 100 runs scored, 169 hits, 33 doubles, 111 walks, a .430 on-base percentage, and an OPS of .905, with each of the last three figures placing him near the top of the league rankings.

Memorable Moments/Greatest Performances

Kruk contributed to a 16–13 victory over the Cubs on August 10, 1989, by going 4-for-5, with a homer, double, three RBIs, and career-high five runs scored.

Kruk gave the Phillies a dramatic 9–5 win over the Cardinals on September 17, 1989, by hitting a grand slam home run off Matt Kinzer with two men out in the bottom of the 12th inning.

Kruk homered again with the bases loaded on September 25, 1991, delivering the key blow in a 5–4 win over the Cubs in Chicago.

Kruk continued to be a thorn in the side of the Cubs on October 1, 1991, going 4-for-6 during a 6–5 Phillies win, with his RBI single in the bottom of the 13th inning providing the margin of victory.

Kruk had another big game against the Cubs on April 18, 1993, hitting a pair of two-run homers during an 11-inning, 11–10 Phillies win.

Kruk helped lead the Phillies to a lopsided 10–3 victory over the Florida Marlins on May 17, 1993, by going 5-for-6, with a double, two RBIs, and three runs scored.

Kruk turned in a similarly impressive performance against the Cardinals on July 27, 1993, going a perfect 5-for-5, with a double, three RBIs, and three runs scored during a 10–7 Phillies win.

Although the Phillies lost the 1993 World Series to the Toronto Blue Jays in six games, Kruk performed extremely well in his only appearance in the Fall Classic, batting .348, with four RBIs, four runs scored, and seven walks.

Kruk experienced the most surreal moments of his career when he faced Randy Johnson in the 1993 All-Star Game. After Kruk feigned heart palpitations when the 6'10" southpaw's first pitch flew over his head all the way to the backstop, he swung feebly at three consecutive 98-mile-per-hour fastballs, before taking a seat on the bench. Commenting on his at-bat afterwards, Kruk said, "When I stepped in the box, I said all I wanted to do was make contact. And, after the first pitch, all I wanted to do was live. And I lived, so I had a good at-bat."

Notable Achievements

- Hit more than 20 home runs once.
- Batted over .300 four times, topping the .320 mark twice.
- Scored 100 runs once.
- Surpassed 30 doubles twice.
- Walked more than 100 times once.
- Compiled on-base percentage over .400 twice.
- Compiled OPS over .900 once.
- Finished second in NL in on-base percentage twice.
- Finished third in NL in batting average once.
- Ranks among Phillies career leaders in batting average (12th) and on-base percentage (7th).
- 1993 division champion.
- 1993 NL champion.
- Two-time NL Player of the Week.
- Three-time NL All-Star (1991, 1992, and 1993).
- Member of Philadelphia Baseball Wall of Fame.

40

WILLIE "PUDDIN' HEAD" JONES

key member of the 1950 Philadelphia Phillies "Whiz Kids" team that captured the National League pennant, Willie "Puddin' Head" Jones proved to be the finest fielding third baseman in the senior circuit for much of the 1950s, leading all NL third sackers in putouts seven times, fielding percentage six times, and assists and double plays turned twice each. Solid at the plate as well, Jones surpassed 20 homers twice, knocked in more than 80 runs three times, scored 100 runs once, and batted over .300 once, with his strong all-around play earning him two All-Star nominations and a spot on the Philadelphia Baseball Wall of Fame.

Born in Dillon, South Carolina, on August 16, 1925, Willie Edward Jones acquired his rather unusual nickname while growing up in Laurel Hill, North Carolina, where he moved with his family at the age of four. Taken from the song "Wooden Head, Puddin' Head Jones" made popular by Rudy Vallee and his Connecticut Yankees in 1933, the moniker "Puddin' Head" originated from the following lyrics:

Oh, Puddin' Head Jones was fat and funny
Dumber than sticks and stones.
Now that is just why the kids all called him,
Wooden head, puddin' head Jones.

A two-sport star at Laurel Hill High School, Jones excelled in both baseball and basketball, before enlisting in the Navy following his graduation in 1943. Discharged from the service almost three years later, Jones began playing semipro ball with the Bennettsville Red Sox of the Palmetto League, where he made a favorable impression on Phillies scout Johnny Nee, who later said, "I followed him for three weeks. They had some smart pitchers in that league—old timers from the Southern Association. They were good, but Jones could hit them."

Willie "Puddin' Head" Jones led NL third basemen in putouts seven times and fielding percentage six times.
Courtesy of Boston Public Library, Leslie Jones Collection

After being signed by Nee, Jones spent the 1947 campaign with Terre Haute of the (Class B) Three-I League, for whom he hit 10 homers, knocked in 107 runs, and batted .307. Called up by the Phillies in September, Jones ended up starting 17 games for them at third base, committing six errors in the field and collecting 14 hits in 62 official at-bats, for a batting average of .226. Jones subsequently split the 1948 season between Utica of the (Class A) Eastern League and Toronto of the (Triple-A) International League, performing well at both stops, although he started a riot in just his second game with Toronto, when, after being hit in the head by a Montreal pitcher the previous day, he responded to another extremely close offering by firing his bat at the opposing hurler. Called up again by the Phillies during the latter stages of the campaign, Jones fared somewhat better this time, compiling a batting average of .333 in 17 games and hitting the first two homers of his big-league career.

Joining the Phillies for good in 1949, Jones had a solid rookie season, hitting 19 homers, driving in 77 runs, scoring 71 times, and ranking among the NL leaders with 35 doubles, although he batted just .244 and committed a league-high 27 errors at third base. Yet, Jones also led all players at his position in putouts and assists, prompting Phillies coach Cy Perkins to respond to a reporter's late season remark about the third baseman's high error total by saying, "Is that so? I've never even noticed it. I haven't seen a third baseman like that in a long time."

Taking great pride in his defense, Jones worked extensively with coach Dusty Cooke during the subsequent offseason to improve himself in that area. After committing fewer errors in 1950, Jones increased his fielding percentage in each of the next three seasons as well, gradually developing into the National League's finest defensive third baseman. In fact, when asked how he compared himself to Jones defensively, Hall of Fame third sacker Pie Traynor replied, "He's better than I was."

Blessed with fast hands, great range, excellent quickness, and a powerful throwing arm, Jones also drew high praise from Robin Roberts, who later rated his former Phillies teammate as the second-best third baseman he ever saw, behind only Brooks Robinson.

Meanwhile, the right-handed-hitting Jones, who stood 6'1" and weighed 190 pounds, soon emerged as one of the better offensive players at his position as well. After helping the Phillies win the NL pennant in 1950 by hitting 25 homers, driving in 88 runs, scoring 100 times, and batting .267, Jones earned his second consecutive All-Star selection the following year by reaching the seats 22 times, knocking in 81 runs, scoring 79 others, and establishing career-high marks with a .285 batting average and an OPS of .828.

Although Jones never again reached the 20-homer plateau or batted any higher than .277, he remained a productive hitter for the next five seasons, averaging 16 home runs and 71 RBIs from 1952 to 1956. Performing especially well in the last of those campaigns, Jones hit 17 homers, knocked in 78 runs, scored 88 times, batted .277, and compiled an OPS of .812, before his offensive skills began to diminish.

After Jones batted just .218, hit only nine homers, and drove in just 47 runs in 1957, the Phillies sought to reduce his salary, with team owner Bob Carpenter saying at the time, "Jones comes right to the door of stardom but never touches the knob." Jones ended up spending one more full year in Philadelphia, rebounding somewhat in 1958 by hitting 14 homers, knocking in 60 runs, and batting .271 after beginning the season on the bench. Jones remained with the Phillies until June 6, 1959, when they traded him to the Cleveland Indians for outfielder Jim Bolger and cash. Sold to Cincinnati less than one month later, Jones continued to serve the Reds as a part-time player until May 16, 1961, when he announced his retirement following his release. Jones ended his playing career with 190 home runs, 812 RBIs, 786 runs scored, 1,502 hits, 252 doubles, 33 triples, 40 stolen bases, a .258 batting average, a .343 on-base percentage, and a .410 slugging percentage, compiling most of those numbers while playing for the Phillies.

Choosing to remain in Cincinnati following his retirement, Jones became an automobile salesman, continuing to function in that capacity until October 18, 1983, when he died from cancer of the lymph glands at the age of 58. Reflecting back on his former teammate, Richie Ashburn said of the man who spoke with a slow Southern drawl, "Willie was unlike any guy I've ever seen. Heck of a ballplayer and a great guy. Southern boy who could charm a bulldog off a meat wagon. Somebody should write a book about 'Puddin' Head.'"

PHILLIES CAREER HIGHLIGHTS

Best Season

Jones posted solid numbers in 1951, earning All-Star honors for the second straight time by hitting 22 homers, driving in 81 runs, scoring 79 others, batting .285, and compiling an OPS of .828. But he performed slightly better the previous year, concluding the 1950 campaign with a .267 batting average, a .793 OPS, and a career-high 25 home runs, 88 RBIs, 100 runs scored, 163 hits, and six triples, while also leading all NL third basemen in putouts and assists.

Memorable Moments/Greatest Performances

Jones starred in defeat on April 20, 1949, going 4-for-4, with four doubles and three RBIs during a 6–5 loss to the Boston Braves.

Jones contributed to a 9–4 victory over the Pirates in Pittsburgh on June 21, 1949, by hitting a pair of homers, driving in three runs, and scoring three times.

Jones proved to be the difference in a 5–2 win over the Cubs on May 3, 1950, hitting two homers and driving in three runs.

Jones helped lead the Phillies to an 8–3 win over the Cubs on July 18, 1950, by going 4-for-5, with a homer, two doubles, and three RBIs.

Jones led the Phillies to a 9–2 win over Pittsburgh on June 19, 1951, by hitting two homers and driving in six runs, with his eighth-inning inside-the-park grand slam putting the game out of reach.

Jones homered twice and knocked in four runs during a 7–3 win over the Reds on July 30, 1952, with his three-run blast in the bottom of the eighth inning proving to be the key blow in a six-run rally that turned a 3–1 deficit into a 7–3 lead.

Jones helped lead the Phillies to a 14–6 win in the second game of a doubleheader sweep of the Cubs on June 9, 1954, by going 3-for-5, with two home runs and five RBIs.

Jones homered twice against Hall of Fame right-hander Don Drysdale during a 6–4 win over the Dodgers on May 24, 1956, finishing the game with three hits and four RBIs.

Jones led the Phillies to a lopsided 12–2 victory over the Cardinals on August 20, 1958, by going 4-for-5, with two homers, a double, and a career-high eight RBIs.

Notable Achievements

- Hit more than 20 home runs twice.
- Batted over .300 once.
- Scored 100 runs once.
- Surpassed 30 doubles once.
- Led NL in sacrifice hits once and games played once.
- Finished third in NL in bases on balls once.
- Led NL third basemen in putouts seven times, assists twice, fielding percentage six times, and double plays turned twice.
- Ranks among Phillies career leaders in bases on balls (8th), games played (11th), plate appearances (11th), and at-bats (12th).
- 1950 NL champion.
- Two-time NL All-Star (1950 and 1951).
- Member of Philadelphia Baseball Wall of Fame.

41
GRANNY HAMNER

The first player ever voted by the fans as an All-Star starter at two different positions, Granny Hamner spent parts of 16 seasons in Philadelphia, serving as the Phillies' primary starter at either shortstop or second base much of that time. Honored by Phillies fans as the franchise's all-time greatest shortstop during professional baseball's 1969 centennial celebration, Hamner proved himself to be a dependable clutch hitter and a natural leader during his time in the City of Brotherly Love, serving as one of the central figures in the team's improbable run to the 1950 NL pennant. Solid both at the bat and in the field, Hamner surpassed 20 homers once, knocked in more than 80 runs four times, batted over .290 on three separate occasions, and led all players at his position in assists and double plays turned once each, with his strong all-around play earning him three All-Star selections and one top-10 finish in the NL MVP voting.

Born in Richmond, Virginia, on April 26, 1927, Granville Wilbur Hamner briefly attended local John Marshall High School, before transferring to Benedictine High when Marshall dropped its baseball program. Starring in multiple sports in high school, Hamner excelled in baseball, basketball, and football, earning All-State honors on the gridiron one year, before choosing to focus primarily on developing his skills on the diamond.

Pursued by several pro teams after batting close to .600 and leading the state in extra-base hits one year, Hamner ended up signing with the Phillies, with whom he made his major-league debut at the tender age of 17 on September 14, 1944, without ever having played a game in the minors. Starting 20 games at shortstop in the season's final three weeks, Hamner committed nine errors in the field and compiled a batting average of .247, before returning to Benedictine for his senior year. Recalling his initiation to big-league baseball, Hamner said, "I was so young I didn't have much of a sandlot background in Richmond. My brother Wes was the best instructor I had as a kid."

Hamner subsequently spent most of the next three seasons in the minor leagues, although he also served in the US Army for 13 months at the Aberdeen Proving Ground in Maryland. After appearing in just 18 games with the Phillies from 1945 to 1947, the 21-year-old Hamner arrived in Philadelphia to stay in 1948, hitting three homers, knocking in 48 runs, batting .260, and committing 27 errors in the field while splitting his time between shortstop and second base. Taking over at short full-time the following year, Hamner remained at that post for the next four seasons, establishing himself as one of the better-hitting middle infielders in the National League.

Granny Hamner earned All-Star honors as both a second baseman and shortstop for the Phillies.
Courtesy of MearsonlineAuctions.com

After hitting six homers, driving in 53 runs, scoring 83 times, and batting .263 in 1949, Hamner helped lead the Phillies to the pennant in 1950 by reaching the seats 11 times, knocking in 82 runs, scoring 78 others, and batting .270, earning in the process a sixth-place finish in the NL MVP voting. Hamner followed that up with a slightly subpar performance in 1951, concluding the campaign with nine homers, 72 RBIs, 61 runs scored, and a .255 batting average, before earning All-Star honors for the first of three straight times in 1952 by hitting 17 homers, knocking in 87 runs, scoring 74 others, and batting .275.

Developing into a solid offensive performer his first few seasons in Philly, the right-handed-hitting Hamner, who stood 5'10" and weighed 165 pounds, became known for his ability to hit in the clutch, with former Phillies teammate Robin Roberts saying, "I'll tell you what. I can't think of a guy I'd rather have up there with the game on the line than 'Hams.' He was tough. He could be 0-for-3, but, put a man in scoring position in the 8th inning, and he'd hit a rope someplace."

Former Phillies president and owner Robert Carpenter expressed similar sentiments when he proclaimed in 1964, "Granny Hamner was the best clutch hitter we ever had."

Meanwhile, longtime Phillies pitcher Curt Simmons described Hamner this way: "A real good hitter. A clutch hitter. Good fielder with a good arm. A real rough, tough guy. He was one of our stars in those days."

A good all-around ballplayer, Hamner also ran the bases well, possessed a strong throwing arm, and displayed outstanding range in the field, although he performed somewhat erratically at times, committing more than 30 errors on five separate occasions, with his 48 miscues in 1950 representing his highest single-season total. Yet, Hamner also consistently ranked among the top players at his position in putouts, assists, and double plays turned.

Hamner, who served as captain of the Phillies from 1952 to 1954, also proved to be an outstanding team leader and one of the league's most durable players, appearing in 473 consecutive games from September 14, 1948, to September 19, 1951.

Perhaps as much as anything, though, Hamner became known for his competitive nature, bad temper, and surly disposition—qualities that prompted Pittsburgh Pirates Hall of Fame third baseman Pie Traynor to identify him as one of the few players of his time who could have competed successfully in the rough-and-tumble era of the 1920s and 1930s. In addition to expressing his distaste for opposing players, Hamner shared a contentious relationship with Phillies management and even some of his own teammates, with Richie Ashburn saying of his lifelong friend in the book, *The Whiz Kids and the 1950 Pennant*, "Granny was a tough kid, let me tell you. When we went to spring training with the Phillies, they had a bunch of veteran ballplayers. . . . He had very little respect for those old players, and he would tell them what he thought. Granny could play better than those veterans. They would try to run him out of the batting cage. Well, Granny was a street fighter. A lot of Granny's friends in Richmond, Virginia, are probably still in prison. He didn't want to put up with all that crap."

Meanwhile, the *Sporting News* reported in 1952, "Hamner is mean, hot-tempered, and plenty rough. He hasn't been in many scraps because opposing players give him a wide berth, respecting his ill temper." The magazine then went on to say that Hamner warned every runner that came into second, "Drop down when you come into the bag when I am the pivot man on double-plays or get hit right between the eyes with the ball."

Hamner continued to perform well for the Phillies after he moved to second base in 1953, having arguably his two finest offensive seasons while manning that post. After hitting 21 homers, driving in 92 runs, scoring 90 times, collecting eight triples and 30 doubles, and batting .276 in 1953,

Hamner homered 13 times, knocked in 89 runs, scored 83 others, batted .299, and finished second in the league with 11 triples and 39 doubles the following season. Named to the NL All-Star team both years, Hamner later expressed great pride in his All-Star achievements, stating, "I was the first to be voted in at two positions. Pete Rose made it at just about all of them later on, but I was the first at second and short. The funny thing was, I was a lousy second baseman. But I was hitting .340 around All-Star time, so my bat got me into the lineup."

Although Hamner remained a starter in Philadelphia for three more years, he never again made much of an impact after 1954. After developing bursitis in his left shoulder during the early stages of the 1955 campaign, Hamner ended up appearing in only 104 games, hitting five homers, knocking in 43 runs, and batting .257, before undergoing surgery to repair his ailing shoulder during the subsequent offseason. Further compromised in future years by an injury to his knee that also required surgery, Hamner proved to be just a shell of his former self by 1957, batting only .227, although he managed to hit 10 homers and drive in 62 runs.

Even though Hamner got off to a good start in 1959, batting .301 in his first 35 games, the Phillies elected to trade him to the Cleveland Indians for journeyman pitcher Humberto Robinson on May 16, thereby ending his 16-year association with the club. Later revealing the disappointment that he felt over having to leave Philadelphia, Hamner stated during a 1972 interview with Duke DeLuca of the *Reading Eagle*, "I was through with baseball the day they traded me. I didn't like it in Cleveland, but the Phillies actually did me a favor. They weren't going anywhere, and Cleveland was battling the White Sox for first place. We lost the pennant in the last two weeks. I really didn't have any reason to beef about the trade. I just hated to leave the organization. I was raised in the organization."

Released by the Indians at season's end, Hamner, who experienced some success on the mound in high school and during his 13-month stint in the Army, subsequently tried to resurrect his career as a pitcher, spending some time in the Cuban Winter League, before serving as a player-manager for two years with a minor-league affiliate of the Kansas City Athletics. Eventually promoted to the parent club, Hamner made three mound appearances for the Athletics in 1962, before announcing his retirement during the latter stages of the campaign. Still only 35 years old at the time of his retirement, Hamner ended his playing career with 104 home runs, 708 RBIs, 711 runs scored, 1,529 hits, 272 doubles, 62 triples, a .262 batting average, a .303 on-base percentage, and a .383 slugging percentage, compiling virtually all those numbers as a member of the Phillies.

Following his playing days, Hamner became involved in many different pursuits, including selling cars and real estate, engaging as a roofing contractor, hosting his own television sports program in Richmond, investing in a motel in Clearwater, Florida, and managing a bowling alley. After settling in Philadelphia during the late 1960s, Hamner eventually rejoined the Phillies organization, assuming various roles over the course of the next two decades, including scout, roving instructor, minor-league manager, and minor-league supervisor. Hamner remained with the Phillies until September 12, 1993, when he died of a heart attack at 66 years of age.

Upon learning of his former teammate's passing, Robin Roberts said, "He was just a tough, tough player, and that really bad injury detracted from his career. Once he hurt his leg, he had no mobility. But during his early years he was something special. He had a phenomenal arm when he was at short, and he had as good of a relay as I've ever seen. He was a natural at short, that's how he should be remembered."

PHILLIES CAREER HIGHLIGHTS

Best Season

Hamner played his best ball for the Phillies from 1949 to 1954, earning three All-Star selections and MVP consideration five times during that six-year stretch. Performing especially well in 1950, 1953, and 1954, Hamner hit 11 homers, knocked in 82 runs, scored 78 times, collected 172 hits, batted .270, and finished second among NL shortstops with a career-high 513 assists in the first of those campaigns, with his solid all-around play for the pennant-winning Phillies earning him a sixth-place finish in the league MVP voting. Hamner had another fine season in 1953, batting .276 and establishing career-high marks with 21 homers, 92 RBIs, and 90 runs scored. But Hamner posted the best overall numbers of his career the following year, concluding the 1954 campaign with 13 home runs, 89 RBIs, 83 runs scored, a .299 batting average, an OPS of .818, 178 hits, 11 triples, and 39 doubles, with each of the last two figures placing him near the top of the league rankings.

Memorable Moments/Greatest Performances

Hamner led the Phillies to an 11–10 win over the Cardinals on July 17, 1948, by going 3-for-5, with two doubles and a career-high seven RBIs.

Hamner contributed to an 8–2 victory over the Cubs in the second game of a doubleheader split on August 28, 1949, by going 4-for-5, with a double, two stolen bases, two RBIs, and two runs scored.

Hamner proved to be a huge factor in a 6–5 win over the Giants on August 10, 1950, going 3-for-4, with a homer, four RBIs, and two runs scored, including the game-winner in the bottom of the 10th.

Although the Phillies lost the 1950 World Series to the Yankees in four games, Hamner excelled in his only postseason appearance, going 6-for-14 (.429), with a triple, two doubles, and one run scored.

Hamner helped lead the Phillies to an 11–6 victory over the Pirates on July 12, 1951, by driving in five runs with a homer, triple, and single.

Hamner homered twice in one game for the only time in his career on July 24, 1953, with his two round-trippers giving the Phillies a 2–1 win over the Cardinals.

Hamner contributed to a 16–4 rout of the Cubs on September 17, 1953, by homering once, knocking in four runs, and scoring three times.

Hamner delivered what proved to be the game-winning hit in a 4–3 victory over the Braves on May 1, 1954, when he doubled home two runs in the top of the 10th inning.

Hamner starred during a doubleheader sweep of the Cubs on June 9, 1954, going 3-for-3, with a triple, double, single, and three runs scored during a 4–0 Phillies win in the opener, before homering and collecting three hits during a 14–6 victory in Game 2.

Hamner helped the Phillies complete a doubleheader sweep of the Pirates on September 3, 1954, by going 4-for-5, with three doubles, one RBI, and four runs scored during a lopsided 10–2 victory in Game 2.

Hamner led the Phillies to an 8–3 win over the Dodgers on May 5, 1958, by driving in five runs with a homer and triple.

Notable Achievements

- Hit more than 20 home runs once.
- Batted over .300 once.
- Finished in double digits in triples once.
- Surpassed 30 doubles four times.
- Led NL in sacrifice hits once, assists once, games played once, and at-bats once.
- Finished second in NL with 11 triples and 39 doubles in 1954.
- Led NL shortstops in assists once and double plays turned once.

- Ranks among Phillies career leaders in hits (11th), doubles (12th), games played (12th), plate appearances (12th), and at-bats (8th).
- 1950 NL champion.
- Finished sixth in 1950 NL MVP voting.
- Three-time NL All-Star (1952, 1953, and 1954).
- Member of Philadelphia Baseball Wall of Fame.

42

LENNY DYKSTRA

Nicknamed "Nails" for his toughness and win-at-all-cost mentality, Lenny Dykstra spent parts of eight seasons in Philadelphia, serving as the Phillies' primary starter in center field in seven of those. An excellent outfielder and tremendous leadoff hitter who possessed occasional power at the plate, a keen batting eye, and outstanding speed on the base-paths, Dykstra emerged as an elite player during his time in the City of Brotherly Love, earning three All-Star selections, two top-10 finishes in the NL MVP voting, and one Silver Slugger, even though he remained fully healthy in just three of his eight years with the Phillies. Nevertheless, Dykstra's accomplishments as a member of the team remain tainted in the eyes of many due to his admitted use of steroids.

Born in Santa Ana, California, on February 10, 1963, Leonard Kyle Dykstra took his last name from his stepfather, Dennis Dykstra, whom his mother married after his biological father, Jerry Leswick, deserted the family when Lenny was a toddler. Raised in the working-class Anaheim, California, suburb of Garden Grove, Dykstra displayed at an early age the feistiness for which he later became so well known, telling anyone willing to listen that his future included a career in major-league baseball, with his older brother, Brian, recalling, "He was always underestimated. People didn't take Lenny seriously because he didn't look all that imposing. But he was a pain in the ass who never took no for an answer."

Far more interested in sports than schoolwork, Dykstra struggled in the classroom but excelled on the ballfield, starring in both baseball and football at Garden Grove High School. After becoming the first and only freshman to play on the school's varsity baseball team three years earlier, Dykstra attended a New York Mets tryout camp during his senior year, telling a team employee who questioned his credentials due to his diminutive stature and slight build, "I'm Lenny Dykstra and I'm the best player you're going to see today."

Ultimately selected by New York in the 13th round of the 1981 MLB Amateur Draft, Dykstra, who had previously committed to play baseball at Arizona State University, decided to sign with the Mets after they agreed to let him bypass rookie ball and begin his pro career at the Class A level. Dykstra subsequently spent the next two seasons with the Shelby Mets of the South Atlantic League, before earning Class A Carolina League MVP honors in 1983 by batting .358, compiling a .472 on-base percentage, and stealing 105 bases for Lynchburg. After one

Lenny Dykstra finished second in the 1993 NL MVP voting.
Courtesy of MearsonlineAuctions.com

more year in the minors, Dykstra joined the Mets during the early stages of the 1985 campaign. Platooning with Mookie Wilson in center field the rest of the year, the left-handed-hitting Dykstra batted .254, homered once, knocked in 19 runs, scored 40 times, and stole 15 bases, in 83 games and 236 official at-bats.

Although Dykstra helped the Mets capture the NL pennant in 1986 by hitting eight homers, driving in 45 runs, scoring 77 others, stealing 31 bases, and batting .295, he found himself being platooned with Wilson much of the time in each of the next two seasons, causing him to grow increasingly unhappy. Finally expressing a desire to go elsewhere early in 1989, Dykstra joined the Phillies when they completed a trade with the Mets on June 18 that sent Juan Samuel to New York for the disgruntled center fielder and reliever Roger McDowell.

Initially struggling upon his arrival in Philadelphia, Dykstra batted just .222 and scored only 39 runs in 90 games over the season's final three and a half months. But, after adding 30 pounds of muscle onto his lean 5'10" frame during the subsequent offseason, Dykstra emerged as a star in 1990, earning his first All-Star selection and a ninth-place finish in the NL MVP voting by hitting nine homers, driving in 60 runs, collecting 35 doubles, stealing 33 bases, leading the league with 192 hits and a .418 on-base percentage, and ranking among the leaders with 106 runs scored, 89 walks, and a batting average of .325, while also topping the circuit with 439 outfield putouts. While some members of the media attributed Dykstra's improvement to his increased playing time, others pointed to his added bulk, which transformed him from a lithe and sinewy 155-pounder into a muscular 185-pound fireplug with a thick neck and rippling biceps. For his part, Dykstra credited the change in his physique to the use of "special vitamins."

Following Dykstra's first full season as an everyday player, he suffered through a horrific 1991 campaign marred by a pair of unfortunate incidents that limited him to just 63 games. After attending teammate John Kruk's bachelor party in early May, an inebriated Dykstra nearly killed himself and Phillies catcher Darren Daulton when he wrecked his sports car. Dykstra, who suffered broken ribs, a broken collarbone, and a broken cheekbone, ended up missing two months. Then, some six weeks after he returned to action later in the year, Dykstra suffered a season-ending injury when he broke his collarbone again running into the outfield wall in Cincinnati. Still, Dykstra performed well in the 63 games he played, batting .297, scoring 48 runs, and stealing 24 bases.

Dykstra subsequently experienced more bad luck in 1992, appearing in only 85 games after having a bone in his wrist broken by a Greg Maddux pitch on Opening Day and breaking a bone in his finger in August. Yet, once again, Dykstra proved to be a productive player whenever he took the field, batting .301, scoring 53 runs, and stealing 30 bases in 35 attempts.

Fully healthy by the start of the 1993 season, Dykstra helped lead the Phillies to the pennant by batting .305 and establishing career-high marks in 10 different offensive categories, including home runs (19), RBIs (66), runs scored (143), doubles (44), hits (194), stolen bases (37), and bases on balls (129), with his 143 runs scored, 194 hits, and 129 walks all leading the NL. Although catcher Darren Daulton, first baseman John Kruk, and third baseman Dave Hollins also had outstanding years for the Phillies, Dykstra, who started all but two games in center field, ignited their offense from his leadoff spot in the batting order, with his contributions to the success of the team earning him a runner-up finish to Barry Bonds in the league MVP voting. And even though the Phillies ended up losing the World Series to the Blue Jays in six games, Dykstra continued to perform at an elite level in the postseason, homering twice, scoring five runs, and batting .280 against Atlanta in the NLCS, before hitting four homers, driving in eight runs, scoring nine times, stealing four bases, batting .348, and compiling an OPS of 1.413 in the Fall Classic.

Extremely confident in his own abilities, and always one to speak his mind, Dykstra, when asked to describe his performance in 1993, said, "I basically went from star to superstar. I basically proved I'm more than the best leadoff hitter in the game. It's nice to have that recognition, but I'm more than a leadoff hitter. I proved I'm the impact player I've always considered myself to be, a situation hitter capable of getting the home run, double, walk, whatever the situation requires. I've worked hard and made myself into one of the top five players in the game. Do they pay leadoff hitters what they're paying me?"

Although Dykstra played the game with wild abandon, diving for balls in the outfield, running into fences, and displaying tremendous aggressiveness on the basepaths, his level of intensity wavered at times, as former Phillies coach John Vukovich acknowledged when he suggested, "He (Dykstra) was a red-light player. But he was a horrible 10–2 player. What I mean is, he hated to play in a 10–2 game, whether we were ahead or behind. He'd lose focus. He only wanted to play with the game on the line all the time."

Dykstra followed up his banner year of 1993 by hitting five homers, driving in 24 runs, scoring 68 times, batting .273, and compiling a .404 on-base percentage during the strike-shortened 1994 campaign, earning in the process his second All-Star nomination. But even though Dykstra gained All-Star recognition once again in 1995, he missed more than half the season with a variety of ailments, limiting him to just two homers, 18 RBIs, 37 runs scored, and a batting average of .264. After appearing in 40 games during the first month-and-a-half of the ensuing campaign, Dykstra left a May contest against the Dodgers in the fifth inning complaining of back stiffness. Subsequently diagnosed with spinal stenosis, Dykstra missed the rest of the season and all of 1997, before announcing his retirement during spring training in 1998 with career totals of 81 home runs, 404 RBIs, 802 runs scored, 1,298 hits, 281 doubles, 43 triples, and 285 stolen bases, a lifetime batting average of .285, an on-base percentage of .375, and a slugging percentage of .419. While playing for the Phillies, Dykstra hit 51 homers, drove in 251 runs, scored 515 times, stole 169 bases, batted .289, compiled an on-base percentage of .388, posted a slugging percentage of .422, and collected 829 hits, 177 doubles, and 26 triples.

Nearly a decade after Dykstra left the game, the 2007 Mitchell Report on steroids in baseball revealed that he admitted to the commissioner's office in 2000 that he used performance-enhancing drugs during his playing career. In attempting to explain his illicit behavior, Dykstra said, "You gotta understand, there were only 28 people who had my job in the whole world. And thousands of people wanted those jobs, and every year there were guys trying to take my job. So, I needed to do anything I could to protect my job, take care of my family. Do you have any idea how much money was at stake? Do you?"

Dykstra attempted to justify his actions once again when he told Scott Miller of Bleacher Report during a 2016 interview that his desire to get paid as an everyday player prompted him to turn to steroids, saying at the time, "I needed to play. I finally got traded to the Phillies in '89, and I'm 150, 140 pounds. So, I knew. [Then-Philadelphia GM] Lee Thomas said, 'Look, we're going to give you 1990. You'll be our everyday guy.' . . . So, I knew '90 was it for me. . . . I literally called up some doctor in Mississippi and told him the story I'm telling you. 'I have a family. I have a chance to make a lot of money. It's not that I can't play. I know how to do that. You don't have to teach me that. But the schedule is six months. I'm just not physically big enough to hold up. If I can just stay strong. . . .'"

Unfortunately, Dykstra has failed to follow the letter of the law in retirement as well, with allegations having been made against him at different times for indecent exposure, sexual assault, real estate fraud, and grand theft auto, forcing him to spend a significant amount of time in jail. Dykstra's troubles began in October 1999, when police arrested him on charges that he sexually harassed a 17-year-old female employee at a car wash he owned in Simi Valley, California. Some 12 years later, in August 2011, Dykstra faced accusations that he exposed himself to six women who answered ads that he placed on Craigslist for a housekeeper or personal assistant. Charged with two misdemeanor counts of indecent exposure, Dykstra received a nine-month prison sentence after pleading no contest. Dykstra later had his prison sentence extended after he pled guilty in 2012 to separate charges of grand theft auto, bankruptcy fraud, and possession of illegal drugs. Continuing to conduct himself in an abhorrent manner following his release from prison in 2013, Dykstra later faced charges of stealing $50,000 in jewelry from a porn star in 2015, trashing and stealing from a hotel room in 2017, and threatening to kill an Uber driver with a gun in 2018. Dykstra, who has spent a total of almost two years in jail, currently lives with his ex-wife, Terri, who says she has no plans to remarry him.

PHILLIES CAREER HIGHLIGHTS

Best Season

Dykstra had an outstanding year for the Phillies in 1990, earning a ninth-place finish in the NL MVP voting by hitting nine homers; knocking in 60 runs; stealing 33 bases; ranking among the league leaders with 106 runs scored, 35 doubles, and a .325 batting average; and topping the circuit with 192 hits and a .418 on-base percentage. But he performed even better in

1993, earning a runner-up finish in the MVP balloting by batting .305 and establishing career-high marks with 19 home runs, 66 RBIs, 44 doubles, 37 stolen bases, an on-base percentage of .420, a slugging percentage of .482, 143 runs scored, 194 hits, and 129 walks, with each of the last three figures leading the National League.

Memorable Moments/Greatest Performances

Dykstra led the Phillies to a 4–0 win over the St. Louis Cardinals on April 15, 1990, by going 4-for-4, with a double and three runs scored.

Dykstra delivered the big blow of a 4–1 win over the Atlanta Braves on May 25, 1992, when he homered off Steve Avery with two men on base in the bottom of the seventh inning.

Dykstra gave the Phillies a 7–6 victory over the Dodgers on July 7, 1993, when he drove in the tying and winning runs with a two-run double in the bottom of the 20th inning, finishing the game 3-for-9, with a homer, double, three RBIs, and two runs scored.

Dykstra helped lead the Phillies to a 10–8 home win over the Chicago Cubs on September 9, 1993, by hitting a pair of homers, knocking in five runs, and scoring three times.

Dykstra delivered what proved to be the game-winning blow of a 4–3 victory over the Braves in Game 5 of the 1993 NLCS when he homered off reliever Mark Wohlers with no one on base and one man out in the top of the 10th inning.

Although the Phillies lost the 1993 World Series to Toronto in six games, Dykstra performed brilliantly, going 8-for-23 (.348), with four homers, eight RBIs, nine runs scored, seven walks, four stolen bases, a .500 on-base percentage, and a 1.413 OPS. Particularly outstanding in Game 4, Dykstra homered twice, doubled, walked, stole a base, drove in four runs, and scored four times during a 15–14 loss.

Dykstra contributed to a 12–1 rout of the Pittsburgh Pirates on May 13, 1994, by going 4-for-4, with a triple, two doubles, and four runs scored.

Dykstra had another big game on April 17, 1996, going 4-for-5, with two triples, a double, two RBIs, and two runs scored during a 9–3 win over the Expos in Montreal.

Notable Achievements

- Batted over .300 three times.
- Scored more than 100 runs twice.
- Surpassed 30 doubles twice, amassing more than 40 two-baggers once.

- Stole at least 30 bases three times.
- Walked more than 100 times once.
- Compiled on-base percentage over .400 three times.
- Compiled OPS over .900 once.
- Led NL in runs scored once, hits twice, bases on balls once, on-base percentage once, plate appearances once, and at-bats once.
- Finished second in NL in doubles once and games played once.
- Led NL outfielders in putouts twice.
- Led NL center fielders in putouts twice and double plays once.
- Ranks 11th in franchise history with .388 on-base percentage.
- 1993 division champion.
- 1993 NL champion.
- Two-time NL Player of the Week.
- May 1994 NL Player of the Month.
- Finished in top 10 in NL MVP voting twice, placing as high as second in 1993.
- 1993 Silver Slugger Award winner.
- 1993 *Sporting News* NL All-Star selection.
- Three-time NL All-Star (1990, 1994, and 1995).

43

BOB BOONE

Part of one of baseball's few three-generation families, Bob Boone spent 19 years in the major leagues excelling for three different teams behind home plate. One of the finest defensive catchers ever to play the game, Boone earned Gold Glove honors seven times over the course of his career, winning the award twice as a member of the Phillies, whom he helped lead to four division titles, one pennant, and one world championship in his 10 years with the club. A three-time NL All-Star, Boone also proved to be a solid offensive performer for the Phillies, batting over .270 five times and driving in more than 60 runs on three separate occasions, with his strong all-around play eventually landing him a spot on the Philadelphia Baseball Wall of Fame and a place in the Philadelphia Sports Hall of Fame.

Born in San Diego, California, on November 19, 1947, Robert Raymond Boone lived a nomadic existence as a youngster, calling six different cities home by the time he reached 13 years of age. The son of Ray Boone, who earned All-Star honors multiple times during a 13-year career that included stints with the Cleveland Indians, Detroit Tigers, Chicago White Sox, Milwaukee Braves, Kansas City Athletics, and Boston Red Sox, young Robert spent his formative years attending three different schools each year, remaining in San Diego during the winter, but attending classes in Florida during spring training and either Detroit, Chicago, or Milwaukee from April through June.

Adopting a more sedentary lifestyle following his father's retirement in 1960, Bob began his baseball career at San Diego's Crawford High School, before enrolling at Stanford University, where he spent his college years starring at third base for the Cardinals. Eventually selected by the Phillies in the sixth round of the 1969 Amateur Draft, with the 126th overall pick, Boone got his start in pro ball in the Florida State League North, before moving on to the A-level Carolina League, where he batted .300 for Raleigh-Durham. Promoted to Double-A Reading in 1970, Boone spent the next two seasons learning the finer points of catching after the Phillies decided to convert him into a receiver. Looking back at his transition from third base years later, Boone said, "I had good hands, a strong arm, and good speed within three feet. I was reticent about moving. Becoming a catcher was the best thing that ever happened to me, considering the way I hit."

Having completed his training behind home plate, Boone began the 1972 campaign at Triple-A Eugene, where he hit 17 homers, drove in 67 runs, scored 77 times, and batted .308, earning him a late-season callup to Philadelphia. Appearing in 16 games with the Phillies over the final three weeks of the

Bob Boone earned two Gold Gloves and three All-Star nominations during his time in Philadelphia.
Courtesy of MearsonlineAuctions.com

season, Boone acquitted himself extremely well, batting .275 and hitting the first home run of his big-league career.

Laying claim to the Phillies' starting catcher's job in 1973, the 25-year-old Boone performed well in his first full season, earning a third-place finish in the NL Rookie of the Year voting by hitting 10 homers, driving in 61 runs, batting .261, and leading all NL receivers in assists and runners caught stealing. Although Boone finished first among players at his position in putouts the following year, he slumped somewhat at the plate, hitting just three homers, knocking in only 52 runs, and batting just .242. Displeased with the right-handed-hitting Boone's offensive output, the Phillies acquired veteran left-handed-swinging catcher Johnny Oates to platoon with him during the early stages of the 1975 campaign, prompting Boone to seriously consider retiring from baseball, as he admitted years later when he said, "I had always worked diligently toward two careers—baseball and medical school. In 1975, I almost quit to go to medical school because baseball wasn't going to be a way to make a lot of money. I put it off, and that winter Andy Messersmith changed all that." (Messersmith, a pitcher for the Los Angeles Dodgers, challenged baseball's reserve clause, paving the way for free agency.)

Assuming a part-time role in 1975 while playing with torn cartilage in his right knee, Boone hit just two homers, drove in only 20 runs, and batted just .246. But Boone improved upon those numbers dramatically in 1976, when, after reestablishing himself as the Phillies' everyday starting catcher, he earned his first All-Star selection by homering four times, knocking in 54 runs, and batting .271. Boone followed that up by hitting 11 homers, driving in 66 runs, and batting .284 in 1977, before earning All-Star and Gold Glove honors in each of the next two seasons. Performing especially well in 1978, Boone hit a career-high 12 homers, knocked in 62 runs, batted .283, and led all NL receivers with a .991 fielding percentage.

Although the 6'2", 200-pound Boone gradually developed into a competent hitter, he always considered himself, first and foremost, a catcher, once saying, "My job is catching. And the biggest part of that job is handling the pitching staff."

Further expounding upon his primary role, Boone stated, "Catching is much like managing. Managers don't really win games, but they can lose plenty of them. The same way with catching. If you're doing a quality job, you should be almost anonymous."

Boone continued, "Calling a game is an art form, not a science. You can't call a game five hours before it begins, or from the bench. There are so many minor adjustments that hitters and pitchers make back and forth during a game, it becomes a sort of mental chess game. I don't believe in going to the mound too often, except to try to relax a pitcher. You can communicate without saying a word, and sometimes it's better that way. . . . There are only a handful of pitches in each game that are crucial, so you'd better not overdo the rest. Getting a young pitcher through a day when he's got mediocre stuff is more fun than going 4-for-5."

Expressing his admiration for the way his fellow receiver plied his craft, longtime Chicago Cubs catcher Randy Hundley stated, "He was a complete catcher—the best at digging the ball out of the dirt. He also knew how to work the pitchers, and he was a tremendous asset as a leader on that team."

Despite batting just .229 in 1980 after undergoing surgery during the previous offseason to repair torn ligaments in his left knee, Boone helped lead the Phillies to their first world championship by hitting nine homers, driving in 55 runs, and doing an expert job of handling their pitching staff. But, after Boone batted just .211, knocked in only 24 runs, and threw out just 22 percent of the runners that tried to steal against him during the strike-shortened 1981 campaign, the Phillies sold him to the California Angels on December 6, 1981, less than three weeks after he celebrated his 34th birthday.

Boone, who left Philadelphia with career totals of 65 home runs, 456 RBIs, 349 runs scored, 957 hits, 172 doubles, and 21 triples, a batting average of .259, an on-base percentage of .325, and a slugging percentage of .370, subsequently began a second career in the American League, starting behind home plate for the Angels for the next seven seasons, before spending his final two years with the Kansas City Royals. And, during that time, Boone earned one more All-Star nomination and another five Gold Gloves, continuing to make a lasting impression on everyone who watched him work behind home plate, with Wade Boggs stating, "He was probably the smartest catcher that I ever had to deal with behind the plate. It was almost like he was in your head, and he would call a game on what you would think and set you up that way."

Boggs continued, "He could get more calls by either sticking his arm out or catching the breaking ball against his chest. He just had an uncanny way of getting strikes when he needed to get them. . . . A guy threw a high breaking ball and he'd just let it sink, and he'd catch it against his chest to give an illusion that it's a strike. Or, if they'd throw a low fastball, he'd stick out his hand before it got any lower to get the illusion that it's a strike. He would catch balls at the end of his glove, half the ball would hang out, this part of the ball is on the corner and the ball is off the plate, so he would give the illusion that he caught it on the corner, but, in actuality, the ball is hanging out of the edge of his mitt, which is that far outside. He was so smart."

Willie Randolph also commented on Boone's ability to impact a game from his catcher's position when he said, "He was one of those guys . . . you didn't like him because it was almost like it was two against one: the pitcher and him. He was very good at knowing what your weaknesses and strengths were. It was like having a coach on the field. . . . He knew how to set you up. He was one of those guys that was always kind of annoying behind you because you always felt he was in your head. He knew how to back you off, go away. He played a lot of psychological games with the hitter."

Meanwhile, Angels pitcher Mike Witt credited Boone for much of the success he experienced on the mound when he suggested, "Boone had a lot to do with my development. He helps in a lot more ways than calling the game. He frames pitches so well that he steals strikes that are four or five inches out of the strike zone. He works so hard to go down in the dirt for the hard curveball that you never worry about bouncing it back to the backstop. With a lot of catchers, you're so afraid of the wild pitch that you choke the curveball and leave it hanging."

Boone also drew praise for his ability to play through pain, with Gene Mauch, who managed him for six seasons in California, telling *Sports*

Illustrated in 1988, "He has the highest pain threshold and the most mental toughness of anyone I ever managed."

Crediting his martial arts training for his ability to stay on the field, Boone stated, "It's an attitude. The kung fu helps because you reach a level beyond pain, beyond exhaustion, and you always know you can do more. I tell myself, 'It's only pain. Can I play or can't I play? If it's just pain, I can play.'"

After starting the vast majority of his team's games in each of the previous 17 seasons, Boone assumed a backup role with the Kansas City Royals in 1990, before announcing his retirement the following spring when he failed to earn a roster spot with the Seattle Mariners after signing with them as a free agent. Ending his playing career with 105 home runs, 826 RBIs, 679 runs scored, 1,838 hits, 303 doubles, 26 triples, a .254 batting average, a .315 on-base percentage, and a .346 slugging percentage, Boone continues to rank third all-time among major-league catchers with 2,225 games played, with only Iván Rodríguez and Carlton Fisk having appeared in more contests behind home plate.

In discussing how he chose to leave the game, Boone told Bob Nightengale of the *LA Times* in 1992, "I think it's hard for people to believe this, but I went out exactly the way I wanted. I told myself years ago I was going to wring it out until the absolute end. And the end is when I can't get employment. Some guys want to dictate how their career ends. They want their farewell tour. But I never wanted a Mike Schmidt press conference, the tears, and all that. You've got to understand, I was never in it for the glory. I was an aberration. God blessed me with skills that didn't deteriorate. And now, I can leave with a certain satisfaction that I did my job for a long time, and I did it well. I did it the right way. And I take great pride in that." Following his playing days, Boone managed the Royals from 1995 to 1997 and the Cincinnati Reds from 2001 to 2003, before eventually accepting the position of assistant general manager and VP of player development with the Washington Nationals.

PHILLIES CAREER HIGHLIGHTS

Best Season

Boone played his best ball for the Phillies from 1977 to 1979, posting his best overall numbers as a member of the team in the first of those campaigns, when he hit 11 homers, batted .284, compiled an OPS of .780, and established career-high marks with 66 RBIs, 55 runs scored, and 26 doubles.

Memorable Moments/Greatest Performances

Boone helped lead the Phillies to a 6–2 win over the St. Louis Cardinals on June 27, 1976, by homering against right-hander Lynn McGlothen with the bases loaded in the bottom of the fourth inning.

Boone collected five hits in one game for the only time as a member of the Phillies on May 7, 1977, when he went 5-for-6, with a double, one RBI, and two runs scored during a 7–4, 13-inning win over the Dodgers in Los Angeles.

Boone proved to be the central figure in a 3–2 victory over the Houston Astros on July 22, 1978, going 4-for-4, with a homer and three RBIs, with his opposite field single in the bottom of the 10th inning driving in Bud Harrelson from second base with the winning run.

Boone contributed to the Phillies' marathon 23–22, 10-inning win over the Cubs on May 17, 1979, by going 3-for-4, with a homer, double, two walks, two runs scored, and a career-high five RBIs.

Boone came up big for the Phillies in Game 1 of the 1980 World Series, going 3-for-4, with two doubles, two RBIs, and one run scored during a 7–6 home win over the Kansas City Royals.

Notable Achievements

- Led NL catchers in putouts once, assists once, fielding percentage once, and runners caught stealing once.
- Ranks among Phillies career leaders with 43 sacrifice flies (tied for 8th) and 77 intentional bases on balls (6th).
- Four-time division champion (1976, 1977, 1978, and 1980).
- 1980 NL champion.
- 1980 world champion.
- July 15, 1979, NL Player of the Week.
- Two-time NL Gold Glove Award winner (1978 and 1979).
- 1976 *Sporting News* NL All-Star selection.
- Three-time NL All-Star (1976, 1978, and 1979).
- Member of Philadelphia Baseball Wall of Fame.
- Member of Philadelphia Sports Hall of Fame.
- Named to Phillies Centennial Team in 1983.

44

TONY TAYLOR

One of the longest-tenured players in franchise history, Tony Taylor spent parts of 15 seasons in Philadelphia during two tours of duty with the club, providing the Phillies with good speed and a solid bat at the top of their lineup and a reliable glove in the field. Playing for mostly mediocre Phillies teams, Taylor batted over .300 twice, scored more than 100 runs once, and stole at least 20 bases four times, while also consistently ranking among the league's top second basemen in putouts, assists, and double plays turned. Extremely versatile, Taylor spent a significant amount of time at other positions as well, starting at third base for one year, and even seeing some action at first base and in left field, with his many contributions to the team and selfless attitude making him one of the most popular players ever to don a Phillies uniform.

Born in Central Alava, Cuba, on December 19, 1935, to a Chinese mother whose parents changed their family name to Sánchez upon their arrival in Cuba and an African-American father who traveled to the region to work in a sugar mill, Antonio Nemesio Taylor grew up on a sugar plantation in Matanzas province, located east of the capital city of Havana. In discussing his childhood, Taylor said, "Central Alava was a quiet place. Nothing to do but play ball or swim in the river. As a boy, I went to school and worked in my cousin's butcher shop. I liked chemistry. If I didn't go into baseball, I would have become a chemist for a sugar company."

After getting his start in organized ball at Central Alava High School, Taylor continued to hone his skills while playing for Estrellas de Colón in the Pedro Betancourt Amateur League. Hoping to pursue a career in major-league baseball, Taylor traveled to the United States at the age of 17 in 1953 and spent one season playing for the independent Texas City team in the Evangeline League, during which time he faced a tremendous amount of pressure as a dark-skinned immigrant who spoke no English. Recalling the problems that he encountered while trying to integrate the circuit, Taylor revealed during a 2009 interview, "It was very difficult for me because they sent me to play in Texas City. I was the first black guy to play in that league. That was in 1954. I had a difficult time, but I knew I came to this country to play baseball, so I didn't care. . . . I had no one to talk to. The only English word I knew was 'Okay,' and I would order meals by pointing at the food. In the middle of the season, the franchise was moved to Thibodaux in Louisiana, and that's when I would have given up the whole deal, had I the money to get back to Cuba. I was so homesick. The fare to Havana was $72. I looked in my pocket, I had only $62. So, I stayed."

Tony Taylor ranks among the Phillies' all-time leaders in games played, plate appearances, and at-bats.

Overcoming the many challenges that he faced his first year in the States, Taylor ended up batting .314, leading the league with 12 triples, and doing a solid job at third base, prompting the New York Giants to sign him as an amateur free agent. Taylor subsequently spent the next three seasons advancing through the Giants' farm system, before being left unprotected in the 1957 Rule 5 Draft, allowing the Chicago Cubs to pluck him from their organization.

Promoted by the Cubs to the major leagues in 1958, Taylor spent the next two seasons starting at second base alongside shortstop Ernie Banks, who tried his best to make the young infielder feel at home at his new position, with the *Sporting News* reporting, "The flashy Cuban had never played at the keystone position in his life. However, he tackled the assignment with determination and plenty of help and encouragement from Banks, his new roomie and sidekick."

Banks also tried to make Taylor feel comfortable in his new surroundings, as the latter recalled in 1970 when he said, "When I first joined the Cubs, I was so lonesome that Ernie tried to talk Spanish with me. Good guy, Banks. Bad Spanish, but good guy."

After getting off to a slow start in Chicago, Taylor gradually developed into a solid player with the Cubs, hitting six homers, driving in 27 runs, scoring 63 times, stealing 21 bases, and batting .235 as a rookie, before reaching the seats eight times, knocking in 38 runs, scoring 96 others, batting .280, and finishing second in the league with 23 stolen bases in his second season. Commenting on the tremendous strides that Taylor made over the course of his first two seasons, Cubs manager Bob Scheffing told writer Sam Lacy in 1960, "Tony didn't have time to break in. . . . . That first season, he did everything wrong. . . . He messed up plays in the field, committed every kind of error imaginable, and didn't hit much either. . . . But he never gave up and had an excellent teacher in Banks, who was understanding, patient, and constantly working at keeping him loose. . . . Next year (1959), he became a big leaguer."

Meanwhile, Cubs batting coach and all-time great Rogers Hornsby noted that the right-handed-hitting Taylor, who stood 5'9" and weighed 170 pounds, had "forearms like Popeye" and suggested, "If he ever learns to stride into the ball and pull it, he'll be a home-run slugger. He sort of falls away from the plate, but he still has so much power that he hits a homer to right field occasionally."

Yet, despite the rave reviews that Taylor received from Scheffing and Hornsby, the Cubs traded him to the Phillies during the early stages of the 1960 campaign for first baseman Ed Bouchee and pitcher Don Cardwell, with Phillies GM John Quinn saying at the time, "We gave up two good players, but you can't make a trade without giving up something of value, and we feel this trade was the best we could make. . . . We now have a fine second baseman in Taylor. He can hit, run, field, and is a fine leadoff man. Besides, he's only 24 years old. The Phils have had a second-base problem for many years, but we have solved that for a long time to come."

Revealing years later that he very much regretted leaving Chicago, Taylor said, "I felt uprooted again. I had to leave behind my bride, Nilda, and she spoke no English. . . . It was tough breaking away from my dear friend Ernie Banks, too."

Despite his initial concerns, Taylor established himself as one of the Phillies' better players over the final 127 games of the 1960 season, batting .287, scoring 66 runs, and stealing 24 bases, earning in the process his lone All-Star nomination. However, he slumped somewhat the following year, batting just .250, scoring only 47 runs, and swiping just 11 bags, later blaming his subpar performance on a 14-pound increase in weight. But, after shedding the added bulk during the subsequent offseason, Taylor arrived at spring training in top shape, prompting manager Gene Mauch to proclaim, "I know we're going to see a different Tony Taylor. I think he's going to cover a lot more ground both ways this season."

Rebounding somewhat in 1962, Taylor ended up hitting seven homers, driving in 43 runs, scoring 87 times, stealing 20 bases, and batting .259, while also ranking among the league's top second basemen in putouts, assists, and double plays. Taylor followed that up with arguably the finest all-around season of his career, concluding the 1963 campaign with five home runs, 49 RBIs, 102 runs scored, 23 stolen bases, a batting average of .281, and a league-leading .986 fielding percentage at second base. Expressing the belief at season's end that Taylor had replaced Pittsburgh's Bill Mazeroski as the senior circuit's top second baseman, Gene Mauch stated, "Bill Mazeroski wasn't close to Taylor this year. Up 'til now, I've said that Maz was the best. But you might have to underline was. This year, I know you'd have to underline was."

Phils teammate Cal McLish added, "You read a lot about guys like Pete Rose. People talk about Taylor like he was just another second baseman, instead of one of the best in the business."

Taylor remained the Phillies' full-time second baseman for one more year, batting .251, scoring 62 runs, and ranking among the top players at his position in putouts, assists, and double plays in 1964, before losing his starting job to Cookie Rojas the following season after being hit twice on the forearm by Don Cardwell pitches on May 31. Finishing the year with a batting average of just .229 and only 41 runs scored in 106 games, Taylor subsequently spent the next two seasons splitting his time between first base, second, and third, although he remained a regular member of the starting lineup. Moved to third base full-time in 1968, Taylor had a decent offensive season, batting .250, scoring 69 runs, and stealing 22 bases, while also finishing third among NL third sackers in both putouts and assists. Displaying his versatility again in 1969 and 1970, Taylor played all over the field, seeing action at first, second, third, and in left.

Commenting on Taylor's importance to the team during 1970 spring training, Phillies manager Frank Lucchesi said, "Taylor is the most underrated player in the league. Every year he comes down here as an extra man, and every year he winds up playing more games than anybody." Taylor then went out and had one of his finest offensive seasons, establishing career-high marks with nine homers, 55 RBIs, and a .301 batting average.

Nevertheless, with the Phillies in a rebuilding mode following a 73-88 finish in 1970, they elected to trade the 35-year-old Taylor to the Detroit Tigers for a pair of minor-league pitchers on June 12, 1971. In discussing the move, Lucchesi stated, "I have nothing but praise for Tony Taylor. But we've come up with a couple of pitching prospects, and we are building."

Meanwhile, Taylor, who lived for many years in the Philly suburb of Yeadon, expressed his sadness to be leaving the place he had come to love, saying, "This is my home; I'll die here."

Taylor ended up spending the next two and a half years in Detroit, serving the Tigers primarily as a part-time player, before being released by the club following the conclusion of the 1973 campaign. Re-signed by the Phillies on December 19, 1973, Taylor subsequently spent the last three years of his career performing almost exclusively for the team as a pinch-hitter, excelling in that role in 1974, when he compiled a batting average of .328 by hitting safely in 21 of his 64 official at-bats. In discussing how he had to adjust to his new role, Taylor said, "I believe the older you get, the harder you have to work. . . . It was hard for me to get used to not playing every day. But I've got to think, concentrate, know my job is to pinch-hit."

Contributing to the Phillies with his leadership, knowledge of the game, and dedication to his profession as well, Taylor drew praise from teammate Larry Bowa, who stated, "His knowledge of the game is unbelievable. Tony will watch a pitcher for an inning, then call me over and explain exactly what the guy is doing, diagnose his move toward first to help me steal."

Phillies manager Danny Ozark added, "Tony Taylor prepares himself like a surgeon. . . . He thinks along the same lines I do, and he is halfway there before I ask him."

Beloved by everyone in Philadelphia, Taylor also found himself being applauded by Milton Richman of United Press International, who wrote in 1975, "Tony Taylor has a special way with people. It doesn't matter who they are, other ballplayers, fans or the press. He's to the Phillies what Ernie Banks was to the Cubs."

With the admiration that Phillies fans felt for Taylor growing even stronger during his second tour of duty with the club, the Associated Press reported in July 1974, "All Tony Taylor has to do is stick his head out of the Phillies' dugout and the fans go wild."

Revealing his mutual love for the fans at Veterans Stadium, Taylor said, "I love those people. If a guy gives 100 percent, they cheer for you. They know baseball, and they know whether a player is playing hard or not."

Taylor continued, "The way the fans received me when I came back, the ovations they gave me, it showed me how much they appreciated the way Tony Taylor played baseball—hard, always hard. It meant so much to me. It showed they remembered. It showed they cared."

Although the Phillies eventually released Taylor on November 2, 1976, he remained with them long enough to take part in their division-winning celebration that year. Announcing his retirement after being let go by the

Phillies, Taylor ended his playing career with 75 home runs, 598 RBIs, 1,005 runs scored, 2,007 hits, 298 doubles, 86 triples, 234 stolen bases, a .261 batting average, a .321 on-base percentage, and a .352 slugging percentage. As a member of the Phillies, Taylor hit 51 homers, knocked in 461 runs, scored 737 times, collected 1,511 hits, 219 doubles, and 63 triples, stole 169 bases, batted .261, compiled an on-base percentage of .322, and posted a slugging percentage of .346.

Summing up Taylor's time in Philadelphia, a 1974 Associated Press article stated, "For 11 ½ years before he was traded by the Phils to Detroit in 1971, Taylor put out, most of the time playing on bad teams. Regardless of the score or the standings, Taylor would come to bat, cross himself, kiss the tip of his bat in his inimitable style, and give any pitcher a tough out."

After retiring as an active player, Taylor spent several years serving the Phillies as a coach at both the major- and minor-league levels, before coaching in the Giants farm system, and, later, for the Florida Marlins. Choosing to end his lengthy association with the game he loved following the conclusion of the 2004 campaign, Taylor announced his retirement, saying at the time, "I put 50 years in professional baseball. I played 19 years in the big leagues, and I coached for 31. . . . My last year when I coached, I said, 'I don't want no more part of baseball. I want to stay home, spend time with my family, travel and forget about everything.'"

Taylor spent the next 16 years enjoying his retirement, before complications from a series of strokes he suffered nearly one year earlier claimed his life on July 16, 2020. Upon learning of the 84-year-old Taylor's passing, Larry Bowa issued a message that read, "Tony Taylor helped me so much in my first year in the big-league camp. He taught me how to play the game the right way, how to act like a big leaguer. Tony, Reuben [sic] Amaro Sr., Cookie Rojas, and Bobby Wine were all so instrumental in my success at the major league level. Rest in Peace TT."

Bobby Wine also had kind words for Taylor, saying, "Tony was a great teammate, a true professional. He loved the Phillies, loved playing, and loved coaching. He was one of Gene Mauch's favorite players. Never heard anyone say a nasty word about him."

PHILLIES CAREER HIGHLIGHTS

Best Season

Taylor had one of his finest seasons for the Phillies in 1970, when, appearing in 124 games at the age of 34, he batted .301, scored 74 runs, and established career-high marks with nine homers and 55 RBIs. Nevertheless, the 1963 campaign would have to be considered the finest of Taylor's career since he earned MVP consideration for the only time by batting .281, stealing 23 bases, amassing 180 hits, placing near the top of the league rankings with 10 triples and 102 runs scored, and leading all NL second basemen with a .986 fielding percentage.

Memorable Moments/Greatest Performances

Taylor starred in defeat on June 2, 1960, going 3-for-4, with a homer, double, walk, and four runs scored during a 9–8 loss to the Braves.

Taylor helped lead the Phillies to a 3–2 win over the Pirates at Forbes Field on September 3, 1960, by going 4-for-5, with one RBI and one run scored.

Taylor gave the Phillies a 4–3 win over the Houston Colt .45s on June 25, 1962, by knocking in Bobby Wine from second base with a single to center field in the bottom of the ninth inning, finishing the game with three hits, a walk, and three runs batted in.

Taylor contributed to a 10–4 victory over the Reds on May 26, 1963, by going a perfect 4-for-4 at the plate and scoring four runs.

Taylor did most of the damage during a 6–5 win over the Dodgers on June 26, 1963, hitting safely three times, driving in five runs, and scoring once.

Taylor helped preserve Jim Bunning's perfect game against the Mets on June 21, 1964, when he made a sensational defensive play at second base in the fifth inning. After knocking down a line drive hit by Jesse Gonder, Taylor scrambled after the ball when it dribbled a few feet away from him and threw from his knees to get the Mets catcher at first base.

Taylor had a big game against the Mets on May 1, 1968, going 4-for-6, with a triple, a stolen base, three RBIs, and one run scored during a 7–2 Phillies win.

Taylor delivered the big blow in a 3–2 win over the Montreal Expos on May 26, 1970, homering off Bill Stoneman with two men on base in the top of the ninth inning.

Taylor proved to be a thorn in the side of the Expos once again two days later, leading the Phillies to a 5–3 win on May 28, 1970, by hitting a pair of solo home runs, reaching the seats twice in one game for the only time as a member of the team.

Taylor experienced perhaps the most memorable moment of his career on August 2, 1970, when he gave the Phillies a dramatic 7–6 win over the

Giants by hitting a grand slam home run off left-handed reliever Mike Davison in the bottom of the ninth inning.

Notable Achievements

- Batted over .300 twice.
- Scored more than 100 runs once.
- Finished in double digits in triples once.
- Stole at least 20 bases four times.
- Finished third in NL with 26 stolen bases in 1960.
- Led NL second basemen in fielding percentage once.
- Ranks among Phillies career leaders in hits (12th), games played (5th), plate appearances (9th), and at-bats (7th).
- 1976 division champion.
- 1960 NL All-Star.
- Member of Philadelphia Baseball Wall of Fame.

45

DARREN DAULTON

The heart and soul of the Phillies' 1993 NL pennant-winning team, Darren Daulton spent parts of 14 seasons in Philadelphia, establishing himself as one of the greatest leaders in franchise history. Starting at catcher for the Phillies from 1989 to 1995, Daulton became known for his extraordinary work ethic, loyalty, and toughness, all of which earned him the respect and admiration of his teammates. Persevering through nine knee surgeries, Daulton also performed extremely well on the field, surpassing 20 home runs and 100 RBIs twice each, en route to earning three All-Star selections and two top-10 finishes in the NL MVP voting.

Born in Arkansas City, Kansas, on January 3, 1962, Darren Arthur Daulton attended Arkansas City High School, where, in addition to starring in baseball, he excelled in football as a defensive back and earned All-State honors in wrestling. Later identified as a true five-tool player by head baseball coach Mike West, Daulton, according to West, also exhibited his outstanding leadership ability in high school, with West recalling, "Darren made people step up. He always gave his very best whenever he stepped on to the field, and he wouldn't tolerate anything less from his teammates. To find someone that young with that kind of passion, selflessness, work ethic, and integrity was truly exceptional."

Selected by the Phillies in the 25th round of the 1980 MLB Amateur Draft, Daulton spent most of the next eight seasons playing in the minor leagues, although he earned callups to the parent club in 1983, 1985, 1986, and 1987, batting .209, hitting 15 homers, and driving in 45 runs in a total of 140 games at the major-league level. Yet, despite the limited amount of action he saw as a member of the Phillies, Daulton learned a great deal about what it took to be a true professional from two of the team's all-time greats, Steve Carlton and Mike Schmidt. Revealing some of the lessons he learned from Carlton to baseball historian William Kashatus in the latter's book *Macho Row: The 1993 Phillies and Baseball's Unwritten Code*, Daulton said, "Lefty showed me how to prepare myself, how to stay in top physical shape. He also taught me about good food and wine by taking me and some of the younger guys out to nice restaurants when we were on the road."

Meanwhile, in discussing Schmidt, Daulton stated, "Schmitty taught me that you have to work at this game to survive in it . . . he spent a lot of time in the batting cages working on his swing. . . . He was always there to encourage us, to share his knowledge. . . . I tried to emulate that kind of leadership later in my career when I saw younger guys coming up."

Joining the Phillies for good in 1988, Daulton spent much of the year backing up Lance Parrish behind the plate, before suffering a

Darren Daulton served as the emotional leader of Phillies teams that won two division titles and two pennants.
Courtesy of MearsonlineAuctions.com

season-ending injury when he broke his hand punching a clubhouse wall. Assuming the Phillies' starting catcher's job the following year, Daulton struggled terribly on offense, hitting eight homers, driving in 44 runs, scoring only 29 times, and batting just .201, in 131 games and 368 official at-bats. However, he improved upon those numbers dramatically in 1990, finishing the season with 12 home runs, 57 RBIs, 62 runs scored, and a batting average of .268, while also leading all NL catchers in assists and double plays turned. But Daulton suffered another setback during the early stages of the 1991 campaign when he and teammate Lenny Dykstra nearly lost their lives in an automobile accident that left Daulton with a fractured eye socket and a scratched cornea. Appearing in only 89 games the entire year, Daulton hit 12 homers, knocked in 42 runs, and batted just .196.

Fully recovered by the start of the 1992 campaign, Daulton emerged as a force to be reckoned with, earning his first All-Star selection and a sixth-place finish in the NL MVP voting by batting .270, scoring 80 runs, leading the league with 109 RBIs, and ranking among the leaders with 27 homers, a slugging percentage of .524, and an OPS of .908. Daulton followed that up with another outstanding season, earning his second straight All-Star nomination and another top-10 finish in the NL MVP balloting by hitting 24 homers, driving in 105 runs, batting .257, and establishing career-high marks with 90 runs scored, 35 doubles, 117 walks, and an on-base percentage of .392 for a Phillies team that ended up winning the pennant.

The unquestioned leader of a motley group of players initially picked to finish last in the NL East, the 6'2", 200-pound Daulton, who acquired the nickname "Dutch" during his time in Philadelphia, provided more than just a powerful left-handed bat in the middle of the Phillies' lineup. Revered by his teammates for his tenacity and old-school toughness, Daulton inspired everyone else on the ballclub with his ability to fight through pain, with Mitch Williams recalling, "With two bags of ice on both knees before every game, he set the tone for us players that year, and probably for the rest of our careers. It's pretty hard to go in and ask for a day off with a guy like that in the locker room."

Williams added, "When he walked in a room, or on the field, he commanded it. And let's be honest, women loved Dutch. I think that a lot of baby boys were named after him, either Darren or Daulton, just to have a piece of him."

Curt Schilling also had high praise for his former teammate, saying, "In my 22 years of baseball, I have never been privileged enough to be around a man who led anywhere near as well as Dutch did. He was perfect in that role in every sense of the word. . . . There's no question in my mind that I don't have the career I had without him. I never played with anybody like him again."

Unfortunately, Daulton never again performed at an elite level after 1993. Although he got off to a fast start the following year, hitting 15 homers, driving in 56 runs, and batting .300 through the season's first 67 games, Daulton had to sit out the remainder of the year after injuring his knee. And even though Daulton earned his final All-Star selection in 1995, he appeared in only 98 games, finishing the season with nine homers, 55 RBIs, and a .249 batting average.

Unable to catch after 1995 due to problems with his knees, Daulton appeared in a total of just 89 games with the Phillies over the course of the next two seasons, splitting his time between the outfield, first base, and DH, before being dealt to the Florida Marlins for outfielder Billy McMillon on July 21, 1997. Daulton spent the remainder of the year playing first base and pinch-hitting for the Marlins, hitting three homers, driving in 21 runs, and batting .262 for the eventual world champions, in helping to lead them to the NL pennant. Choosing to announce his retirement after the Marlins defeated the Cleveland Indians in the 1997 World Series, Daulton ended his playing career with 137 home runs, 588 RBIs, 511 runs scored, 891 hits, 197 doubles, 25 triples, 50 stolen bases, a .245 batting average, a .357 on-base percentage, and a .427 slugging percentage, compiling virtually all those numbers while wearing a Phillies uniform.

Eventually returning to Philadelphia following his playing days, Daulton cohosted the local radio show *Talking Baseball with Dutch* from 2010 to 2016 and established the Darren Daulton Foundation in 2011. Yet, despite his philanthropic work, Daulton ran afoul of the law on several occasions, being arrested four times on vehicle-related charges and once for domestic abuse, which resulted in a two-and-a-half-month jail sentence and another two-and-a-half months in drug rehabilitation.

Diagnosed with glioblastoma, a highly malignant form of brain cancer, after undergoing surgery to remove two brain tumors in June 2013, Daulton lived another four years, eventually dying of brain cancer at the age of 55 on August 6, 2017.

Upon learning of his former teammate's passing, Juan Samuel said, "Darren and I started in the minor leagues together. We worked our way up together to the big leagues, so he was like a brother to me. He was the best teammate I ever had."

Rubén Amaro Jr. stated, "Darren was the teammate and leader I learned more from, respected more, and was honored to call a friend. He wasn't afraid to let you know when you messed up but was also the first to praise you for your effort and dedication to your craft. I love Darren as a brother and will miss him dearly. God bless the Daulton family."

Larry Andersen, who spent parts of five seasons playing with Daulton in Philadelphia, issued a statement that read, "Darren Daulton the ball-player was and ALWAYS WILL BE synonymous with great leadership and winning. Darren Daulton the person was and ALWAYS WILL BE synonymous with caring and compassion. He never turned his back on anyone, whether they were hurting or in need, and was always there even if he merely sensed that someone was on the struggle bus. He may not be in the Baseball Hall of Fame, but he is a Hall of Famer as a person, as most anyone who has known him will attest to. He always greeted you with a big smile, a huge hug, and a kiss on the cheek, and I will forever miss that greeting . . . until we meet again!!!"

Meanwhile, former Phillies GM Ed Wade spoke of Daulton's leadership ability, saying, "Leadership isn't manufactured or contrived. You either have it or you don't. Darren exuded leadership on the field, in the clubhouse, throughout the organization, and in public. The likes of Darren Daulton come along very infrequently."

PHILLIES CAREER HIGHLIGHTS

Best Season

Daulton played his best ball for the Phillies in 1992 and 1993, earning All-Star honors and a top-10 finish in the NL MVP voting each season by hitting more than 20 homers and driving in more than 100 runs. While either of those years would make an excellent choice, I ultimately settled on 1993 since, en route to helping the Phillies capture the pennant, Daulton recorded more than 200 more putouts behind home plate than he registered the previous season (981 to 760), leading all NL catchers in that category.

Memorable Moments/Greatest Performances

Daulton helped lead the Phillies to a 10–4 win over the Cubs at Wrigley Field on August 17, 1985, by going 4-for-5, with two homers, a double, three RBIs, and four runs scored.

Daulton recorded the only five-hit game of his career on September 20, 1989, going a perfect 5-for-5 at the plate during a 9–8 win over the Cubs.

Daulton led the Phillies to a 9–8 win over the Dodgers on July 15, 1991, by collecting five RBIs, four of which came on a fifth-inning grand slam off right-handed reliever Tim Crews.

Daulton homered twice and knocked in five runs during a 7–5 win over the Cardinals on June 5, 1992, with his three-run homer off Todd Worrell in the bottom of the eighth inning providing the margin of victory.

Daulton delivered the pivotal blow of a 5–1 win over the Pirates on May 10, 1993, when he homered with the bases loaded against starter Bob Walk in the bottom of the seventh inning.

Daulton contributed to a 14–6 victory over the Cardinals on July 28, 1993, by hitting an eighth-inning grand slam off Omar Olivares, finishing the game with a career-high six RBIs.

Daulton hit two home runs and drove in five runs during an 8–7 win over the Florida Marlins on August 7, 1993, homering with two men on base in the first inning, before reaching the seats again with one man on in the top of the fifth.

Daulton helped lead the Phillies to a 12–3 win over the Colorado Rockies on April 13, 1994, by going 3-for-4, with a homer, double, four RBIs, and four runs scored.

Daulton had another big game against the Montreal Expos on May 10, 1995, going 4-for-5, with a homer, double, and four RBIs during a 10–1 Phillies win.

Notable Achievements

- Hit more than 20 home runs twice.
- Knocked in more than 100 runs twice.
- Batted .300 once.
- Surpassed 30 doubles three times.
- Walked more than 100 times once.
- Posted slugging percentage over .500 twice.
- Compiled OPS over .900 twice.
- Led NL with 109 RBIs in 1992.
- Finished third in NL with 117 bases on balls in 1993.
- Led NL catchers in putouts once, assists once, double plays twice, and runners caught stealing once.
- Ranks among Phillies career leaders with 607 bases on balls (12th), 57 intentional bases on balls (12th), and 39 sacrifice flies (12th).
- Two-time division champion (1983 and 1993).
- Two-time NL champion (1983 and 1993).
- 1997 *Sporting News* NL Comeback Player of the Year.
- Finished in top 10 in NL MVP voting twice (1992 and 1993).
- 1992 Silver Slugger Award winner.
- 1992 *Sporting News* NL All-Star selection.
- Three-time NL All-Star (1992, 1993, and 1995).
- Member of Philadelphia Baseball Wall of Fame.

46

AARON NOLA

One of the National League's foremost pitchers, Aaron Nola has spent much of the past seven seasons serving as the ace of the Phillies' pitching staff. Since arriving in Philadelphia in 2015, Nola has surpassed 15 victories and compiled an ERA under 3.00 once, recorded more than 200 strikeouts three times, and thrown more than 200 innings twice, with his excellent mound work earning him one All-Star selection and one third-place finish in the NL Cy Young voting. Meanwhile, Nola's stoical nature and cerebral approach to pitching have made him a veritable rock at the top of the Phillies' starting rotation.

Born in Baton Rouge, Louisiana, on June 4, 1993, Aaron Michael Nola started playing baseball at the age of nine, although he did not truly develop a passion for the sport until his older brother, Austin, began competing in tournaments. Hoping to follow in the footsteps of his older sibling, Aaron developed a habit of watching himself in the mirror while mimicking a pitching motion, a gesture that his father later described as "strange gyrations."

After being coached by his father in the Little Leagues, Nola entered Catholic High School in Baton Rouge, where he spent his freshman year suffering from stress fractures in his back caused by a six-inch summer growth spurt, before emerging as a top prospect over the course of the next three seasons. Compiling an overall record of 21-2 and amassing 214 strikeouts in 152 innings pitched at Catholic High, Nola led his team to two state playoff appearances, with the Louisiana Sports Writers Association naming him the top player in the state at the end of his senior year.

Recalling the impression that Nola made on him during their time together at Catholic High, head baseball coach Kyle Achord said, "Aaron was a tall, thin kid with a wiry build, but his innate ability to throw strikes you saw early. That set him apart from an early age. His command was unbelievable, and that's what jumped off the page with me. His velocity was okay, he was 80, 81 mph as a ninth grader—and that's still good."

Aaron Nola finished third in the 2018 NL Cy Young voting.
Courtesy of Keith Allison and All-Pro Reels

Achord continued, "When he toes the rubber, he's out to do everything to help his team win. The demeanor and ability to throw strikes separated him apart, but, as he got older and stronger, the velocity came. The summer entering his sophomore year, he pitched with our varsity. It's when we decided to bypass the junior varsity for Aaron. His junior year, we won the state championship and his senior year, we lost in the semifinals."

Subsequently selected by the Toronto Blue Jays in the 22nd round of the 2011 MLB Draft, Nola elected not to turn pro and instead attend Louisiana State University on a baseball scholarship. Continuing to excel on the diamond in college, Nola posted a composite record of 30-6 for the Tigers the next three years, while compiling an ERA of 2.09 and striking out 345 batters in 332 innings of work. Particularly effective his final two seasons, Nola went 12-1 with a 1.57 ERA as a sophomore, earning in the process SEC Pitcher of the Year honors, while also being named to the National Collegiate Baseball Writers Association (NCBWA), *Baseball America*, and *Collegiate Baseball* All-America teams. Nola followed that up by compiling a record of 11-1 and an ERA of 1.47 ERA his senior year, with his fabulous performance gaining him recognition as the SEC Player of the Year and the 2014 National Pitcher of the Year.

Commenting on the qualities that allowed Nola to dominate the opposition, LSU pitching coach Alan Dunn stated, "Aaron has always had the ability to stay in the moment. He's quiet, but inside, you know he's grinding. He's scary, because he's like that silent assassin. If a team is lucky to get runners on second and third against him, they're not scoring, because he's not going to give in. His command was so good that Aaron did things no SEC pitcher ever did before. There was no question in my mind Aaron was going to do some great things."

Impressed with Nola's superb work at LSU, the Phillies selected him with the seventh overall pick of the 2014 MLB Draft, after which they inked him to a $3.3 million signing bonus and assigned him to their Class A-Advanced minor-league affiliate in Clearwater, Florida. After performing well at Clearwater, Nola finished out the season with the Double-A Reading Phillies, with whom he began the ensuing campaign as well. Continuing to advance through the Phillies' farm system in 2015, Nola went 7-3 with a 1.88 ERA at Reading, earning him a promotion to the Triple-A Lehigh Valley Iron Pigs at midseason. After a brief stay at Lehigh Valley, Nola joined the Phillies in mid-July, making his first start for them on July 21, 2015, when he allowed one run and five hits over the first six innings of a 1–0 loss to the Tampa Bay Rays. Acquitting himself extremely well the rest of the year, Nola went on to compile a record of 6-2 and an ERA of 3.59 in his 13 starts for the Phillies, while striking out 68 batters in 77 2/3 innings of work.

Plagued by a right elbow strain that brought his season to a premature end, Nola proved to be less effective in 2016, going just 6-9 with a 4.78 ERA in his 20 starts, although he still managed to record 121 strikeouts in 111 innings pitched. Rebounding somewhat the following year after getting off to a slow start, Nola finished 12-11 with a 3.54 ERA and a team-leading 184 strikeouts and 168 innings pitched, before emerging as one of the senior circuit's best pitchers in 2018, when he earned All-Star honors and a third-place finish in the NL Cy Young voting by compiling a record of 17-6, finishing second in the league with a 2.37 ERA, and ranking among the leaders with 224 strikeouts, 212 1/3 innings pitched, and a WHIP of 0.975.

Although the right-handed-throwing Nola, who stands 6'2" and weighs 200 pounds, possesses good velocity on his four-seam fastball and sinker, attaining a speed somewhere between 90 and 93 mph with both pitches, he depends primarily on movement, excellent control, an outstanding curveball, and an above-average changeup to navigate his way through opposing lineups, telling the *Philadelphia Inquirer*, "There are different ways to get outs rather than throwing 95, 96, 97. It would be nice to throw 97, but I physically can't."

Nola's greatest strength, though, is his unflappable demeanor and ability to remain on an even keel, a quality he first exhibited as a teenager, with his high school coach, Kyle Achord, saying, "You saw it then, and I still see it when Aaron pitches for the Phillies, his demeanor never changes. I tell people this all of the time. Don't think Aaron is not competitive, and that there isn't a fire burning in there. He never gets real high or real low either way."

In discussing the manner with which he keeps his emotions in check, Nola says, "I try not to get too up or too down. We play a lot of games. You can only control what you can control. If I have a bad start, I try to make the next four days as good as I can. I'm a big process guy. The results will come."

Nola also does an excellent job of preparing himself for each start, both mentally and physically, with former Phillies manager Gabe Kapler saying of his ace, "He's as physically prepared as any pitcher I've even been around. He's as mentally prepared as any pitcher I've ever been around."

After signing a four-year, $45 million contract extension with the Phillies following the conclusion of the 2018 campaign, Nola went 12-7 with a 3.87 ERA and struck out 229 batters in 202 1/3 innings pitched in 2019, before compiling a record of 5-5 and an ERA of 3.28 during the pandemic-shortened 2020 campaign. Although Nola subsequently ranked among the NL leaders with 223 strikeouts in 2021, he pitched less effectively, going just 9-9 with a 4.63 ERA for a Phillies team that finished only two games over .500.

Heading into the 2022 season, Nola boasts a career record of 67-49, an ERA of 3.68, and a WHIP of 1.158. He has also struck out 1,145 batters in 1,023.1 innings of work and thrown three complete games and two shutouts. Since Nola is only 28 years old as of this writing, he figures to add significantly to those totals before his time in Philadelphia comes to an end.

CAREER HIGHLIGHTS

Best Season

Nola had the finest season to this point in his career in 2018, when he earned All-Star honors and a third-place finish in the NL Cy Young balloting by ranking among the league leaders with 17 wins, a 2.37 ERA, 224 strikeouts, 212 1/3 innings pitched, and a WHIP of 0.975. By striking out more than 200 batters and holding his opponents to a batting average under .200, Nola joined Hall of Famer Grover Cleveland Alexander as the only pitchers in franchise history to accomplish both feats in the same season.

Memorable Moments/Greatest Performances

Nola limited the Giants to just five hits and one run in seven innings of work during a 4–2 Phillies win on May 8, 2018, recording a career-high 12 strikeouts for the first of three times during the contest.

Nola defeated the Mets almost single-handedly on July 9, 2018, yielding just one hit and one walk in seven shutout innings during a 3–1 win, while also driving in all three Phillies runs with a bases loaded double in the fifth inning.

Although Nola did not figure in the decision, he dominated the Mets' lineup once again on June 27, 2019, recording 10 strikeouts and allowing just one hit and no runs over the first seven innings of a 6–3 win over the Mets.

Nola proved to be nearly as dominant on August 10, 2020, striking out 10 batters and surrendering just two hits and one run over the first eight innings of a 13–8 win over Atlanta, before the Phillies' bullpen allowed the Braves to score seven times in the top of the ninth.

Nola recorded nine strikeouts and yielded just two hits and three walks in eight innings of work during a 6–0 victory over the Washington Nationals on September 1, 2020.

With the pandemic prompting MLB to limit both ends of doubleheaders to just seven innings in 2020 and 2021, Nola earned a complete-game 11–0 win over the Miami Marlins on September 11, 2020, by allowing just three hits, issuing no walks, and striking out 10 batters in the opener.

Nola threw his first nine-inning shutout on April 18, 2021, surrendering just two hits, issuing no walks, and recording 10 strikeouts during a 2–0 win over the Cardinals, whose only hits came on singles by catcher Yadier Molina and shortstop Paul DeJong.

Nola nearly matched that performance on June 13, 2021, yielding just three hits, issuing one walk, and registering nine strikeouts over the first 7 2/3 innings of a 7–0 win over the Yankees.

Although the Phillies ended up losing the first game of a doubleheader with the Mets on June 25, 2021, by a score of 2–1, Nola performed magnificently, working 5 1/3 scoreless innings, recording 12 strikeouts, and allowing just two hits and one walk. Along the way, Nola tied the major-league record for most consecutive strikeouts by fanning 10 straight batters.

Nola turned in a superb effort against the Atlanta Braves on July 25, 2021, earning a 2–1 victory by recording nine strikeouts and surrendering just four hits and one run in 8 2/3 innings of work.

Notable Achievements

- Won 17 games in 2018.
- Has posted winning percentage over .600 three times.
- Has compiled ERA under 3.00 once.
- Has posted WHIP under 1.000 once.
- Has struck out more than 200 batters three times.
- Has thrown more than 200 innings twice.
- Has led NL pitchers in starts once and complete games once.
- Has finished second in NL in starts once, ERA once, and shutouts once.
- Has finished third in NL in strikeouts once, innings pitched once, and WHIP once.
- Holds Phillies career record for most strikeouts per nine innings pitched (10.070).
- Ranks among Phillies career leaders in strikeouts (8th), strikeouts-to-walks ratio (3rd), and hits allowed per nine innings pitched (5th).
- Finished third in 2018 NL Cy Young voting.
- 2018 NL All-Star.

47

JUAN SAMUEL

Known for his unique combination of speed and power, Juan Samuel proved to be one of the National League's most productive offensive players during his time in Philadelphia. The first player in major-league history to finish in double digits in home runs, triples, doubles, and stolen bases in each of his first four seasons, Samuel accomplished the feat from 1984 to 1987, while also displaying outstanding range and a strong throwing arm at second base. A two-time NL All-Star and 1987 Silver Slugger Award winner, Samuel hit more than 20 homers and knocked in 100 runs once each, scored more than 100 runs three times, and stole more than 50 bases twice. Meanwhile, Samuel also led all NL second basemen in putouts three times and double plays turned once, with his excellent all-around play eventually earning him a spot on the Philadelphia Baseball Wall of Fame.

Born in San Pedro de Macorís, Dominican Republic, on December 9, 1960, Juan Milton Samuel grew up with very little, spending much of his youth playing baseball, before further honing his skills at Licey High School, in Licey, Puerto Rico. Signed by Phillies scouts Kiki Acevedo and Rubén Amaro Sr. for $2,500 on April 29, 1980, Samuel subsequently traveled to Clearwater, Florida, where he joined the team's Bend (Oregon) minor-league affiliate that competed in the Northwest League. Feeling out of place in his new environment, Samuel recalled years later the details of his first spring training: "I went to Clearwater, but many of us actually trained in Sarasota at a complex shared by the Braves and Astros. I was a second baseman, but they kept working me out in right field. I wondered if they confused me with someone else. I remember sitting on the bench and crying. P. J. (Carey, Phillies minor league manager) came up to me and asked what was wrong. I told him I wanted a plane ticket so I could go home. He talked me out of it. He wound up as my manager in Bend. We

In 1987, Juan Samuel became the first player in major-league history to finish in double digits in homers, triples, doubles, and stolen bases in each of his first four seasons.
Courtesy of MearsonlineAuctions.com

became close friends. He came to San Francisco when I played my first game in the majors."

Samuel ended up spending most of the next four seasons advancing through the Phillies' farm system, before finally arriving in Philadelphia during the latter stages of the 1983 campaign. Appearing in 18 games during the season's final month, Samuel acquitted himself well at the plate, homering twice and batting .277. However, he also struck out 16 times and performed erratically in the field, committing nine errors at second base.

Replacing Joe Morgan as the Phillies' starting second baseman in 1984, Samuel earned All-Star honors and a runner-up finish in the NL Rookie of the Year voting by hitting 15 homers, knocking in 69 runs, batting .272, leading the league with 19 triples, and ranking among the leaders with 105 runs scored, 191 hits, 36 doubles, 72 steals, and 310 total bases, although he also topped the circuit with 168 strikeouts and finished second among all NL players with 33 errors in the field. In discussing Samuel at one point during the season, Phillies manager Paul Owens said, "One thing I wanted him to know was that we were going to stay with him no matter what happened. So, the night before our road opener against Atlanta, I called him into my office for a talk. What I told Juan was that I didn't want him to worry about any errors he might make in the field, and not to be disappointed if he didn't hit big league pitching right away. I also told him I knew that eventually everything would come together for him."

Meanwhile, in addressing the right-handed-hitting Samuel's outstanding offensive production, Owens, who had his young second baseman batting leadoff the entire year, stated, "I think the fact that Samuel knew the job was his may have helped him relax. Anyway, he gave us the speed and the on-base percentage that we wanted right away. Frankly, we were a little amazed when he was safe 11 of the first 12 times he tried to steal."

Owens continued, "With most rookies, there is almost always an element of doubt in some area. But the way this kid got to balls in the field and stayed aggressive at the plate, you knew he had the stuff to make it. We didn't feel we were gambling at all by making him our second baseman—just giving up a little time until he got the feel of things."

And, when asked about Samuel's high error total, Owens said, "What was happening was that Juan was rushing everything, getting his feet tangled up, and making errors on balls that he should have handled easily. But once we slowed him down and convinced him he didn't have to throw out every runner by 30 feet, he became much more consistent in the field."

Not totally satisfied with Samuel's performance, though, Owens added, "Now I don't mean that we are satisfied with Juan completely. We'd like to tailor that free swing of his to the point where he is more a contact hitter. We'd also like to improve his conception of the strike zone so that he can get the walks that should come naturally to a leadoff hitter. But what we're pushing for is a gradual change and not an overnight one."

Adapting well to big-league pitching, the 5'11", 170-pound Samuel, who taught himself to speak English as well as most people born in the States, stated, "So far, I haven't had to deal with anything I couldn't handle. Most pitchers try to get me out by moving the ball around, but I also saw a lot of that strategy in the minors."

Samuel, who, in addition to his 168 strikeouts walked only 28 times in his first full season, then added, "I am not a contact hitter. I go up to the plate to swing, not to walk, and I'm not sure if I can or want to change."

Although Samuel managed to draw as many as 60 bases on balls one season, he never truly changed his style of hitting, remaining a free swinger who led the NL in strikeouts in each of the next three seasons as well. Nevertheless, Samuel continued to make significant contributions to the Phillies on offense, hitting 19 homers, driving in 74 runs, scoring 101 times, batting .264, stealing 53 bases, collecting 31 doubles, and finishing second in the league with 13 triples in 1985, before reaching the seats 16 times, knocking in 78 runs, scoring 90 others, batting .266, and placing near the top of the league rankings with 36 doubles, 12 triples, and 42 stolen bases the following year. Samuel then made history in 1987, when, in addition to driving in 100 runs, scoring 113 times, and batting .272, he hit 28 homers, stole 35 bases, and collected 15 triples and 37 doubles, becoming in the process the first player ever to compile double-digit totals in the last four categories in each of his first four major-league seasons. Meanwhile, Samuel, who displayed outstanding range, soft hands, and a quick release at second base, developed into a more consistent fielder, reducing his error total significantly, while also annually ranking among the top players at his position in putouts and assists.

Samuel subsequently experienced a precipitous decline in offensive production in 1988, finishing the season with just 12 homers, 67 RBIs, 68 runs scored, and a .243 batting average. Continuing to struggle at the plate the following year after being moved to center field by new Phillies manager Nick Leyva, Samuel batted just .246 in his first 51 games, prompting the Phils to trade him to the Mets for Lenny Dykstra and reliever Roger McDowell on June 18, 1989.

Expressing his thoughts on the deal, Leyva said, "Len Dykstra will play every day no matter who's pitching and be our leadoff hitter. McDowell will be a closer. He's a durable, steady guy. Samuel is a quality player and a quality person, and I'm sure he'll help the Mets."

Mets manager Dave Johnson countered by saying, "Every time we played the Phillies, I worried about Samuel. He has good power, gets a lot of extra base hits, and can run. He reminds me of Bobby Bonds."

Meanwhile, Samuel, upon learning that he had been traded from the last-place Phillies to the third-place Mets, stated, "I don't know if I won or lost. But I think I picked up about 10 games in the standings. I'm just going to try to help the club as best I can."

Samuel, who left Philadelphia with career totals of 100 home runs, 413 RBIs, 523 runs scored, 921 hits, 176 doubles, 71 triples, 249 stolen bases, a lifetime batting average of .263, a .310 on-base percentage, and a .439 slugging percentage, ended up spending another nine-and-a-half years in the major leagues, never again experiencing the same level of success he attained as a member of the Phillies. After starting in center field for the Mets for the rest of 1989, Samuel spent two-and-a-half years in Los Angeles playing both second base and center field for the Dodgers, earning his final All-Star selection by hitting 12 homers, driving in 58 runs, scoring 74 times, stealing 23 bases, and batting .271 in 1991. He then split the next three-and-a-half seasons between the Kansas City Royals, Cincinnati Reds, and Detroit Tigers. Eventually moving on to Toronto, Samuel spent his final three seasons assuming a backup role for the Blue Jays, before announcing his retirement following the conclusion of the 1998 campaign with career totals of 161 home runs, 703 RBIs, 873 runs scored, 1,578 hits, 287 doubles, 102 triples, 396 stolen bases, a .259 batting average, a .315 on-base percentage, and a .420 slugging percentage.

Since retiring as an active player, Samuel has spent more than two decades coaching and managing at various levels, serving the Tigers as first base coach from 1999 to 2004, before moving to third base in 2005. After spending the 2006 campaign managing in the Mets' farm system, Samuel coached third base for the Orioles from 2007 until June 4, 2010, when he became the team's interim manager following the firing of Dave Trembley. Subsequently replaced by Buck Showalter, Samuel accepted a position elsewhere in the organization as an evaluator for its Dominican Republic academy for the remainder of that season, before returning to Philadelphia, where he has spent the last 11 seasons serving on the Phillies' coaching staff.

PHILLIES CAREER HIGHLIGHTS

Best Season

Samuel compiled excellent numbers for the Phillies in 1984, hitting 15 homers; driving in 69 runs; batting .272; ranking among the NL leaders with 105 runs scored, 191 hits, 36 doubles, 70 extra-base hits, 310 total bases, and 72 stolen bases; and leading the league with 19 triples. But he performed even better in 1987, earning MVP consideration and the second of his three All-Star selections by batting .272, posting an OPS of .837, stealing 35 bases, leading the NL with 15 triples and 80 extra-base hits, and establishing career-high marks with 28 homers, 100 RBIs, 113 runs scored, 37 doubles, and 329 total bases, with each of the last three figures placing him near the top of the league rankings.

Memorable Moments/Greatest Performances

Samuel tripled twice during a 1–0 win over the Giants on May 18, 1984, with his three-bagger in the top of the seventh inning driving in the game's only run.

Samuel contributed to a lopsided 9–1 victory over the Braves on July 19, 1984, by going 4-for-5, with three RBIs, three runs scored, and two stolen bases.

Samuel helped lead the Phillies to a 26–7 thrashing of the Mets on June 11, 1985, by collecting a career-high five hits, knocking in two runs, scoring three times, and stealing two bases.

Samuel starred during a 10–6 win over the Reds in Cincinnati on July 20, 1985, going 3-for-4, with a homer, double, and five RBIs.

Samuel collected a career-high six RBIs during a 19–1 rout of the Cubs on June 23, 1986, finishing the game with two homers, a double, and two runs scored.

Samuel gave the Phillies an 8–7 win over the Cardinals on June 29, 1986, by hitting a grand slam home run off reliever Todd Worrell with two men out in the top of the ninth inning.

Samuel helped lead the Phillies to a 7–6 come-from-behind victory over the Houston Astros on May 11, 1987, by homering twice, driving in five runs, and scoring three others, with his three-run homer off Larry Andersen in the top of the eighth inning tying the score at 6–6.

Samuel had a huge game against the Cubs on August 12, 1987, going 3-for-4, with a homer, triple, five RBIs, and two runs scored during a 13–7 win, with his eighth-inning grand slam off reliever Ed Lynch putting the Phillies ahead to stay.

Notable Achievements

- Hit more than 20 home runs once (28 in 1987).
- Knocked in 100 runs in 1987.
- Scored more than 100 runs three times.
- Finished in double digits in triples four times.
- Surpassed 30 doubles five times.
- Stole more than 30 bases five times, topping 50 thefts twice.
- Posted slugging percentage over .500 once.
- Led NL in triples twice, extra-base hits once, plate appearances twice, and at-bats three times.
- Finished second in NL in triples twice, total bases once, stolen bases twice, games played once, plate appearances once, and at-bats once.
- Led NL second basemen in putouts three times and double plays turned once.
- Ranks among Phillies career leaders with 71 triples (9th) and 249 stolen bases (8th).
- 1983 division champion.
- 1983 NL champion.
- 1984 *Sporting News* NL Rookie of the Year.
- September 1, 1985, NL Player of the Week.
- 1987 Silver Slugger Award winner.
- 1987 *Sporting News* NL All-Star selection.
- Two-time NL All-Star (1984 and 1987).
- Member of Philadelphia Baseball Wall of Fame.

48

MIKE LIEBERTHAL

A solid performer for mostly mediocre Phillies teams, Mike Lieberthal spent parts of 13 seasons in Philadelphia, catching more games, hitting more home runs, and amassing more hits during that time than any other backstop in franchise history. Taking over as the Phillies' primary receiver in 1997, one year after Darren Daulton relinquished his starting catcher's duties, Lieberthal continued to function in that capacity for the next nine seasons, surpassing 20 homers twice and batting over .300 on two separate occasions, while also winning one Gold Glove for his outstanding work behind home plate. A two-time NL All-Star and the 2002 NL Comeback Player of the Year, Lieberthal later received the additional honor of being inducted into the Philadelphia Wall of Fame.

Born in Glendale, California, on January 18, 1972, Michael Scott Lieberthal grew up in a Jewish family headed by his father, Dennis, who served as a scout for the Detroit Tigers and San Francisco Giants for many years. After spending much of his youth playing shortstop in various leagues, Lieberthal, who stood only 5'2" well into his teenage years, moved to catcher after he experienced a seven-inch growth spurt during his sophomore year at Westlake High School. Eventually emerging as a star at Westlake High, Lieberthal gained All-America recognition by setting school records for most career home runs (30), hits (105), and runs scored (79). Making an especially strong impression on scouts one afternoon, Lieberthal homered four times and drove in 10 runs, prompting the Phillies to select him in the first round of the 1990 MLB Amateur Draft, with the third overall pick, even though he weighed only 155 pounds at the time.

Lieberthal subsequently spent most of the next six seasons advancing through the Phillies' farm system, although he appeared briefly with the parent club in both 1994 and 1995, homering once, driving in nine runs, and batting .262 in 40 games and 126 official at-bats. And during that time, Lieberthal added some much-needed bulk onto his lean frame, with Terry Francona, who saw him play in the Arizona Fall League in 1994 before becoming Phillies manager a few years later, describing him as "Skinny, and I mean skinny!"

Close to his normal playing weight of 180 pounds by the time he arrived in Philadelphia to stay in 1996, the 6-foot Lieberthal assumed a backup role to newly signed free agent receiver Benito Santiago, who replaced an ailing Darren Daulton as the Phillies' starting catcher. Performing well in somewhat limited duty, Lieberthal hit seven homers, knocked in 23 runs, and batted .253, in 50 games and 166 official plate appearances, despite having to undergo surgery for torn cartilage in his left knee. Named the Phillies' starting catcher in 1997, Lieberthal had a solid year at the

Mike Lieberthal caught more games than anyone else in franchise history. Courtesy of MearsonlineAuctions.com

plate, hitting 20 homers, driving in 77 runs, and batting .246, while also finishing third among all NL backstops in both putouts and assists. However, after Lieberthal got off to a fast start the following year, a pelvic stress fracture forced him to miss the final 10 weeks of the campaign, limiting him to just eight home runs and 45 RBIs.

Healthy again by the start of the 1999 season, the right-handed-hitting Lieberthal ended up posting the best numbers of his career, earning his first All-Star selection by hitting 31 homers, knocking in 96 runs, scoring 84 times, batting an even .300, and compiling an OPS of .914. Meanwhile, Lieberthal's league-leading .997 fielding percentage and 62 assists earned him Gold Glove honors, allowing him to join Johnny Bench, Lance Parrish, and Iván Rodríguez on an extremely exclusive list of receivers who have hit 30 home runs in the same season that they won the Gold Glove Award.

Although Lieberthal failed to perform at quite the same level the following year, he earned All-Star honors once again by hitting 15 homers, driving in 71 runs, and batting .278, despite missing nearly two months of action due to an assortment of injuries that included a wounded ankle he sustained during a collision at home plate with Yankees center fielder Bernie Williams and a bone spur in his right elbow that required surgery during the latter stages of the campaign. Bitten by the injury bug once again in 2001, Lieberthal appeared in a total of only 34 games after tearing his ACL and MCL and cartilage in his knee while attempting to dive back to first base during a pickoff attempt.

Returning to action in 2002, Lieberthal earned NL Comeback Player of the Year honors by homering 15 times, knocking in 52 runs, and batting .279. He followed that up with another outstanding year, hitting 13 homers, driving in 81 runs, scoring 68 times, and batting .313 in 2003, before undergoing surgery during the subsequent offseason to repair a torn meniscus in the same knee he injured two years earlier.

Although Lieberthal continued to post solid numbers for the Phillies in each of the next two seasons, performing especially well in 2004, when he hit 17 homers, knocked in 61 runs, and batted .271, the many injuries he sustained over the course of his career began to take their toll on him by 2006. Able to appear in only 67 games, Lieberthal finished the season with just nine homers and 36 RBIs, prompting the Phillies to allow him to leave via free agency following the conclusion of the campaign. After signing with his hometown Los Angeles Dodgers, Lieberthal spent the 2007 season serving as a backup to Russell Martin, before announcing his retirement at the end of the year with career totals of 150 home runs, 610 RBIs, 534 runs scored, 1,155 hits, 257 doubles, 10 triples, a lifetime batting average of .274, a .337 on-base percentage, and a .446 slugging percentage.

Making his decision known to the public in January 2008, Lieberthal stated, "I'm done. If the Dodgers had picked up my option, I probably would have played one more year. But I didn't want to go anywhere else. There were a lot of reasons. The money was great as a backup, but I have made enough money in baseball. I just didn't want to go through what I have to go through with my body to play 20-25 games a year. It's not worth it."

Choosing to officially retire as a member of the Phillies, Lieberthal signed a one-day contract with them on June 1, 2008, saying at the time, "Philadelphia has always been a second home to me, so I'm really looking forward to this. I spent half my life there and still follow the team closely on television."

Since retiring as an active player, Lieberthal, who during his playing days served as the 2000 chairman of the Corporate Alliance for Drug Education fund-raising drive and sponsored "Lieby's VIPs," in which he purchased $30,000 worth of tickets for the families of children with cancer, has continued his philanthropic work, cohosting with former Phillies teammates Doug Glanville and Randy Wolf a celebrity billiards tournament on behalf of the Philadelphia Futures mentor program.

PHILLIES CAREER HIGHLIGHTS

Best Season

Lieberthal had easily his finest season for the Phillies in 1999, earning All-Star honors for the first of two straight times by batting .300 and establishing career-high marks with 31 home runs, 96 RBIs, 84 runs scored, 33 doubles, and an OPS of .914, while also leading all NL catchers with 62 assists and a .997 fielding percentage.

Memorable Moments/Greatest Performances

Lieberthal helped lead the Phillies to a 12–8 win over the Colorado Rockies on August 13, 1997, by going 4-for-5, with a homer, three RBIs, and three runs scored.

Lieberthal gave the Phillies an improbable 8–7 victory over the Pittsburgh Pirates on June 16, 1998, when he put the finishing touches on a seven-run rally in the bottom of the ninth inning by hitting a pinch-hit three-run homer with two men out.

Lieberthal proved to be a huge factor in the Phillies' 7–6 win over the Mets on July 19, 1998, collecting four hits, driving in a run, and scoring twice, crossing the plate with the game-winning run in the top of the 10th inning following an RBI double by Rubén Amaro Jr.

Lieberthal contributed to a 7–2 victory over the Rockies on May 8, 1999, by hitting a pair of solo homers.

Lieberthal starred in defeat on May 19, 1999, going 3-for-4, with two home runs and a career-high six RBIs during a 10–9 loss to the Expos, with one of his homers coming with the bases loaded.

Lieberthal led the Phillies to an 11–7 win over the Baltimore Orioles on June 6, 1999, by going 4-for-5, with two homers, two doubles, four RBIs, and three runs scored.

Lieberthal again reached the seats twice during a 9–3 win over the Red Sox on June 3, 2000, finishing the game 3-for-5, with a pair of homers and five RBIs.

Although the Phillies lost to the Dodgers 10–8 on August 10, 2002, Lieberthal had a huge game, going 4-for-5, with three home runs and four RBIs.

Lieberthal led the Phillies to a 14–0 rout of the Florida Marlins on September 16, 2003, by driving in six runs, with four of his RBIs coming on an eighth-inning grand slam.

Lieberthal had another big game three days later, homering twice and knocking in four runs during a 7–3 win over the Cincinnati Reds on September 19, 2003.

Notable Achievements

- Hit at least 20 home runs twice, topping 30 homers once.
- Batted .300 or better twice.
- Surpassed 30 doubles four times.
- Posted slugging percentage over .500 once.
- Compiled OPS over .900 once.
- Hit three home runs in one game vs. Los Angeles Dodgers on August 10, 2002.
- Led NL catchers in assists once and fielding percentage once.
- Tied for eighth in franchise history with 43 sacrifice flies.
- May 23, 1999, NL Player of the Week.
- 1999 Gold Glove Award winner.
- 2002 NL Comeback Player of the Year.
- Two-time NL All-Star (1999 and 2000).
- Member of Philadelphia Baseball Wall of Fame.

49

VON HAYES

A solid all-around player who joined the Phillies near the tail end of one of the most successful periods in franchise history, Von Hayes displayed a tremendous amount of versatility during his nine seasons in Philadelphia, starting at first base and all three outfield positions. Blessed with good power at the plate, excellent speed on the basepaths, and a keen batting eye, Hayes hit more than 20 home runs twice, batted over .300 once, stole at least 20 bases six times, and drew more than 100 bases on balls twice, earning in the process one All-Star nomination and one top-10 finish in the NL MVP voting. Nevertheless, Hayes failed to live up to the enormous hype that surrounded him when the Phillies acquired him in a five-for-one trade, leaving him a disappointment to many.

Born in Stockton, California, on August 31, 1958, Von Francis Hayes grew up some 70 miles west, in the city of Moraga, where he got his start in baseball competing in the Little Leagues and Babe Ruth Leagues. The son of a World War II veteran from Brockton, Massachusetts, and a mother who migrated to the US mainland from Puerto Rico, Hayes attended St. Mary's High School, where he proved to be a mostly ineffective pitcher for the school's baseball team, even though he experienced a six-inch growth spurt his final two years that increased his height to 6'1" by the time he graduated.

Choosing to continue his education in the same system, Hayes enrolled at St. Mary's College of California, where he grew another four inches, prompting him to move off the mound, to first base. Developing into a major-league prospect while manning that post, Hayes earned MVP honors of the US-Japan College World Series in 1979. Meanwhile, the left-hand-ed-hitting Hayes, who modeled his swing after Ted Williams, set school records for triples (17) and slugging percentage (.609) that still stand.

Selected by the Cleveland Indians in the seventh round of the June 1979 Amateur Draft, with the 163rd overall pick, Hayes subsequently spent the next two seasons advancing through the Cleveland farm system, performing especially well for the Class A Waterloo (Iowa) Indians, with whom he earned Midwest League Player of the Year honors by topping the circuit with a .329 batting average, 33 doubles, and 162 hits, while also ranking among the leaders in home runs, RBIs, stolen bases, on-base percentage, and slugging percentage. Promoted to Triple-A Charleston in 1981, Hayes remained with the team until mid-August, when the Indians summoned him to the big leagues. Appearing in 43 games with the parent club over the season's final six weeks, Hayes homered once, knocked in 17 runs, scored 21 times, and batted .257, while splitting his time between the outfield and DH.

The Phillies acquired Von Hayes from Cleveland for five players in 1982. Courtesy of MearsonlineAuctions.com

After beginning the ensuing campaign on the bench, Hayes gradually emerged as the Indians' starting right fielder, although he also spent some time at the other two outfield positions. Starting a total of 127 games, Hayes posted solid numbers in his first full season, finishing the year with 14 homers, 82 RBIs, 65 runs scored, 32 stolen bases, and a batting average of .250. Yet, despite Hayes's strong performance, the Indians decided to part ways with him during the 1982 Winter Meetings when the Phillies offered them a package of five players that included veteran second baseman Manny Trillo and future All-Star infielder Julio Franco.

Recalling his thoughts upon learning of the deal, Hayes said, "The first thing I told myself was, 'You're not going to try and go out there and prove you can play as good as those five combined. You're going to go out there and play your own game. . . . They got me to be Von Hayes.'"

Nicknamed "5-for-1" by new Phillies teammate Pete Rose, the 24-year-old Hayes subsequently found himself being cast in a difficult role in which the hometown fans expected great things from him due to the exorbitant price their team paid to acquire him. Perhaps putting too much pressure on himself his first year in Philly, Hayes hit just six homers, drove in only 32 runs, scored just 45 times, and batted .265. Posting much better numbers in 1984, Hayes homered 16 times, knocked in 67 runs, scored 85 others, batted .292, and finished fifth in the league with a career-high 48 stolen bases, while serving as the team's primary starter in center field. But when

Hayes's offensive production fell off to 13 homers, 70 RBIs, 76 runs scored, 21 stolen bases, and a .263 batting average in 1985, the fans at Veterans Stadium voiced their displeasure over his inability to perform at an elite level, prompting him to state on one occasion, "They can do whatever they want. I'll still be eating steak every night."

After moving to first base in 1986, Hayes finally began to earn the respect of Phillies fans by hitting 19 homers, knocking in 98 runs, batting .305, stealing 24 bases, and leading the league with 107 runs scored and 46 doubles, with his outstanding play earning him an eighth-place finish in the NL MVP voting. Impressed with the exceptional performance of his Phillies teammate, Glenn Wilson said, "I wouldn't be surprised to see Von Hayes win a Triple Crown. That's the kind of ability and determination he has."

Still, Hayes failed to garner much attention on a national level, later saying, "That would've been my year to get recognition. The problem was, I had a teammate (Mike Schmidt) who was the National League MVP."

Although the Phillies experienced very little success as a team during most of Hayes's tenure in Philadelphia, the lanky 6'5", 195-pound outfielder/first baseman proved to be a consistent and versatile contributor to the club. Capable of assuming virtually any spot in the batting order, Hayes had the speed and patience at the plate to hit either first or second, and the power to hit anywhere from three to six. A streaky hitter, Hayes had the ability to carry the team for weeks at a time, with former Phillies manager Lee Elia stating, "There have been times when he was the hottest hitter in the league over a period of months."

Hayes followed up his banner year of 1986 by hitting 21 homers, driving in 84 runs, scoring 84 times, batting .277, compiling an on-base percentage of .404, and finishing second in the league with a career-high 121 walks in 1987, before suffering through an injury-marred 1988 campaign during which he hit just six homers, drove in only 45 runs, and scored just 43 times in 104 games. Healthy again in 1989, Hayes earned his only All-Star nomination by reaching the seats 26 times, knocking in 78 runs, scoring 93 others, stealing 28 bases, batting .259, and drawing 101 bases on balls. After signing a three-year contract extension with the Phillies at midseason, Hayes drew praise from general manager Lee Thomas, who stated, "I really think Von Hayes is going to get better and better." Meanwhile, Hayes proclaimed, "I like Philadelphia very much, and I'm ecstatic."

Unfortunately, Hayes never again performed at the same level. Plagued by a series of injuries in 1990, Hayes appeared in only 129 games, finishing the season with just 17 homers, 73 RBIs, 70 runs scored, and a .261 batting average. After getting off to a slow start the following year, Hayes missed almost three months of the season after a fastball thrown by Cincinnati pitcher Tom Browning broke a bone in his right wrist. With Hayes having concluded the campaign with no homers, 21 RBIs, and a batting average of .225, the Phillies traded him to the California Angels for pitcher Kyle Abbott and outfielder Rubén Amaro Jr. on December 8, 1991. Following the completion of the trade, new Phillies manager Jim Fregosi summed up Hayes's tenure in Philadelphia by saying, "It was very, very difficult for Von to play in Philadelphia. . . . I think he put too much pressure on himself."

Hayes, who hit 124 homers, knocked in 568 runs, scored 646 times, stole 202 bases, batted .272, compiled a .363 on-base percentage, posted a .427 slugging percentage, and collected 1,173 hits, 232 doubles, and 30 triples as a member of the Phillies, ended up being released by the Angels during the latter stages of the 1993 campaign.

After failing to receive an offer from any other team, Hayes announced his retirement, ending his career with 143 home runs, 696 RBIs, 767 runs scored, 1,402 hits, 282 doubles, 36 triples, 253 stolen bases, a .267 batting average, a .354 on-base percentage, and a .416 slugging percentage. Following his playing days, Hayes managed in the minor leagues for three seasons, before spending several more years managing and coaching in various independent leagues.

Looking back on the complex nature of Hayes's stay in Philadelphia, Bill Conlin wrote in the *Philadelphia Daily News*, "Because the Phillies went from perpetual contenders from, say, 1976 to 1983, and then became mostly disappointing for the next several years, Hayes had to live with being both second fiddle to Schmidt and briefly the best player on a bad team. Someone fans couldn't appreciate while he was here but was so frequently part of the city's baseball fortunes that he cannot be forgotten either."

Meanwhile, Lee Elia spoke of Hayes's inability to maximize his full potential when he said, "Sometimes I wonder if it's that he was on a ballclub going through transition. Maybe in a different situation, with a different ballclub, maybe his talents would have been more evident."

Eventually making peace with his time in the City of Brotherly Love, Hayes stated, "Philadelphia fans are the same as fans in other cities. . . . The bottom line is winning. Whenever that happens (losing), people point fingers. I suppose it was tougher on me . . . because of the trade, but I believe I was a better player because of them."

PHILLIES CAREER HIGHLIGHTS

Best Season

Although Hayes hit more home runs in both 1987 and 1989 and stole a career-high 48 bases in 1984, he had his finest all-around season in 1986, when, in addition to hitting 19 homers, swiping 24 bags, and ranking among the NL leaders with 98 RBIs, 186 hits, a .305 batting average, a .379 on-base percentage, and a .480 slugging percentage, he led the league with 107 runs scored, 46 doubles, and 67 extra-base hits.

Memorable Moments/Greatest Performances

Hayes helped lead the Phillies to a 6–3 win over the Cardinals on August 5, 1984, by going 4-for-5, with a homer and double.

Hayes contributed to a 26–7 rout of the Mets on June 11, 1985, by homering twice, driving in six runs, and scoring four times, with both his homers coming during the Phillies' nine-run first inning.

Hayes had another big day against the Mets on September 12, 1986, going 4-for-4, with a pair of doubles, one RBI, and two runs scored during a 6–3 Phillies win.

Hayes led the Phillies to a lopsided 9–2 victory over the Cubs on September 30, 1986, by going 3-for-4, with two homers, a double, five RBIs, and three runs scored.

Hayes delivered the big blow of a 12–7 win over the Cardinals on July 29, 1986, when he connected with the bases loaded against Ray Burris in the fourth inning.

Hayes collected five hits in one game for the only time in his career on April 12, 1987, going 5-for-6, with two RBIs and one run scored during a 9–8 win over the Cubs in 10 innings.

Hayes hit a pair of solo homers during a 7–6 win over the Montreal Expos on June 5, 1987, with his seventh-inning blast off Andy McGaffigan providing the margin of victory.

Hayes contributed to a 13–7 win over the Cubs on August 12, 1987, by going 3-for-5, with a homer, triple, double, five RBIs, and three runs scored.

Hayes gave the Phillies a 7–6 win over the Expos on April 10, 1989, by leading off the bottom of the ninth inning with his second home run of the game.

Hayes defeated the Giants almost single-handedly on August 29, 1989, hitting three homers and knocking in all six runs during a 6–1 Phillies win.

Notable Achievements

- Hit more than 20 home runs twice.
- Batted over .300 once.
- Scored more than 100 runs once.
- Surpassed 30 doubles three times, amassing more than 40 two-baggers once.
- Stole at least 20 bases six times, swiping more than 40 bags once.
- Walked more than 100 times twice.
- Compiled on-base percentage over .400 once.
- Hit three home runs in one game vs. San Francisco Giants on August 29, 1989.
- Led NL with 107 runs scored, 46 doubles, and 67 extra-base hits in 1986.
- Finished second in NL in bases on balls twice.
- Led NL center fielders with .993 fielding percentage in 1985.
- Led NL right fielders with nine assists in 1989.
- Ranks among Phillies career leaders with 202 stolen bases (10th), 619 bases on balls (11th), 74 intentional bases on balls (tied-7th), and 43 sacrifice flies (tied-8th).
- 1983 division champion.
- 1983 NL champion.
- Five-time NL Player of the Week.
- April 1989 NL Player of the Month.
- 1989 NL All-Star.

50

SPUD DAVIS

Although largely overshadowed during his playing days by Hall of Fame receivers Gabby Hartnett, Mickey Cochrane, Bill Dickey, and Ernie Lombardi, Virgil "Spud" Davis proved to be one of baseball's best-hitting catchers for more than a decade, posting a lifetime batting average of .308 for four different teams over the course of his 16-year major-league career, half of which he spent in Philadelphia. Having most of his finest seasons for the Phillies, Davis batted .321 in his two tours of duty with the club, topping the .300 mark on six separate occasions. A solid run producer as well, Davis knocked in at least 65 runs for the Phillies three times even though he garnered as many as 400 official at-bats as a member of the team just twice.

Born in Birmingham, Alabama, on December 20, 1904, Virgil Lawrence Davis grew up in the Birmingham neighborhood of Jefferson, where he acquired the nickname "Spud" as a child, recalling years later, "I liked potatoes so much early in life that I was nicknamed Spud. But I loved baseball more than potatoes, so I cut them out."

Excelling in multiple sports while attending high school at Gulf Coast Military Academy in Gulfport, Mississippi, Davis starred in baseball and football, serving as a running back and defensive lineman for the gridiron squad that won the 1922 Mississippi state title. Eventually, though, Davis decided to focus exclusively on his first love, breaking into professional baseball in 1926 as a member of the Gulfport Tarpons of the Class D Cotton States League, for whom he batted .356 while splitting his time between catcher and third base.

Impressed with Davis's outstanding play at Gulfport, the Yankees purchased his contract in September 1926. However, with Davis failing to earn a roster spot and MLB commissioner Kenesaw Mountain Landis ruling that the Yankees already had too many players out on option, Davis ended up being subjected to waivers, allowing the St. Louis Cardinals to claim him. After spending the 1927 campaign playing for the Reading (PA) Keystones

Virgil "Spud" Davis batted over .300 for the Phillies six times.

of the Double-A International League, Davis arrived in St. Louis the following year, appearing in just two games with the Cardinals, before being included in a multiplayer deal with the Phillies on May 11 that sent him and minor leaguers Don Hurst and Homer Peel to Philadelphia for a package of three players that included veteran catcher Jimmie Wilson. Davis subsequently spent the final five months of the 1928 season sharing playing time with fellow rookie receiver Walt Lerian, hitting three homers, driving in 18 runs, and batting .282, in 67 games and 163 official at-bats.

Continuing to split time behind the plate with Lerian in 1929, Davis performed exceptionally well in a part-time role, hitting seven homers, knocking in 48 runs, and batting .342, in 98 games and 263 official at-bats. Serving as the Phillies' primary backstop the following year after Lerian died in a traffic accident during the offseason, Davis emerged as one of the National League's top receivers, hitting 14 homers, driving in 65 runs, and batting .313, while also ranking third among players at his position with a .986 fielding percentage. Davis posted solid numbers once again in 1931, concluding the campaign with four home runs, 51 RBIs, and a .326 batting average, before having the two finest seasons of his career. After hitting 14 homers, driving in 70 runs, and batting .336 in 1932, Davis earned MVP consideration the following year by reaching the seats nine times, knocking in 65 runs, and finishing second in the league to teammate Chuck Klein with a .349 batting average and a .395 on-base percentage.

Davis's outstanding offensive production his first few seasons in Philadelphia gained him widespread acclaim as one of the finest-hitting catchers in all of baseball. However, his defense left something to be desired. Struggling with weight issues throughout his career, the 6'1", 200-pound Davis did not move particularly well behind home plate, causing him to regularly rank among the league leaders in passed balls and stolen bases allowed. Nevertheless, Davis proved to be adequate as a receiver, leading all NL backstops in assists once, fielding percentage twice, and double plays turned once.

Meanwhile, Davis, who spoke with a heavy Southern drawl, drew praise for the class and sophistication he displayed away from the playing field, with one contemporary writer referring to him as "the personification of the Southern Gentleman" and adding, "He does not strut into hotel lobbies, on main thoroughfares, or on the ball field. The Spud does not poke his nose into an open conversation but is reserved and retiring. He does not hoard his money, dresses in the height of fashion, enjoys good shows and is fond of movies."

Even though Davis batted well over .300 in each of the previous five seasons, the Phillies elected to trade him back to the Cardinals for Jimmie Wilson on November 15, 1933. Upon learning of the deal, Davis expressed the excitement he felt over playing for a pennant-contending team, saying, "Who wouldn't throw his arm off for this bunch after getting away from the Phillies?"

Davis ended up spending three years with the Cardinals, helping them win the NL pennant in 1934 by hitting nine homers, driving in 65 runs, and batting .300 during the regular season, before hitting safely in his only two trips to the plate during the World Series, which resulted in a seven-game win over the Detroit Tigers. After two more seasons in St. Louis, Davis moved on to Cincinnati, where he spent all of 1937 and the early part of 1938 serving as a backup with the Reds. Traded back to the Phillies for pitcher Bucky Walters on June 13, 1938, Davis assumed a part-time role in Philadelphia the next year-and-a-half, compiling a batting average of .307 in 202 official at-bats in 1939, before being sold to the Pittsburgh Pirates at season's end. Davis then served the Pirates as a part-time player the next two seasons, before being released following the conclusion of the 1941 campaign and subsequently named a coach on manager Frankie Frisch's coaching staff. Davis remained a full-time coach in Pittsburgh until 1944, when a shortage of manpower due to World War II forced him to appear in a total of 73 games over the course of the next two seasons. Retiring for good as an active player at the end of 1945, Davis ended his major-league career with 77 home runs, 647 RBIs, 388 runs scored, 1,312 hits, 244 doubles, 22 triples, a batting average of .308, an on-base percentage of .369, and a slugging percentage of .430. At the time of his retirement, Davis ranked second all-time only to Mickey Cochrane among big-league catchers in career batting average. Over parts of eight years in Philadelphia, Davis hit 53 homers, knocked in 363 runs, scored 234 times, batted .321, compiled an on-base percentage of .374, posted a slugging percentage of .449, and collected 790 hits, 134 doubles, and 11 triples.

After turning down an offer to manage Pittsburgh's Double-A minor-league affiliate in Birmingham, Davis scouted for the Pirates for three years, before spending four seasons serving as an assistant coach for the Chicago

Cubs. Released by the Cubs, Davis returned to his hometown of Birmingham, Alabama, where he spent the rest of his life living on his baseball pension and the money that he made during his playing career. Davis lived until August 14, 1984, when he died a little over four months shy of his 80th birthday.

PHILLIES CAREER HIGHLIGHTS

Best Season

Davis performed extremely well for the Phillies in 1932, batting .336, compiling an OPS of .921, hitting 14 homers, and driving in 70 runs in just 402 official at-bats. But he posted slightly better overall numbers the following year, concluding the 1933 campaign with nine homers, 65 RBIs, an OPS of .867, and a career-high .349 batting average, 173 hits, and 51 runs scored.

Memorable Moments/Greatest Performances

Davis made the first home run of his career a memorable one, delivering the key blow in a 6–5 win over the Chicago Cubs on June 8, 1928, when he homered with two men aboard in the bottom of the eighth inning.

Davis collected five hits in one game for the only time in his career on May 17, 1930, going 5-for-5 with three RBIs and two runs scored during a 14–6 home win over the Brooklyn Robins.

Davis homered twice and knocked in four runs during a 10–8 win over the Cubs on August 20, 1930, with his three-run blast in the top of the seventh inning providing the margin of victory.

Davis helped lead the Phillies to a 9–5 win over the Brooklyn Dodgers on July 22, 1932, by going 4-for-5, with two homers, three RBIs, and three runs scored.

Davis had a big day at the plate against Pittsburgh on August 1, 1932, going 4-for-5, with a homer, double, and career-high six RBIs during an 18–5 rout of the Pirates.

Davis's two-out grand slam off Chicago starter Joe Bush in the bottom of the fifth inning proved to be the pivotal blow of a 7–1 win over the Cubs on May 13, 1933.

Davis led the Phillies to a 4–2 win over the Dodgers on July 4, 1933, by going 4-for-4, with two doubles, a triple, and two RBIs.

Davis proved to be the difference in a 2–1 win over the Boston Braves on September 30, 1933, hitting two home runs, the second of which came with two men out in the top of the 10th inning.

Notable Achievements

- Batted over .300 six times, topping the .320 mark on four occasions.
- Surpassed 30 doubles once.
- Posted slugging percentage over .500 once.
- Compiled OPS over .900 once.
- Finished second in NL with .349 batting average and .395 on-base percentage in 1933.
- Finished third in NL with .867 OPS in 1933.
- Led NL catchers in assists once, fielding percentage once, double plays turned once, and runners caught stealing once.
- Ranks ninth in franchise history with career batting average of .321.

SUMMARY AND HONORABLE MENTIONS (THE NEXT 25)

Having identified the 50 greatest players in Philadelphia Phillies history, the time has come to select the best of the best. Based on the rankings contained in this book, the members of the Phillies all-time team are listed below. Our squad includes the top player at each position, a designated hitter, and a pitching staff that features a five-man starting rotation, a setup man, and a closer, whose name I took from the list of honorable mentions that will soon follow. A second team has been listed as well.

PHILLIES FIRST TEAM STARTING LINEUP

Richie Ashburn CF
Chase Utley 2B
Mike Schmidt 3B
Chuck Klein RF
Dick Allen DH
Ryan Howard 1B
Del Ennis LF
Jimmy Rollins SS
Bob Boone C

PHILLIES FIRST TEAM PITCHING STAFF

Steve Carlton SP
Grover Cleveland Alexander SP
Robin Roberts SP
Jim Bunning SP
Curt Schilling SP
Jim Konstanty SU
Steve Bedrosian CL

PHILLIES SECOND TEAM STARTING LINEUP

Sherry Magee LF
Bobby Abreu RF
Scott Rolen 3B
Cy Williams CF
Gavvy Cravath DH
Don Hurst 1B
Darren Daulton C
Tony Taylor 2B
Larry Bowa SS

PHILLIES SECOND TEAM PITCHING STAFF

Chris Short SP
Curt Simmons SP
Cole Hamels SP
Roy Halladay SP
Cliff Lee SP
Jonathan Papelbon SU
Tug McGraw CL

Although I limited my earlier rankings to the top 50 players in Phillies history, many other fine players have performed for the team over the years, some of whom narrowly missed making the final cut. Following is a list of those players deserving of an honorable mention. These are the men I deemed worthy of being slotted into positions 51 to 75 in the overall rankings. The statistics they compiled during their time in Philadelphia and their most notable achievements as a member of the team are also included.

51—CARLOS RUIZ (C, 2006–2016)

Phillies Numbers

68 HR, 401 RBIs, 388 Runs, 898 Hits, 213 Doubles, 7 Triples, 24 SB, .266 AVG, .352 OBP, .393 SLG, .745 OPS

Credit Matthew Straubmuller

Notable Achievements

- Batted over .300 twice.
- Surpassed 30 doubles once (32 in 2012).
- Compiled on-base percentage of .400 in 2010.
- Posted slugging percentage over .500 once (.540 in 2012).
- Compiled OPS over .900 once (.935 in 2012).
- Led NL catchers with 41.7 caught-stealing percentage in 2016.
- Five-time division champion (2007, 2008, 2009, 2010, and 2011).
- Two-time NL champion (2008 and 2009).
- 2008 world champion.
- April 27, 2014, NL Player of the Week.
- 2012 NL All-Star.

52—JOHN TITUS (OF, 1903–1912)

Phillies Numbers

31 HR, 475 RBIs, 649 Runs, 1,209
Hits, 216 Doubles, 64 Triples, 131
SB, .278 AVG, .368 OBP, .379 SLG,
.746 OPS

Notable Achievements

- Batted over .300 once (.308 in 1905).
- Finished in double digits in triples twice.
- Surpassed 30 doubles once.
- Stole more than 20 bases three times.
- Amassed more than 20 outfield assists seven times.
- Finished second in NL with 36 doubles in 1905.
- Finished third in NL in bases on balls once and extra-base hits once.
- Led NL right fielders in putouts twice, assists four times, double plays twice, and fielding percentage twice.
- Ranks eighth in franchise history with 126 sacrifice hits.

53—DICK BARTELL (SS, 1931–1934)

Phillies Numbers

2 HR, 161 RBIs, 386 Runs, 695 Hits, 146 Doubles, 23 Triples, 33 SB, .295 AVG, .358 OBP, .379 SLG, .737 OPS

Credit RMYAuctions.com

Notable Achievements

- Batted over .300 twice.
- Scored more than 100 runs twice.
- Surpassed 40 doubles twice.
- Led NL in games played once, assists once, and sacrifice hits twice.
- Finished second in NL in plate appearances twice, assists once, and sacrifice hits once.
- Finished third in NL in plate appearances once, doubles once, bases on balls once, and stolen bases once.
- Led NL shortstops in putouts three times, assists twice, and double plays three times.
- Ranks 10th in franchise history with 111 sacrifice hits.
- 1933 NL All-Star.

54—STEVE BEDROSIAN (P, 1986–1989)

Phillies Numbers

21-18 W-L Record, .538 Win Pct., 3.29 ERA, 103 Saves, 287 1/3 IP, 241 Strike-outs, 1.253 WHIP

Notable Achievements

- Compiled ERA under 3.00 once (2.83 in 1987).
- Led NL with 40 saves in 1987.
- Ranks third in franchise history in saves.
- Two-time NL Player of the Week.
- May 1987 NL Pitcher of the Month.
- 1987 NL Cy Young Award winner.
- 1987 NL All-Star.

55—DAVE BANCROFT (SS, 1915–1920)

Phillies Numbers

14 HR, 162 RBIs, 331 Runs, 634 Hits, 89 Doubles, 20 Triples, 64 SB, .251 AVG, .330 OBP, .319 SLG, .649 OPS

Credit Library of Congress

Notable Achievements

- Finished second in NL with 77 bases on balls in 1915.
- Finished third in NL in runs scored once and bases on balls twice.
- Led NL shortstops in putouts once.
- 1915 NL champion.
- Elected to Baseball Hall of Fame by members of Veterans Committee in 1971.

56—TUG MCGRAW (P, 1975–1984)

Phillies Numbers

49-37 W-L Record, .570 Win Pct., 3.10 ERA, 94 Saves, 722 IP, 491 Strikeouts, 1.198 WHIP

Notable Achievements

- Compiled ERA under 3.00 five times, posting mark below 2.00 once (1.46 in 1980).
- Posted winning percentage over .600 four times.
- Saved at least 20 games once (20 in 1980).
- Posted WHIP under 1.000 once (0.921 in 1980).
- Ranks among Phillies career leaders in saves (6th) and pitching appearances (4th).
- Five-time division champion (1976, 1977, 1978, 1980, and 1983).
- Two-time NL champion (1980 and 1983).
- 1980 world champion.
- Finished fifth in 1980 NL Cy Young voting.
- 1975 NL All-Star.
- Member of Philadelphia Baseball Wall of Fame.
- Member of Philadelphia Sports Hall of Fame.
- Named to Phillies Centennial Team in 1983.

57—BRYCE HARPER (OF, 2019–2021)

Phillies Numbers

83 HR, 231 RBIs, 240 Runs, 351 Hits, 87 Doubles, 4 Triples, 36 SB, .281 AVG, .402 OBP, .556 SLG, .958 OPS

Credit Keith Allison and All-Pro Reels

Notable Achievements

- Has hit more than 30 home runs twice.
- Has knocked in more than 100 runs once.
- Has scored more than 100 runs once.
- Has surpassed 30 doubles twice, topping 40 two-baggers once.
- Has batted over .300 once.
- Has compiled on-base percentage over .400 twice.
- Has batted over .300 once.
- Has posted slugging percentage over .500 three times.
- Has posted OPS over .900 twice, topping 1.000 once.
- Has led NL in doubles once, bases on balls once, slugging percentage once, and OPS once.
- Has finished second in NL in bases on balls once and on-base percentage once.
- Finished third in NL with .309 batting average in 2021.
- Led NL outfielders with 13 assists in 2019.
- Has led NL right fielders in putouts and assists once each.
- Holds Phillies career records for highest slugging percentage and OPS.
- Ranks sixth in franchise history in on-base percentage.
- 2021 NL MVP

58—JAYSON WERTH (OF, 2007–2010)

Phillies Numbers

95 HR, 300 RBIs, 320 Runs, 507
Hits, 99 Doubles, 9 Triples, 60 SB,
.282 AVG, .380 OBP, .506 SLG,
.885 OPS

Credit Matthew Straubmuller

Notable Achievements

- Hit more than 20 home runs
  three times, topping 30 homers
  once (36 in 2009).
- Scored more than 100 runs once (106 in 2010).
- Stole 20 bases twice.
- Compiled on-base percentage over .400 once (.404 in 2007).
- Posted slugging percentage over .500 twice.
- Compiled OPS over .900 once (.921 in 2010).
- Hit three home runs in one game vs. Toronto Blue Jays on May 16,
  2008.
- Led NL with 46 doubles in 2010.
- Led NL right fielders in putouts once.
- Four-time division champion (2007, 2008, 2009, and 2010).
- Two-time NL champion (2008 and 2009).
- 2008 world champion.
- Two-time NL Player of the Week.
- 2009 NL All-Star.

59—JONATHAN PAPELBON (P, 2012–2015)

Phillies Numbers

14-11 W-L Record, .560 Win Pct., 2.31 ERA, 123 Saves, 237 2/3 IP, 252 Strikeouts, 1.022 WHIP

Credit Matthew Straubmuller

Notable Achievements

- Saved more than 35 games twice.
- Posted winning percentage over .800 once.
- Compiled ERA under 2.50 three times, posting mark under 2.00 once (1.59 in 2015).
- Posted WHIP under 1.000 twice.
- Averaged better than one strikeout per inning once.
- Holds Phillies career record for most saves.
- Two-time NL All-Star (2012 and 2015).

60—DODE PASKERT (OF, 1911–1917)

Phillies Numbers

28 HR, 291 RBIs, 551 Runs, 933 Hits, 175 Doubles, 47 Triples, 149 SB, .272 AVG, .357 OBP, .374 SLG, .732 OPS

Credit Library of Congress

Notable Achievements

- Batted over .300 once (.315 in 1912).
- Scored more than 100 runs once (102 in 1912).
- Finished in double digits in triples once (11 in 1917).
- Surpassed 30 doubles twice.
- Stole more than 20 bases four times, topping 30 steals once (36 in 1912).
- Compiled on-base percentage over .400 once (.420 in 1912).
- Amassed 20 outfield assists in 1911.
- Finished second in NL in doubles once and bases on balls once.
- Finished third in NL in runs scored once, doubles once, and sacrifice hits once.
- Led NL center fielders in putouts once, assists once, double plays once, and fielding percentage three times.
- Ranks sixth in franchise history with 128 sacrifice hits.
- 1915 NL champion.

61—JOHNNY MOORE (OF, 1934–1937)

Phillies Numbers

55 HR, 313 RBIs, 283 Runs, 604 Hits, 107 Doubles, 14 Triples, 14 SB, .329 AVG, .375 OBP, .492 SLG, .867 OPS

Credit Mearsonlineauctions.com

Notable Achievements

- Batted over .300 four times, topping the .320 mark on three occasions.
- Surpassed 30 doubles twice.
- Posted slugging percentage over .500 once (.515 in 1934).
- Compiled OPS over .900 once (.912 in 1934).
- Hit three home runs in one game vs. Pittsburgh Pirates on July 22, 1936.
- Led NL right fielders in assists twice.
- Ranks sixth in franchise history in career batting average.

62—TONY GONZÁLEZ (OF, 1960–1968)

Phillies Numbers

77 HR, 438 RBIs, 514 Runs, 1,110 Hits, 185 Doubles, 50 Triples, 68 SB, .295 AVG, .359 OBP, .433 SLG, .792 OPS

Notable Achievements

- Batted over .300 three times, topping the .330 mark once (.339 in 1967).
- Hit 20 home runs in 1962.
- Collected 12 triples and 36 doubles in 1963.
- Finished second in NL in batting average once and triples once.
- Finished third in NL in doubles once.
- Led NL outfielders in fielding percentage three times.

63—ANDY SEMINICK (C, 1943–1951, 1955–1957)

Phillies Numbers

123 HR, 411 RBIs, 385 Runs, 716 Hits, 102 Doubles, 21 Triples, 20 SB, .244 AVG, .351 OBP, .419 SLG, .770 OPS

Notable Achievements

- Hit more than 20 home runs twice.
- Compiled on-base percentage of .400 in 1950.
- Posted slugging percentage over .500 twice.
- Posted OPS of .925 in 1950.
- Hit three home runs in one game vs. Cincinnati Reds on June 2, 1949.
- Led NL with 15 intentional bases on balls in 1948.
- Led NL catchers in putouts once, assists once, double plays once, fielding percentage once, and runners caught stealing twice.
- 1950 NL champion.
- 1949 NL All-Star.

64—PLÁCIDO POLANCO

(2B, 3B, 2002–2005, 2010–2012)

Phillies Numbers

51 HR, 281 RBIs, 365 Runs, 776 Hits, 127 Doubles, 6 Triples, 31 SB, .289 AVG, .341 OBP, .398 SLG, .739 OPS

Credit Matthew Straubmuller

Notable Achievements

- Batted over .300 once (.316 in 2005).
- Collected 30 doubles in 2003.
- Finished third in NL in sacrifice hits once and sacrifice flies once.
- Led NL third basemen in assists once and fielding percentage twice.
- Led NL second basemen in fielding percentage once.
- Two-time division champion (2010 and 2011).
- 2011 Gold Glove Award winner.
- 2011 NL All-Star.

65—DAVE CASH (2B, 1974–1976)

Phillies Numbers

7 HR, 171 RBIs, 292 Runs, 608 Hits, 80 Doubles, 26 Triples, 43 SB, .296 AVG, .348 OBP, .371 SLG, .719 OPS

Notable Achievements

- Batted .300 or better twice.
- Scored more than 100 runs once (111 in 1975).
- Amassed more than 200 hits twice.
- Finished in double digits in triples twice.
- Collected 40 doubles in 1975.
- Stole 20 bases in 1974.
- Led NL in hits once, triples once, games played once, plate appearances once, and at-bats three times.
- Finished second in NL in runs scored once, hits once, doubles once, games played once, and plate appearances twice.
- Led NL second basemen in putouts once, assists once, fielding percentage once, and double plays three times.
- 1976 division champion.
- Two-time NL Player of the Week.
- Three-time NL All-Star (1974, 1975, and 1976).

66—LARRY CHRISTENSON (P, 1973–1983)

Career Numbers

83-71 W-L Record, .539 Win Pct., 3.79 ERA, 27 CG, 6 Shutouts, 4 Saves, 1,402 2/3 IP, 781 Strikeouts, 1.280 WHIP

Notable Achievements

- Won 19 games in 1977.
- Posted winning percentage over .600 four times, topping .700 twice.
- Threw more than 200 innings three times.
- Led NL pitchers in fewest bases on balls allowed per nine innings pitched in 1978 (1.855).
- Finished second in NL in strikeouts-to-walks ratio in 1978 (2.787).
- Finished third in NL with .760 winning percentage in 1977.
- Ranks eighth in franchise history with 220 starts.
- Five-time division champion (1976, 1977, 1978, 1980, and 1983).
- Two-time NL champion (1980 and 1983).
- 1980 world champion.
- April 9, 1978, NL Player of the Week.
- September 1977 NL Pitcher of the Month.

67—HANS LOBERT (3B, 1911–1914)

Phillies Numbers

19 HR, 212 RBIs, 312 Runs, 549 Hits, 84 Doubles, 30 Triples, 125 SB, .293 AVG, .357 OBP, .400 SLG, .757 OPS

Credit Library of Congress

Notable Achievements

- Batted .300 or better twice, topping the .320 mark once (.327 in 1912).
- Finished in double digits in triples once (11 in 1913).
- Stole more than 30 bases three times, topping 40 thefts twice.
- Led NL with 38 sacrifice hits in 1911.
- Finished second in NL with 26 sacrifice hits in 1913.
- Finished third in NL in runs scored once and stolen bases once.
- Led NL third basemen in putouts twice and fielding percentage twice.

68—JIMMIE WILSON (C, 1923–1928, 1934–1938)

Phillies Numbers

22 HR, 315 RBIs, 305 Runs, 732 Hits, 119 Doubles, 11 Triples, 44 SB, .288 AVG, .334 OBP, .369 SLG, .703 OPS

Credit RMYAuctions.com

Notable Achievements

- Batted .300 or better three times.
- Led NL catchers in putouts once, assists once, double plays once, and runners caught stealing once.
- 1935 NL All-Star.

69—MANNY TRILLO (2B, 1979–1982)

Phillies Numbers

19 HR, 160 RBIs, 197 Runs, 516 Hits, 85 Doubles, 14 Triples, 30 SB, .277 AVG, .321 OBP, .369 SLG, .689 OPS

Credit MearsonlineAuctions.com

Notable Achievements

- Led NL second basemen in putouts twice and fielding percentage once.
- 1980 division champion.
- 1980 NL champion.
- 1980 world champion.
- Two-time Silver Slugger Award winner (1980 and 1981).
- Three-time Gold Glove Award winner (1979, 1981, and 1982).
- 1980 NLCS MVP.
- Two-time NL All-Star (1981 and 1982).
- Member of Philadelphia Baseball Wall of Fame.
- Named to Phillies Centennial Team in 1983.

70—STAN LOPATA (C, 1948–1958)

Phillies Numbers

116 HR, 393 RBIs, 375 Runs, 655 Hits, 116 Doubles, 25 Triples, 18 SB, .257 AVG, .355 OBP, .459 SLG, .814 OPS

Credit Mearsonlineauctions.com

Notable Achievements

- Hit more than 20 home runs twice, topping 30 homers once (32 in 1956).
- Surpassed 30 doubles once.
- Posted slugging percentage over .500 three times.
- Compiled OPS over .900 twice.
- Finished second in NL with 33 doubles in 1956.
- Finished third in NL in extra-base hits once and sacrifice flies once.
- Led NL catchers in double plays once.
- 1950 NL champion.
- Two-time NL All-Star (1955 and 1956).

71—RON REED (P, 1976–1983)

Phillies Numbers

57-38 W-L Record, .600 Win
Pct., 3.06 ERA, 90 Saves, 1 CG,
809 IP, 547 Strikeouts, 1.151
WHIP

Notable Achievements

- Won 13 games in 1979.
- Compiled ERA under 3.00
  four times, finishing with
  mark under 2.50 twice.
- Posted winning percentage
  over .600 three times.
- Posted WHIP under 1.000 once (0.938 in 1976).
- Ranks among Phillies career leaders in saves (7th), winning percentage (tied for 10th), WHIP (10th), and pitching appearances (6th).
- Five-time division champion (1976, 1977, 1978, 1980, and 1983).
- Two-time NL champion (1980 and 1983).
- 1980 world champion.

72—DERON JOHNSON (1B, 3B, OF, 1969–1973)

Phillies Numbers

88 HR, 304 RBIs, 213 Runs, 477 Hits, 82 Doubles, 8 Triples, 4 SB, .251 AVG, .333 OBP, .442 SLG, .775 OPS

Notable Achievements

- Hit more than 20 home runs twice, topping 30 homers once.
- Knocked in more than 90 runs twice.
- Finished fourth in NL with 34 home runs in 1971.
- Hit three home runs in one game vs. Montreal Expos on July 11, 1971.

73—RAÚL IBÁÑEZ (OF, 2009–2011)

Phillies Numbers

70 HR, 260 RBIs, 233 Runs, 421 Hits, 100 Doubles, 9 Triples, 10 SB, .264 AVG, .329 OBP, .469 SLG, .798 OPS

Credit Matthew Straubmuller

Notable Achievements

- Hit 34 home runs in 2009.
- Surpassed 30 doubles three times.
- Posted slugging percentage over .500 once (.552 in 2009).
- Led NL left fielders in assists once and fielding percentage once.
- Three-time division champion (2009, 2010, and 2011).
- 2009 NL champion.
- 2009 NL All-Star.

74—OTTO KNABE (2B, 1907–1913)

Phillies Numbers

5 HR, 280 RBIs, 468 Runs, 856 Hits, 124 Doubles, 43 Triples, 122 SB, .249 AVG, .328 OBP, .315 SLG, .643 OPS

Credit Library of Congress

Notable Achievements

- Stole more than 20 bases twice.
- Led NL in sacrifice hits four times.
- Led NL second basemen in putouts once and assists twice.
- Holds franchise record for most sacrifice hits (216).

75—FRESCO THOMPSON (2B, 1927–1930)

Phillies Numbers

12 HR, 219 RBIs, 369 Runs, 700 Hits, 141 Doubles, 32 Triples, 61 SB, .300 AVG, .353 OBP, .404 SLG, .756 OPS

Notable Achievements

- Batted over .300 twice.
- Scored more than 100 runs once (115 in 1929).
- Surpassed 200 hits once (202 in 1929).
- Finished in double digits in triples twice.
- Surpassed 30 doubles four times.
- Finished third in NL in triples once, stolen bases once, and plate appearances twice.
- Led NL second basemen in putouts twice.

GLOSSARY

ABBREVIATIONS AND STATISTICAL TERMS

1B. First baseman.

2B. Second baseman, or Doubles.

3B. Third baseman, or Triples.

AVG. Batting average. The number of hits divided by the number of at-bats.

C. Catcher.

CF. Center fielder.

CG. Complete games pitched.

CL. Closer.

ERA. Earned run average. The number of earned runs a pitcher gives up, per nine innings. This does not include runs that scored as a result of errors made in the field and is calculated by dividing the number of runs given up, by the number of innings pitched, and multiplying the result by 9.

HITS. Base hits. Awarded when a runner safely reaches at least first base upon a batted ball, if no error is recorded.

HR. Home runs. Fair ball hit over the fence, or one hit to a spot that allows the batter to circle the bases before the ball is returned to home plate.

IP. Innings pitched.

LF. Left fielder.

OBP. On-base percentage. Hits plus walks plus hit-by-pitches, divided by plate appearances.

OF. Outfielder.

OPS. On-base plus slugging (the sum of a player's slugging percentage and on-base percentage).

RBI. Runs batted in. Awarded to the batter when a runner scores upon a safely batted ball, a sacrifice, or a walk.

RUNS. Runs scored by a player.

RF. Right fielder.

RP. Relief pitcher.

SB. Stolen bases.

SHO. Shutouts. Number of complete games pitched in which a pitcher did not allow a run.

SLG. Slugging percentage. The number of total bases earned by all singles, doubles, triples, and home runs, divided by the total number of at-bats.

SO. Strikeouts.

SP. Starting pitcher.

SS. Shortstop.

SU. Setup reliever.

WHIP. The sum of a pitcher's walks and hits divided by the total number of innings pitched.

W-L. Win-Loss record.

WIN PCT. Winning percentage. A pitcher's number of wins divided by his number of total decisions (that is, wins plus losses).

BIBLIOGRAPHY

Books

Cairns, Bob. *Pen Men: Baseball's Greatest Bullpen Stories by the Men Who Brought the Game Relief.* New York: St Martin's Press, 1993.

DeMarco, Tony, et al. *The Sporting News Selects 50 Greatest Sluggers.* St. Louis, MO: *The Sporting News,* a division of Times Mirror Magazines, Inc., 2000.

Kashatus, William C. *Macho Row: The 1993 Phillies and Baseball's Unwritten Code.* Lincoln: University of Nebraska Press, 2017.

Kruk, John, and Paul Hagen. *"I Ain't an Athlete, Lady": My Well-Rounded Life and Times.* New York: Simon and Schuster, 1994.

Leventhal, Josh. *Baseball and the Meaning of Life.* Beverly, MA: Voyageur Press, 2005.

Mann, Michael Francis. *Baseball's Rare Triple Crown.* Bloomington, IN: Xlibris Publishing, 2011.

Roberts, Robin, and C. Paul Rogers III. *The Whiz Kids and the 1950 Pennant.* Philadelphia: Temple University Press, 2000.

Rose, Pete, and Rick Hill. *My Prison without Bars.* Emmaus, PA: Rodale Books, 2000.

Schmidt, Mike, and Glen Waggoner. *Clearing the Bases: Juiced Players, Monster Salaries, Sham Records, and a Hall of Famer's Search for the Soul of Baseball.* New York: HarperCollins, 2006.

Shalin, Mike, and Neil Shalin. *Out by a Step: The 100 Best Players Not in the Baseball Hall of Fame.* Lanham, MD: Diamond Communications, Inc., 2002.

Stark, Jayson. *Worth the Wait: Tales of the 2008 Phillies.* Chicago: Triumph Books, 2011.

Thorn, John, and Pete Palmer, eds., with Michael Gershman. *Total Baseball.* New York: HarperCollins, 1993.

Williams, Ted, with Jim Prime. *Ted Williams' Hit List*. Indianapolis, IN: Masters Press, 1996.

Videos

The Glory of Their Times. Cappy Productions, Inc., 1985.
The Sporting News' 100 Greatest Baseball Players. National Broadcasting Co., 1999.

Websites

The Ballplayers, BaseballLibrary.com
Bio Project, SABR.org
Historical Stats, MLB.com
The Players, Baseball-Almanac.com
The Players, Baseball-Reference.com
The Players, Retrosheet.org
The Teams, Baseball-Reference.com